The Prism of Sex

Proceedings of a symposium sponsored by
WRI of Wisconsin, Inc.
1977
Madison, Wisconsin

THE PRISM OF SEX

ESSAYS IN THE SOCIOLOGY OF KNOWLEDGE

Edited by
Julia A. Sherman
and
Evelyn Torton Beck

The University of Wisconsin Press

Published 1979

The University of Wisconsin Press
114 North Murray Street
Madison, Wisconsin 53715

The University of Wisconsin Press, Ltd.
1 Gower Street
London WC1E 6HA, England

Copyright © 1979
The Board of Regents of the University of Wisconsin System
All rights reserved

First printing

Printed in the United States of America

For LC CIP information see the colophon

ISBN 0-299-08010-2

Contents

PREFACE vii

INTRODUCTION *Julia A. Sherman and Evelyn Torton Beck* 3

HISTORY

Clio's American Daughters: Male History, Female Reality 9
Nancy Schrom Dye

Clio's European Daughters: Myopic Modes of Perception 33
Jane Tibbetts Schulenburg

LITERATURE

The Power to Name: Some Reflections on the Avant-Garde 55
Catharine R. Stimpson

[Why] Are There No Great Women Critics?: And What Difference Does It Make? 79
Susan Sniader Lanser and Evelyn Torton Beck

PSYCHOLOGY

Bias in Psychology 93
Carolyn Wood Sherif

SOCIOLOGY

A Sociology for Women 135
Dorothy E. Smith

PHILOSOPHY

Moral Revolution 189
Kathryn Pyne Parsons

POLITICAL SCIENCE

**Methodological Sophistication and Conceptual Confusion:
A Critique of Mainstream Political Science**   229
Jean Bethke Elshtain

Women's Studies and Political Conflict   253
Virginia Sapiro

AFTERWORD   *Jessie Bernard*   267

CONTRIBUTORS   277

INDEX   279

Preface

■ These papers were part of a conference "Prism of Sex: Toward an Equitable Pursuit of Knowledge" sponsored by WRI of Wisconsin, Inc., and held in Madison, Wisconsin, in the fall of 1977. WRI (Women's Research Institute) is a nonprofit organization incorporated in 1973 under the laws of the state of Wisconsin for educational and research purposes. It is particularly fitting that WRI sponsored this conference, since a major reason for the formation of the institute was to provide an opportunity for the autonomous creation of new knowledge by women. Many universities permit only persons in tenure-track positions to submit research proposals as Principal Investigator, and most granting institutions require a legal entity, not an individual, to be the recipient of a grant. There are very few women in tenure-track positions at research universities. WRI makes available a way around this structural barrier to women's pursuit of knowledge. Formal activities of the institute have included conferences, seminars, workshops, and research.

The editors wish to thank Lydia Bronte and the Rockefeller Foundation for funding which made this conference possible, and the Women's Studies Program of the University of Wisconsin, Madison, for their helpful cooperation. We should also like to thank Corinne Koufacos of WRI, who served as overall director of the project, and the following local persons who served as members of the advisory committee, facilitated the conference, and/or served as discussants: Claudia Card, Kathryn Clarenbach, Dean Robert Doremus, Thomas Kirlin, Diane Kravetz, Diane Lindstrom. Our special thanks to Karl U. Smith for his invaluable support in the early days of the institute's development.

The Prism of Sex

Introduction

Julia A. Sherman
Evelyn Torton Beck

■ From the beginning of recorded history the pursuit of knowledge has been almost entirely in the hands of men. Even the admission of women into institutions of higher learning has not afforded women equal opportunity to participate in intellectual creation. Although some of the more obvious external barriers have been removed, social attitudes and sex-role expectations remain intact and serve to hinder women. Thus, despite affirmative action programs and much noisy publicity about "breakthroughs for women," the pursuit of knowledge remains largely a male domain.

Those statistics most frequently quoted to show progress for women, in fact, disguise the extent to which scholarship continues to be dominated by male thinkers. The typical statistics focus on the rising numbers of women graduates in various fields, without citing what proportion of these students ever find a place within academia; or they focus on the numbers of women employed by universities, without noting that women are clustered on the very lowest rungs of the academic ladder. More accurate indicators of progress for women in the pursuit of knowledge would be increases in the numbers of women in *tenured* positions in the major *research* universities; these increases have been exceedingly slight, and even they do not tell the whole story. For a woman, being a student or *receiver* of knowledge is far more congruent with role expectations than being a theorizer or *producer* of that knowledge. A higher degree is only the first requisite for the pursuit of knowledge. The opportunity and encouragement to pursue scholarly work must follow. Employment in a college or university *in itself* by no means guarantees such opportunity. Time, money, facilities, influence, freedom and autonomy, students, assistants, and a high-level, resonating milieu are necessary for creative intellectual achievement; and these are seldom available to women. Gerda Lerner, a major researcher in women's history, elaborates this point in some detail in connection with the struggle for women's education:

> The achievement of abstract thought and the creation of theories depend on education in the best of the existing tradition and acceptance by a peer group of educated persons, who, by means of criticism and interaction, provide "cultural prodding"; and it demands private time. Women, historically, have been denied all of these. . . . *For women, the most unattainable of the preconditions for abstract thinking has been "cultural prodding," which is institutionalized in the upper reaches of the academic establishment* and in such outside equivalents as "think tanks." Only since the development of the modern feminist movement with its turbulent intellectual activity and its network of female support systems, can a few women hope to share in the preconditions for creative thought which male intellectuals of superior talents have long taken for granted. Thus, the absence of "great" female minds, of women who build theories and systems of theories based on their own ideas and life experiences . . . can be explained as a result of a particular historical deprivation."[1] (Emphasis ours)

For these reasons, more women students and more women in education do not necessarily change the essential circumstances for women scholars: women teach while men research. Women are not expected (nor encouraged) to think deeply, creatively, and with originality. If they persist in spite of this, their work is likely to be devalued and discounted, particularly if it is about women. The best of women's work often becomes respected only when a man produces the same results or if a man supports the work. Sometimes it even becomes wrongly attributed to a male.

Women constitute an enormous, historically submerged group of people, deprived of the power to conceptualize, to name, and to categorize reality. It is indeed difficult to grasp the profound extent of female exclusion from creative intellectual endeavor, grounded as it is in thousands of years of oppression and denigration. Let us look at a few examples taken from actual experiences to illustrate the phenomenon.

Example 1: When asked how she felt about being talented in mathematics, an extremely bright high school senior replied, "Women are supposed to be inferior in mathematics and I'm not. It makes me feel guilty." *Guilty.*

Example 2: A woman has just received tenure in one of the top research universities in the country. She is the first female ever to be granted tenure in her department, but she becomes seriously depressed. Why? She now fears that the academic community will find out she is not so capable after all.

Example 3: In the course of Julia Sherman's research on women and

Introduction   5

mathematics, a man who had otherwise been extremely helpful anxiously inquired, "Do you think that you, being a woman, can be objective in this kind of study?"

What do these incidents mean? They indicate the profound extent to which thinking and the right to say "how it is" has become an attribute of the male sphere. In the first example, the young woman shows us that not being how she "ought to be" is a matter of internal censure. She feels guilty for transgressing. In the second example, the woman professor is unable to accept the recognition she has achieved for her work, and is overcome by doubt and possibly by fear, for her very success makes her a deviant. We may also wonder if on some level she is not punishing herself (before *they* punish her) for her successful trespass onto male territory. In the third example, the helpful and sincere man reveals that he believes objectivity is the province of the male sex. If a man had conducted the same study, it would probably never have occurred to him to question *his* objectivity. As women, we have been told by men not only *what* to think, but also how to perceive ourselves. Ironically, this is true even regarding our own bodies and our own sexuality. Some fifty years ago, Virginia Woolf observed, with considerable irony, that virtually all the books that contained knowledge about women were produced by men, whose major qualifications for the task were "that they were not women."[2] Overwhelmingly this is still the official scholarly view; the situation has only recently begun to change. What is the effect of this imbalance in the power to know? Often, those few women who do achieve positions in the scholarly world do not see as women, but as men have taught them to see —through the prism of the male sex. Sheila Rowbotham, in *Woman's Consciousness, Man's World*, describes the phenomenon in this way: "Every time we mounted the steps of their platforms we wanted to run away and hide at home. We had a sense of not belonging. It was evident that we were intruders. Those of us who ventured into their territory were most subtly taught our place. *We were allowed to play with their words, their ideas, their culture, as long as we pretended we were men*"[3] (emphasis ours). In other words, we could participate so long as we accepted their framework and their scale of values (on which women's experience held a low place).

Women who dare to define reality for themselves are not happily received by men. Their work, often original and brilliant, is among that most frequently cast aside as irrelevant and "unempirical." After thousands of years of female exclusion from the pursuit of knowledge, one must examine the assumptions and question the questions; one cannot merely proceed to give ever more sophisticated answers to questions within a foreign, i.e., androcentric framework. Yet those women who have proceeded in this critical task of questioning the questions have usually paid for their principles and idealism with their academic positions.

This conference, and subsequently this book, emerged from a growing sense of the depth and extent of female exclusion from creative intellectual work. In turn, this led us to wonder what our fields of knowledge would now be like if women had been present in numbers and positions equal to men. Moreover, although women's studies is a resolutely interdisciplinary field, the structure of the academy (which trains us in individual disciplines) affords little opportunity to introduce scholars and students in various fields to each other and to the problems and biases peculiar to each field. For this reason we decided to gather together scholars, some well established and some new, in order to demonstrate how the "prism of sex" has affected several fields of knowledge. We had initially hoped to be able to include in this effort many more fields: anthropology, art, biology, economics, education, law, linguistics, medicine, physical education. Limitations in resources, however, led us to focus on certain core fields in the humanities and social sciences.

The writers responded in various ways to the challenge of our question, sometimes expanding on the theme to deal with bias as it affects class, race, and/or sexual preference, or even questioning the question "What is bias?" The writers also varied in the degree of background information they took for granted. The history papers are more introductory and provide an excellent starting point. Nancy Schrom Dye has presented an overview of American history which allows us to understand some of the biases introduced in that field through the nearly total absence of women. If history is defined simply as a record of public events, what then happens to the history of women, whose experiences have overwhelmingly taken place in the "private world"? And what does such a separation of public/private do to our conception of history? Jane Tibbetts Schulenburg, in her companion essay, surveys European history, especially the medieval period. She points out that periodization in history, and labels such as "the Dark Ages," "the Renaissance," acquired their conceptual basis from a distinctly male vantage point; the experience of women in those eras differs sharply from that of men.

In literature, the production of women has been buried, misinterpreted, misread, and devalued by the male critical establishment. Catharine R. Stimpson shows how the literary "avant-garde," otherwise so progressive in its ideas about literary theory and form, remains biased and narrow in its treatment and assessment of women. Susan Sniader Lanser and Evelyn Torton Beck examine the role of women in critical theory and show how women have consistently been denied a voice as theorizers, critics, and arbiters of literary taste. They bring us the names and works of several women critics and suggest the possibility of uncovering many others, now hidden in history. Both papers on literature show how the inclusion of women might alter our understanding of what literature is and can do.

Carolyn Wood Sherif's paper on psychology provides an excellent foundation for an understanding of perspective in psychological research and theory. She shows the one-sidedness of most research and places sexism in the broader category of biased work—work that disregards the situational context and frame of reference. Her paper calls for a new, more sophisticated psychology that places women's experience at the center of research, a much needed corrective to its almost total exclusion.

Dorothy E. Smith weaves a complex web of thought regarding bias in sociology, a bias which values abstract models, based on male experience and male perception, but omits from its analysis the everyday experiences, the so-called trivia and ephemera that characterize so much of women's world. Smith insists that these concrete, seemingly small bits and pieces of female experience must be included in the theories themselves if sociological studies are to take full account of the data. Women must be written into the studies on the most fundamental levels of experience. Kathryn Pyne Parsons discusses the philosophical basis for the generally accepted system of Western ethics. This system, she believes, is based on a patriarchal scale of values developed within the context of a capitalist concept of ownership that includes the ownership of women's bodies.

In political science, Jean Bethke Elshtain questions the very basis of political philosophy. She asks whether feminist scholarship can rightly proceed within the bounds of logical positivism or even behavioralism, which she believes exclude value from consideration. She also believes that until value is admitted as legitimate, women cannot soundly have a new scholarship. Virginia Sapiro provides an introduction to political science as a whole and at the same time answers Elshtain's questions. She takes the view that bias is bad behavioralism and that some degree of unbiased pursuit of knowledge *is* possible.

Jessie Bernard, in her warm and inimitable way, summarizes her responses to the entire conference—the papers and the ensuing discussions—and gives us her opinion of "What does it all mean? Where do we go from here?"

These essays, each in the context of its own discipline, all point in the same direction. If women's experience has been omitted at the most basic level of conceptualization, then clearly the framework itself must be faulty. The prism of sex has all too often become a prison that has locked male scholars into a one-sided mode of thinking, and has locked women out of the pursuit of knowledge altogether. These essays suggest that we must not only learn to ask new questions, but to challenge the very foundations on which the state of knowledge in each discipline is grounded. Based on this recognition, this volume is meant to provide the beginnings of a dialogue which we hope will continue within and across the many disciplines —those here represented as well as those we had to omit. We intended these essays to raise more questions than they answer, and in this we feel sure we have succeeded.

NOTES

1 Gerda Lerner, ed., *The Female Experience: An American Documentary* (Indianapolis, 1977), pp. 207-8.
2 Virginia Woolf, *A Room of One's Own* (1929; rpt. New York, 1957), pp. 27, 28.
3 Sheila Rowbotham, *Woman's Consciousness, Man's World* (Baltimore, 1973).

NANCY SCHROM DYE

Clio's American Daughters
Male History, Female Reality

■ Historians act as society's memory: what we call history is in good measure what historians decide to study and record. History, then, is an interpretation, not a reconstruction, of past reality; it is the result of a process designed to impose order on the vast and chaotic accumulation of written material handed down from the past. To construct a coherent narrative of some aspect of the past, historians formulate questions and methodologies, sift through documents and statistical data, and, finally, expand some of their materials and delete others. What historians ignore and what they stress depend upon their notions of historical significance. In turn, historians' judgments concerning significance depend upon their personal, political, and social values, their social status, their personal experience, and the cultural milieu in which they work. Not surprisingly, American historians' notions of significance have changed a good deal over the past hundred years: what has been important to one generation of scholars has seldom been compelling to the next. Writing history, then, is a continuous process, not so much because historians uncover new sources or develop new methodologies as because our views of the past and our evaluations of what is important about it are constantly changing.

Two related themes that are evident throughout American historical writing from the middle of the nineteenth century to the very recent present are of special interest to women's scholars. The first is the overwhelmingly political orientation of most investigations and interpretations of the American past. Until very recently, American historians have been preoccupied with questions of politics, public policy, and power. From the days of the first doctoral program at Johns Hopkins, where "History is past politics" was a slogan inscribed on the seminar room wall, historians have defined their subject as a record of the public and political aspects of the American past. As Richard Hofstadter summarized the field in the late

1960s, "Memory is the thread of personal identity, history of public identity. Men who have achieved any civic existence at all must, to sustain it, have some kind of history. . . . That the business of history always involves a subtle transaction with civic identity has long been understood."[1]

The second theme that emerges from an overview of American historical writing, one that is related to the first, is the absence of women from the historical record. Until recently, women have been neither the subjects nor the objects of historical inquiry: they have not been treated as historical actors in their own right nor have their lives been the objects of historical scrutiny. Most historians have written history as if women did not exist or, at best, as if they were some form of rare creature who very occasionally appeared in the background of the historical landscape. Until the last five or six years, historical journals virtually never contained articles dealing with women, and monographs rarely dealt with their situation in the past. Of the dissertations written from 1876, when an American university first granted a doctorate in history, to 1960, only twenty-one can be classified as American women's history.[2] Quite literally our history has been the history of men.

This essay attempts to answer several questions suggested by these themes. Why did history, a field that potentially encompasses every aspect of human experience, develop as a discipline that ignored all but the public aspects of life? Why have historians been blind to women's existence in the past when they have shown themselves capable of seeing and investigating any manner of esoterica? Finally, how has historians' neglect of women distorted the development of history as a field of knowledge? How has it influenced our notions of continuity and change, periodization, historical significance itself?

Typical of a historian, I turned to the past, to the history of American historical writing, in hopes that by learning something about the circumstances in which history developed as an academic field and something about the craft's early practitioners I could suggest some answers to these questions.[3] I began with the obvious assumption that women have not been included in the historical narrative because the field has always been defined as the record of politics and public affairs. Since few women throughout history have been involved in public affairs and far fewer have exercised political power, it would seem to follow naturally and inevitably that women would be excluded from the historical narrative. We are so accustomed to the idea that history is the story of political decision-making, the development of factions, parties, and interest groups, diplomacy and warfare, and the uses and abuses of power that we rarely ask why history as a field of knowledge evolved along these lines.

But as I learned about the history of historical writing and tried to relate the field's development to the role and status of American women, the less satisfactory this explanation became. I wondered, if perhaps just the opposite was true: rather than ignoring women because it was primarily political in orientation, perhaps the field was primarily political because it ignored women. What I am suggesting is that historians have had little understanding or even awareness of the circumstances of women's lives in their own time, let alone in the past, and that their ignorance of female experience and female realities made it inevitable that history would develop areas of inquiry and notions of significance that could not capture women's past. I believe that this was particularly true in the late nineteenth century, when history emerged as a discrete academic discipline, but that, in varying degrees, it has continued to characterize the field throughout the twentieth century as well.

But, one might ask, how could the historians who shaped the field possibly have been ignorant of the realities of women's lives? Certainly all of them knew women; most lived intimately with them. In part, the activities and concerns that have been important aspects of most women's lives, such as childbearing, childrearing, and housework, have been invisible to historians because society has not deemed such activities significant, however essential they may have been to a historian's day-to-day existence and comfort. "Women's work" was part of the background of everyday life, easily blocked out. Perhaps more important to an explanation of how male historians could be unaware of the circumstances of women's lives is increasing evidence that women and men do experience the world in demonstrably different ways, do have separate realities and separate life cycles. As women's historians are just beginning to realize, women have maintained a distinct female culture.

Although history, like other academic disciplines, did not develop as a discrete field until late in the nineteenth century, amateur historical writing flourished throughout the 1800s as an avocation pursued by wealthy, leisured, and cultivated gentlemen. These amateur historians looked upon history as a branch of literature; many of them were also novelists, poets, and essayists. History, such nineteenth-century gentlemen-scholars as George Bancroft, William Prescott, and Francis Parkman believed, served a dual function: it should entertain and instruct. Specifically, they believed that history should imbue Americans with a sense of national pride and identity. Accordingly, they chose subjects that were at once dramatic and patriotic: the lives and careers of the "founding fathers," the day-to-day operations of important military campaigns and battles, the conquest of an immense continent, and what Henry Adams called "the romance and tragedy of statesmanship." Although we now find their romantic prose and grandiose style amusing, these "male crusaders for the Rising Glory of America," as one recent historian dubbed them,[4] established some of the basic themes and assumptions that were to dominate professional American historiography in later years: the achievement of nationhood, the importance of great men, a belief in "progress," a faith in the possibility of man's mastery over the natural environment, and a conviction that America, as a consciously created nation, had a special mission.

Women, needless to say, had little role to play in the panoramic epics that constituted mid-nineteenth-century historical literature. When they did put in a rare appearance, it was usually as extras in the background of an exciting historical landscape.[5] Women also entered the historical narrative briefly as patriotic wives and mothers: George Washington's mother, Mary, and his wife, Martha, made many cameo appearances.[6] The lives of Indian women and the experiences of white female captives drew most attention from the romantic amateurs. Francis Parkman's *Conspiracy of Pontiac*, for instance, contains a long, dramatic digression on the reunion of women captives with their families. Significantly, Parkman chose to dwell upon the fact that many of these women were reluctant to leave their adopted Indian homes. "In the ranks of the Pennsylvania troops," he wrote, "and among the Virginia riflemen, were the fathers, brothers, and husbands of those whose rescue from captivity was the chief object of the march. . . . these men had joined the army, in the feverish hope of winning them back to home and civilization." At the Indian camp, "there were young women . . . who had become the partners of Indian husbands; and who now, with their hybrid offspring, were led reluctantly into the presence of fathers and brothers whose images were almost blotted from their memory. . . . These women were compelled to return with their children to the settlements, yet they did so with reluctance, and several afterwards made their escape, eagerly hastening back to their warrior husbands, and the toils and vicissitudes of an Indian wigwam."[7] For Parkman and other nineteenth-century historians, the essence of the American experience was the triumph of civilization over barbarism, a saga of mastery over the elements and the indigenous population. White men embodied civilization, while the Indian was "a true child of the forest and the desert. The wastes and solitudes of nature are his congenial home. His haughty mind is imbued with the spirit of wilderness."[8] Parkman's treatment of women, however brief, suggests that he identified women with nature and, therefore, with the wilderness to be conquered and subdued.[9]

Near the end of the nineteenth century, historical writing underwent a dramatic transformation. What had been a literary avocation became a professional academic specialty as new research-oriented universities flourished and as increasing numbers of young scholars traveled to Germany for advanced historical study. These first professional historians—several hundred in number when they founded the American Historical Association in 1884—worked to establish history as a discrete discipline that would be an integral part of the new university, distinct from literature and philosophy on the one hand and romantic antiquarianism on the other. The new historians defined themselves as men of science: they believed that by being "objective," detached, and systematic, historians could study their subjects in much the same way that biologists could observe a specimen under a microscope. "Scientific" historians, like their amateur predecessors, were primarily interested in the forging of American national identity. They were also social evolutionists. Accordingly, they tried to trace the origins and evolution of American political and legal institutions.

This first generation of professional historians and a handful of the most influential amateurs, such as Henry Adams and James Ford Rhodes, shaped history as an academic field. They established graduate programs and research collections. They were responsible for identifying institutions, law, diplomacy, and politics as the legitimate areas for historical inquiry. Finally, they determined the major subjects and debates that were to dominate American historiography well into the twentieth century: the causes of the Revolution, the adoption of the Constitution, the nature of the battle between the Hamiltonians and the Jeffersonians, and so on. These late nineteenth-century historians created a field that embodied their personal and social realities and that reflected their cultural milieu. To understand their blindness to women, then, we must look briefly at the society in which these men lived and the place they occupied within it.

The development of history as an academic field coincided with the emergence of the United States as a modern industrial nation and a major world power. Historians' traditional concerns with national identity and with uncovering the special meaning of the American experience were intensified in these decades of rapid social and economic change. Memories of the still recent Civil War, rapid industrialization and massive immigration, the brutal Indian wars that accompanied the last phase of continental settlement, and the beginnings of international economic and political expansion prompted historians to focus their investigations on American character and American nationalism.

Then, too, history developed as a field of knowledge in a culture that made rigid distinctions between public and private aspects of life and the proper roles for men and women. In the genteel world that nineteenth-century historians inhabited, public life was masculine by definition, while the private world of home and family was feminine. Men and women were assigned separate social "spheres." What was more, each sex was endowed with the appropriate character traits to fill their biologically ordained roles. Men were "naturally" suited for the worlds of politics, finance, business, diplomacy, and law: they were aggressive, rational, and strong. Women, on the other hand, had no public role. They were designed by nature to stay within the household and minister to the needs of husband and children. Accordingly, they were "naturally" pliant, emotional, sympathetic, and domestic. Nineteenth-century sex roles were differentiated in another important respect: men were economic producers, while women were consumers.[10]

This cultural ideal, often called the doctrine of spheres, was already disintegrating by the 1870s. Although it would be another half century before women won the right to vote, hundreds of thousands of upper- and middle-class women had already begun to take part in public life through the new women's clubs, the Women's Christian Temperance Union, and the local suffrage associations. New educational opportunities for women, particularly through the eastern women's colleges and the new coeducational land grant universities, also helped weaken the doctrine of spheres. Although it was still rare for women from comfortable backgrounds to work outside the home, the ever-increasing number of working-class women in the labor force helped break down the stereotypic image of feminine idleness and frailty.

It is quite possible, however, that both the amateur and professional historians of the nineteenth century grew up in a world in which women played marginal and largely invisible roles. They were educated without women, their social and professional activities were conducted without women, and the rituals of upper-class courtship probably made spontaneous relationships with women difficult, if not impossible.[11]

At the same time, nineteenth-century women lived in a world that was largely closed to men. Within the private world of the household, women created and maintained what historians such as Carroll Smith-Rosenberg call a female culture. This was a world with its own rites of passage from girlhood to womanhood, and its own ways of transmitting support and knowledge about marriage, pregnancy, childbirth, and childrearing. This was also a world characterized by female friendship networks in which women often formed intense and lasting emotional relationships with one another.[12] This nineteenth-century female culture was, of course, largely invisible to the men who shaped history as a field of knowledge.

Not only the cultural milieu in which early historians wrote, but also the social characteristics of historians themselves help us understand why history developed as a field that excluded women. Early historians' class backgrounds, political and social attitudes, and self-perceptions give us clues to understanding the distorted nature of the discipline.

The most salient characteristic that emerges from a profile of early historians is that most of them were men. Throughout the nineteenth and early twentieth centuries, the writing of history, whether as a literary avocation or as professional scholarship, was a male pursuit. Few nineteenth-century women were among the ranks of distinguished amateur historians. There were exceptions, of course. Mercy Otis Warren, whose career spanned the late eighteenth and first decade of the nineteenth centuries was perhaps the most outstanding. Frances Victor, who anonymously authored at least four volumes of George Bancroft's *History of the Pacific States*, was another.[13] Why so few women wrote history in these years is something of a mystery, especially when we know that many nineteenth-century women were prolific writers in other branches of literature. Americans seem to have perceived history as a male pursuit from its very beginning. As Mercy Warren remarked—no doubt sardonically—in the preface to her *History of the Rise, Progress, and Termination of the American Revolution*, the writing of history was "the more peculiar province of masculine strength."[14] Similarly, women made up only a small minority of the first professional historians.[15] Few women earned doctorates in the field, and substantially fewer found academic positions: universities' discriminatory hiring practices forced women to compete for the small number of posts in the women's colleges, where they usually made up the majority of the faculty and remained throughout their careers.[16]

In addition to being male, most early historians shared other characteristics. Virtually all the nineteenth-century amateurs and a good percentage of the early professionals came from affluent backgrounds; the amateurs in particular were often very wealthy men. To write serious history in the nineteenth century was often a very costly undertaking: it required money for travel, copyists, secretaries, and, of course, an abundance of leisure. Such requirements necessarily made writing history a patrician pastime. The first professional historians were less affluent, but significantly, many moved, or aspired to move, in the same aristocratic social circles.[17] In addition to being wealthy, a good number of prominent amateur historians hailed from powerful families or exercised considerable political or economic power themselves: George Bancroft, Henry Adams, and Theodore Roosevelt are obvious examples.

Early historians' aristocratic backgrounds were often reflected in their choice of subjects. As a group, these men manifested a disdain for the lives and pasts of ordinary people. How blacks, workers, and powerless groups in general fared in the saga of mastery that presumably was the

American experience were not questions that interested them. As one influential amateur historian, James Ford Rhodes, himself a successful iron manufacturer, stated, "The routine of work and the round of pleasures of the majority—those blank pages of history . . ., if written over, could indeed be tiresome."[18]

Both the amateurs and the early professionals thought of themselves as men of action as well as men of scholarship. Theodore Roosevelt, of course, is the best example of the activist historian. A prolific writer, Roosevelt found the study of history perfectly compatible with "the strenuous life." It was, in short, a "manly" activity. Not surprisingly, Roosevelt equated masculinity and nationhood in his writings. His essay "Manhood and Statehood," in which he describes the personal characteristics of the western pioneers, is a good example of the male bias that permeated his views of history. "The *men* who opened the West," he wrote,

> showed practically by their life-work that it is indeed the spirit of adventure which is the maker of commonwealths. Their traits of daring and hardihood and iron endurance are not merely indispensible traits for pioneers; they are also traits which must go to the make-up of every mighty and successful people. . . . There was scant room for the coward and the weakling in the ranks of the adventurous frontiersmen—the pioneer settlers. . . . It is a record of men who greatly dared and greatly did; a record of wanderings wider and more dangerous than those of the Vikings, a record of endless feats of arms, or victory after victory in the ceaseless strife waged against wild man and wild nature. The winning of the West was the great epic feat in the history of our race.[19]

The first professional historians also saw themselves as men of action, albeit in somewhat less strenuous ways than TR. For example, the American Historical Association's first president, Herbert Baxter Adams, insisted upon locating the organization's headquarters in Washington, D.C., because he, along with many of his colleagues, thought historians should be close to the center of political power. Historians, he believed, should be more than academicians; they should help shape public policy and diplomacy. Many early professional historians, then, saw themselves as part of an educated and powerful elite, a kind of intellectual civil service. Because women had no official political role in American society, let alone political power, there was clearly no room for them in this kind of arrangement.

Finally, the men who shaped history as an academic field emerge as supremely confident individuals who identified with American values and entertained few doubts about America as a successful experiment in liberty and democracy. In short, historians as a group were far from marginal social types; they were unlikely to question the assumptions and values, including patriarchy, upon which their culture rested. The history they wrote reflected this confidence as well as mirroring their own social realities: it was history that dealt with progress, the special greatness of American political and legal institutions, and the possibilities of technological mastery.

One of the most important historians of the late nineteenth century, Henry Adams, stands out as an exception to these last generalizations. Unlike his colleagues, Adams consciously defined himself as a marginal individual, personally alienated from late-nineteenth-century American culture, disdainful of Gilded Age political and financial chicanery, and disillusioned with American technology. Significantly, Adams was the one historian of this period who thought seriously about women. "The proper study of mankind is woman," he stated in the beginning of his autobiography, *The Education of Henry Adams.* "Without understanding the movement of sex, history seemed to him mere pedantry."[20] In *The Education* Adams developed a theory of history based on the notion of sexual polarities, which he named the Dynamo and the Virgin. The Dynamo, of course, represented masculinity. Adams defined as masculine precisely what alienated him from American society: the worship of technology, detached and dehumanized rationality, destructive expansion. Woman, on the other hand, was nature; the Virgin represented creative energy, the life force. The tragedy of American society, Adams stated, was that Americans had no interest in or comprehension of the mystical and awe-inspiring Virgin. In consequence, feminine energy was being destroyed by the Dynamo.[21] Adams was not a feminist, either personally or intellectually. His personal attitudes toward women are revealed in his letters. "It is rather droll to examine women's minds," he wrote about his fiancée. "They are a queer mixture of odds and ends, poorly mastered and utterly unconnected. . . . My young female has a very active and quick mind and has run over many things. But she really knows nothing."[22] For one who insisted on the primacy of sexual force in history, Adams's historical writings are "curiously empty" of real females.[23] Adams's work, then, is fraught with contradictions: on the one hand, he was fascinated by Woman as an archetype; on the other, women have virtually no place in his history. In another respect, he perceived and was alienated by the male bias of late-nineteenth-century American life, yet he found women silly and rather uninteresting. In the end, he, like other historians of his generation, was incapable of comprehending the historical realities of women's lives.

But, one might ask, what about the women scholars during the years that history took shape as an academic discipline? Universities barred women from graduate training until the 1890s. From 1893, however, when the University of Wisconsin awarded the first history doctorate to a woman, women earned from 10 to 15 percent of the Ph.D.'s in the field.[24] Female scholars who weathered the formidable discrimination prevalent in academia often went on to distinguished careers within academic departments. In the women's colleges, particularly, women often took the lead in establishing separate departments of history, organizing manuscript collections, and experimenting with new teaching methods. A few individuals, most notably Lucy Maynard Salmon, who served on an early A.H.A. Executive Board, and Nellie Neilson, who was elected president of the association in the early 1930s, were influential in the profession as a whole.

As scholars, however, female historians did not challenge the field's basic assumptions or go beyond established political, diplomatic, and legal parameters in their own research. Thesis and dissertation topics such as "The History of the Appointing Power of the President" and "Anglo-American Isthmian Diplomacy, 1815–1915" were indistinguishable from those of their male colleagues. Nor did female historians before the 1920s investigate women's past once they had completed their graduate training. Although a number of them were well-known feminists and social activists, they kept their research interests separate from their personal and social commitments.[25]

In these respects, female historians differed from their sisters in the new social and behavioral sciences. Women such as Elsie Clews Parsons and Ruth Benedict in anthropology, Jessie Taft in sociology, and Helen Thompson Woolley and Leta Hollingsworth in psychology not only helped shape disciplines that considered questions concerning sex differences, sex roles, and socialization practices, but also were instrumental in changing early social scientists' attitudes toward women's nature. Female social scientists around the turn of the twentieth century were especially influential in weakening the hold evolutionist theories had on American scholars. "Many of those early academic critics [of social Darwinism] were women," Rosalind Rosenberg states in her excellent study of women and early social science, "and those who were men were strongly influenced by their female colleagues."[26] Thus, despite the fact that the number of women in these fields was small, they successfully challenged the biological underpinnings of prevailing definitions of women's nature by empirical research on socialization practices, personality development, and individual differences.

That there were no counterparts in history could have been simply fortuitous, given the small number of women scholars. But it is also possible that history was already defined as a "male" field in which the terms of debate and the areas of inquiry had been firmly established. History, after all, was not a new field in the same ways psychology and the social sciences were, despite the fact that they became professional academic disciplines in the same decades. Graduate training in history may have varied significantly from training in the social sciences, in part because history depended upon archival rather than empirical research and in part because established historians probably assigned dissertation topics to their seminar students. The social sciences may have given women more opportunity to define their own questions and research interests. Elsie Clews Parsons, for example, did a great deal of pioneering work on sex roles, but completed her Ph.D. in history with a standard dissertation on colonial legislation on education. By 1906, with the publication of *The Family*, she had shifted her allegiance to sociology. Although Parsons provides only one example, her experience suggests that female scholars interested in investigating topics concerning women and sex roles may have gravitated to the social sciences.

Just as history established itself as an academic discipline in its own right by the opening of the twentieth century, the field underwent radical internal changes. A new generation of historians, less aristocratic than their predecessors, frequently critical of American political and economic institutions and committed to social reform, worked to redefine the scope of history. These "progressive" historians, who dominated the profession from approximately the second decade of the twentieth century until World War II, called for a dynamic "new history" that would encompass social and economic developments as well as legal and political institutions, that would deal with conflict among classes and interest groups rather than stress national unity, and that would be relevant to contemporary social concerns.

The broad scope of "progressive" history, together with the fact that during the first decades of the twentieth century a feminist movement flourished, would suggest that these new historians' vision of the past would have included women. Indeed, a handful of progressive historians were sensitive to women's past. A small number of dissertations and monographs appeared. The eminent historian Arthur Schlesinger, working to develop the field of social history, recognized the absurdity of neglecting half of humanity in a discipline that purported to embrace the totality of past human experience. "If the silence of historians is taken to mean anything," Schlesinger wrote in his essay "The Role of Women in American History," "it would appear that one half of our population have been negligible factors in our country's history. Before accepting the truth of this assumption, the facts of our history need to be raked over from a new point of view. It should not be forgotten," he concluded, "that all of our great historians have been men and were likely therefore to be influenced by a *sex* interpretation of history all the more potent because unconscious."²⁷ In this essay and in his pioneering volume of urban history, *The Rise of the City*, Schlesinger worked to include women's contributions to the American past and to uncover the specific ways urbanization affected women's lives. Although Schlesinger's conceptualization of women's history was unsophisticated by contemporary standards—he evaluated women's "contributions" to history by the norms of male-dominated society—the fact that he recognized women at all is significant. Two other progressive historians, Charles and Mary Beard, also recognized the importance of women in the past and integrated women into their scholarship. In Mary Beard's *Woman as Force in History*, published in 1946, and in the Beards' joint work, *The Rise of American Civilization*, which appeared in 1930, women appear not as passive and powerless objects of study but as historical actors who exercised influence, made decisions, and occupied central economic roles throughout much of the past.

These first steps toward including women in the historical narrative were shortlived. Despite these historians' prominence, they generated no new movement to investigate women's past. "Progressive" historians, like their predecessors, did not create categories or work with notions of significance that could capture the realities of women's lives. History continued to be the record of public identity.

From World War II to the very recent present, women's history was relegated to what we might call the historical grab bag—a motley collection of quaint or out-of-the-way subjects that could never hope to claim the attention of serious scholars. The handful of serious essays and books on women published during these years—Eleanor Flexner's *Century of Struggle*, for example—received little attention from the profession.

The most likely places in historical writing to find mention of women were male historians' dedications. Prefaces to books and dissertations almost invariably contained tributes to the authors' wives. From these passages we can learn a good deal about male historians' attitudes toward women.²⁸ Ideally, women were wives and mothers possessed of inexhaustible reservoirs of emotional support. They were self-sacrificing, often willing to forsake their own educations or careers for the task of "putting husband through." And, of course, they were talented typists. The ideal woman of the dedications reflected the ideal woman of the postwar era, when social mores encouraged early marriage, large families, and good secretarial skills. Not surprisingly, the number of female scholars declined. Women, who had earned up to 16 percent of the doctorates in the decades before the war, earned less than 10 percent of the Ph.D.'s granted in the 1950s.²⁹

During the postwar era, cultural and social history came of age. But even in these specialities that should by definition have included women's experience, scholars asked few questions designed to uncover the realities of women's past. Instead, cultural historians debated the nebulous concept of "national character" as if women did not exist. Whether Americans were conformists or individualists, inner-directed or other-directed, materialistic or idealistic, were debates that apparently could be resolved without reference to women.[30]

Even many of the studies generated by the "new social history" of the 1960s and 1970s did little to illuminate women's historical experience. The "new social history" marked a significant departure from traditional themes: for the first time, historians asked questions about the private lives of ordinary people. And for the first time historians had methodological tools that enabled them to uncover aspects of everyday life in the past. But even with the new emphasis on private aspects of life, few historians have asked questions about women.

The study of social mobility, one of social historians' major interests, is a good case in point. Historians' assumptions about the significance and extent of social mobility in nineteenth-century America have been predicated entirely on the experience of men. Since the days of Theodore Roosevelt, historians of the west have consistently characterized the westward movement as male, despite the fact that westward migration was generally a family phenomenon. Male bias in the study of vertical social mobility is equally apparent. Mobility studies have been based on the unquestioned assumption that all Americans have regarded "getting ahead" as an important personal priority. Historians have also assumed, if they have given the matter any thought, that women achieved mobility through marriage. Neither of these assumptions has been examined. If the latter notion is correct, how likely were women to move up or down the social ladder by means of marriage? What other avenues of social mobility have been open to them? Studies such as Stephan Thernstrom's *Poverty and Progress* tell us a good deal about what happened to the sons of Newburyport, Massachusetts, immigrants, but they are silent about the daughters. More to the point, how important has the idea of social mobility been to women in the first place?[31] Did women share the individualistic, competitive ethic that historians assumed men possessed?

In a literal sense, then, our history has been manmade. Women, when they appeared in the historical narrative, have been peripheral figures, minor stereotyped characters in a discipline in which issues, periodization, and controversies developed without reference to them. Women's treatment in the historical narrative has reflected their social status in American society. Historians have not thought to write about women's lives in the past or to view history from a female perspective because they have known little about women's lives in the present. As I have indicated, this was especially true in the late nineteenth century, but to a very significant extent, such blindness continues to characterize historians today. Many continue to live in environments in which women play marginal and socially inferior roles. Male historians know little about the world of the women who manage the details of their personal and professional lives—the meal preparation, the care of offspring, the typing of manuscripts. How these tasks are accomplished, and what the life of accomplishing them is like are matters of little significance for the professional academician.

Historians' inability to deal with the realities of women's lives has distorted history as a field of knowledge in two fundamental ways. First, because historians have developed the scope of historical inquiry and defined basic assumptions about the nature of the American experience without reference to women, women have not been integrated into the historical narrative. As a result, our traditional notions of periodization and of social change and our conceptions of American history are flawed, and our interpretations of the impact of basic social, political, and economic developments on Americans' lives are one-dimensional and inaccurate. Just as historians now recognize that it is impossible to comprehend the development of virtually any aspect of American society without understanding the institution of slavery, so too it is impossible to understand America's past without recognizing women's role in the story. Second, historians' blindness to women and their narrow definitions of historical significance have meant that American society as women have experienced it is almost entirely unknown to us. We know little about the basic aspects of women's lives over time. What were their expectations, their options, their perceptions of themselves and others? As Virginia Woolf asks in *A Room of One's Own*, what were women doing "from eight in the morning till eight at night"?[32] What we have not had, in other words, is a history of women in which the questions are drawn from women's experience itself.

Let us look first at the ways historians' blindness to women in the past has distorted the existing historical record. Clearly, the original distortion of history as a field of knowledge was its self-definition as the record of the public past—a definition that may have originated in the nineteenth-century distinctions between public, or masculine, and private, or feminine, spheres. History, then, was truncated from the very beginning because the craft's practitioners confined themselves to a narrow range of questions that could never encompass the totality of human experience. Most of life is lived in private; most people do not have significant public roles—elementary facts that historians have only recently begun to realize.

The periodization of American history has been a second pervasive way in which the neglect of women has distorted our perceptions of the past. Periodization is the ordering of the past into a series of chronological time units; it provides a skeleton upon which historians build analysis and interpretation. In brief, it involves two components: the chronology itself, which includes the generally agreed upon divisions into significant epochs, and the generalizations historians make about each period. Both aspects have been distorted by historians' sexist perceptions of the past.[33]

Traditionally, the major chronology of American history has been political: the Revolution, the early national period, the Jacksonian era, the Progressive era, the New Deal, and so on. Clearly, periodization based primarily on political events and developments is largely irrelevant to women's history. But even when periodization is broader and more flexible, oriented to social and economic as well as political developments, problems in integrating women's experience into the established time periods persist. Historians' demarcations of separate historical epochs do not include significant changes in women's lives. For example, for most of human history, women were prisoners of their reproductive systems; their options were limited by the inevitability of frequent pregnancies and large numbers of children. One of the most profound shifts in women's history occurred over the course of the nineteenth century as the result of the development of an ideology of family planning and the introduction of effective means of contraception. Despite the central importance of this shift in the history of women, however, it occupies no place in historians' notions of periodization.

An even more serious difficulty involving periodization is historians' tendency to make judgments and generalizations about a given historical period that rarely reflect women's experience accurately. For example, historians generally view the years from the mid-eighteenth century through the first decades of the nineteenth century as a period characterized not only by political revolution and the formation of a new government but also by rapid commercial development and the beginnings of industrialization, territorial expansion, and rapid population growth. Increasingly, historians argue that this period can best be understood by subsuming these developments under the rubric of *modernization*. These years, then, mark a period of transition from a traditional society characterized by stability and hierarchical authority patterns to a modern society increasingly characterized by rapid social change, social and geographical mobility, and an individualistic, democratic ethos.

Such generalizations are invariably based on the experience of white males. Thus, whether this period is viewed in the traditional political framework as the years encompassing the American Revolution, the early national period, and the Jacksonian era, or as the period of modernization and economic expansion, historians' judgments are substantially identical: these were years characterized by the extension of political rights, the expansion of economic opportunity, and increased social mobility. But when we look at the same years through the lens of women's experience, the same picture does not emerge. For women, the liberal rhetoric of the American Revolution did not translate into increased opportunities for political expression. Although women played central roles in the economy throughout this period—as home spinners and weavers in the putting-out system and as the major source of early factory labor— woman's economic status declined in an industrial society in which the factory replaced the household as the central economic unit. The process of modernization itself had very different effects on men and women. Women's personal situations improved in modern society—a woman was much more likely to be literate, she was apt to exercise some control over the size of her family, she may have had more say in such basic decisions as who to marry, and she may have had more personal autonomy within her household. Paradoxically, however, although woman's personal status may have improved, her public status appears to have declined in modern American society. By the 1830s, a distinct and limited definition of woman's role had become dominant in American society. While white men's economic and social opportunities were expanding in early-nineteenth-century America, women's place had contracted to the household.[34] Until historians are sensitive to such differences in men's and women's experiences within specific time periods, the framework of history will continue to be sexist.

Historians' blindness to women has impoverished traditional American historiography in other ways as well. The history of institutions, organizations, and social movements in particular have often been misunderstood because historians have been unable to see women as active historical subjects. Women, as feminist historian Gerda Lerner stresses, have been important "institution-builders" throughout American history.[35] It is impossible to understand the establishment and growth of new communities —always a central theme in American historical writing—without taking women's work as institution-builders into account. The history of organizations and social movements has been flawed in similar ways. The Antinomian controversy in early-seventeenth-century Massachusetts is a good case in point. Attempts to interpret the turmoil surrounding Ann Hutchinson and her supporters and their treatment at the hands of the Puritan theocracy have concentrated upon the theological and political aspects of the episode. The fact that Ann Hutchinson was female did not enter into historians' analysis. The first study to consider Ann Hutchinson as a woman was unable to transcend male bias: the work concluded that Hutchinson's "deviant" behavior was menopausal in origin. The same study tried to uncover the motivations of Hutchinson's supporters by examining their husbands' occupations.[36] Not until very recently did it occur to a historian to interpret the Antinomian controversy from the point of view of its female participants.[37] Similarly, one cannot understand a social movement such as abolitionism without realizing that it was women who circulated and provided the majority of signatures on the thousands of antislavery petitions to Congress, women who organized and maintained the boycotts on slave products, women who, in short, provided much of the grassroots activity and moral and organizational impetus for the movement.

Historians' investigations of the nature, acquisition, and uses of power —again, the traditional stuff of historical inquiry—have also been distorted by male bias. Unlike social scientists, historians traditionally have "studied up"; that is, they have investigated powerful individuals and institutions.[38] But despite this emphasis on power and power relationships, it has not occurred to historians to examine patriarchy. We still know very little about the roots of male dominance and about men's uses of power in ways that affect women. What have been the historical connections between patriarchy and capitalism? How have men systematically used power in the family, in the professions, in trade unions, and in other social institutions to subordinate or exclude women? How, for example, were "old boy" networks established? How have they operated?[39] Then, too, we know little about women's uses of power. Although women have generally lacked concrete power resources, they have frequently possessed considerable personal influence. How have women exerted such influence throughout American history?

The first step, then, toward an equitable pursuit of historical knowledge is the integration of women into the existing narrative. To accomplish this involves asking new questions about such traditional concerns as the nature and uses of power. Such integration also involves revising our conceptions of periodization to make our chronology relevant to women's experience. To integrate women into history requires that we look carefully at the major developments and events in the American past to uncover the ways they have affected women as well as men. Finally, to integrate women in American history requires that historians be conscious of gender as well as such factors as race and class in assessing the dynamics of a given historical situation. Historians, in other words, must develop the ability to see women as actors in the past.

The second and more difficult step toward an equitable pursuit of knowledge is to rewrite American history from a female perspective.[40] As it is in the process of being defined, this new women's history is exploring new topics and redefining historical significance with the goal of reconstructing women's experience and consciousness in the past. It is grounded in the conviction that gender, like race and class, is a discrete category of historical analysis and in the belief that women's reality has been significantly different from men's. Such history is also based on the belief that there are universal and uniquely female experiences, such as childbirth, that can be investigated historically. Finally, this new history is concerned with uncovering the ways women have responded to their situation by creating separate female institutions, traditions, and relationships —in a word, by creating a female culture.[41]

Before the last two or three years, historians would have considered any talk of a female culture absurd. Because we never looked for evidence of such a culture, we simply assumed that it did not exist. Because we assumed that the essence of women's oppression throughout much of the past was their physical and psychological isolation from one another, we did not look for ways that women used to transcend the isolation of the individual household, by establishing close friendship networks and by amassing and transmitting specifically female knowledge from one generation to the next.

There are problems with the concept of female culture. We do not know the extent to which it existed. Much of the evidence is scattered and fragmentary. The most serious difficulty is a conceptual one: women's experience has never been shaped exclusively by gender. Women have always had a dual social status: class, ethnic background, and race, as well as gender, have defined women's places in American society. Despite the fact that we can talk about unique and universal female experiences, they have not been identical for all women. Pregnancy, childbirth, and motherhood, for example, have been very different experiences for white middle-class women and southern mountain women. Such difficulties notwithstanding, however, women's historians are increasingly interested in understanding women's past on its own terms, without imposing external notions of historical significance upon their findings.

What are some of the questions this new history should explore? Because women's lives have always been integrally tied to the family and the household, we need to know much more about the family from a female perspective. How have women perceived marriage and motherhood over time? How have they related to their husbands, their children, other women? One area that is already being explored is housework. Although housework is a virtually universal aspect of female experience, it has been inadequately explored—in part because housework is deemed socially and economically insignificant (it is not "real" work) and in part because most historians know nothing about it. As a result, we have assumed that housework and the role of housewife have not changed significantly over time. Recent historical overviews of housework indicate, however, that this is an aspect of women's lives that has changed dramatically over the course of American history, first as production shifted from home to factory and housewives lost their central economic role, later with the broad movement to systematize women's work within the home.[42] There are still many questions left unanswered about housework and the social and economic role of the housewife. How did housewives in the past perceive their role and their work? How have they structured time around the rhythms of housework and child care? When did women become American society's primary consumers? By what processes did they internalize this role?

The history of childbirth is another good example of an area women's historians are beginning to investigate. Because childbirth is an unchanging biological process, we have assumed that it had no history, properly speaking. But childbirth is a cultural as well as a biological event, and as such its management and the traditions that surround it have changed a great deal over time. Until very recently, our only insights into the history of childbirth were through the history of obstetrics. That story, which is usually told as a saga of male technological and professional mastery over the forces of primitive female ignorance and superstition, tells us little about the realities of childbirth from a female perspective. We know very little about maternal mortality or about the incidence of diseases such as toxemia and puerperal septicemia at different times and among different groups of women. We know even less about female perceptions of childbirth in the past. How did an awareness of the dangers of parturition affect women's consciousness in the past? How did women respond to the shift from midwives to predominantly male doctors and the later shift from home to hospital births?

In short, an equitable pursuit of knowledge must involve the willingness of historians to view women's past as significant in and of itself. In addition, our questions must be drawn directly from women's experience in the past, rather than dictated by conventional notions of historical significance. Because our perceptions of historical reality are largely what historians choose to record, women, in a very real sense, have had no history. And because history is knowledge and knowledge is a form of concrete power, women, by being denied access to their past, have also been excluded from this power source. By restoring women to the historical narrative and by uncovering women's unique experiences in the past, women's history revolutionizes the scope of historical inquiry.

NOTES

1 Richard Hofstadter, *The Progressive Historians* (New York, 1968), p. 3.
2 Compiled from Warren F. Kuehl, ed., *Dissertations in History: An Index to Dissertations Completed in History Departments of United States and Canadian Universities, 1873–1960* (Lexington, Ky., 1965).
3 The two excellent studies of American historical writing and the historical profession upon which I have relied most heavily are John Higham, *History: The Development of Historical Studies in the United States* (Englewood Cliffs, N.J., 1965), and Hofstadter, *The Progressive Historians*.
4 Lawrence Friedman, *Inventors of the Promised Land* (New York, 1975).
5 William Prescott's brief mention of women in his *Conquest of Mexico* (1843) was typical. "Above the combatants," he wrote, "rose a wild and discordant clamor, in which horrid shouts of vengeance were mingled with groans of agony . . . and with the screams of women; for there were several women, both natives and Spaniards, who had accompanied the Christian camp." Quoted in Frank Freidel, ed., *The Golden Age of American History* (New York, 1959), p. 45.
6 See Friedman, *Inventors of the Promised Land*, for a discussion of "patriotic mother" imagery in nineteenth-century popular historical writing.
7 Francis Parkman, *The Conspiracy of Pontiac and the Indian War after the Conquest of Canada* (Boston, 1901), 2: 246–48.
8 Ibid., 1: 1.
9 For discussion of imagery linking women and nature, see Friedman, *Inventors of the Promised Land*. For a general conceptual treatment of this idea, see Sherry Ortner's pioneering essay, "Is Female to Male as Nature Is to Culture?" *Feminist Studies* 1 (Fall 1972): 5–31.
10 The classic article on nineteenth-century sex role stereotypes is Barbara Welter, "The Cult of True Womanhood," *American Quarterly* 18 (Summer 1976): 151–74.
11 The best personal account of a nineteenth-century gentleman-scholar's upbringing and early adulthood is Henry Adams, *The Education of Henry Adams*.
12 The best treatment of nineteenth-century female culture is Carroll Smith-Rosenberg, "The Female World of Love and Ritual: Relations between Women in Nineteenth-Century America," *Signs* 1 (Autumn, 1975): 1–29.
13 Significantly, there is no discussion of even outstanding female historians in conventional treatments of nineteenth-century historical writing, such as David Van Tassel, *Recording America's Past: An Interpretation of the Devel-*

opment of *Historical Studies in America, 1607–1884* (Chicago, 1960). An excellent overview of the lives and careers of female historians is Kathryn Kish Sklar, "American Female Historians in Context, 1770–1930," *Feminist Studies* 3 (Fall 1975): 171–84. Also see the biographical essays on outstanding women historians in *Notable American Women*.

14 Quoted in Friedman, *Inventors of the Promised Land*, p. 151.
15 Precisely how small a minority we do not know. The American Historical Association has not kept ongoing records of the percentage of women in the historical profession. Statistics available on the percentage of doctorates going to women reflect all fields.
16 See Sklar, "American Female Historians in Context," for discussion of job discrimination and female historians' career patterns.
17 John Higham estimated that virtually all of the nineteenth-century amateurs and at least 26 percent of the first generation of professional historians were men of aristocratic background. Higham, *History*, pp. 9–10, 63–65.
18 Quoted in Higham, *History*, p. 155.
19 Theodore Roosevelt, "Manhood and Statehood," in *The Strenuous Life: Essays and Addresses* (New York, 1918), pp. 252–54 (emphasis mine). "Manhood and Statehood" was written in 1901.
20 Quoted in Elizabeth Waterson, "The Gap in Henry Adams' Education," *Canadian Journal of American Studies* 7 (Fall 1976): 138.
21 *The Education of Henry Adams* (Boston, 1974), pp. 379–90.
22 Quoted in Waterson, "The Gap in Henry Adams' Education," pp. 133–34.
23 Waterson makes this point in her fine analysis of Adams's views on women, "The Gap in Henry Adams' Education," p. 138.
24 This is an estimate based on information in the Report of the American Historical Association's Committee on the Status of Women, 1970.
25 This is a speculative conclusion based on biographical information on distinguished women historians in *Notable American Women* and in Sklar, "American Female Historians in Context."
26 Rosalind Rosenberg, "In Search of Woman's Nature, 1850–1920," *Feminist Studies* 3 (Fall 1975): 146.
27 Arthur Schlesinger, "The Role of Women in American History," in *New Viewpoints in American History* (New York, Macmillan, 1921), p. 126.
28 For a discussion of male historians' dedications and the attitudes they reveal, see Linda Gordon, Persis Hunt, Elizabeth Pleck, Rochelle Goldberg Ruthchild, and Marcia Scott, "Historians' Phallacies: Sexism in American Historical Writing," in *Liberating Women's History*, ed. Berenice Carroll (Urbana, Ill., 1976), pp. 55–74.
29 American Historical Association, Report by the Committee on the Status of Women in the Historical Profession, 1970, p. 11.
30 One brief attempt to deal with women and American national character is David Potter, "American Women and the American Character," in *American History and the Social Sciences*, ed. Edward N. Saveth (New York, 1964), pp. 427–45.
31 See James Henretta, "The Study of Social Mobility: Ideological Assumptions

and Conceptual Bias," *Labor History* 18 (Spring 1977): 165–78, for an excellent critique of the class and ethnic biases of existing social mobility studies. Many of Henretta's points can be applied to the male bias in the study of social mobility.
32 Virginia Woolf, *A Room of One's Own* (New York, 1929), p. 48.
33 The best discussion of the conceptual problems involved in periodizing women's history is Joan Kelly Gadol, "The Social Relation of the Sexes: Methodological Implications of Women's History," *Signs* 1 (Summer 1976): 809–23.
34 For appraisals of the impact of social and economic change on women's lives during this period, see Joan Hoff Wilson, "The Illusion of Change: Women and the American Revolution," in *The American Revolution: Explorations in the History of American Radicalism*, ed. Alfred Young (DeKalb, Ill., 1976), pp. 383–445; Nancy Cott, *The Bonds of Womanhood: "Woman's Sphere" in New England, 1780–1835* (New Haven, 1977); Gerda Lerner, "The Lady and the Mill Girl," *Midcontinent American Studies Journal* 10 (Spring 1969) pp. 5–14; and Daniel Scott Smith, "Family Limitation, Sexual Control, and Domestic Feminism in Victorian America," in *Clio's Consciousness Raised: New Perspectives on the History of Women*, ed. Mary Hartman and Lois Banner (New York, 1974), pp. 119–36.
35 Gerda Lerner, "The Majority Finds Its Past," *Current History* 70 (May 1976): 193–96.
36 Emery Battis, *Saints and Sectaries: Anne Hutchinson and the Antinomian Controversy in the Massachusetts Bay Colony* (Chapel Hill, 1962).
37 Lyle Koehler, "The Case of the American Jezebels: Anne Hutchinson and Female Agitation during the Years of Antinomian Turmoil, 1636–1640," in *Our American Sisters*, ed. William Shade and Jean Friedman, rev. ed. (Boston, 1976), pp. 52–75.
38 For a short but incisive critique of this phenomenon in social science research, see Laura Nader, "Studying Up," *Psychology Today* 11 (September 1977): 132.
39 Recently there has been some exciting work along these lines. See especially Heidi Hartmann, "Capitalism, Patriarchy, and Job Segregation by Sex," *Signs* 1 (Spring 1976, Supplement): 137–69, and Mary Walsh, *"Doctors Wanted: No Women Need Apply": Sexual Barriers in the Medical Profession, 1835–1975* (New Haven, 1977).
40 Such a reconstruction of female experience is just beginning. Examples of works along these lines include Smith-Rosenberg, "The Female World of Love and Ritual"; Gerda Lerner, ed., *The Female Experience: An American Documentary* (Indianapolis, 1977); Johnny Faragher and Christine Stansell, "Women and Their Families on the Overland Trail," *Feminist Studies* 2 (1975): 150–66.
41 For conceptual discussions of female culture, see Carroll Smith-Rosenberg, "The New Woman and the New History," *Feminist Studies* 3 (Fall 1975): 185–98, and Gerda Lerner, "Placing Women in History: Definitions and Challenges," *Feminist Studies* 3 (Fall 1975): 5–14.

42 Some excellent work has already been done on the history of housework. See especially Barbara Ehrenreich and Deirdre English, "The Manufacture of Housework," *Socialist Revolution* 26 (October–December 1975): 5–40; and, for the English experience, Ann Oakley, *Woman's Work: The Housewife, Past and Present* (New York, 1976). Also see Nona Glazer-Malbin, "Housework: Review Essay," *Signs* 1 (Summer 1976): 905–22.

JANE TIBBETTS SCHULENBURG

Clio's European Daughters
Myopic Modes of Perception

■ Recognition that women have been denied an equitable history is neither a modern phenomenon nor limited to this side of the Atlantic. Perhaps one of the best and earliest observations of the basic distortion of history dates to a medieval figure, that caustic critic, Chaucer's Wife of Bath. This articulate archwife notes:

> For take my word for it, there is no libel
> On women that the clergy will not paint,
> Except when writing of a woman-saint,
> But never good of other women, though.
> Who called the lion savage? Do you know?[1]

With her indomitable sense of humor, Dame Alice, the Wife of Bath, skillfully relates a number of problems basic to the structure of history that were evident during her own age. First of all, the writing of history was totally monopolized by men. For much of the Middle Ages, celibate clerics were the articulate sector of society; history was thus a function of their class. Historical works, coming from this single male vantage point (often as moral commentary), necessarily presented a slanted view of women, a perspective that emphasized women's essential inferiority. Thus, an unequal treatment of the sexes, a sexual stratification based essentially on ecclesiastical patriarchal values, underlines much of the history of the period. Visible female figures, worthy of historical ink, were stereotypically depicted as dichotomized beings, viewed through the medieval clerical condensing lens as either saints or sinners, Marys or Eves.[2] According to Dame Alice, positive treatment of women was limited to a few elite, exceptional women—specifically, women saints, whose lives served an edifying or didactic purpose. These medieval "Women Worthies,"[3] saints-virgins by definition, denied their sexuality and in this condition came closest to approximating men. Therefore, they alone were seen as worthy of compliment or praise—"faint praise" though it may have been.

The Wife of Bath also remarks, refreshingly, that if women had in fact written history, as the clergy had traditionally done, a radically different emphasis or slant would have resulted:

> By God, if women had but written stories
> Like those the clergy keep in oratories,
> More had been written of man's wickedness
> Than all the sons of Adam could redress.
> (p. 239)

Dame Alice thus contends that if female values and interests had determined the writing of history, the record would have been completely reversed; man would now become subject or victim of historical license. Indeed, Chaucer's Wife of Bath presents a rather enlightened consciousness of the inequitable treatment of the sexes in history. Her delightfully blunt responses to the underlying tensions created by patriarchal assumptions are unequaled in the literature of this period.

Christine de Pisan (ca. 1363–1431), the first feminist in the Western tradition, examines at some length the basic distortion of women in history. Her feminist tract, the *City of Ladies*, opens with her description of the immense depression she had experienced in her research. With the repetition of negative remarks by scholars about women—the male consensus in "slandering" all women—her disillusionment increased. (In many ways Christine de Pisan's experience is similar to that described so vividly by Virginia Woolf, some five hundred years later, in *A Room of One's Own*.)[4] De Pisan tells us that whatever author or volume she read, some chapters or certain clauses were intent on blaming women. She realized that women had indeed suffered much wrong from these biased writings; yet, faced with this consistent negative reinforcement, she began to doubt herself, thinking her own reasoning powers must be faulty.[5]

Reason, one of the female allegorical figures who come to aid and comfort de Pisan in the *City of Ladies*, answers her despair and confusion in regard to the misogynist tradition. She astutely observes that male accusations directed against women in fact contradict experience; they are "pure legends right shrewdly colored."[6]

Christine de Pisan then directs her attention to analyzing the origins of misogyny. What were the reasons for man's distorted view of womankind? Some men, she notes, blamed women, but supposedly with good intent, i.e., to warn other men of women's evil ways. De Pisan, however, says that these men are unjust and should not blame all women, many of whom are "right excellent," for the faults of a few. Some men write against women simply to show that they are well grounded in the Scriptures. Others espouse misogynism out of envy and sorrow. As old men they have become resentful because younger men have superseded them in their activities with women. They therefore project their sexual frustration, their "failings," ("Old, full of will and no power") on women. Another, most perceptive reason which Christine de Pisan suggests for the basic distortion of women is simple male ignorance of women's accomplishments through the ages, i.e., of women's history. Many believe that women, in fact, have contributed little to the world, their only service being that of bearing children and spinning.[7]

De Pisan then asks if there were any great women of high understanding and of science (great writers and philosophers). She is answered by Dame Reason: "If it were the custom to put the little maidens to school and that they were made to learn the sciences as do the male children, they should learn as perfectly and they should be as well entered into the subtleties of all the arts and sciences as they [the boys] are."[8] Dame Reason's observation embodies a remarkable feminist spirit for this period. In her perceptive criticism of society, de Pisan speaks out against the discriminatory educational policy of her age. With women being equally talented and having the same aptitude for education as men, she believed that they had an equal right to education.[9] The repercussions of this unfortunate educational exclusivity were, according to de Pisan, partially responsible for women's low profile among men of great learning and science.

Christine de Pisan is then charged with the building of the City of Ladies. This was to be a utopia populated exclusively by women, women of past history and myth as well as contemporary women distinguished for their achievements and virtues. Through the use of example, of "Women Worthies," she would be able to prove to "mankind" once and for all that women were in fact equal to, or even greater than, men. The city was to serve a number of purposes. Women would be included or harbored in the city so as not to be forgotten "as though they were strangers."[10] Thus, the city would provide historical immortality to its selected inhabitants. The feminist citadel would also serve as a defense to protect women against all detractors, such as those who say that God gave women only two positive attributes—the ability to bear children and to spin—or, at best, the three proverbial qualities of weeping, speaking, and spinning.[11] It was to be "a perpetual dwelling as long as the world shall last."[12]

This, then, was a type of early "compensatory history,"[13] perhaps a historical vindication, in which women would prove themselves capable of establishing and maintaining a thriving civilization. This early example of women's history, an anthology of famous women or collective biographies of women, was not original with Christine de Pisan. One of the earliest works of this type was a book on famous women written by the Greek biographer Plutarch.[14] Another anthology, Boccaccio's *De claris mulieribus* [Concerning famous women], written in the fourteenth century, provided at least three-quarters of the examples which de Pisan utilized in her *City of Ladies*.[15] Despite its borrowings from Boccaccio, the significance of the *City of Ladies* lies in how de Pisan used these examples. By providing a positive historical heritage for women (Boccaccio's work was definitely not in this "feminist" tradition),[16] she showed women, through the wide variety of roles they had played in the past, what they had been historically and what they could be in the future.[17] Thus, her selected examples of female achievement, bolstered by her critique of male conventional wisdom, provided an effective attack on the distorted view of women of her period. It also offered encouragement to others who, like de Pisan herself in the depths of depression at the beginning of her research, felt "that God made a foul thing when he formed woman . . . alas good lord why haddest thou not made me to be born into this world in the masculine kind?"[18]

Christine de Pisan's sensitive perception of the inequitable pursuit of knowledge and her energetic denial of this tradition were most extraordinary for the Middle Ages. In accord with the Wife of Bath, she notes that one of the basic reasons for the gross distortion of women in books is that women were not the authors. She observes essentially that one may plead a case well without party—"and I promise thee that books that so saith women made them not."[19] She also criticizes the bias of male authors who directed their works ostensibly toward the good of the commonweal but were in reality speaking to only one-half of the world, men. These authors should understand the two parts of the commonweal: "It is no doubt that the women be as well in the number of the earthly creatures as be the men."[20] Perhaps her most articulate concern for the equality of women in historiography came after studying her impressive catalogue of "Women Worthies." She states that it is time to right the scales, to rectify the blatant bias of male authors: "Madame, ye have showed me enough great constancy in the courage of women and all other virtues that truly no more may be said of any man. So I marvel greatly how so many worshipful ladies that have been so wise and so well lettered and that have gotten the fair style of writing and have made fair books have suffered so long without speaking out against the many errors directed against them by diverse men when they knew well that it was a great wrong."[21] Here then is a very "modern" voice, a timely observation and plea: women scholars must address themselves to the task before them. Her statement that she marvels at how these women could "have suffered so long without speaking out" against misogynism "when they knew well that it was a great wrong" is especially forceful, and it was written over five centuries ago!

These two late medieval sources—Chaucer's Wife of Bath and Christine de Pisan—which recognized the inequitable treatment of women, coincide with a period in which women's experiential realm had become substantially circumscribed; in general, their previous options in political, religious, and economic spheres had sharply contracted. It is thus a period in which divergencies between the historical experience of men and women had become more pronounced.

The compartmentalization of historical experience, with its concurrent narrowness of perception, can be traced with some consistency from the beginnings of historical writing. Western civilization has always been extremely attentive to its past and especially over the last 1,500 years a vast quantity of historical writing has emerged. The two great traditions which have influenced European historiography have been the classical and Christian legacies. One of the formative themes which emerged from the classical heritage was the treatment of political success, of the rise of a people to universal power.[22] The basic parameters of historical investigation were essentially determined by this interest in political development. A similar mode of historical perception underlines the biblical tradition. In Ecclesiasticus, for example, the following criterion of historical selection can be noted: "Let us now sing the praises of famous men, the heroes of our nation's history. . . . Some held sway over kingdoms and made themselves a name by their exploits. Others were sage counsellors. . . . Their line will endure for all time, and their fame will never be blotted out."[23] The world reflected by the ancient historians was populated essentially by prominent male figures. The emphasis on political power and success, and the general relegation of women to a secondary position in society, necessarily excluded most women from equally participating in the "making of history." Indeed, the visibility of women was often rather ingloriously predicated on their relationships to famous male figures: acting as wives, mothers, temptresses, and disastrous influences, singled out as the cause of war, etc.

Despite the rather consistent androcentric aims and emphases of traditional historiography, there were certain periods in which the historical experience of women came closer to approximating that of men. The early Middle Ages (ca. 500–1000) is a period in which this seems to be especially true. It is perhaps ironic that this era of female prominence has traditionally been designated as the "Dark Ages." (More will be said about the subjectivity of periodization later in this essay.) Before turning specifically to examples of historiography and the mental climate of two early medieval chroniclers, let us look briefly at some basic modes of historical perception. How did these early medieval historians perceive their world? How did they order their perception in view of their own condensing lens? As noted in a recent study of medieval chroniclers, "The medieval chronicler was an interested and partisan witness not only to the events of his time but to its tastes, prejudices, and preferences as to what was visually and perceptually significant. More than a mere scribe who contented himself with recording dates, facts, and gossip, the chronicler endowed his narrative with an intense view of the world and a projection on the world of acquired and often unconscious perceptual modes."[24] Although theoretically the chronicler was an impartial observer and recorder of events who narrated happenings in a somewhat chronological order, his task involved from the first a basic criterion of selection. And as Archambault points out, there is necessarily something arbitrary about choice! The chronicler reported those events and activities which were important to him and basically in accord with the condensing lens of his period. What is incorporated in history, and how it is incorporated, as well as those aspects that are neglected or excluded, depend in the final analysis on the chronicler's historical observation. Whether something is viewed as interesting and important (worth recording), or uninteresting and mundane (worth omitting), is part of a learned response or of unconscious assumptions. The chronicler's sense of importance was therefore in a large measure taught to him; and as a mode of perception it, in turn, affected reality.[25] Thus, this rather straightforward, matter-of-fact function was inevitably dependent on the writer's basic perceptual mode, his way of seeing experience, and on his value system.

Since history is based on a criterion of selection, biases appear in even the most objective attempts. As Marc Bloch noted, "The steadiest minds did not and could not escape the commonest prejudices of the time."[26] Thus on one level, predetermined, deliberate errors that skew historical fact are not uncommon in historiography. In order for an error to take hold, or spread, however, it had to comply with an age and its needs; it had to conform with the collective prejudice of the time. In other words, it was necessary for social conditions to favor the circulation of false rumors.[27]

But of perhaps more importance for women in historical writing is the area of unconscious distortion. This is most telling in regard to basic beliefs and prejudices of a period. In the gathering, sorting, and sifting of information, the general unconscious omission of women, for example, tells us much about the "mental equipment," the "intellectual presuppositions and environment" of the writer.[28]

The early Middle Ages seems to have fostered a rather positive mental climate in regard to the historical perception of women. The milieu reflected in the chronicles of this age was one of a rough-and-ready, *de facto* equality for women. In this frontier type of existence, women were looked upon as truly indispensable assets and as partners. Their high respect and prominence rested on a practical appreciation. The basic demographic imbalance, fewer women than men, helped to enhance women's position and worth in Germanic society.[29] Their strength of position in areas of public power (political and ecclesiastical) was predicated on the rather "irregular powers" held by the families of the period.[30] Queens and noblewomen were unusually prominent in the early medieval Church as proselytizers, generous benefactors, and powerful abbesses, especially of the double monasteries of Anglo-Saxon England.[31] The age also boasts a rather high percentage of women saints, again an indication of a basic prominence and visibility for women within society.[32]

Thus, life itself in early medieval society provided chroniclers with an opportunity to observe many able women participating in a wide variety of activities.[33] With the merging of public and private realms, the historical experience of women for this period rather closely approximated that of men; the dichotomy between male and female "spheres" was not artificially fixed or narrowly circumscribed as it would become in the twelfth and thirteenth centuries. Therefore, women, as visible and integral members of society, are not excluded from an active role in the shaping of history.

The sixth-century *History of the Franks*, written by Gregory of Tours, provides an extremely rich and invaluable perspective on early medieval society. As a French bishop, Gregory came into contact with a wide variety of experiences and people. Although his chronicle focused on the history of the French monarchy and Church, he records the activities of common people, women and men, alongside those of the most powerful rulers of the age.[34] In his position of authority, Gregory was acquainted with many of the women he described in his history. Women wielding religious or political power were especially visible in his society and were thus noted in some detail by Gregory. Therefore, one of the striking aspects of his history is the inclusive condensing lens, and specifically the natural and positive integration of women into the narrative of events. No special effort was made to isolate women in his history, or to evaluate them differently from men; for both women and men are described very simply by their actions.

Gregory's history is what is known as "exemplar history." Through the utilization of examples, models, it was to serve as a guide to proper action: "The function of this type of history is to select the relevant example (*paradeigma, exemplum*), in the didactic sense of being illustrative of what the society, through the historian, desires to inculcate and what it wants to warn against."[35] In describing his subjects, Gregory, as an ecclesiastic, utilizes moralistic terms, exaggerating both their "evil" and "holy" actions. His rather extensive treatment of the political quarrels of Brunhild and Fredegund is colored by this judgmental perspective; Brunhild is depicted as a very pious, competent woman and Fredegund as the "enemy of God and man."[36]

The History of the Franks provides a wealth of information on the multifarious activities of Germanic women. Gregory describes women's crucial roles in the proselytization movement, queens participating in royal conferences, queens appointing bishops to sees and endowing the Church with property from the royal domain, women going on pilgrimages to Jerusalem, women involved in lawsuits and pleading their own cases before the king, women active as wives of bishops, nuns criticizing bishops, and so on.[37] He recounts a very interesting case involving an attempted rape of a free woman by a local duke. The victim killed the duke, escaped, and was finally granted royal protection.[38] Gregory describes another woman as "a woman of great wisdom."[39] One of the most fascinating and detailed accounts in his chronicle is that of the revolt of the nunnery of Holy Cross.[40] Gregory himself was involved as an arbitrator in this rebellion, which took the authorities several years to quell.

Thus, Gregory of Tour's *History of the Franks*, as an example of a universal chronicle (which tends to be comprehensive and inclusive), mirrors a society with a natural integration of experiences for women and men. The artificial, constricted existences that will be prescribed in many of the writings beginning with the twelfth century are not part of the early medieval historical tradition.

Just as Gregory of Tours has been called the "Father of French History," so the Venerable Bede is often designated as the "Father of English History." In Bede's very influential *History of the English Church and People* we can note the assumptions, values, and basic perceptions of reality of an eighth-century monk. Despite the fact that Bede spent most of his life in the monasteries of Wearmouth-Jarrow in the north of England, his history exhibits a rather healthy attitude toward women. Again, within this early medieval society, the experiential realms between men and women were not highly differentiated, and this, in turn, is reflected in the historiography.

Bede's own exceptional personality pervades his entire history; and it is a key to understanding his rather positive views on women. In the preface to his ecclesiastical history, and in the introduction to his life of Saint Cuthbert, he underlines the importance of intellectual objectivity in both his source materials and his own writing.[41] Another important aspect of his personality defining the scope, emphasis, and general tone of his history is what has been called his "intellectual humility." Bede tells us that the purpose of history is to record what ordinary people believed: "The opinion of the common people is the true law of history."[42] Thus, Bede's appreciation of human variety, his observations of individual women and men, peasants, queens and kings, abbesses, nuns, abbots and monks, found throughout his history, underline his basic criterion of selection.

Although Bede saw the contemplative monastic life as the ideal type of existence, throughout his history one can note his essential practicality.[43] He understood the practical importance of women in the conversion of the English to Christianity and in the development of the English Church. The very presence of a substantial number of women in his history points up the fact that they were definitely worth Bede's attention and were of interest to him as a person and writer. Thus, in his ecclesiastical history, Bede shows a great deal of practical admiration and respect for the English women of his time. He depicts them as bright, aggressive women; able administrators; and extremely influential people. Bede notes, for example, that Abbess Ethelburga "runs her convent in a manner worthy of her brother"[44] (the highest compliment for this period). Or he writes of Abbess Hilda of Whitby, "So great was her prudence that not only ordinary folk, but kings and princes used to come and ask her advice in their difficulties and *take it*."[45] In his life of Saint Cuthbert, he describes Abbess Aelfflaed as a "wise woman and learned in the Holy Scriptures"; but of greater significance was the fact that she acted with "womanly daring" (*audacia feminea*).[46]

Bede's history has been read for over 1,200 years and has served as a prime source of information about the early history of Christianity among the English.[47] Written in the north of England, in a monastery far removed from the ancient centers of civilization, it is truly a remarkable work. Despite Bede's cultural isolation, his viewpoint is by no means parochial nor limited; rather, through his well-endowed monastic library he was acquainted with a variety of classical sources and had also assimilated the idioms and traditions of the Church Fathers.[48] Still, Bede was by no means servile to their authority and traditional mental attitudes. He obviously disregarded their work if it seemed "unreasonable" to him; and this proved to be especially true in regard to the negative patristic perception of women. His world was definitely a different practical and intellectual world from theirs; his scholarship and outlook were indeed unique.[49]

As a "grandchild of pagans" and a "child of barbarians,"[50] Bede's history is a product of pagan barbarism.[51] And as such, it represents new beginnings. Although cognizant of past historiographic traditions—classical and patristic works—his approach reflected a new world and its mindsets. Removed from and perhaps less encumbered by traditional modes of thought, Bede seems to have approached reality with a less constricted, or at least a different, view. Bede, then, should be singled out for his broad conceptual framework of human history, and for his remarkable sensitivity and understanding, which later historians, more restricted and rigid in their perception, more specialized and "professional" in their task, would lack.

The centuries that followed Bede's, specifically the eleventh and early twelfth centuries, witnessed a silent revolution.[52] Nearly all areas of life were affected by change. As society and its institutions became more stabilized, more highly structured and organized, and as the Church became reformed and more "rightminded," women were denied the active roles which they had previously *assumed.* They "found their own spheres of influence beginning to shrink, especially in the upper reaches of political and economic power."[53] The historical experience of women also began to diverge substantially from that of men. Victims of a rationalized confinement of women, they became isolated from the "mainstream of history." Their previous visibility became faded and obscured. These societal shifts are reflected in some of the basic changes in historiography of the central and late Middle Ages.

While the twelfth and thirteenth centuries were centuries favorable to systematization, they were basically "unhistorical" in their approach to knowledge. In other words, in their search for "truth" about the universe and the nature of "Man," in the creation of their summas, they in fact agreed to ignore the specifics, to ignore history.[54]

With a decline in clerical history writing, the aristocratic chronicle became one of the popular forms of historical writing from the twelfth to fifteenth centuries. In the same tradition as the medieval romances, the aristocratic chronicles were extremely narrow, limited to celebrating the values of the knightly class. Activities of the "other," the nonnoble classes, those existing outside of the pale of aristocratic privilege, were seen as not worthy of the aristocratic chronicler's attention. The emphasis of this literary genre was on the personal honor of the knight. Public posture, the heroic, aristocratic stance, based on the chivalric code of behavior, was now of prime importance.[55]

Aristocratic women were "altered" to be made to fit into this value system "more or less badly." As might be expected in this highly restrictive atmosphere, aristocratic women were not provided active roles; rather they served a secondary, subordinate function, as sources of inspiration for the knights' heroic acts. This obviously was not a very satisfactory role for women, "since most of the time they were a mere excuse for the hero's usual hyperthyroid activity."[56] But at the same time that women's experience in real life was becoming more and more circumscribed—as they were increasingly displaced from an active role with very real power—the literary pretensions, women's images in history and literature, became more extravagant. The loss in real power was neatly masked by a chivalric veneer providing women with an illusion of power and prestige. This fantasy of power was created in the aristocratic woman's ability to ensnare and captivate her courtly lovers. She was accorded a superficial respect with a highly conscious emphasis on physical attributes (male-defined anatomical perfection) and proper courtly deportment.

The historical model for women, illustrative of the moeurs the fashionable aristocracy wished to inculcate, no longer incorporated the early medieval "positive" characteristics of intelligence, leadership, administrative skills, and others. Instead of figures of action, women now worthy of historical ink were passive creatures; they served society as ornaments, as mere objects to be won over. Highly constricted by the codes of proper deportment, the aristocratic "lady" was nearly "refined out of existence." Her elevation to the pedestal, as noted by Eileen Power, was much like that of a stylite, and "few human beings are suited to the part of Stylites, whether ascetic or romantic."[57]

The ideals found in the aristocratic writings of the central and late Middle Ages were limited, however, to a small aristocratic caste. They were simply projections of an idealized life that suited the aristocracy's aspirations and standing.[58] Their real existence, then, was not necessarily in accord with this mode of perception. Nevertheless, as ideals, they were widely disseminated and became very influential. And even long after their "usefulness" had passed, they have lingered on, partially assimilated into very different societies. (A similar mind-set, for example, can be found in nineteenth-century romanticism and the Cult of True Womanhood.) It indeed points up how tenacious such ideologies can be!

Thus, the historical experience of the aristocratic chronicle was extremely narrow, rigid, class conscious, and exclusive. The main concentration was on heroic actions of knights in battle, their crusading efforts, and chivalric biographies of kings, tracing their heroic descent and justifying their rule. The active heroic existence of aristocratic men was sharply differentiated from the explicit passiveness expected of women.[59] In sum, the aristocratic mental climate stressed a total separation of male and female roles.

The hypocrisy of this type of chivalric viewpoint, with its inherent assumption of the amelioration of womankind, provided part of Christine de Pisan's frustration described in her *City of Ladies*. Whereas conceptually, women were accorded an honorific position—worshipped and placed on a pedestal—in reality, women consistently experienced heavy antifeminism and less-than-equitable treatment. Thus the appearance of the eternal dichotomized woman, a figure similar to Virginia Woolf's monstrosity, "a worm winged like an eagle."[60]

For centuries scholars have questioned and criticized the aims, methods, and especially the limitations of traditional historiography. The eighteenth-century critic Voltaire delivered an early and famous protest. "It seems," he wrote, "that for fourteen hundred years, there have been none but kings, ministers, and generals in the Gauls."[61] While he recognized the need for political history, the study of battles and dynastic quarrels, Voltaire stressed that history should also include a history of customs and culture.[62] Despite the attempt by the Enlightenment *philosophes* to change the canons of traditional historiography and to write social history, they were basically uninterested in history *per se*. Their main interest was in using past evidence to prove their general philosophical tenets. The nineteenth-century Romanticists also had a new appraisal of historiography. In their historical studies they attempted to be more comprehensive and to utilize a wide variety of sources and disciplines. Despite this new "interdisciplinary" approach, however, political history remained the main focus of research.

It was only in the late 1920s that a truly new history began to emerge, under the tutelage of Lucien Febvre and Marc Bloch, two of the greatest and most influential French historians. They established what has been called the *Annales* school, named after the journal they set up in 1929 to publish new research in social and economic history. In their work they waged a common battle against political and narrative history, striving constantly for a "new and even revolutionary history."[63] Febvre and Bloch labored to supplant traditional historiography with a "wider and more human history," a "living history," a people-oriented history. Their goal was to study whole social units, to produce "total history," history without compartments.[64]

In his classic *The Historian's Craft*, Marc Bloch defines history as a human science, one that could learn much from the other social sciences. According to Bloch, written historical records—"intentional evidence"—were no longer sufficient for historical inquiry. Historians needed to test everything which might in fact fill in the gaps and provide a better understanding of the past. Bloch advocated that historians discover and use new methodologies and especially new types of source material. They must avoid excessive historical specialization and instead have a smattering of knowledge in a wide range of subjects and techniques, employing an integrated, interdisciplinary research. Historians were then to place more and more confidence in a second category of source material, that of "unintentional evidence," i.e., "evidence of witnesses in spite of themselves." Only by this means could scholars reconstruct, or fill in, whole sections of the past that had been missing. Bloch notes that without the aid of "unintentional evidence" historians would simply perpetuate the same "false prejudices, false inhibitions and myopias which had plagued the vision of those same generations."[65]

Yet despite Febvre's and Bloch's perceptive and valid critiques of traditional historiography and their pleas for emancipation from the narrow constraints of the past, their own historical models contained both internal and external contradictions. Traian Stoianovich, in his excellent study *French Historical Method: The Annales Paradigm*, points out that while the title of their journal, *Annales: Économies, Sociétés, Civilisations*, encompassed a commitment to social history, *Annales* scholars consistently remained ambivalent at best in regard to the whole area of social history. Social history continued to be poorly defined; and economic change, material structures, and "mental equipment" remained the main focus of their research and interest. *Annales* scholars similarly neglected research on the family and the history of women and children.[66]

The tradition of neglect, or unconscious omission, of women in historiography is apparent in the *Annales* models established by Febvre and Bloch. Their paradigms, their own language, their definitions, all unfortunately belie the actualization of a new, comprehensive history. For example, throughout many of Febvre's essays defining his new approach, methodology, and techniques, a most glaring "inconsistency" plagues the modern reader. Nearly every page is permeated with exclusively masculine references: the reader, the researcher, the object of this new history is man/men.[67] In Marc Bloch's definition of history, the tenacity of traditional habits in concept and language are again telling:

> Long ago, indeed, our great forebears, such as Michelet or Fustel de Coulanges, taught us to recognize that the object of history is, by nature, *man*. Let us say rather, *men*. Far more than the singular, favoring abstraction, the plural which is the grammatical form of relativity is fitting for the science of change. Behind the features of landscape, behind tools or machinery, behind what appear to be the most formalized written documents, and behind institutions, which seem almost entirely detached from their founders, there are *men*, and it is *men* that history seeks to grasp.[68]

Although in this definition Bloch obviously intends the term *men* to be generic, all-inclusive, to encompass both men and women, his history in fact comprehends only the specific, i.e., men. Whereas this new history was to be *histoire totale*, "a wider and more human history," no special effort is made to fill this all-too-obvious gap in traditional historiography.

Marc Bloch's great classic, *Feudal Society*, which has become a model for the new generations of medieval social and economic historians, has indeed very little to say about women.[69] In fact, there are only two general references to women—"women and the inheritance of fiefs" and "great ladies"—and a mere four others referring to such *femmes extraordinaires* as Brunhilde, Kreimhild, Edith, Queen of England, and Joan of Arc. The attention devoted to women is about on a par with the index entry "horses and their role in England."

Stoianovich argues that this neglect of family history (and women's history) was predicated on the "old habit" of traditional history, developed when historians had been solely interested in the growth of political power. He notes: "Historians among whom political history became unfashionable, on the other hand, could not formulate new historical facts in regard to the family with ease until the assertion of a climate of opinion favorable to the study of nonconsensual and vanquished groups." It is this favorable new climate which seems to have influenced the "new history" of the third generation of the *Annales* school. *Annales* scholars are now focusing their research on "all groups previously considered historyless."[70] Again according to Stoianovich,

> The object of *Annales* work is to construct a history of every group and subject whose investigation has been suppressed or neglected. . . . It aims similarly at the "demasculinization of history" and at the development of a history of women, of youth, of childhood, of oral cultures, of voluntary associations. . . . To achieve their exalted goal of penetrating the arcana, they [the *Annales* scholars] are ready to use linguistics, demography, folklore, psychology, and psychoanalysis. They will look at a text not only for what it says but for its silence as well, which may relate to the said or the written as the unconscious relates to the conscious.[71]

Thus, especially during the early 1960s, there occurred a growing interest among historians in the hidden, the "historyless," the "nonconsensual."[72] Studies in historical demography and the history of childhood became "legitimized" as valid areas of research. And with this new interest and scholarly acceptance, the family became a primary *Annales* concern; in fact, the 1972 issue of the *Annales* was entitled "Famille et société."[73] Within this same climate of favorable opinion, women's history has slowly emerged from the periphery of historiography and has been recognized as a vital component of total history.

Yet despite these very exciting and revolutionary changes in recent historiography, with the new emphasis on social history—the family, women, and childhood—the old traditional models of neglect still persist in new scholarship. The continuity with old habits remains incredibly strong. Stoianovich notes, for example, one aspect of continuity in the *Annales* journal: that is, its use on the cover of every issue of the messenger god Hermes (mediator between gods and men) as a symbol of *Annales* scholarship. He then observes:

> Behind or beside the revealed Hermes stands, we presume, an invisible or concealed Hestia, as in classical Greek tradition. As in Greece, too, the Hestia of the *Annales* represents an enclosed, domestic, feminine space, with a fixed center (the hearth), while Hermes represents movement, passage, repeated change of condition, mobile wealth, constant and repeated intercourse with the outside world. The space of human collectivities, in *Annales* thought as in Greek tradition, has a dual aspect—Hermaean and Hestian. It is at once fixed and mobile, autarkic and interdependent. Nor can one stress sufficiently the constant presence of these two aspects in general human experience.[74]

It is only over the last fifteen or twenty years, then, with the climate of opinion favorable to the study of neglected groups, that scholars have become increasingly sensitive to the need of considering this dual aspect in history: the necessarily complementary roles of women and men in society. But for many historians, conditioned in the habits of traditional historiography, women continue to exist within the time-honored, truly hidden Hestian tradition, as either the "invisible or concealed," as definitely "historyless" entities.

A final limitation of traditional historiography which this essay will briefly examine is that of conventional periodization and its effects on the evaluation of women in history. Marc Bloch, in *The Historian's Craft*, criticized the unreality of the traditional periodization of history.[75] Conventional terms such as the "Middle Ages" and "Renaissance" are simply intellectual conveniences that serve only a pedagogical function. They are concepts, convenient mental categories, and not a reality. These "modern" terms do not necessarily coincide with critical points in human development. Based on perceptual modes, they are subjective and imply value judgments. As Bloch has noted, "The worst of it is that since the name, as always, carries the idea along with it, these false labels end by misrepresenting the merchandise."[76]

The critical questioning of traditional historical periodization is especially crucial for women's history. Joan Kelly-Gadol's excellent pioneering studies on women in European history have dealt with this problem. She points out, for example, that during the Italian Renaissance the historical experience for women differed substantially from that of men; in fact, "there was no renaissance for women—at least, not during the Renaissance."[77] For medieval history, the conventional historical periodization is also most arbitrarily conceived; and this seems to be especially true viewed in light of women's experience. The early Middle Ages (500–1000) has traditionally been denoted, in a somewhat condescending fashion, as the "Dark Ages," whereas the twelfth century usually is described in terms of a rebirth or renaissance. Yet for women, as we have previously noted, the period of the early Middle Ages (the "Dark Ages") was a very positive period indeed. This was an age when women played a vital role in society and were extremely visible in a wide variety of roles. And interestingly enough, it is in the period of the twelfth-century renaissance that women's roles substantially contracted; they experienced a loss in nearly all areas of prominence. Nonetheless, the Enlightenment's invention of the "Dark Ages" has remained very influential in perpetuating a myth about this "brutish" and barren period. One of the popular misconceptions which the historical formula "Dark Ages" has encouraged is that this was indeed the nadir in women's historical existence, that it was an age of women's total subordination and subjugation. One author notes:

> The persistence of this myth of woman's abject subordination is partially attributable to what may be termed the "masculine historical rationalization," which assumes that modern women are much better off when compared with the miserable lot of their forebears, and its corollary, the "male argument from progress," which concludes that men are much more enlightened now when compared with the barbaric practices of their ancestors. The more we get ourselves to believe the sexual injustices of the "Dark Ages," the more we are able to persuade ourselves of our own evolutionary progress.[78]

Thus, this attempt to impose arbitrarily chosen formulae to realities and provide a "false precision" to an age often falls short of coinciding with the actual historical experiences of the period.[79] These judgmental tags frequently end up furthering misconceptions of the past, and subsequently provide a convenient rationale for the inequities of the present. Historians must challenge traditional periodization. They need to look more closely at the wide experiential variants of a period.

In this essay I have attempted to survey a few indices of the inequitable pursuit of knowledge in European historiography. Though the creative force of history is the female muse Clio, and the very Roman letters used in the writing of history were, according to tradition, invented by a woman,[80] women have not fared at all well in the discipline. Across the centuries, the historiographic tradition has been conspicuously narrow, political, didactic, and uncompromisingly androcentric. We find few women historians, and in general, few women as the subject matter of intentional historical evidence. Needless to say, it is high time to rectify the biases of the past, to redress the balance as Christine de Pisan so valiantly attempted over five hundred years ago.

An immense amount of creative research is needed to fill the blatant lacunae of traditional historiography. The sources are indeed available: women in the past have not been mute, historyless nonentities. There is a great wealth of information on women in historical sources—hidden within the annals of intentional evidence, or especially prominent in the "unintentional" sources, such as censuses, wills, parish records, cartularies, hagiography, and iconography. In many cases this evidence, as it pertains to women, remains essentially untouched. New and creative minds are needed to analyze it, to ask new questions, and to apply new methodologies. In these investigations, an increased emphasis will need to be placed on "unintentional evidence," and also on studying sources for their silences as well as for what they say.[81] Considering the incredible dimensions of the task before us, this will be an ongoing project for many generations of historians.

The goals, the actual methodology, and the basic definition of the task remain a point of contention among scholars. One of the confusing issues in our research on women is that it is often extremely difficult to know what is uniquely female over and against what is human, to know, in surveying historical change, to what degree problems are a function of being a woman, and to what degree they are common to both women and men during a certain period. Therefore, we must in our research move beyond a compartmentalized perception of society and expand our vision to truly encompass a "wider and more human history." We must enlarge our condensing lens to reveal a total landscape, a "total history," and not perpetuate in our attempts to "right the scales" a type of myopic perception suspiciously reminiscent of traditional historiography. Since no true understanding can be attained without a certain range of comparison, this necessarily means the integration of both women and men in our historical ventures. As Natalie Zemon Davis puts it in a recent article:

> ... it seems to me that we should be interested in the history of both women and men, that we should not be working only on the subjected sex any more than an historian of class can focus exclusively on peasants. Our goal is to understand the significance of the *sexes*, of gender groups in the historical past. Our goal is to discover the range in sex roles and in sexual symbolism in different societies and periods, to find out what meaning they had and how they functioned to maintain the social order or to promote its

change. Our goal is to explain why sex roles were sometimes tightly prescribed and sometimes fluid, sometimes markedly asymmetrical and sometimes more even.[82]

NOTES

1 Geoffrey Chaucer, *The Canterbury Tales*, trans. Nevill Coghill (Baltimore, 1952), p. 293. All quotations of *The Canterbury Tales* are from this edition.
2 Eileen Power, "The Position of Women," in *The Legacy of the Middle Ages*, ed. C. G. Crump and E. F. Jacob (Oxford, 1926), pp. 401-2.
3 The term "women worthies" is from Natalie Zemon Davis, "'Women's History' in Transition: The European Case," *Feminist Studies* 3 (Spring-Summer 1976): 83-103.
4 Virginia Woolf, *A Room of One's Own* (New York, 1957), esp. pp. 31-37.
5 *Here begynneth the boke of the Cyte of Ladyes*, trans. Bryan Anslay (London: H. Pepwell, 1521), pt. I, chap. i.
6 Ibid., chap. ii.
7 Ibid., chaps. viii, xxxvii.
8 Ibid., chap. xxvii.
9 Lula McDowell Richardson, *The Forerunners of Feminism in French Literature of the Renaissance from Christine de Pisan to Marie de Gournay*, The Johns Hopkins Studies in Romance Literatures and Languages, 12 (Baltimore, 1929), p. 28.
10 *Cyte of Ladyes*, pt. II, chap. lxvii.
11 Ibid., pt. I, chaps. xxxvii, x.
12 Ibid., pt. II, chap. lxviii.
13 The term "compensatory history" is taken from Mari Jo Buhle, Ann G. Gordon, and Nancy Schrom, "Women in American Society: An Historical Contribution," *Radical America* 5 (July-August 1971): 3-66.
14 See Plutarch, "Concerning the Virtues of Women," in *Plutarch's Essays and Miscellanies*, ed. A. H. Clough and William W. Goodwin (Boston, 1909), 1: 340-84; Philip A. Stadter, *Plutarch's Historical Methods: An Analysis of the 'Mulierum Virtutes'* (Cambridge, 1965).
15 Richardson, *Forerunners of Feminism*, p. 26. See Giovanni Boccaccio, *Concerning Famous Women*, trans. Guido A. Guarino (New Brunswick, 1963). The idea for Boccaccio's *De claris mulieribus* was taken from Petrarch's *De viris illustribus*.
16 In *De claris mulieribus* Boccaccio notes that he has marveled in regard to those who have written of the illustrious deeds of noble men and "why they have not somewhat touched on the glorious acts of women, when it is evident that divers and sundry of them have done right notable things." He then reviews the deeds of some three hundred notable women. This work is essentially a didactic tract, providing admonishments for the women of his own day. In part

Boccaccio praises the positive behavior of women in the past to accentuate the "depraved" characteristics of "modern," Renaissance women. Another of Boccaccio's works, *The Corbaccio* (1354–55), underlines his blatant antifeminism. This work becomes an arsenal of misogynist thought, as it continues and further elaborates upon the early writings of the Church Fathers. According to Boccaccio, *The Corbaccio* was provoked by his rejection by a Florentine widow. Her husband's spirit apparently returned to have Boccaccio tell the "bitter" truth about this woman and all women!

17 Davis, "'Women's History' in Transition," p. 83.
18 *Cyte of Ladies*, pt. I, chap. i.
19 Ibid., pt. II, chap. xiii.
20 Ibid., chap. liii.
21 Ibid.
22 Marc Bloch, *The Historian's Craft*, trans. Peter Putnam (New York, 1959), p. 4; R. W. Southern, "Aspects of the European Tradition of Historical Writing, 1: The Classical Tradition from Einhard to Geoffrey of Monmouth," *Transactions of the Royal Historical Society*, 5th ser. 20 (1970): 175, 188–89.
23 Ecclesiasticus 44:1–3, 13, in *The New English Bible: The Apocrypha* (Oxford, 1970).
24 Paul Archambault, *Seven French Chroniclers: Witnesses to History* (Syracuse, 1974), p. ix.
25 William J. Brandt, *The Shape of Medieval History: Studies in Modes of Perception* (New York, 1973), p. 105.
26 Bloch, *The Historian's Craft*, p. 134.
27 Ibid., pp. 106, 107.
28 Southern, "The European Tradition of Historical Writing," p. 173. The term "mental equipment" (*l'outillage mental*) is found in L. Febvre's writings and is the title of volume 1 of his *Encyclopedie française*. See Peter Burke, ed., *A New Kind of History from the Writings of Febvre*, trans. K. Folca (London, 1973), p. xiii.
29 See David Herlihy's *Women in Medieval Society* (Houston, 1971), p. 5; and idem, "Life Expectancies for Women in Medieval Society," in *The Role of Woman in the Middle Ages*, ed. Rosemarie Thee Morewedge (Albany, 1975), pp. 5–10.
30 Jo Ann McNamara and Suzanne Wemple, "The Power of Women through the Family in Medieval Europe: 500–1100," in *Clio's Consciousness Raised: New Perspectives on the History of Women*, ed. Mary Hartman and Lois Banner (New York, 1974), p. 113.
31 Double monasteries, consisting of separate houses for nuns and monks within one physical unit, were usually under the jurisdiction of an abbess. This provided abbesses with a great deal of real power and visibility during the early Middle Ages.
32 See my article, "Sexism and the Celestial Gynaeceum: From 500–1200," *Journal of Medieval History* 4 (1978): 117–33.
33 Betty Bandel, "The English Chroniclers' Attitude toward Women," *Journal of the History of Ideas* 16 (1955): 144.

34 Gregory of Tours, *History of the Franks*, trans. Lewis Thorpe (Baltimore, 1974), pp. 34–35.
35 Traian Stoianovich, *French Historical Method: The Annales Paradigm* (Ithaca, 1976), p. 26. I would like to thank Shelia Cooper of the Department of History, Indiana University, Bloomington, for calling my attention to Stoianovich's work.
36 Gregory of Tours, *History of the Franks*, bk. ix, chap. 20.
37 Ibid., bk. ii, chaps. 29–31; bk. ix, chap. 10; bk. x, chap. 31; bk. i, chap. 39; bk. ix, chap. 33; bk. ii, chap. 17; bk. iv, chap. 36; bk. ix, chap. 40.
38 Ibid., bk. ix, chap. 27.
39 Ibid., chap. 24.
40 Ibid., chaps. 39–43; bk. x, chaps. 15–17.
41 Bede, *The History of the English Church and People*, trans. Leo Sherley-Price (Baltimore, 1968), pp. 33–35; idem, *Two Lives of St. Cuthbert*, trans. Bertram Colgrave (New York, 1969), p. 143.
42 Peter Hunter Blair, "The Historical Writings of Bede," *La Storiographia altomedievale* 17 (Spoleto, 1970): 200, 202.
43 Ibid., p. 204.
44 Bede, *History*, bk. iv, chap. 6.
45 Ibid., chap. 23 (emphasis mine).
46 *Two Lives of St. Cuthbert*, bk. xxiv.
47 Blair, "The Historical Writings of Bede," p. 221.
48 Gerald Bonner, "Bede and Medieval Civilization," in *Anglo-Saxon England*, ed. Peter Clemoes, vol. 2 (Cambridge, 1973), pp. 72–73.
49 Ibid., pp. 74–76.
50 Jean Leclercq, *The Love of Learning and the Desire for God*, trans. C. Misrahi (New York, 1961), p. 45.
51 Blair, "The Historical Writings of Bede," p. 198.
52 See R. W. Southern, *The Making of the Middle Ages* (New York, 1953), esp. pp. 219–57.
53 Jo Ann McNamara and Suzanne Wemple, "Sanctity and Power: The Dual Pursuit of Medieval Women," in *Becoming Visible: Women in European History*, ed. R. Bridenthal and C. Koonz (Boston, 1977), p. 92.
54 Southern, "The European Tradition of Historical Writing," p. 163.
55 See Brandt, *The Shape of Medieval History*, pp. 81–146.
56 Ibid., p. 143.
57 Power, "The Position of Women," p. 406. The phrase "refined out of existence" is from a paper presented by Judith M. Davis at the Seventh Conference on Medieval Studies, April 30–May 3, 1972, at Western Michigan University, Kalamazoo, entitled "Courtly Love-Ethic and Medieval Romance: The Role of Women as Love Objects and Narrative Devices."
58 D. J. A. Matthew, *The Medieval European Community* (London, 1977), p. 110.
59 Brandt, *The Shape of Medieval History*, pp. 139–45.
60 Woolf, *A Room of One's Own*, p. 46.
61 Quoted in Bloch, *The Historian's Craft*, p. 178.

62 Stoianovich, *French Historical Method*, p. 29.
63 Ibid., p. 11.
64 Burke, *A New Kind of History*, pp. xii, 27-43; Bloch, *The Historian's Craft*, pp. x, 18.
65 Bloch, *The Historian's Craft*, pp. 61-62. Bloch defines "intentional evidence" as "accounts which are consciously intended to inform their readers."
66 Stoianovich, *French Historical Method*, pp. 9, 95-96, 167-68, 170-80.
67 See, for example, pp. 27-43 in Burke, *A New Kind of History*.
68 Bloch, *The Historian's Craft*, pp. 25-26 (emphasis mine).
69 Marc Bloch, *Feudal Society*, trans. L. A. Manyon (London, 1961).
70 Stoianovich, *French Historical Method*, pp. 171, 158.
71 Ibid., pp. 158-59.
72 Ibid., chap. 6, "Historyless and Nonconsensual." The following is a very incomplete list of some of the most prominent scholars working in this area: Braudel, Duby, Herlihy, Ariès, Le Goff, Le Roy Ladurie, Laslett, Meuvret, and Goubert.
73 Ibid., pp. 172, 176.
74 Ibid., pp. 62-63.
75 Bloch, *The Historian's Craft*, pp. ix, 180-89.
76 Ibid., p. 182.
77 Joan Kelly-Gadol, "Did Women Have a Renaissance?" in Bridenthal and Koonz, *Becoming Visible*, p. 139. See also Joan Kelly-Gadol, "The Social Relations of the Sexes: Methodological Implications of Women's History," *Signs* 1 (1976): 809-23; and idem, "Notes on Women in the Renaissance and Renaissance Historiography," in *Conceptual Frameworks for Studying Women's History*, Sarah Lawrence College Women's Studies (Bronxville, N.Y., 1975), pp. 1-11.
78 Michael Kaufman, "Spare Ribs: The Conception of Woman in the Middle Ages and the Renaissance," *Soundings: An Interdisciplinary Journal* 66 (1973): 139-40. There have been a number of studies on the evolutionary scheme and women's history. See, for example, J. Z. Giele, "Centuries of Womanhood: An Evolutionary Perspective on the Feminine Role," *Women's Studies* 1 (1972): 97-110.
79 Bloch, *The Historian's Craft*, p. 184.
80 *Cyte of Ladyes*, pt. I, chap. xxxiii. Here de Pisan discusses in some detail how Carmentis had made the significant discovery of Roman letters and how these letters in turn were rather ungraciously utilized by men in their condemnations of women!
81 Stoianovich, *French Historical Method*, p. 159.
82 Davis, "'Women's History' in Transition," p. 90.

CATHARINE R. STIMPSON

The Power to Name
Some Reflections on the Avant-Garde

■ We know more, in our books and in our bones, about the effects of sexism on literature than we think we do. Scholars have shown that Western culture has propagated an ideology of creativity that says men produce art, women children; that literary texts both reflect and reinforce sex/gender systems; that literary critics may judge those texts more favorably if they believe they were written by a man rather than by a woman; that literature classes tend to concentrate on books by and about men; that colleges and universities, particularly the more prestigious, prefer to hire male literary scholars rather than female; and that language itself, a system that ought to be as neutral as the laws of nature, has been used to press a male advantage.[1] Moreover, such demonstrations have gone on within a contemporary intellectual climate that distrusts broad scholarly claims to objectivity and value-free inquiry. What more, then, is there to say?

If the study of bias in literature and literary studies is now too advanced to permit easy revelations, it still can use refinement. I wish to offer a notion of "benign blindness." That is, as literary critics have sorted out what literature means and what texts are like, they have ignored discrimination against women. This has not happened because they are vicious, but because, as they work, they tend to believe themselves to be too decent to be guilty of such crude errors. Several elements make up this flattering sense of self. First, in the twentieth century, the study of literature is remote enough from centers of political and economic power to permit people to think that it can be relatively uncorrupt. Accompanying this, implicitly or explicitly, is the residue of humanistic and romantic beliefs about the ennobling nature of the free exercise of consciousness. As people respond to a text, their sensibilities are to be enhanced. Next, because literature deals with feelings as well as with facts, with moral issues as well as with logical structures, its students necessarily talk about the "softer" elements of experience, and reveal their own humanity. They may believe in magical links between their discourse and their behavior.

Next, because books have women characters, women writers, and women readers, their professional guardians and interpreters can, correctly, tell themselves that they are aware of the complexities and contributions of women to their field. Maynard Mack, then a great professor of English at Yale, could, in his 1970 presidential address to the Modern Language Association, allude to Dido, Artemis, and Iphigenia. Indeed, the awareness of women can be cheerful enough to permit literary people, if often quaintly, to feminize their own profession. One French scholar, helping to celebrate the seventy-fifth anniversary of the MLA, said: "The Modern Language Association was already a buxom middle-aged lady, clad in dignified petticoats of erudite parchment . . . when, in 1926, a new-born babe, the [American Association of Teachers of French] . . . made its joyful entry into the world."[2] Such metaphors suggest several possible states of mind: a comfort with women sufficient to permit badinage; an internalized sense of gender flexible enough to admit that a man's vocation might comprise both masculine and feminine elements; or a contemporary use of a classic theme—the male (now a scholar) evoking his Muse (now a bourgeois Sarah to his Abraham).

Yet literary texts do have the strength to subvert ordinary modes of consciousness. Naming the strange, unfamiliar, unpalatable, and alarming, they can, potentially, rearrange habitual modes of thought and feeling. In much modern literature and literary theory, this ability is construed less as one option for the text than as a necessity. Such an influential idea, often advocated polemically, is loosely expressed in the term *avant-garde*. Avant-garde art demands that the artist self-consciously and aggressively plan for the "dissolution of the relationship between the writer or artist and the public." She or he may then seek "to restore, to recreate the unity of art and public, and bring about a radical change in art and society, even if these attempts at a solution are sometimes utopian and anarchic."[3] The phrase was first used in the late eighteenth century in a military sense, to refer to the troops who marched out before a larger mass of other soldiers. *Avant-garde* has never lost the connotation of small-group daring, of assault, of militant antagonism, of a fusion of beauty and threat. It appeared again in the 1830s to represent political and artistic radicalism, utopian socialism and artists who might work to realize it. It served as a label for "social progress, for socialist ideas and the collective efforts of artists."[4] It then accumulated several meanings—to become a bundle of mutually contradictory relationships among politics, culture, and abrupt change. One critic has catalogued three relationships:

> The most violently apocalyptic one was advancing toward nothing less than the full transformation of social, political and personal life, through imaginative exploration and discovery, the creation of opposing values, the reconstruction of consciousness and the erection of models for true, liberated behavior. A much more modest progress was toward the creation of alternate realms of existence, to be inhabited by all imagination-summoned refugees from modern social horror and psychic oppression. . . . The third . . . was moving into the elaboration of wholly self-contained new artifacts . . . pure, noncontingent, unapplicable works . . . rid . . . of all nonaesthetic categories, including those of progress, discovery and cultural renewal.[5]

No matter what the particular meaning, the notion of the avant-garde necessarily implies change. Its supporters and interpreters have probably inflated how fast and how much cultures and societies do change. They have probably miscalculated how old the apparently new can actually be. Nevertheless, logically inseparable from the avant-garde is "the idea that art must evolve,"[6] especially away from a corrupt or inadequately represented present. The novelist Bryher, for example, writes of her generation:

> We were the last group to grow up under the formidable discipline of the nineteenth century whose effect, however much we resented it, cannot be entirely eradicated from our systems. All of us had been taught as soon as we could speak that abnegation and hard work would give us security and peace. The battle of the trenches cracked this myth from one end of Europe to the other. . . . In such a seething epoch of personal tragedy, the only thing left in which we could believe was art. . . . Only art, if it were to fill the hollow left by chaos, must be revolutionary and new. It must find words that were not tainted by nineteenth-century associations, rhythms that fitted the purr of machines rather than the thudding of hooves, different colours and, above all, a sternly truthful approach.[7]

In the twentieth century, some avant-garde groups, such as the surrealists, wedded revolutionary political and aesthetic activity, though their sense of what it meant to be a political revolutionary shifted for many of them. Nevertheless, after the late nineteenth century, the term *avant-garde* became more and more purged of politics, more and more restricted to art. So Lucy R. Lippard, the diligent and responsive feminist art critic, could write about a self-conscious and self-defined "women's art": "Some women artists are consciously reacting against avant-gardism and retrenching in aesthetic areas neglected or ignored in the past. . . . One of the major questions facing feminist criticism has to be whether stylistic innovation is indeed the only innovation. . . . perhaps women . . . differ . . . from the traditional notion of the avant-garde by opposing not styles and forms, but ideologies."[8]

Whether an avant-garde text elides or separates politics and art, it—with some arrogance—confronts readers with an event designed to shatter their expectations of what a text ought to do, be, and say. They can initially feel that the text has rejected them and display such features of the psychology of rejection as irritation, frustration, and huffy boredom. In revenge, readers can next reject the text. A student, puzzling out a page of Gertrude Stein, can threaten to throw the book against the wall. But even if readers fail to persist in following the text as far as possible, their world will have been altered, no matter how slightly.

In addition, the creation of avant-garde art—the writing of its texts and antitexts; the production of its dramas, rituals, and happenings; the construction of its sculptures, canvasses, and collages—has tended to take place in subworlds of such urban centers as New York, Chicago, Tokyo, London, Paris, or Berlin. Named bohemias, such subworlds often flout *bourgeois* sexual conventions and the legalized institutions of marriage and the family. Ironically, that pugnacious disregard has not always guaranteed a vital respect for the dignity and autonomy of women. The mocking of tradition has not always resulted in the transformation of traditions of masculinity and femininity. At times, women are still asked to embody only the principles of sexuality and of beauty. Bryher, remembering her discomfort in Paris bars after World War I, writes: "It was quite another story at the Boeuf. There I was a dismal failure and I remember Cocteau's expression of horror when he looked at me as we were introduced. He was right. The Boeuf was a place for men and for decorative women."[9] At other times, the proper function of women is construed as motherhood. In a study of avant-garde artists in New York after World War II, two sociologists discovered that many of them, particularly the older ones, disliked women artists. Their attitude was "negative. They direct a good deal of their 'ire' toward what they see as her abrogation of the only 'proper' role, which is motherhood."[10] At still other times, women are accepted if they inspire or support men, if they act out the role of Muse or patron. That role, though, need not consistently provoke male gratitude or affection. The biographers of Harriet Weaver, the English friend and publisher of James Joyce in London, talk about his reaction to a conversation she had with Sylvia Beach, his American friend and publisher in Paris: ". . . Joyce was outraged when he heard that Harriet had discussed him behind his back. . . . Like many men with a habit of dependence on women, he had a wild terror of being trapped in their monstrous regiment. Their compassion, eagerly sought, wove a net round him, detested and feared whether or not it was meant for his own good."[11] Finally, some bohemians of both sexes still subscribe to theories of sex and gender that ascribe one set of characteristics to men, another to women.

So Janet Flanner, writing about the devotion of Sylvia Beach to James Joyce, could say: "All of Joyce's gratitude, largely unexpressed, should have been addressed to her as a woman. For the patience she gave to him was female, was even quasi-maternal in relation to his book."[12] Yet, in spite of all this, the student of avant-garde art who explores the lives of avant-garde artists will enter circles, settings, studios, and homes in which previously held notions of social decorum and propriety will be dethroned.

The avant-garde, then, ought to work in at least two ways—aesthetically and biographically—to shock literary scholars and critics out of their benign blindness, so sufficiently to disrupt them that they must regard the world, including its sex/gender arrangements, anew. Literary scholars and critics can respond to the avant-garde in a complex fashion, however. First, the usual job of scholars and critics—to interpret, codify, judge, and explain—tempts them to impose their will upon a work and to control it. Instead of letting a poem or a novel act upon them, they act upon it. They can, in effect, smother its force. Next, they can respond to the avant-garde in a contradictory way—at once freshly and dully. They might, for example, accept a more open notion of literary form, but not of sex/gender arrangements. If this happens, the study of literature will parallel those bohemian minority cultures in which novelty was praised about most things, but rarely about the abolition of sexism. The precise nature of that mixed response can be pertinent to those of us who ask—in wonder, rage, and rue—why sexism persists so stubbornly in our institutions of knowledge and why feminism is so threatening.

In America during the central part of the twentieth century, two journals have exerted a powerful influence in helping to decide what literature is and what books matter. So doing, they themselves have become institutions, their titles symbols for their audiences, acquaintances, and detractors. Though their contributors disagree among themselves, often vitriolically, each journal has built and accrued a reputation that is more than the sum of its parts. The response of each to the avant-garde shows the process of an encounter with the new that wishes to stimulate and rearrange human perceptions, beliefs, and actions.

The first journal is the *PMLA*, the official organ of the Modern Language Association.[13] Some policies of the journal have changed over time. It has become more open to younger members of the profession. It has, since 1973, sought to make its articles of genuine interest to the membership of the profession at large. Despite such responses to diachronic pressures, *PMLA* has also had stable aims. First, it has consistently sought to reflect the concerns of its members. If they change, it will, if erratically, change too. Yet, given *PMLA*'s reputation, when it publishes something, it also endorses both the author and the subject. The journal, then, plays a mediating role among various segments of the profession, speaking for some, speaking to others. Next, the mental exercise that the MLA supports is scholarship and research. During the twentieth century, its sense of purpose has widened. In December 1969 it amended its constitution to read: "The object of this Association shall be to promote study, criticism, and research in modern languages and their literatures, and to further the common interests of teachers of these subjects." Nevertheless, the intellectual skeleton and heart of the MLA is scholarship, that discreet engagement of the human mind and human life that seeks

> to define, develop, criticize and transmit those bodies of data held to be significant reality by the society within which they function;
>
> in so doing, to eliminate falsehoods; to integrate isolated discoveries and facts into systematic and coherent wholes;
>
> and thereby, to advance the development of that set of intellectual products known *in toto* as "the body of learning," the "scholarship," or, in a stricter sense, the "knowledge," of a particular society, culture, or era.[14]

Not surprisingly, the MLA as an organization and the *PMLA* as a journal embody the proud claim of modern scholarship: that it transcends politics; that the researcher's "discoveries and facts" float above any specific power group and its ideologies. In the late 1960s, that claim was passionately debated as part of a larger struggle for governance of the organization. In 1968, at a plenary meeting of the standing committees of the MLA in New York, one scholar stated: "I emphatically deny . . . that social and political issues are the proper business of the Modern Language Association."[15] At the same time, another, one of the most intelligent in the profession, accused the MLA of practicing "the politics of inadvertence," the refusal to recognize how political it was. In another example of the male scholar's use of sexual and female imagery, he added: "I take it that no one, including myself, wants the MLA to relinquish its chastity: virginity, rather, is at stake. For the Association seems to have retained about ninety per cent of its virginity thus far . . . a dubious commodity."[16] Though the association now suffers less from the politics of inadvertence, another form of the benign blindness that can be pernicious, many of its members would still deny that social and political issues are its business.

The second journal is *The Partisan Review*. It began as the official organ of a small Communist group, the John Reed Club of New York. The editorial of the first issue of the "Bi-Monthly of Revolutionary Literature" in 1934 said that this voice of the revolutionary working class would "combat not only the decadent culture of the exploiting classes but also the debilitating liberalism which at times seeps into our writers through the pressure of class-alien forces."[17] As students of American cultural history know, *Partisan Review* also developed over time. In 1935, it broke from the John Reed Club, but vehemently retained its radical spirit. It would be "a revolutionary literary magazine edited by a group of young Communist writers, whose purpose will be to print the best revolutionary literature and Marxist criticism in this country and abroad."[18] Then, in 1937, it severed itself from the American Communist Party and from any allegiance to Stalin and Stalinism. Its commitment would be simultaneously to radical politics, to free thinking and "democratic controversy," and to a cultural criticism that celebrated certain autonomous qualities of works of art. Its editors, at once besieged and bold, announced: "Any magazine, we believe, that aspires to a place in the vanguard of literature today, will be revolutionary in tendency; but we are also convinced that any such magazine will be unequivocally independent. *Partisan Review* is aware of its responsibility to the revolutionary movement in general, but we disclaim obligation to any of its organized political expressions."[19] In 1938, it endorsed an organization that the surrealists André Breton and Diego Rivera were founding, the manifesto of which declared:

> Our aims:
> the independence of art—for the revolution;
> the revolution—for the complete liberation of art![20]

The mental exercise that *Partisan Review* supported, and supports, in the fulfillment of such hopes is discursive reasoning, in theory, the work of the highly informed, analytical, speculative intelligence, the effort of the human mind, through natural language, to become conscious of its own condition and to measure it both with full accuracy and with humanistic sympathy.

Obviously, *Partisan Review* accepts, even celebrates, the complex inseparability of culture and politics, of art and society, of the imagination and history. It has presented some of the most provocative and shrewd writing ever done in America about those relationships. Though its ideology, particularly about Communism, has shifted, the journal has consistently assumed that artists and intellectuals have a responsibility to the larger world, though they may act it out in subtle ways. In 1936, in still another use of female imagery, a contributor stated: "*Culture herself* demands that we put the right social values ahead of the right literary values."[21] If *Partisan Review* was to become less rigid and more flexible in the setting of its ideological priorities, if it was to become more suspicious of apocalyptic ambitions, millenial hopes, and flagrantly didactic and authoritarian impulses, it still retained a sense of "the impossibility of the modern writer's escaping his social responsibilities."[22]

Each journal's attitude towards the avant-garde is consistent with its nature. Indeed, these two journals, as enterprises, contain few surprises. I was unable to find in *PMLA* one article on the avant-garde as such. The struggle within the MLA and the *PMLA* has been to accept the modern at all, let alone its flamboyantly radical fringe. Only after World War II did *PMLA* discuss Henry James, or the Victorians, to any extent. That opening to the present accompanied a greater interest in American literature, more thematic essays and fewer philological articles, and the recognition, at once irascible, baffled, and delighted, that the profession was part of the expansion of American higher education itself.

On the other hand, *Partisan Review* welcomed the avant-garde, sought to define and explain it, and helped to name, no matter how narrowly, those authors that were to constitute for years what passed for the modern tradition. The journal was a participant-observer in the institutionalization of a dominant sense of what modern culture is. So Philip Rahv, whose sturdy and sapient essays are still compelling, could write in 1939 of the relationship of modern capitalism to a "group-ethos . . . the proud self-imposed isolation of a cultivated minority." He could wonder if a new avant-garde movement, "in the proper historical sense of the term, can be formed in this pre-war situation," and then conclude, with despairing courage, "that all we have left to go on now is individual integrity—the probing conscience, the will to repulse and to assail the forces released by a corrupt society."[23]

The history of such intrepid adventurousness is well-known. In part, it recapitulates the narrative of the revolutionary prodigal son who became, not simply a family member again, but a patriarch. *Partisan Review*'s writers became famous and respectable, the pride of academic institutions—especially, though not exclusively, Columbia. Its location until the 1960s in New York helped to attach it to a national network of book publishing. Indeed, some of its most distinguished contributors sponsored a book club. It supplemented Marx with Freud as a primary source of ideas. Disenchanted with the practice of Russian Communism, irritated by "bohemian radicals," it generated a new respect for the America it had once sought to alter so radically. Its study of the avant-garde often narrowed itself to aesthetic concerns.[24] Towards those who might say that they represented the new radicalism or the new avant-garde *Partisan Review*'s texts could be hortatory, aloof, cold, contemptuous, or insulting. Norman Podhoretz, comparing the bohemianism of the 1950s to his sense of it in the 1920s and 1930s, could snort: "It is hostile to civilization. It worships primitivism, instinct, energy, 'blood.'"[25] In addition to poverty of mind and feeling, Podhoretz raged, the Beats lacked even the capacity for stylistic modernity. A symbol of *Partisan Review*'s stability, superficially a condition antithetical to avant-garde practice, is the fact that one man, William Phillips, has held a vital editorial position since 1936. An extreme symbol of its shift from an aggressive support of the avant-garde to an aggressive defense of given cultural and political principles is the philosopher Sidney Hook. In 1968, the same year his name left the *Partisan Review* masthead, he belligerently attacked the know-nothing destructiveness of MLA radicals at the association's general meeting.[26]

The solidifying of *Partisan Review* was part of the historical process that transformed the aesthetic experiments of the late nineteenth and early twentieth century from new to known works. Just after World War II, a philosopher warned that the avant-garde had been institutionalized. Unfortunately, the university had become its home. He said: ". . . you cannot live in the midst of an English faculty . . . without becoming infected, especially under the urgency of academic advancement, with the point of view of your colleagues, who for their part have stakes in preserving their own form of bureaucratic specialization expressed by *PMLA*."[27] Significantly, some of the most cogent descriptions of the hard, ironic maturing of *Partisan Review* and of modernism were written for *Partisan Review* itself. Its early revolutionary skepticism, tempered by the self-inquiry of psychoanalysis and the demands of cultural criticism, enabled it to reflect upon itself. In general, if the journal is now more *about* the avant-garde than a sample of it, if it has become as reactive as innovative, it can still explore the concept of the avant-garde brilliantly.[28] In addition, it remains committed to an open inquiry that creates a climate for politically and aesthetically radical activities. In 1972, for example, the editors, organizing another of their symposia on big questions, worried about a new conservatism, "a hostility to anything exploratory, problematic, and disquieting . . . [which] often goes along with a rejection of the whole modernist impulse in art."[29]

The particulars of the play between the presentation of the avant-garde and residual sexism can be seen in the way each journal handled two avant-garde writers who were contemporaries: James Joyce (1882–1941) and Gertrude Stein (1874–1946). Though both lived in Paris—Joyce in voluntary exile from Ireland, Stein from America—they were not friends. To oversimplify, Stein "was irritated to have her position as arch-experimentalist challenged," and Joyce once "pointedly" told a woman friend, 'I hate intellectual women."[30] They probably met but once. Sylvia Beach, Stein's friend as well as Joyce's publisher, recalls a party at a sculptor's in Paris: "They had never met, so, with their mutual consent, I introduced them to each other and saw them shake hands quite peacefully."[31] Joyce's reputation today, though subject to revision, is impeccable. A genius, he did transform imaginative literature. Stein's reputation is still controversial. To some, her intelligible prose is trivial gossip; the rest, a babble of nonsense. To others, she too transformed imaginative literature, but so radically that even the daring and sympathetic do not yet know how to explain her compositions.

The first essay on Joyce that *PMLA* published appeared in 1939. Called "James Joyce: A Study in Words," it initiated one of the two dominant methods of analysis that *PMLA* scholars were to use on Joyce: the study of language and the analysis of structure. The second was to place him historically: to trace the influence of Ibsen, Mozart, Nietzsche, or Irish folklore, and to explore correlations between his life and art. As the journal exalted Joyce through the scrupulous devotion of the scholars whom it permitted to appear there, so did the association through the attention given to him at annual meetings. After 1948, about one-third of the English II sessions (the contemporary literature section) were devoted, wholly or in part, to Joyce.

Joyce's appeal to literary scholars is obvious. His biography is dramatic, but not uncomfortably so. He suffered exile, poverty, illness, censorship, and indifference, but triumphed in the end. His work calls for detailed, burrowing exegesis. It demands the industry the academy has supplied. Moreover, decoding him seems to end in the discovery of coherence; surface chaos reveals structure and order. In brief, lots of people can say lots of things about Joyce and his predecessors for a long time. In addition, his portrait of the artist, if not his art, is a deeply conventional one. It flatters and sustains a male-dominated, but female-infiltrated, profession. Though women and female principles may help, men do the serious writing. Shem is Joyce's pen man. The first *PMLA* article on Joyce implicitly recognized this. It spoke of younger artists imitating "the Master."[32] Subsequent essays, from both female and male scholars, keep on bowing to a tradition in which fatherlike founders have sonlike disciples, who then become fathers themselves with their own spiritual sons.

Such habits of thought, which affect the analysis of both the conditions of creativity and books themselves, were at their most florid in the 1950s. During that decade a male scholar presented the *PMLA* with an apparent paradox: Joyce was "one of the most domestic of modern writers," but Stephen Daedalus, his character, had to free himself from home and family. Joyce, the scholar suggested, "equated woman with life."[33] Unhappily, life—which such icons as the moon and water picture—can overwhelm man: ". . . The woman-trapped artist . . . may lose his independence as artist by submerging in life." He may, however, "transcend mundane life by continuing to produce art which is universal and timeless." After dying in the light of the moon or in the river of life, he may be reborn. Joyce, the scholar concludes, apparently "did both—fulfilled Stephen's mission as artist and became what Stephen feared to become, a participant in life, a family man with responsibilities to others as well as to himself and his art."

If the man had stopped there, he would have given one plausible interpretation of Joyce's work. But writers in *PMLA* tend to be less psychologically sophisticated than writers in *Partisan Review* and so more apt to give themselves away. Joyce's scholar went on to lecture about art at large. So doing, he displayed an ideological sexism that shaped his criticism as education does the mind. He wrote:

> The artist is an artist literally only when he is creating art, but he is a man too, and when he descends from his highest elevation he is likely to find that he wants such things as a drink, a dinner, some conversation, a woman. If he does not find them at home, he is all too likely to dissipate his creative energy in the search for them. Joyce's union with Nora was a form of economy. It was a partial compact with life which, while taking care of his mortal needs and rescuing him from that restless quest for distraction in Bohemias and Nighttowns . . . yet left the creative personality free to produce art.

No refutation of such notions appeared. Later, however, one article did question, not the masculinizing of the role of the artist, but the warmth and richness of Joyce's insights into sex. "In some respects", the essay carefully stated, "compulsive and unhealthy, Joyce is like a lapsed priest in his reactions."[34] The author of the article, a Jesuit priest, provides evidence, in the quarrel about whether "insiders" or "outsiders" are better critics of anthropological phenomena, for the special powers of the alert insider.

If more than twenty articles and essays have appeared in *PMLA* on Joyce, only one has been published on Stein. In part, it is a dazzling example of intellectual agility—a brilliant theory about connections among avant-garde writing, avant-garde filmmaking, and the use of repetition. In part, it is a numbing example of intellectual opacity. In 1970, the author declared firmly: "Gertrude Stein belongs to the past now, and her works are generally unread. For most people, the questions her works raised are now answered, and all negatively."[35] The texts about texts in *PMLA* are often etiological blanks. They document all quotations and credit their sources, but they fail to reveal the origins of their large, governing perspectives. Though one is tempted to say that behind the judgment on Stein is sexist bias, one cannot do so responsibly. Stein may have been subjected to the penalty of false prophecy because her critic misreads women writers, or because he misreads the future of experimental writers, or because he misreads more than he should.

The disproportion of attention, let alone reverence, between Joyce and Stein that *PMLA* shows appears much less in *Partisan Review*. From its first issue, *Partisan Review* recognized Joyce as a major reference point. In its early period as a "revolutionary literary magazine," it loathed him. His "modernistic posture" was thought to deploy apparently new aesthetic forms only to deflect the birth of genuinely new aesthetic and political ones. To one Communist critic, he was a paradigm of bourgeois art: "What social mind exists today that includes both a complete acceptance of the value of MacLeish, Proust, Joyce, on the one hand, and of the growing proletarian literature on the other? The former are merely in a precarious predominance over the latter."[36] To Philip Rahv, he exemplified the weakness of the rebellious, but nonrevolutionary imagination: "From the initial social resentment in *Dubliners* Joyce developed toward a demoralized consciousness of social impotence and hence toward a desire for liberation from the social. The result is a sinking into imaginative life, regarded as the self-contained domain of art: thus art becomes a barrier between his disgust with reality and his impulse to change it. The perfect stasis is the idealized negation."[37]

As *Partisan Review* came to see the imagination less as a pit and more as a copious protection against authoritarianism and simple-mindedness, it transformed its evaluation. Joyce—like Rilke, Stevens, Yeats, Eliot, Dostoevsky, Proust, Kafka, Mann, Faulkner, or Beckett—had the wit to respond to the terrible conditions of modern life with art that was at once patterned, yet complex; intelligible, yet intricate; difficult, yet humane; anguished, yet brave. He pictured "alternate realms of existence." In 1939, a critic wrote about *Finnegans Wake*, published in full that year. He praised the seriousness of Joyce's quest and "the piety that is involved in the energetic and still uncorrupted affirmation of life that is implicit in every movement of his writing. This is the seriousness of the greatest comedy, which always keeps in recollection the tragic knowledge that is at its base."[38]

By 1952, *Partisan Review* cast Joyce as an avatar of the avant-garde. Yet its definition of the avant-garde had sufficiently altered to become nearly a self-contradiction. The best of the moderns, living on the edge of the present for the sake of the future, also fed on the past. William Phillips said:

> On the positive side, we have become aware that literature cannot subsist only on advanced attitudes and tributes to internationalism; it must also relate itself to the indigenous and homely strains of a culture. An avant-garde is necessary to keep the spirit of intransigence alive, but by some irony of the imagination the best literary works have also gone back to more classic and conservative influences. In the modern period, for exam-

ple, writers like Proust, Kafka, Mann, Eliot or Faulkner cannot be defined simply as rebels. Not that they have been in any sense conformists, but their new vision has been tied to many myths of the past and to the idea of a common experience. Even Joyce, who produced a kind of monumental avant-gardism, is a rock-ribbed traditionalist as compared with his co-experimenters in *transition*. While most avant-garde writing of the Joycean school was aimed chiefly at the breakdown of syntax, Joyce himself tried to recreate the folklore of consciousness.[39]

Inhabiting the various realms of time, Joyce was simply *there*, for critics to interpret, judge, and use in the construction of their theories about modern culture. Once established as a great figure, he became the focus of tautological inquiry. Some might try to see him in a historical perspective, to sort out what was late Victorian about him, what modern, what postmodern.[40] None ever questioned the greatness. Indeed, the presumption of it encouraged them to take him on in the first place.

Partisan Review believes that thought is dynamic and that the ethics of the intellectual demand fair-mindedness. Amidst the analyses, exegetical forays, memoirs, and reviews of Joyce criticism and scholarship was some skepticism about him. Philip Rahv, exploring the tension between a writer's use of history and of myth, said that in *Finnegans Wake* "the mythic bias is in ascendant, the historical element recedes, and the language itself is converted into a medium of myth."[41] To abandon history, of course, is to abandon that sense of the possibility of change which is a conceptual necessity for those who long for a different political order. Only one article, however, questioned Joyce's ideas about sex and gender. Frank Budgen, in an autobiographical essay, recounted a conversation with an angry Joyce who decried women and their putative urge "to usurp all the functions of the male—all save that one which is biologically pre-empted."[42] When Budgen reminded him that women were artists, performers, and scientists, Joyce responded, in a "tirade," that no woman had ever authored a complete philosophical system. Budgen noted wryly: "So that was it. The creator of Molly Bloom and Anna Livia Plurabelle could never of course be a misogynist. . . . But . . . the demesne of philosophical inquiry . . . [is] the one impregnable province of the mind reserved exclusively for the male."[43] For others, Joyce's theories about male and female principles, about male and female symbols, were almost as much an article of faith as his reputation. Indeed, one critic so internalized the notion of man-the-writer (the equivalent in literary criticism of man-the-hunter in anthropology) that he schematized Joyce as the modern voice of the male and D. H. Lawrence as that of the female, of womanhood and "her mysteries."[44]

Clearly, *Partisan Review* does not wholly endorse such beliefs. In the late 1930s, it published Gertrude Stein, sent her copies, and solicited her opinion about American writing.[45] In the early 1940s, with a small joke about the oddness of her latest manuscript, it included her in a directory of artists and writers living in a Europe at war.[46] Yet her work is treated peripherally. The closest account of it occurs in the context of an answer to an attack upon her that is construed as an implicit argument against the moderns in general. Stein herself is described as an egoist and child "under the spell of the private life."[47] An early Communist abhors her, with Joyce, as a swimmer in the backwards-flowing "currents of aestheticism."[48] A historian of an earlier avant-garde contemptuously dismisses her as a literary failure: "The avant-garde of the heroic period (except for Gertrude Stein) drew the line between experiment and absurdity."[49] A critic whose interest in style grew more and more consuming took her, with the later Joyce, to demonstrate a point about modern form.[50]

Not until *Partisan Review*, in the late 1960s and early 1970s, published a younger critic willing to support the possibility of radical rearrangements of natural language itself did Stein's form really receive praise. Skeptical of progress in art, in itself an agnostic attitude towards past notions of the avant-garde, Ronald Sukenick saw Stein and Joyce as precursors of a renewed fiction. Both "raise the question of whether it is really the pragmatic, discursive, rationally intelligible side of language that best puts us in touch with our experience of the world and of ourselves." To understand them "requires a release from understanding."[51] Only one commentator—though he thought Stein "a trifle peculiar," her "intuitions those of a gifted child setting out to write history merely from the sound of names"—began to see Stein for what she is: a representative of the avant-garde in art *and* in politics. He admired her feminism, among other qualities, and wrote: ". . . this is meant to be a tribute. . . . I had the feeling that one of the lost, late children of the '20s had arrived home for good."[52]

Why should the prevailing blankness about Stein be the case? That *PMLA* articles might ignore feminism as politically avant-garde is understandable. *PMLA* has persistently declared that its scholars abjure all politics. *Partisan Review*, however, was created, not simply to reflect, but to lead thinking about culture and politics. It prided itself on the taut dragnet of its dialectic. Stein, of course, would not want to have been thought of as a political writer. She instructed *Partisan Review*: "Writers only think they are interested in politics, they are not really, it gives them a chance to talk and writers like to talk but really no real writer is really interested in politics."[53] Yet, *Partisan Review*'s editors and writers could have ignored that if they had wanted to. Certainly, they proved capable of ignoring another and far more intense of her hopes: to be thought of as a genius worthy of belonging to, perhaps even worthy of dominating, the post-Victorian, modern tradition. They accorded no women that status. Overlooking both Stein's claims to glory and her brand of feminism, they necessarily failed to investigate a weird aspect of that feminism: the belief that genius, even in a woman, was male.[54]

My answers to the question will be incomplete rather than complete, suggestive rather than definitive. In part, some *Partisan Review* people may never have fully escaped the ideology of the 1930s, which said that the solution to the woman problem lay, not in feminism as a separate movement, but in socialism. Their radical politics rationalized women away, an error the New Radicalism of the 1960s was at first to repeat. Moreover, especially after World War II and before Vietnam, many *Partisan Review* people subscribed to a psychology—at once prescriptive, descriptive, and poetic—that told men and women to "prize" their "specific sexuality."[55] So doing, women would be torn between being feminists, which meant accepting "male values" of achievement, and being female, which meant accepting traditional maternal and erotic patterns of behavior. Though feminism might once have been a boon, it was now a problematic source of conflict. It might also be inseparable from homosexuality. In 1950 Diana Trilling worried that "the homosexual story of this century at least seems to suggest a connection between the increase in women's rights and an increase in inversion."[56]

Diana Trilling's essays of this period are painful reading—less for their conscious ambivalence about a narrowly construed feminism, common to the period, than for their far less conscious revelation of some of the humiliations of the bright woman in a world of bright men. She writes, for example, of coming home from a poetry reading. In the living room are several men, among them her husband and the poet W. H. Auden. Chivalrous, they stand up for her, but then they wait for her to leave so that they can sit down and begin to talk again.

Finally, some *Partisan Review* people used a vocabulary of values that made the term *masculine* a sign of the good, the term *feminine* a sign of the feeble and weak. In 1941, Lionel Trilling was fastidiously put off by an "obtrusively 'literary' and oddly 'feminine'" aspect of Ernest Hemingway's style.[57] A few years later, another critic boxed with the same terms. He wrote, with special reference to the academic world he was himself to join: "Like Eliot, Joyce makes wonderful material for the favored mode in contemporary criticism, the feminine and subservient elucidation of a difficult text in which the critic, giving himself up completely to the work of art, takes on himself for a time its glory and its power."[58] The fabric of such language covers the tired bones of the same ideology of gender that Joyce and Stein endorsed: the justification of leaving the production of real arts and letters to men. When it appears to accept that, *Partisan Review* joins the contributors to the *PMLA* it enjoyed tweaking. Perhaps humanly guilty of a narcissism that demanded that a male image be projected and enshrined, both used culture—its sources, its history, and its power—as their vast reflecting pool. What blinded *PMLA* to such a deformation was its organizational ego-ideal of objectivity. What blinded *Partisan Review* was its group ego-ideal of a broad, yet subtle vision of the many activities of man.

Yet, as I have said, neither journal embodies a pig-eyed bigotry. *PMLA* often published articles by and about women. In 1923, for example, Walter Edwin Peck wrote an essay "The Biographical Element in the Novels of Mary Wollstonecraft Shelley."[59] If some pieces were patronizing, others conveyed a quasi-feminist perspective. In 1954, a man said of Nathaniel Hawthorne: "Unlike his judicial ancestor, who consigned a witch to the gallows with an undismayed countenance, Hawthorne would have sprung the trap with a sigh. If one were the witch, one might well wonder wherein lay the vital difference."[60] *Partisan Review* has also had material by and about women, though more by than about. It has published many of the most powerful, talented women writers of the twentieth century: Tillie Olsen (as Tillie Lerner), Agnes Smedley, Elizabeth Bishop, Mary McCarthy, Hannah Arendt, Elizabeth Hardwick, Dorothy Van Ghent, Susan Sontag, Iris Murdoch, Sylvia Plath, Anne Sexton, Doris Lessing, Adrienne Rich, Denise Levertov, Joyce Carol Oates. The material it has had about women has often been feminist. In 1959, a woman who was then a frequent contributor declared:

> ". . . even novelists and poets only express *themselves* and, so far as the opposite sex is concerned, proceed largely by projection, and of course by observation, which is behavioristic and inevitably conventional to some extent, evading the question of an inner life. And most artists have been men anyway and have invented and re-invented women for the world and for themselves, without consultation. Artistically women have been less articulate and their education has often encouraged them to reticence and duplicity. It is not surprising that with so little to go on in the way of honest and unaided documents, Freud should have left the "thinking" female of my generation with an odd picture of herself . . . surely the enormous importance given by Freud to the castration complex is a sign of his inability to think in any but masculine terms. . . . Simone de Beauvoir and others have produced good evidence that a more common female preoccupation is fear of penetration, of *damage*, . . . which may or may not be directly sexual.[61]

After 1970, *Partisan Review* presented formidable feminists: Kate Millett, Marge Piercy, Juliet Mitchell, Adrienne Rich. Although it also issued an asinine attack on feminist critics, it did apologize for it, if grudgingly.[62]

On balance, the women in the literary scholarship and criticism I have discussed are less objects of simple hostility (though they might be) than of a gamut of emotions ranging from attraction to indifference, less an absent or obsessive category than a secondary one. That secondary status is parallel to, and probably partially caused by, the administration of the journals themselves. Though women are on the staff, men have nearly all the editorial positions. The governing structure of the MLA tends to resemble that of *PMLA*. Between 1945 and 1969, for example, less than 1 percent of the MLA's Executive Council was female. In brief, both *PMLA* and the MLA treat women as if they were a part of the human landscape that ought to be substantively described and properly named. Women, especially if they are really able, can do some of the naming. Nonetheless, the power to name the namers rests, to a great degree, with men.

The distribution of power within the realm of culture is a comparatively genial microcosm of society at large. That such inequalities have gone on for so long reflects a psychic and social version of a law of inertia: bodies in power tend to stay in power, unless external forces disturb them. Ironically, the slow and fusty *PMLA* may be easier to disturb than the lively and modern *Partisan Review*. Though the process is frustrating, slow, and cumbersome, the MLA itself has mechanisms through which its members can force the organization to do their bidding. It has been somewhat responsive to feminist protest, organization, and activity. In 1974, there were two seminars on Gertrude Stein. In 1975, there was a seminar entitled "Women in Works by James Joyce."[63] By 1977, 50 percent of the Executive Council was female. Persistent pressure will probably eventually affect the *PMLA*. In contrast, a self-perpetuating group governs *Partisan Review*. If such a process protects it from reactionaries, it also insulates it from the reinvigorating energies of those who offer new definitions of the radical, new ways of being avant-garde.

The distribution of power between men and women is inseparable from the allocation of tasks between the sexes first outlined in the Lord's punishments for a sinning Adam and Eve. Men, except under special circumstances, toil in the public world. Women, except under special circumstances, toil in the private world. If secondary in the public world, they are primary in the private world—as faithful wives, as lovers, as mothers. The pressure of a conservative fear of any real change in such domestic arrangements—a fear the powerful and the powerless share—circles back to reinforce the unequal distribution of power and the genderizing of labor, including the work of culture, literature, and art. Symbolically, in an early issue of *Partisan Review*, only one contributor's family life was brought up—that of Tillie Lerner. She was "at work on a novel of mining life. . . . Last year she took a leave of absence from the Young Communist League to produce a future citizen of Soviet America."[64]

Even people who support women's right of access to public culture tend to fear a fundamental shift in the putative norms of family and domestic life. In 1970, members of the MLA voted by mail ballot on resolutions about education; foreign writers, scholars, and teachers; minority culture; interdisciplinary work; exchange with Cuba; and women's status. Measures that might prove reasonably easy for institutions to enact and that might give women a fairer economic deal were supported. Measures that might expand sexuality and childcare arrangements were controversial. Measures that might guarantee women's departure from the home and into the profession were strongly opposed.[65]

Behind men's fears of a transformation in the relation between public and private realms may be still another fear, too regressive to mention openly, too subterranean to grasp directly. Men might wonder if the women, from whom they wish to remain detached and yet to whom they wish to remain attached, might not withdraw and leave them all darkling. An oblique expression of such an emotion might have appeared in a notice in *Partisan Review* of three contemporary novels by women. The male reviewer first evoked Joyce's parody of an old-fashioned women's fiction; next outlined the anatomy of a new; and, finally, warned: ". . . in the long run . . . the goal may not be a new 'woman's fiction' as such but a fiction that can represent the lives of women as part of the general life of people. This would require women writers to write about *men* as George Eliot . . . did."[66]

It is perhaps an unyielding law of change—be it in consciousness or in institutions or in their union—which we can never wholly choreograph nor decipher that those who want change must do what their opponents most fear. The test, then, of a self-proclaimed avant-garde movement will be the wrath it provokes. Today, some of the most radical writing that women are doing, both politically and aesthetically, concerns a world of women. In some texts, a world of men and a world of women impinge upon each other—with love, in terror, with suspicion. In other texts, women have left men, for a while or forever. So far, most of these books, are novels. There, the imagination has seen and transformed reality to create, through language, the contours of rebellion and desire.

Nobody, in conventional or avant-garde circles, has yet developed a criticism strong and supple enough to interpret these new texts.[67] Whether this will happen, and whether it will be accepted if it does happen, is unclear. Its success will depend upon pervasive efforts to make sexism obsolete and to generate new structures of the self and of community. In literary terms, this process of deconstruction and construction will mean that women will both name their own experience and the forms that best embody it. Such an effort will be genuinely avant-garde.

NOTES

1 For articles that demonstrate a number of these points, see "Women in the Colleges: Status, Teaching, Feminist Criticism," an issue of *College English* 32 (May 1971). A recent bibliography of work on women writers, feminist and otherwise, is Barbara A. White, *American Women Writers: An Annotated Bibliography of Criticism* (New York, 1977).
2 Henri Peyre, "Commentary by the Presidents of Fifteen Sister Organizations on the Occasion of the Seventy-Fifth Anniversary of the Modern Language Association," *PMLA* 83 (1958): 11.
3 Miklós Szabolcsi, "Avant-garde, Neo-avant-garde, Modernism: Questions and Suggestions," *New Literary History* 3 (Autumn 1971): 54-55.
4 Ibid., p. 49. See, too, Clement Greenberg, "Avant-Garde and Kitsch," *Partisan Review* (hereafter *PR*) 6, no. 5 (1939): 34-49; Clement Greenberg, "Towards a Newer Laocoon," *PR* 7, no. 4 (1940): 296-310; Renato Poggiolo, *The Theory of the Avant-Garde* (New York, 1971); first Italian edition, 1962; first English edition, 1968; and Linda Nochlin, "The Invention of the Avant-Garde: France, 1830-80," in *Avant-Garde Art*, ed. Thomas B. Hess and John Ashbery (New York, 1967-68), pp. 3-24. For a study of revolutionary art in a revolutionary society, see Robert A. Maguire, *Red Virgin Soil: Soviet Literature in the 1920s* (Princeton, 1968). For provocative suggestions that demand exploration about the role of women as aesthetic innovators, see Grace Shulman, "Women the Inventors," *Nation*, 11 December 1972, pp. 594-96.
5 Richard Gilman, "The Idea of the Avant-Garde," *PR* 39, no. 3 (1972): 388-89.
6 Susan Sontag, "Nathalie Sarraute and the Novel," *Against Interpretation* (New York, 1966), p. 100. The essay was first written in 1963 and revised in 1965.
7 Bryher, *The Heart to Artemis: A Writer's Memoirs* (New York, 1962), pp. 203-4.
8 *From the Center: Feminist Essays on Women's Art* (New York, 1976), p. 6.
9 Bryher, *The Heart to Artemis*, p. 211.
10 Bernard Rosenberg and Norris Fliegel, *The Vanguard Artist: Portrait and Self-Portrait* (Chicago, 1965), p. 258. For a too-brief, but interesting study of women in a New York bohemian setting in the first part of the twentieth century, see June Sochen, *The New Woman in Greenwich Village, 1910-1920* (New York, 1972).
11 Jane Lidderdale and Mary Nicholson, *Dear Miss Weaver: Harriet Shaw Weaver, 1876-1961* (New York, 1970), p. 323. For a sardonic view of female

patrons and male artists in bohemian circles, and of books about them, read Bertha Harris's review of Adrienne Monnier's autobiography, *The Very Rich Hours of Adrienne Monnier* in *Christopher Street* 1 (July 1976): 44–47.

12 Janet Flanner, foreword to *Published in Paris: American and British Writers, Printers, and Publishers in Paris, 1920-1939* by Hugh Ford (New York, 1975), p. xii.

13 I will talk about the *PMLA* since 1920, a date chosen because, by then, avant-garde practices ought to have come to the attention of MLA members, who are *PMLA* contributors.

14 Mary E. Payer, "Is Traditional Scholarship Value Free? Toward a Critical Theory," in *Papers from the Morning Session of the Scholar and the Feminist IV: Connecting Theory, Practice, and Values: A Conference Sponsored by the Barnard College Women's Center* (New York: Barnard College, The Women's Center, 1977), p. 28. Payer's paper should be required reading for those concerned with the theoretical foundations of feminist scholarship.

15 O. B. Hardison, "The MLA and Social Activism," *PMLA* 83, Supplement (1968): 985.

16 Richard Ohmann, "The MLA and the Politics of Inadvertence," *PMLA* 83, Supplement (1968): 988. Two years later, the critic Frederick Crews made a similar point: "I believe that our literary studies generally do have an ideological cast, less in what they say than in what they refuse to consider. Plausible lines of investigation that might lead to disquieting conclusions, or that would employ politically alien categories of thought, are not pursued, while dubious but politically reinforced assumptions are elevated into articles of faith." "Do Literary Studies Have an Ideology?" *PMLA* 85 (1970): 424. Though Ohmann's focus was the Vietnamese War and Crews's was American capitalism in both domestic and international forms, their analyses can be applied to sexism in the profession as well.

17 *PR* 1, no. 1 (1934): 2.

18 *PR* 2, no. 8 (1935): 2.

19 *PR* 4, no. 1 (1937): 3.

20 "Manifesto: Towards a Free Revolutionary Art," trans. Dwight Macdonald, *PR* 6, no. 1 (1938): 53.

21 Louis Kronenberg, "Criticism in Transition," *PR* 3, no. 6 (1936): 7.

22 Dwight Macdonald, "The Tower beyond Politics," *PR* 4, no. 2 (1938): 60. Macdonald resigned in 1943, saying that *PR* was becoming too academic, too literary, too indifferent to Marxist values, charges the remaining editors refuted. In his letter of resignation, Macdonald also announced that Nancy Macdonald was leaving as business manager, for reasons similar to his. See *PR* 10, no. 4 (1943): 382. Macdonald did continue to write for *PR*.

23 Philip Rahv, "Twilight of the Thirties," *PR* 4, no. 4 (1939), 12, 14, 15.

24 See, for example, Max Kozloff, "Art and the New York Avant-Garde," *PR* 31, no. 4 (1964): 535–54.

25 "The Know-Nothing Bohemians," *PR* 25, no. 2 (1958): 307–8.

26 "The Barbarism of Virtue," *PMLA* 84 (1969): 465–75.

27 William Barrett, "The Resistance," a review of *The Little Magazine: A History and a Bibliography,* PR 13, no. 4 (1946): 486. About twenty years later, another professor also wrote that the avant-garde was a permanent aspect of modern culture, though its recent phase of "experimentalism" may be "exhausted." See Richard Chase, "The Fate of the Avant-Garde," PR 21, no. 3 (1957): 364.
28 An example? Norman Birnbaum, "The Making of a Vanguard," PR 36, no. 2 (1969): 220-32.
29 "On the New Cultural Conservatism," PR 39, no. 3 (1972): 397.
30 Richard Ellmann, *James Joyce* (New York, 1959), p. 543.
31 Sylvia Beach, *Shakespeare and Company: The Story of an American Bookshop in Paris* (New York, 1959), p. 32. Ellmann, *Joyce,* p. 543, gives a different version of the encounter.
32 Joseph Prescott, "James Joyce: A Study in Words," PMLA 54 (1939): 314.
33 This quote, and all others from the same source, are in Maurice Beebe, "James Joyce: Barnacle Goose and Lapwing," PMLA 71 (1956): 302-20.
34 William T. Noon, S. J., "James Joyce: Unfacts, Fiction, and Facts," PMLA 76 (1961): 265.
35 Strother B. Purdy, "Gertrude Stein at Marienbad," PMLA 85 (1970): 1096.
36 Wallace Phelps, "The Anatomy of Liberalism," PR 1, no. 1 (1934): 48.
37 Philip Rahv, "How the Waste Land Became a Flower Garden," PR 1, no. 4 (1934): 42.
38 William Troy, "Notes on *Finnegans Wake,*" PR 6, no. 4 (1939): 110.
39 William Phillips, "Our Country and Our Culture," PR 19, no. 5 (1952): 587.
40 Read, for example, Robert Martin Adams, "The Bent Knife Blade: Joyce in the 1960s," PR 29, no. 4 (1962): 507-18.
41 Philip Rahv, "The Myth and the Powerhouse," PR 20, no. 6 (1953): 644. For similar comment, see Steven Marcus, "The Novel Again," PR 29, no. 2 (1962): 195.
42 Frank Budgen, "Further Recollections of James Joyce," PR 23, no. 3 (1956): 534.
43 Ibid., p. 535. Budgen's use of the word "impregnable" is interesting. The genderizing of creativity works on tight structural principles: the interplay and opposition of maleness/masculinity and femaleness/femininity. The male artist often incorporates the female in the act of creativity. For example, Sylvia Beach, remembering, perhaps kindly, how she felt when she lost the American publication rights for *Ulysses,* says, "In the case of *Ulysses,* I gave Joyce leave to do whatever he wishes. And, after all, the books were Joyce's. A baby belongs to its mother, not to the midwife, doesn't it?" *Shakespeare and Company,* p. 205. But the female is much less frequently permitted to incorporate the male. When she does, she may be either praised (i.e., told approvingly that she has a "masculine mind" or "thinks like a man") or blamed (i.e., told disapprovingly that she "acts like a man").
44 John Henry Raleigh, "Victorian Morals and the Modern Novel," PR 25, no. 2 (1958): 260.

45 See "The Autobiography of Rose," *PR* 6, no. 2 (1939): 61-63; "A Letter," *PR* 6, no. 3 (1939): 127; and an answer to a questionnaire, "The Situation in American Writing," *PR* 6, no. 4 (1939): 40-41.
46 "What Has Become of Them?" *PR* 8, no. 1 (1941): 61.
47 Josephine Herbst, "Miss Porter and Miss Stein," *PR* 15, no. 5 (1948): 570.
48 Phelps, "The Anatomy of Liberalism," p. 50.
49 Dwight Macdonald, "Masscult and Midcult II," *PR* 27, no. 4 (1960): 613. Also see David Paul, "Time and the Novelist," *PR* 21, no. 6 (1954): 644.
50 Clement Greenberg, "The Crisis of the Easel Picture," *PR* 15, no. 4 (1948): 483.
51 Ronald Sukenick, "The New Tradition," *PR* 39, no. 4 (1972): 585-86. See, too, Martin Duberman, "The Season," *PR* 35, no. 3 (1968): 427-28. Duberman, not coincidentally, supports both women's liberation and gay liberation.
52 R. W. Flint, "Cambridge Theatricals," *PR* 23, no. 2 (1956): 285-86.
53 "The Situation in American Writing," p. 41.
54 For more detail, consult my essay, "The Mind, the Body, and Gertrude Stein," *Critical Inquiry* 3 (Spring 1977): 489-506.
55 Diana Trilling, "Men, Women and Sex," *PR* 17, no. 4 (1950): 376.
56 Ibid., p. 373.
57 Review of *For Whom the Bell Tolls* by Ernest Hemingway, *PR* 8, no. 1 (1941): 63.
58 Robert Gorham Davis, "Narrow Views of Joyce," *PR* 15, no. 9 (1948): 1016.
59 *PMLA* 38 (1923): 196-219.
60 Morton Cronin, "Hawthorne on Romantic Love and the Status of Women," *PMLA* 69 (1954): 89-98.
61 Kathleen Nott, "Notes on Feeling and Ideology," *PR* 26, no. 1 (1959): 67.
62 The piece, by Robert Boyers, appeared in *PR* 43, no. 4 (1976): 602-11. The apology was in *PR* 44, no. 1 (1977): 111. Two items help to illustrate *PR*'s commitment to a feminist perspective. Steven Marcus, who had written for the journal since the 1950s and served in an editorial capacity since the 1960s, was the adviser for Kate Millett's doctoral dissertation at Columbia. Her *PR* piece, "The Balance of Power," 37, no. 2 (1970): 199-218, was taken from that work, which became *Sexual Politics*. Next, a story by William Phillips, "Lives and Wives of a Genius," *PR* 19, no. 2 (1952): 152-68, is a sardonic and accurate picture of a bright, undisciplined male intellectual who devours women. Whether or not it was meant to do so, it dramatizes a feminist analysis.
63 One of the listed participants was Florence L. Walzl, who had earlier published "The Liturgy of the Epiphany Season and the Epiphanies of Joyce," *PMLA* 80 (1965), an utterly dutiful reading of *Dubliners*, in which she thought "the artist's creative act was analogous to the eucharistic change effected by the priest," at least in Joyce (p. 437). She did not conclude from this that Joyce thought only men could be artists.
64 *PR* 1, no. 2 (1934): 2.

65 The actual votes, as recorded in *PMLA* 85 (1970): 649–52, were as follows:

Issue	Yes	No
"Preference" to women in hiring until they are 51% of profession	1,639	2,767
Abolish nepotism	3,526	754
Support of day-care centers on campus	2,246	2,149
Support of paid parenthood leave for women and men	2,026	2,321
More flexibility between full-time and part-time work	3,368	821
MLA should work for better birth control and abortion measures	2,304	2,057
Fringe benefits for all employed women	3,900	178
Space given to women's concerns in *PMLA* and MLA newsletter	3,268	922
Support women's studies courses	2,866	1,270

66 Thomas R. Edwards, "Women Beware Women," *PR* 41, no. 3 (1974): 476.
67 For a beginning, see Suzanne Juhacz, *Naked and Fiery Forms: Modern American Poetry by Women, A New Tradition* (New York, 1976); Ellen Moers, *Literary Women* (Garden City, N.Y., 1976); Elaine Showalter, *A Literature of Their Own* (Princeton, 1977).

SUSAN SNIADER LANSER
EVELYN TORTON BECK

[Why] Are There No Great Women Critics?
And What Difference Does It Make?

■ By uncovering the androcentric bias of the established literary tradition, feminist scholarship has changed our understanding of literary history and sharpened our perception of how it operates to include or exclude individuals or groups of writers. By undertaking a reevaluation of literature by and about women, it has succeeded in bringing to public attention scores of women writers who were previously neglected, undervalued, or misread. The same, unfortunately, cannot be said of women critics, for whom no similar body of material has been uncovered. Why this discrepancy, and what difference does it make?

It is useful to remind ourselves that in a patriarchal society, the idea of woman as thinker or theoretician is seen virtually as a contradiction in terms. While the term *woman writer* is clear evidence of society's basic conception of the artist as male, our comfort with the phrase does suggest some recognition of women as creators. Because the artist has always been permitted a few of those qualities historically attributed to women (sensitivity, expressiveness, sensuality), patriarchal culture has grudgingly learned to tolerate the woman artist; yet it continues to resist, denigrate, and mistrust woman as critic, theory-builder, or judge. The tasks which "literary criticism" subsumes—research, evaluation, and analysis—are still viewed as exclusively male activities requiring "masculine" powers (logic, judgment, the ability to abstract) unlikely and improper in a woman. For this reason, the term *woman critic* sounds like an awkward, faulty construction, not corresponding to any verifiable reality.

An overview of twenty-four widely used anthologies of literary criticism reveals that, without doubt, the literary critical establishment is in the hands of men.[1] Of a total of 653 essays, only 16 (2.4 percent) represent the work of women.[2] While the vast majority of the essays by men are of a theoretical nature, only a few women (Madame de Staël, Virginia

Woolf, Maud Bodkin) are presented as literary theorists. Well over half the essays by women are examples of "practical criticism"—men's theories applied to the works of men, or essays by novelists on the craft of fiction. Conspicuously absent are writings about the work of women and essays that challenge patriarchal norms.

Can it be, we wondered, that women have really produced so very few critical judgments or theories worthy of being passed on? Did no women concern themselves with women's texts? Scholarly investigation shows that, lacking training and encouragement, many women have been squeezed out of "male" fields, but it also shows that at least since the eighteenth century some women did produce in virtually all academic fields. This recognition led us to question the process by which literary history has selected its canon, and to doubt that the anthologies give us an accurate picture of women's contributions to the study of literature. To verify these claims, a more thorough investigation of primary sources was needed.

The task of unearthing critics is particularly frustrating, because the "official" histories of criticism, while naming dozens of men whose work is never anthologized, are almost as silent about women as the anthologies themselves. (Histories of primary literature, in contrast, are far more likely to contain names of women writers, however disparagingly treated and however briefly discussed.) In our search for clues we resorted to scanning the indexes of standard literary histories, alert for the presence of a female name; more often than not, the textual reference was fleeting.

Our search through the standard reference work in the field, René Wellek's four-volume *History of Modern Criticism, 1750-1900*, provides a useful illustration of the complexities of this type of spadework.[3] Of the relatively few women whose names found their way into these volumes, the overwhelming majority were not critics at all, but either writers— discussed briefly in terms of male critics' opinions of their fiction—or confidantes of male critics, who are assumed to have a function so passive that Wellek says, for example, of Flaubert's relationship to Louise Colet: "He writes to [her] as if she were a good dog."[4] In the history of criticism, then, women are viewed mainly as *objects*: material for critical opinion if they are writers, receptacles for critical opinion if they are mistresses or friends. In neither case are they autonomous agents as far as literary criticism is concerned.

In Wellek's four-volume *History*, comprising over 1,500 pages of text and including literally hundreds of critics, only thirteen female practitioners are discussed. Nine of these women are mentioned only in passing and usually in relation to a male critic. For example, Elizabeth Montagu's work on the "marvellous" in Shakespeare is not examined for its own merits, but is mentioned only in comparison to work done by Samuel Johnson and Ludwig von Tieck. Anna Brownell Jameson's work on Shakespeare is mentioned because Heine used it in his own scholarship.[5] Q. D. Leavis is brought up briefly, but her conception of criticism is mentioned only after she is identified as F. R. Leavis's wife. Even George Eliot's critical writings are linked with those of George Henry Lewes, the man with whom she lived. Only four women—Eliot, Bettina von Arnim, Margaret Fuller, and Madame de Staël—receive more than a sentence of discussion. Even in these fuller treatments, however, the women's relationships to men remain in the foreground, and any relevant feminist material is omitted. In the bibliography that Wellek appends to his history—a listing of several hundred important literary essays—de Staël and Fuller alone represent women's contribution to 150 years of literary scholarship.

Had Wellek—and the sources from which his work derives—not been, as Virginia Woolf would say, "blinded by the . . . spectacles which sex puts on his nose," his *History of Modern Criticism* could have included literally dozens of women whose work is no more "minor" than that of the scores of men whom Wellek does include.[6] Many of the female critics whom Wellek mentions only in passing[7] merit considerably fuller discussion. And women's writings about women and literature constitute a tradition of criticism which Wellek and his colleagues completely ignore.[8]

An adequate history of women critics in Western culture would require years of research, so deeply is the female critical tradition buried and obscured. Following some of the leads which Wellek and other literary historians provide, we have investigated the circumstances of several women critics of the past three centuries. We offer here, not a comprehensive survey, but several cases which seem typical. We intend them as a bare beginning, as markings on a path which will allow us to explore woman's place within the mainstream of literary criticism and which will help us understand what the omission of women's critical perspectives has done to the discipline.

In our exploration of literary history, we encountered female critics who are almost totally forgotten, women whose work lives on in the writings of men, and women who have been acknowledged but whose criticism has been selectively (mis)read. Among those long forgotten is Anne Lefevre Dacier (1654–1720), whom Wellek calls the first modern-day female critic. Though this is not quite accurate, Dacier is one of the earliest women whose career rests entirely on her scholarship. Dacier is responsible for a brilliant translation of Homer and for several critical essays;[9] she was a central figure in the "querelle des Anciens et des Modernes" which raged during the reign of Louis XIV.

The *Memoires* of Saint-Simon provide a clue to the appropriate mask necessary for the woman thinker of that time, especially if she was also a scholar's wife. Saint-Simon notes that Madame Dacier was "far more naturally learned" than her husband, and therefore "very useful to him" and to the many scholars who consulted her. But he praises her most lavishly for her properly feminine demeanor:

> She was a scholar only at her desk or in the company of other scholars; everywhere else she was simple, plain, intelligent, agreeable in conversation; and one would not have suspected that she knew more than the most ordinary woman. . . .
> . . . [She] spoke of fashions and hairdos with the other women . . . with an artlessness and a simplicity that suggested she was capable of nothing better.[10]

One can hardly imagine a similar statement being made about a male scholar, nor would it credit him in the least. If Madame Dacier was encouraged to hide her talents, it is little wonder that literary history forgot her name.

As Dacier was "useful" to her husband and his friends, so literary history is filled with women who functioned, wittingly or not, as scholarly servants to men. Two examples from British literature are illustrative. The eighteenth-century novelist and scholar Charlotte Lennox (1720–1804) was a friend and colleague of Samuel Johnson, who professed strong admiration for her work. Johnson encouraged Lennox to undertake a study of Shakespeare's literary sources, and he apparently wrote the dedication to Lennox's three-volume *Shakespear Illustrated* (1753). This study, which uncovers source material for twenty-two of Shakespeare's plays, was a task of scholarship from which, Karl Young surmises, "Johnson's natural indolence may well have recoiled,"[11] but which would provide him with invaluable material for his own *Preface to Shakespeare* (1765). In his 1756 "Proposals for Printing, by Subscription, the Dramatick Works of William Shakespeare," Johnson had promised "to read the books which the authour read, to trace his knowledge to its source, and compare his copies with their originals."[12] In Johnson's *Shakespeare* the sources for the plays are discussed, and though Johnson refers readers to Lennox's work for some matters which he does not treat, he consistently fails to credit her with her discoveries; these appear in Johnson's text as if they were his own, while men like Alexander Pope are duly credited for their research. Johnson not only fails to credit Lennox but, as Wellek comments, apparently "used the information . . . without . . . adding anything of his own"[13]—a double deceit at a woman's expense.

In his 1923 study of Johnson's *Shakespeare*, Karl Young attempts to account for this omission, noting that it may have stemmed in part from

Johnson's sharp disagreement with some of Lennox's judgments of Shakespeare; but ultimately Young finds "no satisfactory explanation . . . no reason that is creditable to [Johnson]," and he concludes: "It is hard to forgive him for ignoring the fact that [Lennox] laid at his door very considerable amounts of fact."[14] We must wonder, though Young does not, Is it easier for a critic to forget his debt to a *woman* who has served him, or to assume that his encouragement of her entitles him to the fruits of her research?

The case of Vernon Lee (1856-1935) is similar. Her 1895 essay on point of view in fiction, "On Literary Construction,"[15] predates by several years Henry James's work in a similar vein. Lee's essay, as Kenneth Graham notes:

> contains not only a full exposition of point of view in its modern sense, but is in many other respects one of the most remarkable of all late-Victorian pronouncements on the craft of fiction—and one that appears to have gone largely unremarked. . . . Many partial anticipations of James' later criticisms are obvious . . . [and] in some ways, Vernon Lee's theory is more comprehensive and more sympathetic than James'.

Graham concludes: "A more incontestable and more relevant point is that her article deserves to rank beside any single similar piece of writing by James for its qualities of originality, reasonableness, and devotion to the craft of novel-writing."[16]

In a footnote to this discussion, Graham comments that Lee and James "enjoyed a fairly close acquaintance from the seventies or eighties until a breach in 1892."[17] Vineta Colby indicates the source for this rift: in that year Lee published a short story which contained a very thinly veiled portrait of Henry James. Apparently with the best of intentions but insufficient fictional finesse, Lee's portrayal of James was not entirely complimentary.[18] Whether, as a result, James failed to credit Vernon Lee with her contributions to his own theory and whether the failure of acknowledgment was deliberate or simply an oversight, are open to speculation. It is extremely unlikely that James did not read, and use, Lee's work.

Many of Vernon Lee's other theories have also become mainstays of twentieth-century criticism. Her aesthetic theories, especially the concept of empathy, her explorations into the psychology of reading and the active nature of the writer-reader relationship, and her close analysis of literary texts are all pioneering efforts. But even Lee's use of a male pseudonym (her real name was Violet Paget) did not ensure her a place in literary history; her sex did not remain concealed for long.

Clara Reeve (1729-1807) is another pioneering critic who has been forgotten. Her *Progress of Romance,* published in 1785 and only reissued in

1930, was the first book-length treatment of narrative art. Reeve offers a historical, generic, and social analysis of fiction that Scholes and Kellogg (who are among the few critics to give Reeve's work the slightest attention) consider more comprehensive than almost all but premodern efforts at narratology. Reeve formulated the crucial distinctions between novel and romance, which, as Scholes and Kellogg note, have not basically been altered since she set them forth nearly two hundred years ago.[19]

Reeve's narrative theory is surely as important as the gothic novels for which she is far better known. But literary history allows women to be novelists far more readily than it accepts them as critics. Dozens of women who practiced both modes seem to have been selectively perceived. Some twentieth-century examples are instructive: Edmund Wilson and Mary McCarthy are both critics and novelists. Wilson is remembered primarily as a critic; McCarthy, primarily as a novelist. Virginia Woolf and T. S. Eliot are both artists of great stature and achievement; both have written extensively about literature as well. Eliot's essays, especially "Tradition and the Individual Talent," appear in virtually every anthology of modern criticism. Woolf's equally ground-breaking essays, such as "Mr Bennett and Mrs Brown," are rarely anthologized. Alain Robbe-Grillet and Nathalie Sarraute are considered the two leading practitioners of the French *nouveau-roman*. Robbe-Grillet's book of essays, *Pour un nouveau roman*, is far more widely read, at least in English translation, than Sarraute's *L'Ere de soupçon*, which does not exist in paperback in English and, in general, remains considerably less well-known. And it is Robbe-Grillet's name which comes up when the *nouveau-roman* is discussed, though Sarraute is equally prolific and equally instrumental in shaping the mode.

Another twentieth-century example leads to the suspicion that women whose theorizing is overtly feminist are even more likely to be ignored or dismissed. Dorothy Richardson (1873–1957) originated both the theory and practice of the stream-of-consciousness technique in fiction, yet her contribution to the modern novel is often overlooked. Perhaps one reason for Richardson's fate is that she used this new technique explicitly to provide a form adequate to female experience: "a feminine equivalent of the current masculine realism." For this Richardson was accused "of feminism, of failure to perceive the value of the distinctively masculine intelligence,"[20] and of inadequate punctuation, a fault which became a virtue when other (male) writers began to practice it! One major theorist of stream-of-consciousness literature, Robert Humphrey, offers this denigrating analogy for Richardson's intent:

> Unfortunately, the dichotomy between the feminine and masculine viewpoints is too tenuous, if not wholly inadequate, for any degree of profundity.

> . . . One might as well propose that Faulkner writes in order to present a psychotic equivalent of the current sane realism! Faulkner has, certainly, advantages . . . in presenting life from an abnormal person's point of view, and likewise there are certain values inherent in the presentation of life from a feminine point of view—but . . . an adequate purpose is not found in presenting these viewpoints merely for the sake of novelty.[21]

Writing from a woman's perspective, in other words, is an interesting gimmick, like Faulkner's use of Benjy in *The Sound and the Fury*, but it is hardly a justification for developing a whole new literary mode. Thus Humphrey dismisses Dorothy Richardson's theory, and her practice of it in *Pilgrimage*, and reserves his praise for her followers.

Other feminist critics have received similarly inadequate treatment. René Wellek declares his esteem for the critical theories of Margaret Fuller, which he finds superior to those of the other American transcendentalists, but he omits all reference to her feminist ideology. We should also remember that until the last decade, Virginia Woolf's inclusion in the canon had been based on a partial reading of her work; the emphasis was on her brilliant formal achievement, not on the feminist consciousness that informs all her writing. It is hard to believe today that *A Room of One's Own* lay forgotten for almost forty years.

What, then, is the status of the woman critic in the literary world? She will be ignored, undervalued, or dismissed if at all possible, especially if she challenges the status quo. Though she may be well known in her lifetime, in time her name will be forgotten, her works unread. It seems that women's theories, like women themselves, are ultimately viewed as ephemeral, earthly, of the flesh. Mary Ellman has said that "the male body lends credence to assertions, while the female takes it away."[22] It is this fact of patriarchal culture—and not an absence of women critics—which accounts for the erasing of women from the "official" versions of literary history. Certainly women have never been as plentiful in any intellectual/theoretical discipline as men, but a paucity is not an absence. Small numbers, however, are easier to erase; thus, paucity allows the creation of an *illusion* of absence, and this illusion in turn perpetuates the paucity. The fewer women critics there are, the more easily they can be ignored, and the fewer will be the women who follow them. The first task of patriarchal myth-making has been to wash away the "traces" women leave on history; it must then be our first task to recover what has been lost, and to substitute realities for myths.

As we begin to write ourselves into literary history, we must also ask what difference such a re-vision will make. Obviously it is to the benefit of any silenced group to become conscious, visible subjects. But what of literary scholarship itself? Would the presence of a viable tradition of female critics make a qualitative difference in the way literary thinking is carried out?

Given the sharp differences in the socialization of men and women in our society, and given the fact that women are oppressed, a woman's perception of reality must differ significantly from that of a man. But despite the chasm forged by gender polarization, it is theoretically possible for large numbers of women to participate in any discipline without affecting the philosophical premises or methodology of that field. If a woman wishes to be a literary critic but accepts androcentric definitions of her nature and capabilities, her goal would logically be to "think like a man." Such a "masculinization" of women's minds is a patriarchal commonplace: where men hold power and define women in relation to themselves, the price for participation has been just such an acceptance of androcentric epistemologies, and a parallel sacrifice of woman-centered modes of perception. Androcentric thinking—which in our day usually masquerades as scientific objectivity—is rewarded in the woman scholar, while thinking within a gynocentric frame of reference is dismissed as emotional, subjective, specialized, or intuitive—i.e., not scholarly as the patriarchs have defined the term. As a result, many female thinkers have been reduced to parroting the patriarchy or remaining silent. The writings of women who are struggling to define themselves but have not yet given up a patriarchal frame of reference may betray a tension so strong as to produce a virtually "double-voiced" discourse.

But the lessons of history are instructive: whenever women have had sufficient individual or collective power, they have been likely to perceive the contradictions in their own situation, and to recover an autonomous woman-centered epistemology. It is this gynocentric way of knowing that we have come to call feminist. While such a changed mode of perception is never inevitable, we have learned that it becomes most possible when women are freed from economic, psychological and social dependence on men. The building of female support networks helps to reinforce the validity of this epistemology and to minimize the sanctions against it.

Virginia Woolf has described the recognition of Otherness with which a gynocentric way of knowing begins: it is "a sudden splitting off of consciousness . . . when from being the natural inheritor of [this] civilisation, she becomes, on the contrary, outside of it, alien and critical."[23] It was this kind of recognition which led Charlotte Perkins Gilman, in 1911, to expose the androcentrism of the literary tradition, whose major categories—the story of adventure and the story of love—were based on an ideology of male conquest.[24] Similarly, in examining the tradition of critical discourse, we have noticed that the language in which the patriarchal critic conceives his task reveals an underlying ethos of power, battle, possession, and control. It seems unlikely that women would see themselves in terms of these models; and, in fact, we suggest that women critics are more likely to conceive their task in terms of illumination, co-creation, and partnership.

We believe that not only the conception of criticism, but the critical theories themselves, have been seriously distorted by the omission of women's thought. Some of the standard assumptions and classifications used in literary criticism betray an exclusively male frame of reference, which, by excluding women at the most basic levels of definition, creates categories that are inaccurate and incomplete.

We might begin with a challenge to traditional generic classifications, which are based almost exclusively on a body of man-made texts. Feminist critics have observed that women's writings do not easily fit these categories and for this reason are often judged to be defective. If our generic postulates were based entirely on women's texts, or even on a truly integrated canon, our conception of genre might take an altogether different shape. Moreover, even our idea of what constitutes "literature" would be considerably altered, since letters and diaries, two of the literary forms most frequently used by women (especially before 1800), are rarely included in the definition of literature as an art form.

Similarly, we must question descriptive terms such as "fragmented," often used to devalue women's forms, for they are meaningful only if we are measuring women's art against some preestablished norms of "wholeness" and "seamlessness." There may well be a correlation between the fragmentation of women's time and experience in the real world and the structures of women's texts. If women's work were at the center of our definitions, our hierarchy of values would very likely be changed.

Another significant illustration is provided by our understanding of the comic mode, usually defined in terms of a "happy resolution" through marriage. If we looked at our texts from a woman's point of view (if, for example, we analyzed *The Taming of the Shrew* from Kate's perspective), we might not see "resolution" at all, but rather tragic surrender to the status quo. A historical category such as the *Bildungsroman* (defined as a young man's progression to adulthood, complete with sexual initiation and artistic success), might also need to be modified. If we posit a female hero, the same growth pattern is not only viewed as inappropriate, but yields disaster and decline. How then do we name the female *Bildungsroman*?

Women theorists might also make far different decisions about what to name and what to ignore. Instead of positing a category of "unhappy housewife" novels, which emphasizes the problem and makes it look like women's fault, women critics might classify such texts by their impulse toward change, thus emphasizing the solution. We might ultimately want to dismiss some of those categories which seem necessary to us now. Now, for instance, it is important to bring lesbian literature out of hiding and dare to give it its proper name. At some future time, when lesbian texts are not seen from a heterocentric reference point, they will perhaps be taken for granted as part of other categories: Rita Mae Brown's *Rubyfruit Jungle* could easily be taught in a course on the modern picaresque novel, for example, and Olga Broumas's *Beginning with O*, within a study of lyric poetry. In fact, just as women have begun to stress the need for a more flexible canon, so we might also create fluid literary theories which are predicated not on stasis but on the fact of process, on the very possibility of change.

We can also significantly alter the foundations of criticism by challenging the accepted hierarchy of values that dominates patriarchal critical judgment. For example, why should such qualities as "irony" and "complexity" be considered the epitome of excellence, while "sentiment" and "simplicity" (usually associated with women's texts) are disparaged? On what unspoken assumptions are these values based? Such a hierarchy clearly gives preference to men's texts and a male world view, which at this moment in history seem to be moving rather steadily toward increased alienation and anomie. This same hopelessness is not in the least characteristic of contemporary women's texts, nor is it valued by feminist critics. If we permitted our own epistemology and our own needs as women readers, writers, and critics to determine our norms, we might find that qualities of accessibility and involvement would serve us considerably better. Furthermore, a rethinking of established aesthetic norms would permit us more easily to see, apart from patriarchal judgments and preconceptions, what we as women have produced, and in what forms. Such reconsideration would also help us avoid thinking in polarities, and would enable us to move toward distinctions based on a spectrum of values, which, in turn, would lead us to more openness and greater flexibility.

In this way, then, we begin to decondition ourselves as critics. We can recognize the dangers of playing by the established rules, for how we conceptualize and describe determines how we judge. We can reject patriarchal categories and terms; we can refuse to name their names. But refusal and rejection are not sufficient. We must also move ahead, rename, and reclaim, particularly those of our works that the patriarchy has named (falsely) for us. In West Germany, for example, the response to Verena Stefan's *Häutungen*, a feminist text that fits no categories, has been vitriolic, and its author has been vilified by the establishment press, which does not understand Stefan's perspective. Male critics fail to see what she is trying to do or say. Thus, they misread the content and misjudge the form of her text.

Having ourselves been trained to think in patriarchal terms, we can only offer glimpses of what a nonpatriarchal, nonandrocentric, nonheterocentric criticism might look like. We can continue the process of developing a less deformed critical perspective by constantly questioning the categories and the terminology of critical discourse. Does women's literature (as well as other "outsider" literature) fit a given construct? If not, perhaps it is the construct that is partial or distorted, not the literature that is defective. In using traditional critical concepts, we can be wary and attentive to the underlying perspective. When any one aspect is stressed or put in the foreground, we can look at what is ignored in the process. To forge this kind of criticism we need continually to jar our thinking out of its androcentric ruts. Such a perspective is difficult to maintain because it is not reinforced by our patriarchal institutions, and is often actively derided. The critical establishment has as its most powerful weapon the charge that it we do not accept its judgments, let alone its categories, then we are losing our critical acumen, our standards, and our taste—worst of all, we are not doing real literary criticism, but engaging in some kind of make-believe work that is not properly "literary" nor properly "critical."

We need not, of course, continue to argue against patriarchal norms. Perhaps it is no longer productive to expend our energies refuting them. If we are really ready to place ourselves at the center of our thinking, we will begin to develop a criticism that does not justify itself against patriarchal conceptions, but simply ignores them, taking the useful components of the past, and leaving behind the regressive elements. In so doing, we truly begin taking the power to name, and with it, the power to create a criticism of our own.

NOTES

1 The anthologies we examined contained essays from the Greeks to the present, with an emphasis on twentieth-century material. Among them were collections edited by Allen and Clark; I. Babbit; L. S. Hall; O. B. Hardison; I. Howe; C. Kaplan; Lieder and Withington; G. Poulet; Rajan and George; Schorer, Miles, and Mackenzie; Smith and Parks; R. Stallman; Sutton and Foster; and R. B. West. The typical anthology contained twenty to forty essays, with no more than one text written by a woman. Irving Howe's *Modern Literary Criticism* (1958) had the largest proportion of women's writings: five of thirty-one texts.
2 The sixteen essays are by Madame de Staël (three occurrences), Maud Bodkin

(two), Virginia Woolf (two), Elizabeth Bowen, George Eliot, Selma Fraiberg, Helen Gardner, Dorothy Van Ghent, Mary McCarthy, Katharine Ann Porter, Olive Schreiner, and Susan Sontag.

3 René Wellek, *History of Modern Criticism, 1750–1900*, 4 vols. (New Haven, 1955–65).

4 Ibid., 4:26. Wellek's *History* makes no pretense at objectivity. Among the targets for his frequent negative judgments are men who showed any degree of enthusiasm for women writers whom Wellek himself dislikes. For example, the praise given Joanna Baillie by Robert Southey and Sir Walter Scott leads Wellek to comment that Southey "was too generous, too uncritical to be a good judge of his contemporaries" (2: 121), and that Scott "lacked discernment, and even critical pretensions and principles" (2: 122). Baudelaire's esteem for the novels of Marceline Desbordes-Valmore is characterized as a "weak spot" (4: 450), and everyone is accused of "grossly overpraising" George Sand (e.g., 3: 260). Instead of questioning twentieth-century mainstream judgments of these women writers, Wellek assumes they have no intrinsic merit, and therefore sees the praise of these women by *their* contemporaries as a flaw in critical evaluation.

5 Wellek neglects to note that one of Jameson's achievements is a work entitled *Characteristics of Women; or, Shakespeare's Heroines* (1832). However forgotten today, Jameson, as Ellen Moers notes, "wrote books on art that were immensely successful . . . and played a significant share in forming Victorian taste." Ellen Moers, *Literary Women* (Garden City, N.Y., 1976), pp. 187–88.

6 Virginia Woolf, *A Room of One's Own* 1929; rpt. New York, 1957), p. 86.

Many women known primarily for their fictional works, letters, poetry, or plays were also literary critics. A partial listing of critics is appended to this essay.

7 Anne Brownell Jameson, Mary Fitton, Clara Reeve, Elizabeth Montagu, Q. D. Leavis, Marie Rose Stuart, and George Sand. Wellek's failure to discuss the critical writings of George Sand, although he mentions her many times in passing, is inexplicable.

8 Women frequently wrote about women and literature, but such writings constitute a double "outsiderhood": they are both *by* women *about* them. Men's writings about women, however, *are* included in the *History*.

9 For example, *Des Causes de la corruption du goust* (1714; rpt. Geneva: Slatkine Reprints, 1970); and *Homere defendu contre l'Apologie du R. P. Hardouin* (1716; rpt. Geneva: Slatkine Reprints, 1971).

10 Quoted in Paul Mazon, *Madame Dacier et les traductions d'Homere en France* (Oxford, 1936), p. 11. Translation ours.

11 Karl Young, "Samuel Johnson on Shakespeare: One Aspect," *University of Wisconsin Studies in Language and Literature*, no. 18 (1923), p. 180.

12 Quoted in ibid., p. 146.

13 Wellek, *History*, 1: 102.

14 Young, "Samuel Johnson on Shakespeare," pp. 222, 213.

15 In Vernon Lee, *The Handling of Words* (1927; rpt. Lincoln: University of Nebraska Press, 1968), pp. 1–33.

16 Kenneth Graham, *English Criticism of the Novel, 1865–1900* (Oxford, 1965), pp. 135, 138.
17 Ibid., p. 135n.
18 Vineta Colby, *The Singular Anomaly: Women Writers of the Nineteenth Century* (New York, 1970), pp. 253ff.
19 See Clara Reeve, *The Progress of Romance* (1785; rpt. New York: The Facsimile Text Society, 1930), esp. pp. 110–11; and Robert Scholes and Robert Kellogg, *The Nature of Narrative* (New York, 1966), pp. 6–7.
20 In the 1938 Foreword to *Pilgrimage* (London, 1967), 1 : 9–12.
21 Robert Humphrey, *Stream of Consciousness in the Modern Novel* (Berkeley, 1954), p. 11.
22 Mary Ellmann, *Thinking about Women* (New York, 1968), p. 138.
23 Woolf, *A Room of One's Own*, p. 101.
24 Charlotte Perkins Gilman, *The Man-Made World; or, Our Androcentric Culture* (New York, 1911), chap. 5, pp. 87–106, esp. pp. 94ff.

APPENDIX: Some Women Critics, 1700–1900

This list is not comprehensive; it is simply a sharing of names that seem worthy of further investigation.

Name	*Country*	*Dates*
Bettina von Arnim	Germany	1785–1859
Lucy Baxter	England	1837–1902
Anne Lefevre Dacier	France	1654–1720
Lady Eastlake (Elizabeth Rigby)	England	1809–1893
George Eliot	England	1819–1880
Anne Finch, Countess of Winchelsea	England	1661–1720
Margaret Fuller (Ossoli)	U.S.	1810–1850
Stephanie de Genlis	France	1746–1830
Anne Brownell Jameson	England	1794–1860
Vernon Lee (Violet Paget)	England	1856–1935
Charlotte Lennox	England; U.S.	1720–1804
Mary Manley	England	1663–1724
Alice Meynell	England	1847–1922
Mary Wortley Montagu	England	1689–1762
Elizabeth Montagu	England	1720–1800
Lady Morgan (Sydney Owenson)	Ireland	178?–1859
Clara Reeve	England	1729–1807
George Sand	France	1804–1876
Olive Schreiner	S. Africa; England	1855–1920
Mme. de Staël	France	1766–1817
Mary Wollstonecraft	England	1759–1797

CAROLYN WOOD SHERIF

Bias in Psychology

■ Almost a decade ago, Naomi Weisstein fired a feminist shot that ricocheted down the halls between psychology's laboratories and clinics, hitting its target dead center. The shot was a paper, of course; and thanks to the woman's movement, it later found its way into print under the title "Psychology Constructs the Female, or The Fantasy Life of the Male Psychologist." Her thesis was that "psychology has nothing to say about what women are really like, what they need and what they want, essentially because psychology does not know."[1]

Weisstein's critique focused on the male-centeredness of psychology and upon theories that attribute women's lower status in society and personal problems to psychological qualities that make both appear to be inevitable. She correctly directed attention to social-psychological research demonstrating the impact of social circumstances upon an individual's private experiences and actions.

Still earlier, a woman whose academic study had been in psychology made similar critical points in *The Feminine Mystique*.[2] The year that book appeared I spoke at a symposium at Rice University on the status of the "educated woman," declaring that ignorance about women pervaded academic disciplines in higher education, where the "requirements for the degree seldom include thoughtful inquiry into the status of women, as part of the total human condition."[3] A reading of Georgene Seward's *Sex and the Social Order*[4] had long ago convinced me that the orthodox methods of studying and interpreting sex differences were capable of delivering only mischievous and misleading trivia. Apart from the hoary sex-differences tradition (euphemistically called the "study of individual differences"), psychology's treatment of the sexes contained several brands of psychoanalytic thought and a growing accumulation of research on socialization to "sex-appropriate behaviors," which was actually the old sex-difference model mixed with psychoanalytic notions and served in a new disguise.

Since the 1960s, the woman's movement has provided the needed context for critical examination of biased theoretical assumptions and working practices in psychology's diverse areas. While referring to that critical literature and the more positive efforts to proceed toward reconstruction, I will concentrate here on examining the following questions, which I believe must be answered if there is to be an equitable pursuit of knowledge about human individuals in psychology:

1. Why have demonstrations of theoretical and research bias, some dating to the earliest days of academic psychology, been no more effective than they have been in correcting theory and research practice? Is the problem simply that there have not been enough women in psychology, or is there something in psychology's assumptions and working practices that also needs attention?
2. What are the dominant beliefs in psychology about the proper ways to pursue knowledge? Where do they come from and what supports them, despite the documented fact that they can encourage biased perspectives?
3. What assumptions about the human individual lie beneath the diversity of psychological theories and their associated procedures for studying that individual?
4. What can we learn from an examination of the state of psychology today that will further an equitable pursuit of knowledge?

Ethnocentrism, Androcentrism, and Sexist Bias in Psychology

The growth of academic psychology over the past century has been compellingly a United States' phenomenon, despite European origins and the non-American backgrounds of a number of its stimulating theorists and researchers. A few decades after William James at Harvard and Wilhelm Wundt at Leipzig started psychological laboratories (1875, according to Boring's history),[5] their students had started psychology departments or laboratories at major universities, including the newly forming women's colleges. Work by women Ph.D.'s began to appear, and two of them (Mary Calkins and Margaret Washburn) served early in this century as presidents of the American Psychological Society, which had formed toward the end of the nineteenth century. In Cattell's *American Men of Science* of 1903, three women were included among fifty psychologists starred as "eminent," two ranked in twelfth and nineteenth ranks (Mary Calkins and C. Ladd-Franklin, respectively), and the third among the last twenty (Margaret Washburn).⁶ Not a high proportion, to be sure.

The problem of bias in psychological research was encountered early in the discipline's history, as E. G. Boring's *History of Experimental Psychology* makes clear. "Laboratory atmospheres," or the little Geister within the Zeitgeist (to use his favorite term), were repeatedly found to affect the results coming from different laboratories on the same problem, whether the problem concerned such issues as the presence or absence of images in thought, insightful learning vs. slow trial-and-error learning, or the accumulating research on sex difference. In his history, Boring dismissed sex bias once and for all when assessing the results of Francis Galton's psychological assessments on 9,337 persons at the 1884 International Health Exhibition: "No important generalizations as regards human individual differences appeared, however, unless we should note Galton's erroneous conclusion that women tend in all their capacities to be inferior to men."⁷

Helen Thompson Woolley had critically exposed the bias in sex-difference research, dismissing much of it as drivel, in 1903 and 1910.⁸ Leta S. Hollingworth completed doctoral research at Columbia on whether performance on several tasks suffered during menstruation, finding no decrement despite the contrary conviction of her major professor, E. L. Thorndike. Like Mary Calkins earlier, she repeatedly wrote against the hypothesis that women's intellectual capacities varied less than men's. She penned an article in 1916 called "Social Devices for Impelling Women to Bear and Rear Children" that can still rock complacent heels.⁹

And surely someone must have read the dissertation by Mary Putman Jacobi that won the distinguished Boylston Prize from Harvard University in 1876 on the question, "Do women require mental and bodily rest during menstruation, and to what extent?" Dr. Jacobi began her dissertation with the following caution: "An inquiry into the limits of activity and attainments that may be imposed by sex is very frequently carried on in the same spirit as that which hastens to ascribe to permanent differences in race all the peculiarities of a class, and this because the sex that is supposed to be limiting in its nature, is nearly always different from that of the person conducting the inquiry."¹⁰ Then she reviewed historical evidence both on medical views of menstruation and on women as workers. She collected complete case histories on 268 women, including on their health, took physiological measures during one to three months, and conducted a small performance experiment. She concluded that, yes, short rest periods during the working day would be helpful for menstruating women, as they also would be for women and men during the rest of the month, all of whom would benefit even more by an eight-hour day in place of the twelve or more hours they then labored.

Admittedly, I have chosen cases of women who were keenly aware of the actualities of sex bias, and who were vigorously protesting its manifestations. If, instead, we were to look at the work of the other forty-seven eminent psychologists on Cattell's list in 1903 or at the bulk of writings on sex differences during the early part of this century or at the writings of Sigmund Freud, we would find tons of exemplars for the conclusion reached by my colleague and former student, Stephanie Shields, in her highly original paper reviewing the early years to document social myth in psychology. Her conclusion was as follows: "That science played handmaiden to social values cannot be denied."[11] A similar conclusion could be reached by examining the literature in psychology on race. Yet some mental testers will deny that racism has anything to do with contemporary controversies over intelligence testing.[12]

One could go on and on with further examples of theoretical and research controversies involving bias in psychology on large and on small problems. But I come to a major question: If the possibility and the existence of sexist bias was recognized by the turn of this century, why and how could academic and nonacademic psychology continue to perpetuate its myths up to the present?

Hierarchy in Psychology

It has been thirty-four years since I entered psychology as a graduate student, having learned as an undergraduate at Purdue University that there was such a thing as social psychology. My desire to be a social psychologist was then unorthodox. Nevertheless, I was accepted, even welcomed into the psychology department of the University of Iowa as a graduate assistant. It was 1943, during World War II, when qualified male applicants to graduate programs were scarcer than hen's teeth. As we should know, women are valued more when men are scarce, as today's volunteer army demonstrates. My first lessons at Iowa concerned the status criteria and norms valued by psychologists.

At the peak of the status hierarchy were the experimentalists. At that time and place, being an experimentalist meant being self-consciously scientific, reading the philosophy of science as expounded by logical positivists, and studying hungry rats learning the way to food, or humans responding to a puff of air to the eyelid. One way to determine who "counts" to an elite is to learn whose arguments the elite attends to and whose viewpoints they try to demolish. At the time, the only people worthy of attention from experimentalists were other experimentalists.

The next rung in the hierarchy was occupied by the "mental testers" and statistical buffs, who represented a quite different tradition in psychology but had to be listened to by experimentalists who wanted to analyze their data in the currently fashionable way. The testing tradition, which began in Great Britain, had been fueled by the practical success of the French psychologists Binet and Simon in developing a workable test for singling out school children with potential learning problems. The Stanford version of their test, the development of group tests, and their use during World War I put testers of all kinds into an orbit that is now a $120 million industry by conservative estimate.[13] Interestingly enough, a survey of the interests of women psychologists just after World War II revealed that proportionally more were in the ranks of the testers than of the experimentalists.[14] So perhaps it is no accident that the two women (Anne Anastasi and Leona Tyler) who were elected presidents of the American Psychological Association in the past decade were recognized as experts in the mental testing tradition of differential psychology as well as active contributors to the professional organization. Somewhat more predictably, their terms followed immediately upon that of the first and only black president of the association (Kenneth B. Clark).

On the next lowest rung of the hierarchy at Iowa in 1943 were the developmental psychologists, whose work at the time focused heavily on preschool children. They were housed in the same building, but under the separate roof of the Institute for Child Welfare (a less prestigious locale, you may be sure), and included the only women faculty. Although regarded as the "child study people," they were headed by an experimentalist from the same major university as the psychology chairman; hence, a few of them were regarded as acceptable by experimentalists. But the testers and the developmentalists had more to talk about, since Iowans were in the forefront of the attack on a fixed, inherited "intelligence," battling Minnesotans and Californians who defended the alleged constancy of IQ.

One distinguished member of the Child Welfare faculty was Kurt Lewin. Lewin had published the famous studies on the effects of adult modes of interaction on the behavior of small boys in leisure-time groups, the authoritarian, democratic, and laissez-faire leadership experiments.[15] At the time, he was often in Washington, involved in the equally well-known studies on group decision. (These studies demonstrated that women volunteers in Red Cross activities were not easily persuaded by lectures to alter long-ingrained food customs, but were quite capable of changing the family diet to include unpopular foods to help the war effort when presented with the problem of food shortages and encouraged to arrive at a joint decision to make the change.)[16] Like many of their experimental colleagues in Washington, in military service, or with the Office of War Information, the experimentalists at Iowa regarded these as "applied" activities, necessary at the time but not the stuff of which a science is made. At the bottom of the Iowa ladder and also classified as "applied" were the one other social psychologist and the clinical psychologists.

The hierarchy was male, of course. Thirty years ago, it was the experimentalists at the top, the testers and statisticians next, then the developmentalists, and finally the social psychologists, including some interested in what was called personality, along with the clinicians. After World War II, there were notable changes, the most striking being the enormous increase in number of clinical psychologists, with federal funds to support their activities and student training. Today, about 40 percent of APA members are clinical psychologists. The numbers and the standing of social psychologists changed, less through their following the example of Kurt Lewin than through their self-conscious efforts to be accepted as *experimental* social psychologists and their quoting Lewin's injunction against historicalism, one of his least defensible points. A host of new specialties was born of postwar prosperity. You name it, we have it, including in 1973 a division on psychology of women and by 1976 a division "interested in religion."

So why do I bring up the hierarchy of three decades ago? It is my contention that each of the fields and specialties in psychology sought to improve its status by adopting (as well and as closely as stomachs permitted) the perspectives, theories, and methodologies as high on the hierarchy as possible. The way to "respectability" in this scheme has been the appearance of rigor and scientific inquiry, bolstered by highly restricted notions of what science is about. The promise was that theirs was the true path to general psychological principles, applicable with slight modification to any human being and, in some cases, to any organism, even rats, monkeys, and chimpanzees.

Never mind that in practice, psychology treated women, blacks, and other minorities, as well as residents of certain other countries, as more "different" than a well-behaved laboratory chimpanzee. We are talking of myth, or more accurately, the ideology of psychology's elite. In that perspective, work outside of the laboratory was suspect. Research in naturalistic settings was regarded as necessarily less "pure," even "contaminated." Efforts to change social life or individual circumstances were regarded as merely "applied" work, typically as premature attempts to apply psychological principles.

The irony is that the preservation of psychology's hierarchy and the expansion of the entire enterprise was supported by those psychologists making inroads into major institutions—educational, business, industrial, military, governmental, the growing mass media, and the "mental health" institutions and industry—in short, the "applied" psychologists. Without their inroads, psychology would have been small potatoes in academia, but it need not have worried. The growing number of psychologists in major institutions needed the academic hierarchy to support its claims at being scientific.

Dominant Beliefs Conducive to Bias in Psychology

Certain of its dominant beliefs about the proper ways to pursue knowledge have made psychological research peculiarly prone to bias in its conception, execution, and interpretation. It is on these that I shall focus here —and I shall be highly critical. If I thought that these were the only beliefs in psychology or that they characterized everything within its bounds, I would not still be a psychologist. But I have seen a number of battles and skirmishes over psychological findings, many of them possible because of fundamental flaws in the orthodox modes of seeking knowledge.

A historical perspective is useful in understanding the issues. One year after psychology's entry onto the academic scene, the Centennial Exposition of 1876 opened in Philadelphia. As the Smithsonian's 1976 recreation vividly reminds us, rhapsodic praise of science and technology was a major theme. From its birth, academic psychology cast its lot within the bright promise of a scientific future. Similarly, founders of the notion of psychotherapy—all physicians, including Sigmund Freud— were immersed in that same promise. Freud reserved special indignation for those critics, like Havelock Ellis, who suggested that he was dealing in allegory and myth rather than in science.[17] In this respect alone, Freud was brother under the skin to the best-known psychologist of our day, B. F. Skinner.

I shall not be exploring the larger historical trends toward faith in science. Instead, I am concerned with the subsidiary impulse of psychologists to seek acceptance and prestige for their new discipline through imitating the more established scientific disciplines. Over time, those who became the most prominent psychologists were those who imitated the most blindly, grasping what brought prestige in their society even though it was more a caricature of the more established sciences.

Undeniably, the prestigious and successful sciences in the late nineteenth and early twentieth century were those securely focused on the physical world and the physical processes of the organic world. Psychologists, in their strivings to gain status with other scientists, did not pause long on issues raised by the differences between studying a rock, a chemical compound, or an animal, on one hand, and a human individual, on the other. Instead, methods that had been successful in the physical and biological sciences were embraced as models for psychology. Researchers were soon deep into analogy, comparing the human individual to the chemical compound or to the animal as the subject of research, with all of the power that such an analogy gives to the scientific investigator, at least if the animal is captive and small. Unlike the natural scientist, however, the psychologist had only social power over the research subject, not the greater power to explore, observe, and analyze that had unlocked so many of nature's secrets for the physical sciences.

Beliefs about What Is "Basic"

The methodology promoted in psychology, in its strivings for social acceptability and prestige, rested on the assumption that the causes of an event can be determined by breaking down the event into component parts, or elements, and studying those parts and their relationships to one another. The more "basic" these parts or elements are, the more "basic" is the inquiry.

What psychology defined as basic was dictated by slavish devotion to the more prestigious disciplines. Thus, a physiological or biochemical part or element was defined as more basic than a belief that Eve was created from Adam's rib, not because the former can necessarily tell us more about a human individual, but because physiology and biochemistry were more prestigious than religious history or sociology. On the environmental side, a physical element that could be counted or that one of the physical sciences had already measured was regarded as more "basic" than poverty; thus, the social disciplines that wrote about poverty in any way other than by counting income had even less standing than psychology. Turning to the humanities for an understanding of what is basic in being human was considered absurd. What could scholars in English or Spanish, in history or classics, possibly tell psychologists? Psychologists did look to history and philosophy to find out about the history and philosophy of science, but then, that was all about mathematics, physics, and chemistry, and therefore respectable.

Narrowing the Space and Time Framework

The event to be studied and the elements to be considered basic or peripheral were to be those that occurred in the here-and-now of the researcher's observation or of the other techniques for data collection. In many respects, Kurt Lewin's call for ahistoricalism in psychology—that is, for concerning oneself with history only as its forces were revealed in the immediate situation at the time of study—was merely confirmation of existing research practice.[18] Nonetheless, it provided justification for developmental, social, and personality psychologists to view as "scientific" the conduct of research on human individuals about whose past, personal loyalties, and social ties, about whose place in a larger historical-cultural nexus, they knew next to nothing. Consequently, they seldom looked for or found evidence of history, culture, or organizational ties in the specific research situations they studied. Mary Putnam Jacobi's surveys of the history of cultural and medical thought about menstruation and of the historical experiences of working women were now to be considered excess baggage in a study of particular women at a particular period of time. Even her case histories would come to be seen as unnecessary, except insofar as they contained evidence of physiologic malfunction, since physiological factors were defined as basic.

"Objective" Language as a Disguise for Ignorance or Bias

By the mid-twentieth century the elementism practiced by orthodox psychology became thoroughly blended with the language of applied mathematical statistics, especially as applied to biological and agricultural research. Thus, the elements became abstract "variables." The psychologist in pursuit of knowledge was attempting to seek causation by discovering lawful relationships among variables. Paraphrasing E. L. Thorndike, the psychologist came to believe that "anything that exists, exists in some quantity, hence can be measured" and hence is a variable.[19]

In causation, not all variables are created equal, however. Some are designated "independent variables," and it is to these that one looks for causality, despite textbook cautions to the contrary. One may find the independent variable in nature, as when an agronomist selects garden plots with soil rich or poor in nitrogen in which to plant corn. The yield or height of the growing corn is then the "dependent" variable caused by the independent variable (rich or poor soil), unless the soil or the seed or the air contain other "contaminating" variables.

It goes without saying that a person's sex is considered an independent variable, not a dependent one, despite the fact that everyone and no one knows what that means. Psychologists seem to think they know, when they pronounce that the sex of the researcher or the sex of the research subject, or both, are independent variables in research; but it should not take a Renée Richards to demonstrate that the assumption of causality by the "independent variable" of sex is misleading. Why? Because the "variable" called sex is like a railroad boxcar: everyone knows what it is called and what it is used for, but no one knows what is inside. Older psychologists had no doubt that it contained "biology." Modern psychologists follow suit, or add culture, or subtract biology as well. Result? Utter confusion in almost all discussions of the variable "sex" or of sex differences.

Glorifying the Experiment: An Example

The highly abstract belief that knowledge is to be gained by studying parts, elements, or variables and by seeking lawfulness in their relationships, is translated into reality during psychological research. The most prestigious way to make this translation is the experiment. In the experiment, certain selected "independent," presumably causative, elements are deliberately varied, while other possible choices are controlled or kept in a constant state.

What this description of the experiment means is that in the human experiment much of what goes on is simply ignored. The researcher may choose the independent variable by selecting persons according to sex, race, etc., or according to their performance on a psychological test. But the experiment is considered much more valid if the researcher attempts to create the independent variable by "manipulating" the circumstances in the research situation—for example, by controlling what people see or hear or do. Thus created, the variable is somehow regarded as purer, less "contaminated" by past experiences. History is ignored, and the researcher has the illusion of creating history at the moment.

While I was looking for an example of an experiment, the mail brought the current issue of the *Journal of Personality and Social Psychology,* the most widely read and cited journal in that area of psychology. The second article, by the journal editor and his students, concerned the effects of three "independent variables" upon reactions to messages intended to persuade college students for or against some viewpoint, for example, for or against faculty tenure. Other independent variables were also introduced in a series of eight separate experiments. All of these experiments studied the ratings of messages on thirty-six different topics made by persons described as follows: "Subjects were either unpaid undergraduate volunteers who were enrolled in introductory psychology courses or were paid respondents to classified advertisements in the university newspaper. . . . Subjects were recruited without regard to sex and were assigned randomly to a persuasion . . . group and to an identification number within that group. . . . a total of 616 subjects provided data."[20]

Eighteen of the messages concerned past presidents of the United States, and eighteen others concerned arbitrarily selected social issues—that is, the researchers simply picked them. The experiments are presented as a novelty, with considerable pride, because the messages were presented to subjects by computer on video screen, and the subjects responded to them by pushing the computer's buttons. "The computerized method assures a standardized experimental procedure for each subject . . . it minimizes interaction of the subject with a human experimenter. These characteristics are responsible for a desirably high degree of situational control and assurance that possible sources of experimenter bias are minimized."[21] But it was the researchers who selected the topics, presented them in certain orders, varied the contents of the screen, etc. Moreover, the researchers were forced to add the caution that "although the relationship of experimenter to subject is mediated by the computer, that relationship nonetheless exists."[22] They make less issue about the undeniable possibility of significant effects from interacting with a computer.

The researchers present their findings on the persuasive effects of the messages in typical fashion, as the means or averages of all the students' single ratings on each issue after they had read the message. The individual differences among the students, including what their opinions about the presidents or the social issues were before messages were presented, were treated in the statistical analysis as a "random-effect" factor.

In short, this experiment typifies the assumption in a great deal of experimentation that "general laws" about the relationships among variables can be obtained by comparing averages of the responses made by a sizable number of individuals, who are regarded as being without a background, personal history, or gender that might have anything to do with their response in the situation. In this case, the situation itself is described only in terms of the equipment, which is shown in a photograph. Its duration appears to have been well within the academic hour.

Are These the Beliefs of "Hard Science"?

Doing "basic" research on "variables" that are given numbers, and hence can be treated statistically, and, especially, performing experiments are sometimes called the "hard science" ways of seeking knowledge in psychology. What these beliefs describe, instead, are efforts by some members of a newer, less established discipline to imitate what they, as outsiders, see as the ways the physical sciences achieved knowledge successfully. It is the physical sciences that are called "hard sciences," as we all know, and the human disciplines that are "soft."

The adoption of the "hard" and "soft" analogy within psychology and within other social disciplines obscures the real issues, which are about the ways to extend scientific methods to the study of human beings by other human beings. Those who use these adjectives have almost always been men trying to put down other men and their work, attempting to enhance their own status by associating their own efforts with the more prestigious physical or natural sciences.[23] For this reason, I think it particularly misleading to suggest that "hard" also implies "masculine," while "soft" implies "feminine." After all, in the physical sciences there have been a few women, and some of the women minority in the "soft" disciplines follow the hard line.

Within psychology, the "hard" vs. "soft" name-calling is also to be heard when issues of "scientific" vs. "humanistic" psychology are discussed. Again, the controversies do not divide the men from the women; they have been quite divisive of male psychologists. But "humanistic" psychologists need to cease accepting their opponents' definitions of what is "scientific" and start to assess science as a human endeavor. The self-consciously scientific experimental psychologists need to start thinking about the unique problems raised in the history of science when human individuals turn to studying other individuals.

Meanwhile, the equitable pursuit of knowledge will be better served if we recognize psychologists' self-annointment as "hard" researchers for what it is: a put-down of critics who do not accept their orthodoxies. Those who proclaim the hardness of their methods and their hardware the loudest are the most guilty of producing research findings with the durability of a marshmallow. And now, we shall see why.

Critique of Psychological Orthodoxy's Beliefs on Its Objectivity

I have intended my description of the standard in psychological research, which admittedly was almost a caricature, to make clear that the standard research situation is loaded with opportunity for bias. The opportunity starts when a researcher decides what to study and it continues to widen during decisions about how to study the subject. What is the individual being studied to do during the research? The researcher decides, of course, often in highly arbitrary ways dictated by custom in previous research, not by what the person does or is doing in daily life. What are to be included as the all-important independent variables? Which aspects of the individual's behavior are to be noticed and which ignored during the research experience? The researcher makes all of these decisions, often forgetting at times that he or she is a human being who is part of the research situation too.

Research as an Interpersonal and Cultural Event

Now we can see, I trust, why Robert Rosenthal and many others after him were able to demonstrate in the late 1950s and the 1960s the phenomenon of researcher bias—specifically, that the researcher's expectations of the outcome in research affect what is actually found.[24] Rosenthal's findings should have come as no surprise. Studies of interviewing had already shown that middle-class interviewers obtained answers from working-class respondents that differed from those obtained by working-class interviewers, that white interviewers got answers from black respondents differing from those obtained by black interviewers, and that women respond differently to men and to women, as men respond differently to women and to men.[25]

Why should the effect of one human being upon another be a surprise, especially the effect of a much more powerful researcher upon a person who has agreed to cooperate in an institutional setting that defines the person as "subject"? Did someone believe that the psychology of researcher and the psychology of subject, both human beings, are altogether different?

There was also the failure to recognize other sociocultural aspects of the research situation. The research setting, whether experiment or interview, packs a cultural wallop through its physical location, especially if defined as a place to do research, and through the plethora of equipment, clipboards, forms, tape recorders, and audiovisual equipment that researchers pack about. Two-way mirrors, intended to hide the researcher, in fact alert the person observed that his or her actions are being watched and evaluated. A simple button placed in the room in the event that the subject wants to leave becomes a signal to "panic" ("if it's there, it's there to be used"). The supposedly neutral and objective paper-and-pencil test or information blank turns out to be a signal to the individual that someone who knows more than she does is evaluating something about her, perhaps even her worth as a person—an unnerving thought at best and at worst a promoter of apprehension or of an active effort to appear "socially desirable." Finally, evidence has accumulated indicating that people who volunteer for research tend to be those with more interest in psychology, research, and science, who do respond to the research situation differently from a person somehow mousetrapped in the research situation. The difference is typically in a direction congenial to the researcher's interest, although it need not be, especially since the researcher has often been unaware of the impact of these research impedimenta or of the active attempts by subjects to evaluate and deal with the research situation.[26]

The impact of the research situation is nowhere more convincingly shown than in Stanley Milgram's study of obedience by research subjects to a researcher's commands to deliver increasingly more severe electric shocks to another person who is ostensibly another innocent subject. Actually, the latter played a prescribed role, exhibiting discomfort and objecting to the procedures, though never actually being shocked. Once a "subject," man or woman, agreed to participate in the experiment, typically for pay, the highly institutional setting, the white-coated experimenter, and the structured procedures took precedence, at least for 65 percent of the subjects, so long as the apparent victim was out of sight in the next room. Milgram understood the power of that institutional setting, its equipment, and the authoritative researcher. He showed that obedience dropped sharply when the procedures called for closer proximity to the apparent victim, and that another person refusing to cooperate blew the game. The standard personality tests purporting to measure proclivities toward aggression proved worthless in predicting reactions to the research situation. On the other hand, certain past experiences in the subject's life did appear to relate to his or her decision on whether to continue shocking the victim or whether to stop, as 35 percent of Milgram's subjects did even in his most compelling situation. These past experiences related much more to the individual's perspectives on authority, on science, and on self than they did to abstractly defined personality characteristics.[27]

More Culture in Study of Persons

The final cultural wallop packed by a research situation concerns the activity performed by the research subject. What is the individual to do for research? How does she or he regard the task—as easy or difficult, fun or boring, familiar or strange? The researcher's choice of what is to be done, and hence, of what behaviors are to be examined, is critical.

By now, we know that the standard procedures developed in an influential line of research to study achievement motivation were biased by the choice of tasks and of instructions that were male-oriented. They were inappropriate for studying achievement orientations of women who had been brought up to believe that certain activities and institutions—e.g., the military—were off-limits for women.[28] We also know that the effort to patch up that theory on achievement by adding a new motivation— avoidance or fear of success—produced over two hundred studies with conflicting results.[29]

Both efforts failed largely because the researchers, in defining the research situation, forgot that outside of it and for years, success had been defined by others who count in our eyes—our reference persons and groups—and that what success meant has been quite different for the reference persons and groups of different men and women in our society. In fact, *success* has been defined so differently that both women and men who have tried to achieve success in ways ruled more appropriate for the other gender—for example, career women or male ballet dancers—have been targets for derogatory labels and negative adjectives so widely used as to be social stereotypes. Especially in a society where some of these divisions have begun to change, indeed where some people are actively rejecting both the definitions and the possibility of "success" in traditional terms, what kind of a theory on motivations to achieve, or fears of failure, or motives to avoid success, can ignore the issues of who defines success or failure for whom, and whether individuals accept those definitions as their own? A little history, a little sociology and economics, a little attention to the historic pleas of feminists and antiracist movements, would have helped.

Another example of bias induced by the selection of activities is a whole line of research on influenceability or suggestibility. One of the old saws in many social psychology texts up through 1974 (though not in any of the four authored by the Sherifs) was that women are more susceptible to persuasive influences or suggestions than men. The research evidence to lay that old saw to rest was collected by my former student Ben Tittler over ten years ago, when he showed that both men and women were more suggestible when the topic at hand was of very little concern to them (e.g., the reputation of General von Hindenburg) than when the topic was deeply and personally involving (e.g., the appropriate personal qualities for men and women). More recently, Judy Morelock's Ph.D. research at Pennsylvania State University has demonstrated that whether men or women are easily influenced by persuasive suggestions depends upon the gender of the researcher in relation to the topic—specifically, that women are more suggestible with a male researcher when the topic is socially defined as one of male interest, while men respond in parallel fashion when a woman researcher tries to influence them on a topic socially defined as interesting to women. Finally, Alice Eagley has performed the arduous task of surveying all available research on short-term persuasion and suggestion, and has found no basis whatsoever for the blanket conclusion that one sex is more suggestible than the other.[30] There is, however, a great deal of evidence that anyone may be suggestible or influenced when he or she is placed in an ambiguous situation where one's responsiveness to the situation itself seems more important at the time than personal integrity or self-definition as individual man or woman. When some aspect of the person's self becomes highly involved or is at stake, neither sex is readily or easily influenced by the opinions or persuasiveness of another person during a brief encounter, especially if that other person is a stranger.[31]

Short Course in How to Perpetuate Social Myth

The lesson for those who want to perpetuate sex bias in psychological research is clear: Restrict the framework for study to a narrow span of time. Attend only to what you decide is important, ignoring as much else as possible. Label these important aspects in the language of "variables," both to sound objective and to mask your ignorance. Arrange the research situation as you choose. If you are biased, the situation will be. Record your selectively chosen data and discuss them as though dealing with eternal verities.

If anyone tries to refer to historical, cultural, or organizational circumstances outside of your own narrow framework, either (1) derogate such talk as referring to "soft" facts and "soft" disciplines which you see as being of little relevance to your carefully controlled variables and findings; or (2) suggest that everyone has different interests, and that yours happens to be in psychology, whatever its limitations, not in history, culture, etc. In either case, you will have removed the most effective and, ultimately, the only effective means by which your critic can expose your bias and show what you have done wrong. You will have put the critic in the position either of confining the discussion to your limited framework, or of going out to do another study to show that your research does not hold up—that it cannot be replicated or that it crumbles when another variable is introduced.

Suppose that your critic does the latter. The attempt to replicate a study with a few well-chosen variations is the means many psychologists choose if they want to do serious battle in order to gain victory within the establishment's walls. The history of our field and the analysis of the "social psychology of the psychological experiment" that I just reviewed both suggest that the critic's chance of scoring a critical point is very high. Findings in the area will become "controversial."

Now, what should you, the researcher, do to your critic? By far the best tactic is to withdraw from the field, murmuring about the weaknesses of the research design that has become controversial. Find another way to score your point with a research design so different that the ongoing controversy is no longer relevant.

In fact, that is exactly what has happened over and over again in psychology on many topics, but almost invariably on topics where sex bias is charged. For example, most research from Putnam-Jacobi's and Hollingworth's to the present shows insignificant variations in women's performance attributable to the menstrual cycle on a variety of laboratory tasks. So proponents of the view that menstruation is debilitating by definition switched grounds. Instead of looking at what women do, they started looking at the way women said they *felt*—at their reported moods and especially at their bad ones. The switch amounted to saying, in effect, that bad moods *are* debilitating, whether women perform differently or not. Then new critics showed quite convincingly that the culture is loaded with stereotyped notions about menstruation and bad moods, some authors almost seeming to say that women report bad moods because they think they are supposed to. The debilitator school chuckles tolerantly and points to hormonal fluctuations during the cycle. Can such hormonal "storms" be ignored?

Meanwhile, women who experience discomfort during menstruation are wondering whether to blame the experience on their *really* being the "weaker sex," or on their society, or on themselves. Women who experience no discomfort wonder what all the fuss is about. Fortunately, a small minority of researchers is beginning to realize that an unbiased view of this universal, greatly neglected cyclic phenomenon can be developed only over considerable time through enlarging the framework for study. That framework has to include historical perspective and study, as well as unbiased physiological study that sees hormonal variations as normal and universal for both genders, each with characteristic patterns. It has to include a vastly expanded perspective on what women and men do, their relationships to one another and in a variety of periodic activities, as these relate to the most underdeveloped problem area in psychological research—namely, how people feel and experience themselves, and why, when, and how these self-experiences affect their actions.

If the issues of bias in psychological research were as simple as turning the methods and instruments prized by psychology into the service of defeating bias, many battles would have been won long ago. My short course in how to perpetuate myths has already been learned too well by too many to allow such a defeat. The long course in how to destroy myths has to begin with the essentials: Broaden the framework within which knowledge is sought, then persist in the difficult tasks of relating events within that broadened framework through a variety of methods and research techniques. This is the only course toward an unbiased psychology. Otherwise, those who hold biased viewpoints, either wittingly or unwittingly, will return a decade later, dredge up the old research evidence, reinterpret it by clothing it in new words, and start the argument again before public audiences who like the message. This is what happened in the so-called race and intelligence controversy, which many psychologists believed had been laid to rest a generation ago.

Buttresses in Society for Psychology's Orthodoxy

In view of the openness of psychological research to bias, who in society buttresses the continuation of its research traditions by supporting them or by drawing upon their conclusions? It is popular in academia to say "no one"; but such scholarly aloofness is far from true, historically. Since World War I, the military has been one of the strongest sources of support for psychological tests on what psychologists called "intelligence," then came to define as "what my test measures." Tests of "abilities" and of variously labeled aptitudes followed. Another source of support has been our vast educational system, from preschool through graduate school, in order to place students into educational tracks and channel them into different slots for future training or education. In fact, the goals of education became defined in terms of test performance, rather than tests serving as a means of seeing whether the educational establishment was meeting its own goals or those considered desirable in society.

The logical extension of the so-called intelligence or ability tests to the assessment of various aspects of the personality and of motivation followed, especially after World War II. These tests became so standard that incoming freshmen at the University of Minnesota accepted the practice of taking the Minnesota Multiphasic Personality Inventory along with placement tests in academic subjects. They were widely used in government and industry, which also adopted large batteries of aptitude tests for use in selecting employees and in promotion. Desirous of an "instant criterion" for selecting able and docile employees, these institutions did not, typically, develop tests demonstrably predictive of success in a job, but purchased commercial tests often developed for entirely different purposes. The use of such tests, both in educational placement and in fateful decisions about employment, have figured recently in several court decisions on affirmative action practices.[32] I am told also that a well-known vocational interest test for high school students has ceased printing its separate tests for women and men, which were on pink and blue forms.

Aside from the testing industry, the military and other agencies of government have poured huge sums into research on problems that concerned them at the moment. During and after World War II, the popular topic was propaganda; then came studies of small groups and leadership; and by the early sixties all the money was for cross-cultural research and studies on how to change people's attitudes. The relationship between what was supported, what psychologists in those periods studied, and what problems were concerning government and the military is clear, though seldom discussed. Similarly, the record of what is supported in the study of child development mirrors the social problems of concern to authorities at the time and the programs they hope to justify by research. A whole new research industry whose sole aim is to evaluate social programs by the government has recently been born in academia and in commercial firms. Such evaluation research is prone to bias in the direction of confirming what policymakers want to perpetuate and what they hope fails, as one of the earliest papers on the topic makes abundantly clear.[33] More recently, we learn from daily papers that, all the while, the CIA has been supporting research through a variety of phony foundations and social agencies.

Finally, the emergence of clinical psychology as the largest specialty by psychologists after World War II reflects the fact that wars are very hard on people, creating problems that last far beyond their duration. Clinical psychology grew from the lack of enough psychiatrists to handle war-related human problems and from the growing numbers of human casualties at the community level who raised community, hence governmental issues. And once we had the problems and a growing army of professionals, the definition of what is to be done with human problems in living changed: many now required, not friends, not better working conditions, not a social worker, not a job interview, not a minister or loving parent, but a therapist. Benefitting from the aura already created by the medical profession, clinical psychologists came into demand, in preference to a minister or a social worker or a counselor, because their claims to expertise rested on a discipline that said it was scientific, that based its procedures on research findings.

It has become customary for women to deplore the practices of testing for psychological assessment, placement, and hiring, but to regard these practices as not expecially biased against their gender. This misconception probably arose because the early intelligence testers in this country made the deliberate decision not to construct tests indicating overall male-female differences in intelligence. The decision was dictated perhaps less by lack of sex bias (though indeed, it was made when the suffrage movement was at its height), than by the necessity of having a test that correlated with the only available criterion of validity—performance in elementary school, in which the sexes did not differ systematically. Nevertheless, this sagacious decision by the early testers did not apply to those women, or men, who happened to have been born into a poor family or came from a minority group with problems and opportunities differing markedly from those more fortunate.

The extension of the early testers' logic to issues of aptitudes, personal motivation, and interests has been loaded with gender bias. Society has persisted in attempting to define women and men as creatures with entirely different capabilities and fates, despite the historic social trends in employment, family, and other activities of the kind documented so well by Jessie Bernard in discussing "tipping points."[34] The indiscriminate use of tests developed primarily for males is both biased and inappropriate as society changes. Necessarily their use assumes that the standards based on male performance in the past will be retained when the very institutions in which performance is to occur will have changed by admitting women. The situation is remarkably similar to that in cross-cultural research when the researcher attempts to use the methods and procedures developed in the United States to study, say, India.

The Indian psychologist Durganand Sinha has commented on this practice perceptively. "Psychology," he said, "appears to be method-bound. Sometimes it is ridiculed as a science without content but with plenty of methodology. Modelling itself after physical sciences and in its zeal for precision and universality of its principles, it has not only adopted a micro approach but has fought shy of highly complex social processes. When the study of a social phenomenon is not easily amenable to its methods, it is ignored." Sinha then goes on to relate his own experiences in attempting to apply standard research methods and procedures in Indian villages, giving examples of the need for "culturally appropriate models, tools and techniques."[35] With the same logic, we may see that particular methods and procedures which may have been useful to a society content with its unequal division of labor and unequal opportunities in education are misleading when the same society finds its institutions changing to include those hitherto relegated to different or markedly inferior status.

Thus, U.S. society contains many major and central institutions with interests bolstering psychology's claims to be scientific and bolstering the particular version of scientific methodology adopted as its most prestigious resource. I do not intend at all to pose a dichotomy between so-called basic and so-called applied research. On the contrary, both have been constrained by a particular vision of what is worth doing and how to do that scientifically. That particular vision is not the only one available, nor does it lead to unbiased definition of problems, results, or conclusions. Its most powerful weapons against charges of bias have been, not dazzling scientific accomplishments, but its support by elites in psychology and the larger society based on consensus of opinion.

Assumptions (Theories) about the Individual

At the basis of the natural science model of psychological research there are assumptions about the individual that, when formally stated, we would call psychological theory. In fact, there is no generally accepted perspective in psychology, much less a generally accepted theory. There is, instead, a jungle of rival schools, situation-specific and person-specific generalizations, and mini-theories developed to explain what went on in a particular experiment. Nevertheless, the rival schools share some or many common assumptions about how to pursue knowledge, they use each other's methods, and their interests reveal certain patterns.

I think it is not unfair to say that experimental orthodoxy in psychology has most purely revealed a lack of interest in research problems or theoretical statements that concern women and men in the problems of living in their families, with friends, and in working and raising children. From the beginning, experimental psychology's assumptions about the individual have regarded individual and social differences as something to be treated as "error," in the sense that its experiments and its laws would not try to explain them. Individuals are different, that's all. The result has been an experimental psychology that appears to treat everyone equitably, but in fact makes decisions arbitrarily about when to study women or men, blacks or whites, rich or poor, in terms of the researcher's convenience, their likelihood of performing appropriately for the researcher, or the source of research funds.

Watching Out for Other Animals

Many (though fortunately not all) experimentalists have also adopted a peculiarly American view of the evolutionary process, one that places less emphasis on Darwin's original interest in explaining the origins of the *different* species than on continuity in evolutionary development. The emphasis on continuity is sometimes so extreme that the human individual is seen as differing from individuals in other species only in terms of increased quantity and complexity of the human central nervous system, and in a few other details, including the undeniable absence of a tail.

Such views are the basis for the enthusiasm exhibited by some psychologists for the current fad called sociobiology. Their enthusiasm is also aided by near total ignorance of elementary anthropology, especially about kinship systems.[36] The uncritical assumption that the human individual is a somewhat more complicated white rat or hairless ape has been criticized valiantly by European researchers and by outstanding researchers in this country.[37] But our texts are still full of animal research placed side by side with human research on, say, the "maternal drive." It is now considered necessary to include a well-placed warning that, of course, one should not ignore the complicating factors that differentiate human mothers from rat mothers. But new students and often their teachers proceed to analyze the human mother on the basis of what rats have done when separated from their pups by an electrified grid.

The importance of a genuinely comparative study of animal behavior does not need defense. But the uncritical acceptance of the assumption that apparent similarity in behaviors by a human individual and by individuals in another species is evidence for a "biological" basis in the human behavior is both erroneous and an obstacle to the equitable pursuit of knowledge. In the larger sense, all human behavior has a biological basis. Little is added to that statement by seeking surface resemblances between the human being and other animals, while ignoring the processes underlying the analogous actions.[38]

As others have said, the cat and the human individual both act, but the human knows that he or she is acting, thinks about it, and can talk about it. It is of interest that chimpanzees are bright enough to learn to communicate by gestures or through a computer, painfully taught by human beings. It is nonsense to conclude that the chimpanzee is learning in the same way that a human child learns to communicate. By about the age two, any normal human child in any culture outstrips the chimpanzee without special instruction, provided only that there are other human individuals about who speak.[39]

It should not be necessary to reiterate such observations, except that the simple and universal phenomenon of human consciousness, of awareness of self in relation to others, is not at all central in orthodox psychology's assumptions or its methodology. How else can we explain that some psychologists still have great difficulty in believing that what the human research subject thinks, how he or she sizes up the research situation and the research, how he or she hopes to appear to the researcher, are critical events in the sequence that leads to the researcher's so-called hard data?

Why else should it be a mystery to some that a woman and a man in the same situation might size up the situation differently? Instead, the orthodox proclivity is to attribute any differences in the reactions by a man and a woman in what researchers see as the "same" situation to some hypothetical attribute, often biologically determined. If, as often happens, they react in the same way, that similarity is then seen as irrelevant to the subject's gender.

The Study of Sex Differences and Trait Theory

The reason that only differences between the genders are considered of research or theoretical significance is not hard to uncover. Many psychologists, including Julia Sherman in her notable survey of research on women as well as Eleanor Maccoby and Carol Jacklin in their survey of early childhood literature on sex differences, have noted the remarkable tendency not to publish, to ignore, or even to distort findings of no differences.[40] Jessie Bernard has commented trenchantly on the study of individual differences in psychology, warning us once again of the dangers of looking only at arithmetic averages and ignoring overlaps in the frequency distributions of individual measures.[41] They and many others have analyzed the reasons for the resulting distortions in the literature, which are undeniably biased against women. That is why any difference is better for publication than no difference.

In reviewing the literature, Maccoby and Jacklin complained that the nature of most of the research on sex differences forced them into being "trait" psychologists.[42] Jessie Bernard correctly cautioned psychologists against their usual practice of reporting a difference between averages with language that implied the uniform possession of attributes, for example, by saying that girls are less aggressive than boys when what was found was that more boys than girls performed an aggressive action or that some boys performed more aggressively than most boys, thus creating a higher average for boys than for girls. In fact, the shape of the distribution of individual differences is seldom even described in research on sex differences. It is assumed to be a "normal" curve for each gender.

The entire literature on sex differences reflects certain assumptions of its founding father, Sir Francis Galton, who also is responsible for the research tradition comparing racial and national differences. Of course, Galton found that women are inferior, just as he found the British superior to those of their subject peoples who visited the Exposition. He was interested in proving the superiority of British males to women and to the colored peoples they ruled, founding a Eugenics Society for the purpose of improving and purifying British blood, even if it had to be contaminated by that of women. Later psychologists improved the research model he developed to make the tests more "workable," but it is still the same model with the same assumptions about what a human individual is.

The image of the human individual is that of a bundle of abilities, capacities, skills, and personal traits. The assumption is that the psychologist can develop a test of each of these traits, either through a set of tasks to be performed or a set of questions to be answered. With little concern about the research situation itself, and certainly not assigning it major importance, the researcher selects the tasks or tests, judging what is appropriate to study. The more abilities or traits one can measure, the merrier, of course. In fact, most research concentrates on a few at a time.

The assumed validity of the test rests theoretically upon some criterion measure—for example, the actual performance by a child in school, his/her actual frequency of aggressive actions in a sample day, or actual performance on the job. In fact, such criterion tests of validity are seldom available in research on sex differences. Instead, psychologists have devised a host of subterfuges to escape them. The criterion is established in the same situation in which the test is given, then called "internal validity," while "external validity" outside of the research situation is merely fervently hoped for. Or they talk of "construct validity," in which one test correlates with another test called by the same name.

The score on the test or the level of task performance is taken as indication that the person *is* intelligent, or aggressive, or submissive, or anxious, or *has* this or that motive. By verbal magic, a specific set of actions in a specific research situation is transformed into the label for something that the person has, is, or possesses as a trait.

In the early days, it was assumed that any differences so obtained between males and females were biologically determined. Wasn't sex a biological variable? The two sexes evolved through biological evolution, didn't they? What's the problem in finding cause in biology? By the 1930s many psychologists had been exposed to the findings of cultural anthropology, especially to the early writings of Margaret Mead and Ruth Benedict. Becoming reluctant to assign all sex differences to biology, when the two genders differed so noticeably from one culture to another, they began the more usual practice of assigning some to cultural socialization, or to both biological and cultural influences in some undetermined mix. But they had bought into a theoretical and research model that, in itself, contained no possibility of assessing the cause of anything. On the contrary, the assumptions and the research procedures were ideal for promulgating or perpetuating myths.

Even in developmental psychology, the search for causation was not included in the rationale for testing "traits," so it was added, in the form of partial information about the child's family or how teachers treat boys and girls. Great joy is expressed by environmentalists if these agents can be blamed for sex differences that result. But what one comes out with is a girl or boy that *has* such-and-such a trait in some degree, to which the psychologist attributes the cause for the behavior that had intially provided the basis for the trait attribution. It is a beautifully circular argument with no escape route.

When research efforts have turned to whether the traits allegedly discovered in research are evident in the behavior of the same individuals on a variety of tests or across several situational contexts, the results have included many negative outcomes. Consistency in behaviors defining the alleged traits is hard to come by. Yet every generation of researchers manages to turn up one finding that may provide a clue out of the trait trap, whether concerning gender differences or not. When a person believes that he or she possesses a personal characteristic and when, furthermore, that characteristic is personally important to him or her, then that person is more likely to be consistent in manner of behaving across different situations.[43] In short, the key to consistent social behavior appears to lie in whether or not and to what extent the person values consistency in that respect.

Going a step further, let us recall Woodworth's caution long ago about the characteristics of trait names. Although usually regarded as qualities describing the *person,* most are in fact adverbs or evaluations of social interaction. If a person behaves aggressively, isn't it often toward another person? Can one be submissive by oneself, or doesn't one need someone or something else to submit to? Thus, it would seem that what the person *has* is not a trait, but some or many highly charged convictions about what kind of a person he or she is or wants to be, relative to others, in certain activities and circumstances. Such a notion leads to quite a different view of the human individual.

It would seem logical to extend these implications to greater exploration of the individual's self-system, which is linked in all major theoretical statements since the time of William James to the person's establishment of relationships—conceptual and motivational—with other persons, social values, groups, and institutions. Such a direction seems preferable to attempting to build on the old trait theory to develop a set of traits to be emulated by the individual seeking androgyny. Emphasizing personal flexibility, this work has concentrated on demonstrating the superiority of a person who feels she or he exhibits traits traditionally incorporated in both the stereotypical masculine and feminine roles in our society.[44] In view of the extreme susceptibility to bias in the trait theory model for research, I would feel more comfortable with a definition based, not on traits, but on cross-disciplinary study of the human self-system. Similarly, I am troubled by the rush of young researchers attempting to prove that females are not inferior to males in such-and-such an ability or such-and-such a trait, especially when it is by no means clear what difference it makes.

Behavioristic Images of the Individual

The many versions of behavioristic theorizing since John Watson's triumphant proclamations of its advent should have altered the study of sex differences a great deal more than they have. Watson and behaviorists since him proclaimed that psychologists had to concentrate on observing concrete actions relative to specific environmental circumstances, eliminating reliance on the plethora of instincts, drives, traits, and other hypothetical and unobservable concepts that psychologists used to explain the causes of behavior. The strong environmental determinism in behavioristic theories has been appealing to some feminists, but the virtual dominance of behavioristic theories in psychology over several decades has not reduced the frequency of stereotypes and myths about sex differences. One explanation, of course, has been that most behaviorists have been men. Yet, despite its healthy correctives to biological determinism and unbridled speculation about what goes on inside the human mind, behaviorisms as currently formulated have been inadequate to the task of explaining the psychosocial differentiation of the two genders, even in our own society.

It is worthwhile, I believe, to comment on behavioristic theories from this perspective. First of all, each has insisted that it is totally unscientific to include human consciousness or self-awareness in its explanations. The result has been failure to deal with the human experience, whether male or female. Second, though environmental determinists of one kind or another, behaviorists have been weaker than other schools in psychology in specifying the human social environment. Environmental influences have been confined to rewards and/or punishments or, in the extremity of a B. F. Skinner, to any state of affairs that increases the probable frequency of a particular response. Few behaviorists regard it as worthwhile to turn to the social disciplines in order to understand the distinctively human parts of the social environment, wherein other individuals are labeled by society as male or female, child or adult, weak or powerful. To most behaviorists, it is irrelevant or boring to emphasize that individuals develop in more or less organized groups and institutions, including families, circles of peers, churches, schools, and so on, each with social values invested in the criteria for being man or woman; that one's own groups are juxtaposed with others seen and treated as superior or inferior, powerful, less powerful, or powerless; that the very objects and technologies are symbols of differing personhoods and of different genders. This sociocultural environment does not include merely goodies for the good and punishment for the bad, but rules for evaluating how the individual *should* behave, what he or she should strive for and what avoid, what individual variations will be tolerated by individuals in different social classifications and what variations will be punished. Such general rules are the social norms of the culture, invested with values that traditionally differ for men and women.

The neglect of the human social environment by behaviorists has left their theories based on naïve notions about pleasure and pain, reward and punishment. The issues of why one individual tolerates or even wants to be dominated by another, or why a boy learns to become unemotional to the point of being unable to shed a tear, remain mysteries that their most cynical adherents toss off with flippant phrases such as, "Well, some people get their kicks out of the darndest things." The various theories of "social exchange" now current in social psychology are guilty of similar assumptions and similar neglect of the social environment, of which the give-and-take among individuals is an important part. What is exchanged are rewards and punishments, according to some inner calculus that the adherents of the theory understand because they are parts of the same culture.[45] Projections of the calculus and the rewards into the minds of another sex, another group, or another culture produce a bizarre psychology, replete with androcentric, ethnocentric, or nationalistic biases.

Furthermore, the behavioristic emphasis in psychology has produced theories capable only, in the last analysis, of explaining how certain se-

Bias in Psychology

lected aspects of the environment determine certain individual behaviors. They are quite helpless in the face of individuals who actively participate in the process of changing the social environment or of altering their own actions. Finally, they appeal at last resort to such inner forces as "self-reinforcement" or "intrinsic motivation," for which there is no provision in behaviorism. The accumulating research evidence that bribery is not the most effective means to improve learning or skills is admission of the failures of strict behaviorisms.[46]

Psychodynamic Visions of Woman's Place

Of course, the most devastating power plays through psychological theorizing ignore both the social environment and behavior as much as possible by focusing exclusively upon the internal psychological world—on so-called psychodynamics. If one were to design a theory to keep women in inferior position and at lowered worth, none is more suitable than one locating the causes of women's behavior and problems inside the woman. In many ways, the old sex-difference researchers who firmly believed in innate and inevitable female inferiorities were easier to refute than those psychodynamicists who admit some environmental influences into the picture in order to create the motivations and complexes that would hold women in bondage.

Julia Sherman's review of the research literature on psychosexual development was a healthy corrective and commentary on the unbridled influence of the forefather of psychodynamists, Sigmund Freud. Like Maccoby and Jacklin, who found themselves trapped in research inspired by trait theories, Sherman often found herself enmeshed in research (a lot of it not very good research) inspired by Freudian formulations.[47] She found her way out of it with level head, careful assessment of the evidence, and some gentle humor.

In my view, the equitable pursuit of knowledge is totally impossible within a Freudian framework, no matter how nice Freud was to individual women nor how many patients lacking money for his own fees he sent to Anna Freud or other women analysts. According to Gilman, Sigmund Freud continued to emphasize his conclusions that women are morally and ethically deficient as well as masochistic and more prone than men to neuroses as a weapon against feminists five years after U.S. women achieved the vote. "We must not allow ourselves to be deflected from such conclusions," he wrote, "by the denials of the feminists who are anxious to force us to regard the two sexes as completely equal in position and worth."[48]

Nor do I regard it as accidental that the most quoted writer on adolescence in the United States today, Erik Erikson, who loaded his writings with cultural influences and humane concern for women, concluded as follows: ". . . womanhood arrives when attractiveness and experience have succeeded in selecting what is to be admitted to the welcome of the inner space 'for keeps.'" Thereby, he defines maturity, concluding an identity search which "must keep itself open for the peculiarities of the man to be joined and of the children to be brought up" although "already defined by her kind of attractiveness and in the selective nature of her search for the man (or men) by whom she wishes to be sought." Erikson pronounced that "successive stages of life offer growing and maturing individuals ample leeway for free variation in essential sameness."[49] Hasn't there been more leeway for some than for others?

Erikson's position, like Freud's, can be understood only as the tacit assumption that all is inevitable in the world. Women and men must adjust to their destinies, which are both sexual, except that men can have all that and outer space too. If it is still necessary to pay homage to those early pioneers who, like Freud, dared to talk about sex, I suggest that we turn our attention outside of psychology to Margaret Sanger or to Havelock Ellis, who hit it right on the head when he suggested that Freud was spinner of myth. Explanations of a person's experiences and actions in terms so inevitably focused on hidden processes and complexes formed prior to earliest memories, with minimal regard for the differing cultural conditions of development, are bound to be unverifiable and open to the arbitrary interpretations of someone else's "great mind." Psychoanalytic theory has been under attack for years from several sources, but it is my hope that the movement toward equality of men and women will deliver the final blow to any attempt to explain behavior in terms of inner psychodynamics alone.

Critiques and Changes within Psychology

In the vast and diversified halls of psychology, there is something for almost everyone. Psychologists themselves, however, are becoming increasingly concerned about the state of their domain, especially as provoked by the considerable changes in society and the movements toward a more equitable society among blacks, students, and other war protesters and, or course, among women. Some even listen to the criticism from abroad, which is growing. The signs of change are evident in the organizing of the Association for Women in Psychology and, later, Division 35 of the American Psychological Association, and in the founding of journals like *Sex Roles* and the *Psychology of Women Quarterly*. The language in psychology journals no longer commits atrocities like that of referring to the research subject as "he" in an experiment in which all of the subjects were women. It even appears that the report of the Task Force on Sex Bias and Sex Stereotypes in Psychotherapy will not be altogether forgotten.[50]

But much business goes on as usual. Changes in thinking and in research practice are slowest of all. Therefore, I must confine my remarks to a few trends that seem to be in the direction of healthy correction. These trends are accompanied by quite a bit of in-fighting and considerable confusion. Some writers refer to the "crisis" (in social psychology), to the "jungle" (in the literature on learning), to the "misery" (of psychotherapy), in psychology.[51] Nevertheless, the signs are hopeful and the trends necessary.

1. The first is toward broadening psychologists' perspectives on the pervasive influences of cultural institutions, of ways of living and working, and of social values upon the individual in any research situation. The androcentrism of psychology until recent years is really but one sign of its narrow perspective. No amount of technical refinement and replication of findings within a restricted sociocultural and institutional setting will broaden the perspective. Comparative research within the same country, cross-cultural research, and an eye to history are the first essentials in enlarging this vision of human beings, male and female.[52] It is hoped that the several volumes on cross-cultural research forthcoming may aid in the broadening process and in delineating the problems.[53]

2. Second, there is great need for psychology to extend its cross-disciplinary borrowing beyond the biological disciplines, to which it has continually turned with pride. It needs to learn from the social disciplines and humanities, which it has treated like poor relatives for many years, about significant and enduring problems in human relationships. Such cross-disciplinary borrowing and perspectives are most natural in social psychology, which has in recent decades gotten itself into difficulties by seeking respectability within the cloistered confines of the laboratory without attending to relevant field research and the actualities of real life. The self-defined crisis in social psychology, discussed by a score of its leading practitioners, is in large part a product of attempting to be really acceptable to psychological orthodoxy while neglecting contributions from the other social disciplines on the scope and importance of the larger social environment. Women in psychology should be and are in the forefront in this relevant cross-disciplinary borrowing, in order to understand their own status and subsidiary roles in many spheres of living, including the politics of housework and childcare.[54]

3. There is another trend that some call a "cognitive revolution" in psychology. It is not a revolution except to those dyed-in-the-wool behaviorists who once really believed that human beings do not think or ponder or worry, but instead only *think* that they do. The trend toward cognitive theories (that is, theories about knowing and how we know) varies in different parts of psychology. For example, among experimentalists who used to be studying "verbal learning" and among many developmental psychologists, it is closely linked to renewed interest in language and language development. Strongly influenced by Piaget, whose work was once brushed over lightly with complaints about broad theory and anecdotal research, the study of child development has come to focus heavily on cognitive development. On the other hand, in social psychology, the interest in cognition is manifest in hundreds of studies on the attribution process, that is, how individuals make decisions about what caused behavior they observe in another or in themselves.

This generally healthy trend entails some dangers, particularly in the tendency to propose cognition as some kind of "pure" mental event that is altogether different from feeling or wanting. Psychologists are prone to separate off the latter as problems of emotion or mood, on one hand, or of motivation, on the other. In truth, the human individual is a small system, whose mind, emotions, and desires cannot be compartmentalized into neat pigeonholes to be worked over one at a time. When a person tries to know or does know something, she or he almost invariably evaluates the process and what is known. The tendency to deal with human cognition in terms of "information processing" or "pure cognition" derives prestige from analogy with computer technology. You can be sure, however, that unless evaluation, feeling, and wanting are allowed into cognitive processing for everyone, it will be women who will be accused of "irrationality." One need look only at what male psychologists have thought that they knew about women in the past to know that cognition is affected by evaluations, feelings, and desires. Yet they did not think themselves irrational. Therefore, the old dichotomy of rational vs. irrational had better be eliminated in favor of a unified perspective that sees some emotion and some motivation in every cognitive process.

4. There is growing acceptance in psychology of the necessity for a perspective on the individual that sees his or her experiences and actions as jointly and intimately affected by internal events (past experiences, thoughts, feelings, and desires) and by a continuing interaction with a social environment, which includes much more than other individuals, as I noted earlier. The spelling out of such a coordinated perspective is diffi-

cult. Available formulae (such as Kurt Lewin's that behavior is a function of the person *in* the environment) cannot tell us how to study the personal and environmental influences that jointly affect behavior. I suspect that the tasks of translating the perspective into research practice are essential to an equitable pursuit of knowledge. Therefore, I will devote the rest of this paper to exploring the problems. They are not separate from the three trends previously noted.[55]

Needed Perspective: Coordinating Psychological and Sociocultural Influences

I will illustrate the needed perspective through research on a set of problems that are intimately related to bias in psychology, namely social stereotypes and their psychological ramifications. Social stereotypes consist of consensual and evaluative judgments on the character, attributes, and personal qualities of individuals classified into one common social category (e.g., by national origin, race, social class, or sex) by members of another social category. The agreement among individuals on such attributions is naïvely viewed as evidence of their truth. Indeed, such agreement may extend beyond the social boundaries of the judges and be shared by many of those judged.

Thus, research findings in the United States and in many other countries document men's stereotyped images of women and women's stereotyped images of men as well as considerable agreement between the genders on the characteristics of both. Such documentation has been interpreted in many ways, the naïve realist concluding: "Well, if everyone agrees, the stereotypes must be true of individual men and women—or most of them." The impulse of a psychologist with orthodox training in one of the perspectives already discussed would be to challenge the naïve realist: "Let me study individuals to see whether, indeed, men are more competent or aggressive than women, women more emotional, passive, or nurturant than men." Depending upon the psychologist's training, tasks, tests, or situations will be devised to assess the behaviors of individual women and men in order to test the stereotypes.

As we have seen, the test of "truth" in any specific social situation is hazardous, in that the researcher's bias (pro or con) can enter at any step: in defining the task or test, in setting up the situation, in selecting the particular behaviors that are to be recorded and assessed. Consequently, the eventual outcome of a series of such experiments is likely to be contradictory evidence. The sensible conclusion, in line with that of Maccoby and Jacklin's on young children, is that we do not know very much about gender-related differences in behavior and that many stereotyped attributions are made with little or no support from research findings on how males or females actually behave.

What the psychologist has failed to grasp is that consensual agreement on psychological or social "reality" is also one evidence in history, political science, or anthropology for the existence of social myth. Other indicators of myth include those that turn up in psychological studies to test social stereotypes: they may exist in the face of conflicting, contradictory, or ambiguous evidence. Their challenge is met by emotional refutation, even elaborate defense. Clear exceptions to the myth are celebrated as amazing phenomena, by no means altering the general rule (hence the "exceptional women" who "thinks like a man").

The study of those myths called social stereotypes in history, political science, and sociology clarifies the psychological problems, especially when the study examines the origins of social stereotypes and their changes over time. Invariably, social stereotypes reflect the history of relationships between groups or classes of people. Mutually supportive alliances promote mutually positive images of the other group or class. Competition for mutually exclusive ends, conflict, or domination-subordination promote negative, even derogatory, images.

The focus on the relationship among people, rather than on the characteristics or specific actions of individuals, is a point of departure at a historical and sociological level of analysis for reformulating a variety of issues in the psychological study of the genders. Such reformulations have already been attempted on group stereotypes through a series of three naturalistic experiments in summer camps directed by Muzafer Sherif, in a study of competitive and cooperative relationships between girls' groups by Rozet Avigdor, and in the many studies of adults in workshops by Robert R. Blake and Jane Mouton.[56] These studies all concentrated on the relationships between individuals belonging to informally organized groups whose initial contacts were arranged to preclude preexisting stereotyped views of the other group. When interacting over a period of time (e.g., a week) in repeated circumstances that pitted each group against the other toward highly desirable ends and valued status available to only one group, the group members not only became hostile and aggressive toward one another, but also formed clear-cut, negative, and stereotyped images of individuals in the other group.

The individuals on each side blamed those on the other for their conflicting relationships, attributing the blame to personal qualities shared by the other side. These images, in turn, strongly colored the perceptions and actions of individual participants, leading to derogation of observed performance by the other side that did not differ from their own, to self-justified acts of dominance and aggression, to distorted appraisals of actual events. And, it should be emphasized, these were "normal, healthy" individuals, carefully selected for the research and initially unacquainted (in the Sherif experiments).

The same individuals, however, changed their behaviors and their views of one another when the relationships between groups changed. Rozet Avigdor compared the stereotyped images held by groups of young girls when in conflict and when cooperating for common ends, showing beautifully how the particular characteristics attributed to the other group under these varying circumstances were related to the intergroup relationships. For example, in conflict, the sterotyped attributions pertained to aggressiveness, undesirable motivations, self-seeking, and the like, but not to a number of other unfavorable traits that were included on the list to be used in evaluation. The Sherif research showed that, most reluctantly, the boys in summer camps began to cooperate when faced with a series of events which affected both groups equally and whose undeniably preferred outcomes required the joint efforts of all individuals in both groups (superordinate goals). Then their images of one another changed to favorable attributions. They explained their own ability to interact with the others on the basis of changes in the other individuals.

In brief, these studies showed that major psychological phenomena associated with invidious stereotyping of others occur within specific contexts of human relationships. Stereotypes and their psychological consequences reflect those relationships. No amount of detailed study of the individuals apart from those relationships could serve to test the truth value of the stereotyped images that had formed. To the contrary, short-term tests of the perceptions, judgments, and actions of the individuals apart from the intergroup relationships might have led a psychologist to conclude that individuals on one side or the other, or both, were psychologically aberrant.

The histories of relationships between the genders differ in many ways from intergroup conflict, notably in the absence of well-defined groups of men and women separated by geographic as well as social space. On the contrary, even the most gender-polarized patriarchal societies necessarily admit women into kinship structures, men's sexual activities, and the division of productive work, including child care and food production and preparation. Thus, while gender relationships share the dominant-subordinate structure to be found in many intergroup relationships, they are also sufficiently different to make cliches about "the longest war" or about "sleeping with the enemy" misleading for analytical purposes (as contrasted with their possible utility as slogans). In fact, as Julia Sherman has suggested, the rise and change of social sterotypes among individuals classified by virtue of uniquely different and significant capabilities (comparable to the sexual capabilities of women and men) as well as by division of labor and social status remains to be studied systematically.

Steps toward the Future

If there is a parallel between intergroup relations and relations between men and women, I believe that it lies in the primacy of the relationships between the genders, which must change if lasting changes are to occur in their respective self-definitions and the mutual views that the two genders maintain in our society. The woman's movement offered glimpses of what might happen by showing that the "raising" of one's own consciousness as a woman required rejection of others' definitions of self coupled with an understanding of the relationships in which women become enmeshed. Annette Brodsky has reported on the therapeutic value of such efforts toward redefining self.[57] As Martha Mednick has pointed out, self-definition has to be accompanied by rejection of the system of relationships that had produced acceptance of a lowered status for women. The consolidation of the renewed self-definition as woman can only occur through actions consonant with the new definition.[58] Julia Sherman has similarly emphasized the therapeutic effects of new activities with the social support of others.[59] Yet, here is where the rub lies. The rest of the world changes more slowly than the new awareness of self, and parts of both resist change or simply stay the same. Social power is not equitably distributed.[60]

The woman's movement has been responsible for wonders in the last ten years in bringing awareness of the issues to women and to men and in pointing to the permeation of sexism throughout our lives. Many women and men have accepted viewpoints, tasks, and changed relationships that they would not have dreamed of a mere decade ago; they might have laughed at the thought. Meanwhile, as in any social movement, countermovements and reactions have also grown up and strengthened.[61]

One of the first systematic studies of an educational scheme to alter sex-related stereotypes in the public schools has reported mixed results. According to Guttentag and Bray, the educational materials had the greatest impact on kindergarten children, especially girls, followed by fifth graders, chiefly the girls; but their impact on ninth graders was most mixed of all. Some changes were evident for some ninth-grade girls, but this seemed to depend upon having a teacher truly dedicated to using the materials and on the cooperation of peer groups. In some schools the girls were so oriented toward boys that the boys' derogation of the effort soured the girls as well. On the whole, the ninth-grade boys reacted to the educational materials by being more stereotyped and negative than previously, while the girls showed some gains in the desired direction.[62] Apparently, changes by the more advantaged boys would require some changes in what they are doing, in their relationships with girls, and in how they see those relationships in the future.

Rebecca, Hefner, and Oleshansky have commented upon the requirements of work situations and the self-definitions of men and women in a way particularly appropriate to conclude this discussion. Noting that the emphasis has been on women and men's changing themselves, they inquire why it is not also reasonable to emphasize changing the roles in which men and women live and work, separately or together.[63] Institutional change seldom gets handed down from above as a free gift. Even if it did, such suggestions imply a process of change over time, wherein individuals change themselves as they change their practices, and their practices as they change themselves.

The challenge to psychology as such actualities occur and as future possibilities appear is the development of methods and practices that can encompass the events. To meet this challenge, we shall have to be developing ways of seeking knowledge that are not stereotyped as "hard" or "soft," but that obtain information on a broader spectrum of the social world, through several disciplines and with comparative methods and techniques as well as those now commonly used. I do not propose that every study be done in naturalistic circumstances or that we all emulate Jane Goodall's example by spending five years to investigate the social behaviors of chimpanzees for a dissertation. I do believe that we must change the notion that anything of great value can be learned about human beings in the quick study with canned procedures. These characterize the kind of research in psychology that promotion committees have come to count, rather than to read. What goes on in our laboratories, clinics, and classrooms must be seen for what it is, cultural phenomena and events where we can learn about individuals, provided we understand the times and the larger societies of which they are parts.

NOTES

1 Naomi Weisstein, "Psychology Constructs the Female, or The Fantasy Life of the Male Psychologist," in *Roles Women Play: Readings toward Women's Liberation*, ed. Michele H. Garskof (Belmont, Calif., 1971), pp. 68-83.
2 Betty Friedan, *The Feminine Mystique* (New York, 1963).
3 Carolyn W. Sherif, "Women's Role in the Human Relations of a Changing

World," in *The Role of the Educated Woman*, ed. C. M. Class (Houston, 1964), pp. 29–41.
4. Georgene Seward, *Sex and the Social Order* (New York, 1946).
5. E. G. Boring, *A History of Experimental Psychology*, 2nd ed. (New York, 1950), p. 509.
6. Ibid., p. 548.
7. Ibid., p. 487.
8. Helen B. Thompson, *The Mental Traits of Sex* (Chicago, 1903), Helen T. Woolley, "Psychological Literature: A Review of the Recent Literature on the Psychology of Sex," *Psychological Bulletin* 7 (1910): 335–42.
9. For an account of Leta S. Hollingworth's career and the views of prominent male psychologists during the early period of her work, see Stephanie A. Shields, "Ms. Pilgrim's Progress: The Contributions of Leta Stetter Hollingworth to the Psychology of Women," *American Psychologist* 30 (1975): 852–57. The title quoted was published in *American Journal of Sociology* 22 (1916): 19–29.
10. Mary Putnam Jacobi, *The Question of Rest for Women during Menstruation* (New York, 1877), pp. 1–2.
11. Stephanie A. Shields, "Functionalism, Darwinism, and the Psychology of Women," *American Psychologist* 30 (1975): 739–54.
12. See Lee J. Cronbach, "Five Decades of Public Controversy over Mental Testing," *American Psychologist* 30 (1975): 1–14.
13. *AAP Advance*, August–September 1977, p. 2.
14. Boring, *A History of Experimental Psychology*, p. 583.
15. See Ronald Lippitt and Ralph K. White, "An Experimental Study of Leadership and Group Life," in *Basic Studies in Social Psychology*, ed. Harold Proshansky and Bernard Seidenberg (New York, 1965), pp. 523–37. Lewin's first publication on this research appeared in 1939.
16. Kurt Lewin, "Studies in Group Decision," reprinted in *Group Dynamics: Research and Theory*, ed. Dorwin Cartwright and Alvin Zander, 2nd ed. (New York, 1956).
17. See Carol Tavris and Carole Offir, *The Longest War* (New York, 1977), pp. 151–52.
18. A penetrating critique of ahistoricalism and its psychologizing of the social environment was written by one of Lewin's most ardent admirers, Roger G. Barker, "On the Nature of the Environment," *Journal of Social Issues* 19 (1963): 15–38.
19. Masculinity-femininity as a "variable" or polarized dimension is one example of the mischief created in psychology by "thinking in variables" and accepting the implied dictum about measurement. See Anne Constantinople, "Masculinity-Feminity: An Exception to a Famous Dictum?" *Psychological Bulletin* 80 (1973): 389–407; and Lawrence Kohlberg, "A Cognitive-Developmental Analysis of Children's Sex-Role Concepts and Attitudes," in *The Development of Sex Differences*, ed. Eleanor E. Maccoby (Stanford, 1966), pp. 82–173. Very different views on the proper way to seek knowledge are achieved when the definition of what is "masculine" and "feminine" is sought by analyzing divisions of people

and their activities in human social life. See Muzafer Sherif and Carolyn W. Sherif, *Social Psychology* (New York, 1969).
20 D. L. Ronis, M. H. Baumgardner, M. R. Leippe, J. J. Cacioppo, and A. G. Greenwald, "In Search of Reliable Persuasion Effects, I: A Computer-Controlled Procedure for Studying Persuasion," *Journal of Personality and Social Psychology* 35 (1977): 551.
21 Ibid., p. 567.
22 Ibid.
23 For a sociological analysis of conditions promoting such efforts by psychologists, see J. Ben-David and R. Collins, "Social Factors in the Origin of a New Science: The Case of Psychology," *American Sociological Review* 31 (1966): 451–65.
24 Robert Rosenthal, *Experimenter Effects in Behavioral Research* (New York, 1966).
25 See Hadley Cantril, *Gauging Public Opinion* (Princeton, 1944); Howard Schuman and Shirley Hatchett, *Black Racial Attitudes: Trends and Complexities* (Ann Arbor, 1974); Charles F. Cannell and Robert L. Kahn, "Interviewing," in *Handbook of Social Psychology*, ed. Gardner Lindzey and Elliott Aronson, (Reading, Mass., 1968), vol. 2.
26 Some of the vast literature on the "social psychology of the research situation" is summarized in Robert Rosenthal and Ralph L. Rosnow, eds., *Artifact in Behavioral Research* (New York, 1969). A more recent and readable introduction is James G. Adair, *The Human Subject: The Social Psychology of the Psychological Experiment* (Boston, 1973). Both tend to ignore the earlier work on "social desirability" effects; see Allen L. Edwards, *The Social Desirability Variable in Personality Assessment and Research* (New York, 1957). Both also tend toward trying to "eliminate" or reduce the effects they have studied, rather than using their understanding toward reconstruction of psychology's methodology. For alternative perspectives with the latter aim, see Sherif and Sherif, *Social Psychology*, esp. chap. 6, and Carolyn W. Sherif, *Orientation in Social Psychology* (New York, 1976).
27 The most complete review of the obedience research is in Stanley Milgram, *Obedience to Authority* (New York, 1974). Cross-cultural comparisons leading to similar conclusions are summarized in M. E. Shanab and Khawla A. Yahya, "A Behavioral Study of Obedience in Children," *Journal of Personality and Social Psychology* 35 (1977): 530–36.
28 Aletha H. Stein and Margaret M. Bailey, "The Socialization of Achievement Orientation in Females," *Psychological Bulletin* 80 (1973): 345–66. See also Martha T. S. Mednick, Sandra J. Tangri, and Lois W. Hoffman, eds., *Women and Achievement: Social and Motivational Analysis.* (Washington, D.C., 1975); Virginia O'Leary, "Some Attitudinal Barriers to Occupational Aspirations in Women," *Psychological Bulletin* 81 (1974): 809–26.
29 John Condry and Susan Dyer, "Fear of Success: Attribution of Cause to the Victim," *Journal of Social Issues* 32 (1976): 63–83; David Tresemer, "The Cumulative Record of Research on 'Fear of Success,'" *Sex Roles* 2 (1976): 217–36.
30 See Carolyn W. Sherif, Merrilea Kelly, Lewis Rodgers, Gian Sarup, and Ben-

net Tittler, "Personal Involvement, Social Judgment, and Action," *Journal of Personality and Social Psychology* 27 (1973): 311–28; Judith C. Morelock, "Sex Differences in Compliance," *Sex Roles; A Journal of Research*, in press; Alice H. Eagley, "Sex Differences in Influenceability," *Psychological Bulletin* 85 (1978): 86–116.

31 This analysis of the persuasion or "suggestibility" research follows that in Muzafer Sherif and Carolyn W. Sherif, *An Outline of Social Psychology* (New York, 1956); and idem, *Social Psychology*.

32 See, for example, Phyllis A. Wallace, ed., *Equal Employment and the AT&T Case* (Cambridge, Mass., 1976). Judith Long Laws's chapters in this book are excellent examples of the broadened perspective on women's interests and motivations that becomes possible when conditions of work and living are included in the framework of study. Other chapters particularly relevant in the present context reveal sharp divisions among psychologists on the use and interpretation of tests and interviews used in hiring or promotion.

33 Donald T. Campbell, "Reforms as Experiments," *American Psychologist* 24 (1969): 409–29.

34 Jessie Bernard, *Women, Wives, Mothers: Values and Options* (Chicago, 1975).

35 Durganand Sinha, "Social Psychologists' Stance in a Developing Country," *Indian Journal of Psychology* 50 (June 1975): 98–99.

36 In reviewing Marshall Sahlins's *Use and Abuse of Biology* (Ann Arbor, 1976), M. H. Fried of Columbia's anthropology department finds it amusing that geneticists should accept the kinship genealogies used in different cultures as genetic genealogies. Sahlins had remarked that the lack of correspondence is "merely Anthropology I. Is it too much to ask that our colleagues in contingent biological fields raise their sights to a somewhat more sophisticated level?" M. A. Fried, "The Use and Abuse of Biology," *The American Scientist* 65 (1977): 352–53. Meanwhile, some of what is taught in Anthropology I is being questioned by Mary K. Martin and Barbara Voorhies, *Female of the Species* (New York, 1975), and by others, though not the lack of correspondence between social and genetic genealogies noted above.

37 François Jacob, professor of cell genetics at Institut Pasteur in Paris, provided an interesting view of evolutionary possibilities, including both continuities and discontinuities in species evolution. François Jacob, "Evolution and Tinkering," *Science* 196 (1977): 1161–66. Among psychologists, T. C. Schneirla and his students have consistently pursued comparative studies within an evolutionary framework encompassing both species-specific and continuity assumptions. See T. C. Schneirla, "Levels in the Biopsychology of Social Organization," *Journal of Abnormal and Social Psychology* 41 (1946); and Lester R. Aronson, Ethel Tobach, D. S. Lehrman, and J. S. Rosenblatt, eds., *Development and Evolution of Behavior: Essays in Memory of T. C. Schneirla* (San Francisco, 1970).

38 Schneirla made trenchant criticisms of attributions to "biology" or nature based on no more than surface similarities.

39 See Roger Brown, "Development of the First Language in the Human Species,"

American Psychologist 28 (1973): 107-28; Kingsley Davis, " A Final Note on a Case of Extreme Isolation," *American Journal of Sociology* 52 (1947): 432-37; Eric H. Lenneberg, *Biological Foundations of Language* (New York, 1967).
40 Julia A. Sherman, *On the Psychology of Women: A Survey of Empirical Studies* (Springfield, Ill., 1971); Eleanor E. Maccoby and Carol N. Jacklin, *The Psychology of Sex Differences* (Stanford, 1974).
41 Jessie Bernard, "Sex Differences: An Overview," in *Beyond Sex-Role Stereotypes: Readings toward a Psychology of Androgyny*, ed. Alexandra G. Kaplan and Joan P. Bean (Boston, 1976), pp. 9-26.
42 Maccoby and Jacklin have been praised for what they did not do (for example, they did not abolish differences between the sexes or conclude that there were none) and blamed for what they did not try to do (for example, examine the research literature on adult women). They were attempting to evaluate the congruence of research findings on alleged differences in early childhood. What they found was, in the words of one reviewer, "a sprawling, unruly body of data." Jeanne H. Block, "Debatable Conclusions about Sex Differences," *Contemporary Psychology* 21 (1976): 517-22. Since most of those data were also obtained within the research model for personality traits, it seems less than judicious to suggest that the authors should have organized the data differently. In fact, the contrast between the pontifical conclusions in many texts about early childhood differences and the mess Maccoby and Jacklin exposed is genuinely amusing. Thus, while some reviewers bemoan the Maccoby-Jacklin effort, I take it as one more indication that a trait approach to personality will invariably produce a mess.
43 Gordon W. Allport, "The Ego in Contemporary Psychology," *Psychological Review,* 50 (1943): 451-78; Muzafer Sherif and Hadley Cantril, *The Psychology of Ego-Involvements* (New York, 1947); Sherif et al., "Personal Involvement, Social Judgment, and Action;" Daryl J. Bem and Andrea Allen, "On Predicting Some of the People Some of the Time: The Search for Cross-Situational Consistencies in Behavior," *Psychological Review* 81 (1974): 506-20; Hazel Markus, "Self-Schemata and Processing Information about the Self," *Journal of Personality and Social Psychology* 35, no. 2 (1977): 63-78.
44 Sandra L. Bem, "The Measurement of Psychological Androgyny," *Journal of Consulting and Clinical Psychology* 42 (1974): 155-62.
45 See Michael Billig's *Social Psychology and Intergroup Relations* (London, 1976), chap. 6, for a trenchant critique from a European perspective of the assumptions of "interpersonal games" in U.S. social science.
46 John Condry, "Enemies of Exploration: Self-Initiated Versus Other-Initiated Learning," *Journal of Personality and Social Psychology* 35 (1977): 459-77.
47 Julia A. Sherman, *On the Psychology of Women.*
48 Richard Gilman, "The FemLib Case against Sigmund Freud," *The New York Times Magazine,* 31 January 1971, pp. 42-47.
49 Erik H. Erikson, *Identity: Youth and Crisis* (New York, 1968), pp. 282-83.
50 American Psychological Association, "Report of the Task Force on Sex Bias and Sex-Role Stereotyping in Psychotherapeutic Practice," *American Psychologist* 30 (1975): 1169-75. A fuller mimeographed report is also available

from the APA. The report is providing the basis for a National Conference on Psychotherapy Research sponsored by the association.
51 The *Personality and Social Psychology Bulletin*, official publication of APA's Division 8, has carried a dozen or more articles on the "crisis" in the last year. See M. Brewster Smith, "Social Psychology, Science, and History: So What?" *Personality and Social Psychology Bulletin* 2 (1976): 438-44; Muzafer Sherif, "Crisis in Social Psychology: Some Remarks towards Breaking through the Crisis" ibid. 3 (1977): 368-82. See also H. Rachlin, "A Guide through the Jungle of Animal Learning," *Contemporary Psychology* 22 (1977): 165-66; A. M. Des Lauriers, "The Greatness and the Misery of Clinical Psychology," ibid., pp. 169-70; J. F. Rychlak, "Personality Theory: Its Nature, Past, Present and—Future?" *Personality and Social Psychology Bulletin* 2 (1976): 209-25.
52 Sherif and Sherif, *Social Psychology*, chap. 1.
53 Harry C. Triandis, University of Illinois, is editor. See also idem, "Social Psychology and Cultural Analysis," *Journal for the Theory of Social Behaviour* 5 (1975): 81-106.
54 See Florence L. Denmark, "The Psychology of Women: An Overview of an Emerging Field," *Personality and Social Psychology Bulletin* 3 (1977): 356-67.
55 In fact, a coordinated interactionist perspective guided this entire chapter, which reflects my recent book, *Orientation in Social Psychology*. References to the specific researches cited in the next sections are in that book.
56 See Carolyn W. Sherif, *Orientation in Social Psychology*, Chapter 5 for summaries of this research. For complete accounts, see Muzafer Sherif, O. J. Harvey, B. Jack White, W. Robert Hood and Carolyn W. Sherif, *Intergroup Conflict and Cooperation: The Robbers Cave Experiment*. Norman, Okla.: University Book Exchange, 1961; Rozet Avigdor, Étude expérimentale de la genèse des stéréotypes. *Cahiers Internationaux de Sociologie*, 14 (1953): 154-68; Robert R. Blake, Herbert Shepard, and Jane S. Mouton, *Managing Intergroup Conflict in Industry*. Houston: Gulf Publishing Co., 1964.
57 Annette Brodsky, "The Consciousness-Raising Group as a Model for Therapy with Women," *Psychotherapy: Theory, Research, and Practice* 10 (1973): 24-29.
58 Martha Mednick, "Social Change and Sex Role Inertia: The Case of the Kibbutz," in Mednick, Tangri, and Hoffman, *Women and Achievement*, pp. 85-103.
59 Julia A. Sherman, "Social Values, Femininity, and the Development of Female Competence," *Journal of Social Issues* 32 (1976): 181-95.
60 Rhoda Unger, a psychologist trained in physiological psychology, is among those whose study of male-female interactions has led her to the concept of social power or status as the key to such a study. Phyllis Chesler, a clinical psychologist, came to similar conclusions. For an intriguing survey of the research literature on male-female interactions and an application to training, see Marlaine E. Lockhead and Katherine P. Hall, "Conceptualizing Sex as a Status Characteristic: Applications to Leadership Training Strategies," *Journal of Social Issues* 32 (1976): 111-24.

61 For a social-psychological perspective on this process, see my *Orientation in Social Psychology*.
62 Marcia Guttentag and Helen Bray, *Undoing Sex Stereotyping: Research and Resources for Educators* (New York, 1976).
63 Meda Rebecca, Robert Hefner, and Barbara Oleshansky, "A Model of Sex-Role Transcendence," *Journal of Social Issues* 32 (1976): 197–206.

DOROTHY E. SMITH

A Sociology for Women

The Line of Fault

■ This inquiry into the implications of a sociology for women begins from the discovery of a point of rupture in my/our experience as woman/women within the social forms of consciousness—the culture or ideology of our society—in relation to the world known otherwise, the world *directly* felt, sensed, responded to, prior to its social expression. With this as the starting point, the next step locates that experience in the social relations organizing and determining precisely the disjuncture, that line of fault along which the consciousness of women must emerge. Inquiry does not begin within the conceptual organization or relevances of the sociological discourse, but in actual experience embedded in the particular historical forms of social relations which determine it.

As women members of an intelligentsia and therefore trained in the modes of acting, thinking, and the craft of working with words, symbols, and concepts, we have both a special responsibility and a special possibility of awareness at this point of rupture. The disjuncture which provides the problematic of this inquiry is that between the forms of thought, the symbols, images, vocabularies, concepts, frames of reference, institutionalized structures of relevance, of our culture, and a world experienced at a level prior to knowledge or expression, prior to that moment at which experience can become "experience" in achieving social expression or knowledge, or can become "knowledge" by achieving that social form, in being named, being made social, becoming actionable. The work of inquiry on which I am engaged proceeds by taking this experience of mine, this experience of other women—this line of fault—and asking how it is organized, how it is determined, what the social relations are which generate it.

This actual or potential disjuncture between experience and the forms in which experience is socially expressed (becoming thereby intelligible and actionable) is the break along which much major work in the women's movement has focused. Perhaps de Beauvoir's radical and scholarly analysis in *The Second Sex* failed to enliven a movement in the way in which Friedan's *Feminine Mystique* or Millett's *Sexual Politics* did, in part because the latter make the critique of ideology central whereas de Beauvoir does not.[1] As a participant in that period, one who shared in that change in consciousness and who had read de Beauvoir at an earlier stage, my sense is that books such as de Beauvoir's or Bernard's *Academic Women*[2] were of importance in establishing a sense of powers and possibilities, but that they did not do what Millett and Friedan (very different though they are) did, or what others of that period also did. Millett and Friedan unveiled the ideological nature of the "values," "norms," and "beliefs" concerning women's role and the relations between the sexes which we had taken for granted even when we had struggled with the divergence between the normative and the actually practiced. These norms, values, and beliefs were received as a social reality, however resentfully or uneasily, or with those feelings of guilt that Bart has so justly and precisely described: "not only were we depressed, but we were depressed because we were depressed. Since according to the experts we suburban housewives should have been happy, contented, fulfilled and pregnant. What was wrong with us?"[3] Through these works and others we became aware of the feminine mystique *as* a mystique which served to keep us in our places by invading our own consciousness as our beliefs, our values, our sense of morality, fitness, and obligation. In Kate Millett's *Sexual Politics*, the syntactic analysis de Beauvoir had provided of how women are constituted as other in relation to men as subject was given power and substance by Millett's analysis of the work of writers who for many of us (for my generation at least) had been held up as exemplary—not just as writers but as exemplars and teachers of the legitimate forms of relations between the sexes. These forms we had learned directly or indirectly from these men, among others. Though we might have found them repellant, horrific, and humiliating, the moral practices of that ideological mode, drawing its pieces of machinery from Freud, among others, ensured that just those reactions affirmed the legitimacy and correctness of the prescription. Such responses were defined as defenses, pathologies, or resistance—causes for precisely the cure laid out plainly before us: be other than you are! Surely the dilemma I had experienced in relation to the work of D. H. Lawrence was, in various forms and in various relations, a common one. I was constrained to acknowledge his work both as genius and as moral authority. His ultimate idealization of sexual relations between women and men was one where women's consciousness, her sensation, was so totally annulled before the man's that she should

A Sociology for Women

forego even orgasm and accept essentially the annihilation of her own consciousness in the sexual act. This totality of subordination, this annihilation of self, was something I resisted without knowing how to resist. But that rebellion at an earlier time had no ground to stand on, no rightful means of expression, and thus no authority for me. It certainly had no possibility as a topic for talk with others, since to do so would have been to exhibit publicly the psychological flaws the ideology defines: an unwillingness to "accept our femininity," a secret desire to castrate men.

As we explored the world from this place in it, we became aware that this rupture in experience, and between experience and the social forms of its expression, was located in a relation of power between women and men, in which men dominated over women. Millett, not alone and not first but in terms specifically relevant here, identified this relation of dominance as the patriarchy. The forms of thought, the means of expression, which we had available to us to formulate our experience were made or controlled by men. From that center women appeared as objects. In relation to men (of the ruling class) women's consciousness did not, and most probably generally still does not, appear as an autonomous source of knowledge, experience, relevance, and imagination. Women's experience did not appear as the source of an authoritative general expression of the world. Women did not appear to men as men do to one another, as persons who might share in the common construction of a social reality where that is essentially an ideological construction. There was, we discovered, a circle effect—men attend to and treat as significant what men say and have said. The circle of men whose writing and talk has been significant to one another extends back in time as far as our records reach. What men were doing has been relevant to men, was written by men about men for men. Men listened and listen to what one another say. A tradition is formed, traditions form, in a discourse with the past within the present. The themes, problematics, assumptions, metaphors, and images form as the circle of those present draws upon the work of those speaking from the past and builds it up to project it into the future. From this circle women have been almost entirely excluded. When admitted, it has been only by special license, and as individuals, never as representatives of their sex. They could share in this circle only by receiving its terms and relevances. These have been and still are to a large extent the terms and relevances of a discourse among men.

We had learned to practice what Rowbotham describes as a nihilistic relation to our own consciousness. As members of an intelligentsia, we had learned, furthermore, to work inside a discourse which we did not have a part in making, which was not "ours" as women. The discourse expresses, describes, and provides the working concepts and vocabulary for a landscape in which women are strangers. That strangeness is an integral part of the socially organized practices which constitute it. In a short story Doris Lessing tells of a girl growing up in Africa whose consciousness has been wholly formed by traditional British literary culture. Her landscape, her cosmology, her moral relations, her botany, are those of English novels, poetry, and stories. Her own immediate landscape, its life forms, the character of her everyday world, the actuality of Africa, do not fully penetrate and occupy her consciousness. They are not named.[4] This is paradigmatic of the same rupture in consciousness—the line of fault from which this inquiry begins.

The ideologies of our society have provided us with forms of thought, images, modes of expression, in which we were constrained to treat ourselves as looked at from outside, as other. Rowbotham describes this at a point where the split has already appeared:

> I had yet to understand the extent to which I identified with men, used their eyes. I was really sliced in two. Half of me was like a man surveying the passive half of me as a woman-thing. On Boxing Day in 1967 the Beatles' *Magical Mystery Tour* appeared on television. A group of people including the Beatles go on a coach trip. There is the atmosphere of excitement, of all being on the bus together and enjoying a treat. When they get off all kinds of things happen: tugs-of-war which remind you of the desperate tugging you felt you had to do when you were a child; a woman who eats and cries and cries until you can't imagine how a human being could carry so many tears around inside her. Then at one point all the boys in the bus are separated from the girls. You follow the boys in the film, wriggling around in your seat in front of the telly, in mounting excitement. It's like going into the Noah's Ark at Blackpool when you're six or listening to very loud rock music when you're thirteen. I got the same tightening down at the bottom of my spine. Well there I was clenching my cunt and where should they go but into a strip-tease. I had caught myself going to watch another woman as if I were a man. I was experiencing the situation of another woman stripping through men's eyes. I was being asked to desire myself by a film made by men. Catching myself observing myself desiring one of my selves I remained poised for an instant in two halves.[5]

Women's means to reflect upon themselves is a reflection from outside themselves, the structuring of themselves not as subjects, but as other. Furthermore, in its contemporary terms, it appears not as men's view of women, but in impersonal and general terms. De Beauvoir describes it thus:

> A man never begins by presenting himself as an individual of a certain sex; it goes without saying that he is a man. The terms *masculine* and *feminine* are used symmetrically only as a matter of form, as on legal paper. In actu-

ality the relation of the two sexes is not quite like that of two electrical poles, for man represents both the positive and the neutral, as is indicated by the common use of *man* to designate human beings in general; whereas woman represents only the negative, defined by limiting criteria, without reciprocity. In the midst of an abstract discussion it is vexing to hear a man say: "You think thus and so because you are a woman," but I know that my only defense is to reply: "I think thus and so because it is true," thereby removing my subjective self from the argument."[6]

In so replying, she has already forfeited her position, because she has necessarily taken it up on his ground, an apparently neutral but covertly masculine position. Imagining this as exemplary of actual conversations, we can ask, How is it that what he says proceeds from a position on this general ground? that he speaks not merely with authority, but with authority of this kind and in this form, the authority of the impersonal, neutral, the detached, the factual? How is it that her options are either to speak as a woman and therefore as limited, restricted, and subordinate, or else to speak on his ground, to speak as a man or rather to be neutered? Her subjectivity does not draw upon the implicit authority of the generalizing impersonal mode. His does.

The critique of the institutions which alienate women from their experience has taken many forms in the women's movement and developed very rapidly: attacks on stereotyping in advertising and the media in general; the critique of sexism in school reading materials, and of the exclusion of women's interests and news relevant to women from the news media;[7] of history for its exclusive focus on men and of the historical traditions organized and maintained by men;[8] the critique of theology and religious institutions;[9] of the social and behavioral sciences;[10] of art, both in exemplary practices such as Women's House in Los Angeles and also in teaching and writing.[11] Another critical approach has focused on the professionally organized institutions of social control, the health care systems, law, and psychiatry in particular. The same line of fault is identified in their practices. The critique of medical institutions has been both of the failure to take up and treat as legitimate women's experience of their bodies[12] and of the historical transformation of the healing arts in the process of excluding women from its practice as men came to appropriate and exert monopolistic control over the technical practices becoming dominant in contemporary Western medicine over the last two hundred years.[13] The critique of medicine and in particular of gynecology has been also a practical one. Women have developed alternatives for women, which have been radical both in providing for woman a place to begin from her knowledge of her own body and also in representing a radical departure from the professional forms of social relations in which knowledge is appropriated and controlled by "experts." The critique of psychiatry as among those institutions which serve the oppression of women has again been both of its ideologies and of its practical political dimensions in relation to the oppression of women.[14] It has also been concerned with the development of alternative approaches in therapy.[15]

In the disclosures and discoveries of the women's movement, women's experience breaks away along this line of fault. It makes thus observable an apparatus of social controls in part ideological in the sense of being images and symbols, and in part an organization of specialized practices. This comes into view as a whole which, though loosely organized, is not made up of discrete and singular functional domains (as we have in sociology tended to conceptualize them), but rather, constitutes a differentiated but coherent structure, an apparatus of "ruling," of organization and control over the society. This apparatus is occupied almost exclusively by men, whose participation in it is also differentiated by social class (working-class men are not part of it; women are not part of it).

In analyzing the ideological phases of this "apparatus," I make use of Marx and Engels's concept or formulation of "ideology." In returning to their usage in *The German Ideology*,[16] I am bypassing some of the rather different usages which have developed since that time and are now current in the social sciences. I am not using the term to refer to political beliefs, though political beliefs would be one instance or aspect of ideology. Nor am I using the term to draw the boundaries between an impartial and disinterested social science and "ideology" as an interested and partial perspective biased by its roots in a particular group or class.[17] I am concerned, rather, with ideology as those ideas and images through which the class which rules the society by virtue of its domination of the means of production, orders, organizes and sanctions the social relations which sustain its domination. Further, in following Marx and Engels's use of ideology, I view the ideas, images, and symbols in which our experience is given social form not as that neutral floating thing called culture but as what is actually produced by specialists and by people who are part of the apparatus by which the ruling class maintains its control over the society. Thus, the concept of ideology provides us with a thread through the maze different from our more familiar notions of "culture," for it directs us to look for and at the actual practical organization of the production of images, ideas, symbols, concepts, vocabularies, as means for us to think about our world. It directs us to examine who produces what for whom, where the social forms of consciousness come from.

Marx and Engels's account of ideology allows us to make a preliminary sketch of the social relations organizing the rupture which is women's experience in this social form. Specifically, their formulation provides a method enabling us to see how ideas and social forms of consciousness may originate outside experience, coming from an external source and becoming a forced set of categories into which we must stuff the awkward and resistant actualities of our worlds. Marx and Engels held that how people think about and express themselves to one another arises out of their actual everyday working relations. Their view of this is not, however, as simple-minded as it has sometimes been represented. Their analysis shows how the ideas produced by a ruling class may dominate and penetrate the social consciousness of the society in general, and thus may effectively control the social process of consciousness in ways which deny expression to the actual experience people have in the working relations of their everyday world. It offers an analysis which shows how a disjuncture can arise between the world as it is known directly in experience and as it is shared with others, and the ideas and images fabricated externally to that everyday world and provided as a means to think and image it.

The social forms of thought, according to Marx and Engels, arise in people's immediate working relations, their immediate and directly experienced world as it is shared with others: "The production of ideas, of conceptions, of consciousness, is at first directly interwoven with the material activity and the material intercourse of men, the language of real life. Conceiving, thinking, the mental intercourse of men appear at this stage as the direct efflux of their material behavior. The same applies to mental production as expressed in the language of politics, laws, morality, religion, metaphysics, etc. of a people."[18] Before the development of a class structure, the kind of rupture I am attempting to explicate is one that could emerge only in biographical idiosyncracies, and not as a "social" phenomenon. With the emergence of a class society, however, "mental production" becomes the privilege of the class which dominates the means of production and appropriates the means of mental production. The contrast which the Marxist formulation allows us to conceptualize is between, on the one hand, ideas and images—the social forms of thought —directly expressive of a world known directly and shared, arising where things need to be thought, said, sung, or imaged in paint or sculpture, enacted in ritual, or formulated as rule; and, on the other hand, the social forms of thought which are made for us by others, which come to us from outside, and which do not arise out of experience, spoken of and shared with others, or out of the need to communicate with others in working contexts. The concept of ideology brings into focus the conscious production of the forms of thought by a ruling class or that section of a ruling class known as the intelligentsia, which serves to organize and order the expression of the local, particular, and directly known into forms concordant with its interests, aims, and perspectives. Thus, experiences, concerns, needs, aims, interests, arising among people in the everyday and working contexts of their living are given expression in forms which articulate them to the existing practices and social relations which constitute its rule.

Sociology is part of this ideological structure. Its themes and relevances are organized by and articulate the perspectives of men—not as individuals floating vaguely as sexual beings in a social void, but as persons playing determinate parts in the social relations of this form of society, occupying determinate class positions in it, and participating in networks of relations, which link their work to that of other professionals, in the health and educational institutions of the society, and to its more direct practices of ruling, whether in business, in government, or elsewhere. The perspectives and interests, the experience and anxieties, that are incorporated into sociology and integrated to the sociological discourse, arise out of a determinate range of social institutions forming the governing apparatus of the society—management, government, military organization, health institutions, psychiatry, education, and the social and psychological sciences, the media, and other specialized ideological institutions—the institutions which form the Marxist's understanding of the "superstructure."

In describing the ideological rupture and locating it in a ruling class, I am not using the model of manipulation of ideas from behind the scenes, the model of ideology as ideas designed to deceive and fool the innocent, put forward consciously and with malign intent by a ruling elite. This model is quite inadequate to analyze the phenomenon we are concerned with. We are describing, rather, a set of positions in the structures which "rule" (manage, administrate, organize, and otherwise control). These constitute the bases of common perspectives. Thinking, informed by interests arising in the work of ruling and relevant to getting that work done, develops in overlapping circles of discourse. People who occupy such positions come to view the world in distinctive ways by virtue of their participation in the ruling structure. They have working relations with others similarly placed. They have similar problems, experiences, concerns, and interests. In the formally and informally organized circles of discourse the "social" or intersubjective character of their interests and experience is accomplished. A ruling class does not exist merely as an ideologically homogeneous collection of individuals standing in an identical relation to the means of production. Rather, a ruling class is the basis of an active process of organization, producing ideologies that serve to organize the class itself, and its work of ruling, as well as to order and legitimize its domination. Ideologies take for granted the conditions of ruling-class experience. They give social form to its interests, relevances, and objectives. In its specific historical character ideology builds the internal social organization of the ruling class as well as its domination over others. Its overall character, however, depends upon, and takes for granted, the social relations that organize and enforce the silences of those who do not participate in this process, who are outside it.

It is important to keep in mind that we are not talking only about the control of ideas in an abstract sense. Rather, we are talking about control over the means of producing and disseminating ideas and images—that is, control over the educational process, over the media, and so on. The silence of those outside the apparatus is a silence in part materially organized by the preemption, indeed virtual monopoly, of communications media and the educational process as part of the ruling apparatus.

During the last fifty years these developments have deepened and intensified in the society to a very great degree, with the extension of the educational process, with the development of news media, with the encompassment of so many more aspects of our lives within the framework of commodity production. We may imagine earlier the existence and persistence of folk tradition—of a working-class culture, for example—so that disjunctures such as we are describing were accessible directly to consciousness in the confrontation of local and special traditions with ideologies. In comparing women's situation with that of the working class, Rowbotham identifies just such a submerged tradition among the British working class in the "divorce between home talking and educated language." Here, experience *has* a language.

> There is a long inchoate period during which the struggle between the language of experience and the language of theory becomes a kind of agony. In the making of the working class in Britain the conflict of silence with "their" language, the problem of paralysis and connection has been continuous. Every man who has worked up through the labour movement expressed this in some form. The embarrassment about dialect, the divorce between home talking and educated language, the otherness of "culture"— their culture—is intense and painful. The struggle is happening now every time a worker on strike has to justify his position in the alien structures of the television studio before the interrogatory camera of the dominant class, or every time a working-class child encounters a middle-class teacher.[19]

Such submerged traditions survive in many sections of our society—to some extent among black people, in certain rural areas, in Canada notably among native peoples (Indians and Inuit). But they have largely disappeared for women and most particularly for middle-class women—that is, women who have in common relatively highly developed skills in literacy and are oriented towards written media, the authority of women's magazines, professionals (psychiatrists, psychologists), and so on. For women, education has in the end meant intense exposure to the invasion of consciousness by interpretations systematically developed by such specialists as psychologists, historians, and sociologists, as well as exposure to short stories, novels, and other literature, which in other ways form our dreams, wishes, visions, and fantasies.

The penetration of the society by the ideological process includes, particularly for the relatively highly educated, an "in-depth" organization of consciousness. Freud's work represents the major technical breakthrough of extending the imperialism of "rationality" over personal experience, beyond the immediately practical organization of participation in professional, occupational, and womanly roles. In this way psychiatry provides a set of techniques for examining one's life and experience in relation to an ideology which legitimates and enhances conformities of feeling and disposition as well as of action and offers an elaborated technique for separating out what is "healthy" and putting away what is not. We have been left with very few places to hide.

In the emergence of modes of speaking our experience, of making it social and hence in this context political, there is, as Rowbotham has described, "a long inchoate period." For women particularly, there has not even been a "home talking" to contrast with an educated language. In beginning to find out *how* and *what* to speak, we had to begin from nowhere, not knowing what it was we would have to say and what it was we would need to know how to speak. In almost every area of work, therefore, in opposing women's oppression we have had to resort to women's experience as yet unformulated and unformed; lacking means of expression; lacking symbolic forms, images, concepts, conceptual frameworks, methods of analysis; more straightforwardly, lacking self-information and self-knowledge. The distinctive and deep significance of consciousness raising at an earlier period of the women's movement was precisely this process of opening up what was personal, idiosyncratic, and inchoate and discovering with others how this was shared, was objectively part of women's oppression, finding ways of speaking *of* it and ways of speaking it politically. It is this essential return to the experience we ourselves have directly in our everyday worlds that has been the distinctive mode of working in the women's movement—the repudiation of the professional, the expert, the already authoritative tones of the discipline,[20] the science, the formal tradition, and the return to the seriously engaged and very difficult enterprise of discovering how to begin from ourselves.

The resort to beginning from our experience and from our own subjectivities has been a fundamental and essential resource in the work of radicalizing (remaking from the root) the various ideological structures of this social form. In art and in poetry the artist begins with the problem of having learned her craft in an alienated mode and must discover methods of working that allow her to begin from herself distinctly as a woman or, perhaps even more simply, to begin from herself who is a woman. Judy Chicago's autobiographical account of her "struggle as a woman artist" is an account of just this process by a politically conscious, feminist artist.[21] The same struggle is expressed in the work of women poets, whether consciously, as in the work of a poet like Adrienne Rich, whose sense of the lack of language to express women's experiences is a powerful theme in her later poetry, or as a submerged but important organization of her relation to language, as Juhasz has suggested for the work of Emily Dickinson.[22]

In their work at the point of rupture between experience and the ideological modes of interpreting and reading it, women have had to resort to their experience unmade, because there has been no alternative. We can speculate that the "subjectivity" of women, their "intuitiveness," their "insight," as qualities identified in them by men, represent incursions of an underground of unformed and unsystematically developed knowledge of experience excluded, repressed, and lacking the means to become shared. When Dorothy Richardson in the early twentieth century introduced her radical stylistic innovations, she was in search of a style that would and did express the consciousness of women, of a particular woman, as actual experiencing. Her aim to become a women's Balzac meant an exploration of the experiencing of an everyday world from within a particular individual subjectivity.[23] In Chicago's account of how the women of the Fresno Women's Program went about discovering how to express their experience as women, we find another method relying on the same basic resource:

> In one of our sessions, we discussed how we felt when we were walking down the street and were harassed by men. Everyone had very strong attitudes about these experiences, and we decided to try to make images of the feelings. I asked the women to deal with the sensation or experience of being psychically invaded by a man or men. There was no media restriction. They were free to paint, draw, write, make a film, or do a performance. On the day the work was presented, we were downstairs in the basement of one of the students' homes. Everyone was trembling because women were showing images of feelings and experiences that none of us had every seen portrayed before: paintings and drawings, poems, performances, and ideas for films, all revealing the way women saw men. These perceptions were considerably different from the way men saw and depicted themselves in their art.[24]

This beginning "from the centre," to use Lucy Lippard's phrase, has been a powerful source for women poets and for women artists.[25] Juhasz has suggested that it is the emergence of this that constitutes a new tradition in poetry:

> The new tradition exists: wrought slowly through the century with pain and daring, it daily encounters and confronts a growing audience. No one style or form defines it, yet certain qualities do characterize the poetry of contemporary women poets: a voice that is open, intimate, particular, involved, engaged, committed. It is a poetry whose poet *speaks as a woman, so that the form of her poem is an extension of herself. A poetry that is linked to experience through the active participation of the poet herself.* A poetry that seeks to affect actively its audience. A poetry that is real, because the voice that speaks it is as real as the poet can be about herself. A poetry that is revolutionary, because by expressing the vision of real women it challenges the patriarchal premises of society itself.[26]

Those of us who have been working in relation to disciplines such as sociology, psychology, and anthropology confront different constraints and possibilities. The problem seems to be of a different kind. In history, for example, though women historians have advanced very rapidly indeed, perhaps more so than in any other field, the problem of what it means to do a history of women, what the methodology and founding of such a history is, still remains.[27] The professional discourse has a momentum of its own. The canons of science as a constitutional practice require the suppression of the personal. The structures developed become the criteria and standards of proper professional performance. Being a professional involves knowing how to do it this way, how to produce work which conforms to these standards, addressing these topics and following these methodologies. Further, doing it this way is how we recognize ourselves as professionals. We begin from a position in the discourse as an ongoing social process of formally organized interchange. We begin from a position within a determinate conceptual framework which is identified with the discipline (though there are many), and by virtue of our training and of what it means to do the professional work in our disciplines we begin from outside ourselves, to locate problematics organized by the sociological, the psychological, the historical discourse. The perspective of men institutionalized as the "field" or the "discipline" cannot, it seems, be so directly confronted with a personal source of experience, because to do so is to step outside the discipline, to cease to do sociology or history, and, with whatever virtue or value, to be found to be doing something else.

Sociology: Women Are Outside the Frame

The concepts, methods, relevances, and topics of sociology are accomplished in the social organization of the discourse. A discourse (the term is

A Sociology for Women

borrowed from Foucault)[28] is like a conversation in which utterances are abstracted from particular participants located in particular spatiotemporal settings. Certain journals and occasions such as classes, conventions, and the like are warranted sites for the presentation of sociological work. Work is accomplished as sociological in part by its presentation at such sites. By virtue of publication or appropriately sited public reading, a text becomes part of the literature that *is* sociology. This literature is exemplary in the sense that sociologists look to what has already been done and is already identifiable as a legitimate piece of sociological work to exhibit what is recognizable as sociology. The discourse is maintained by practices that determine who can participate in it as fully competent members. It develops as a process of organization and reorganization of relations among participants through the medium of their work. To be recognized as a proper participant, the member must produce work that conforms to appropriate styles and terminologies, makes the appropriate deferences, and is locatable by these and other devices in the traditions, factions, and schools whose themes it elaborates, whose interpretive procedures it intends, and by whose criteria it is to be evaluated. This system continually regulates the topics, themes, problematics, and conceptual practices of sociology and ensures that the relevances of sociological work are the relevances of the discourse.

The virtual exclusion of women from positions of influence in the discipline has meant that we have been unable until very recently to give themes and topics to the sociological discourse.[29] In proposing remedies, we have in general, as in other fields of intellectual work, drawn on women's experience as the primary source to correct the situation. Oakley, for example, has made a critique of sociology as "concealing" women. She suggests that the definition of subject areas in sociology—social stratification, political institutions, religion, education, deviance, sociology of work, and so on—has been determined by a male focus of interest and that it "reduces women to a side-issue from the start." Her critique is formulated in terms of bias and distortion; the measures of these she proposes involve "the extent to which the experiences of women [are] actually represented in the study of these life-areas." She proposes that the major subject areas be evaluated with respect to "the extent to which women are studied in each subject-area, and their actual role in the sphere of social life that the subject-category represents. For example, in the case of housework the omission of this topic from both family sociology and the sociology of work clearly conveys a distorted impression of women's situation."[30] The remedy is to take women's experience into account so that the balance can be redressed and women's perspectives and experiences represented equally with men's.

Oakley's proposal for correction is, at that stage of her work at least, largely additive. McCormack's approach suggests a critique that aims to modify the organization of the field. She proposes that we should work by identifying the male bias in established approaches. These must be examined from the perspective of women, and the implications for the field of incorporating the perspectives and interests of women must be followed through. In her own field of specialization, political sociology, she points out that women's relation to the political process is very different from that of men. Differences between women's political behavior and that of men have generally been understood in terms of deviations from a male norm of political behavior. Explanations in terms of differences in socialization, or of "backwardness," have been used. Her own proposal is that women represent, in fact, a separate political culture from that of men, one that adds "up to a female design for political living that is dissimilar from that of the male." She insists, furthermore, that the interpretation of women's experience as a basis for modifying political sociology must not be interpreted as women's special interest in or "title" to topics traditionally and sterotypically identified with women, such as the political socialization of children.[31]

The problem is that this procedure is one which, whether it is additive (Oakley) or truly critical (McCormack), treats the "agenda" of the discipline as given. But this agenda, embodied in the organization of sociological "domains," is grounded in the working worlds and relations of men, whose experience and interests arise in the course of and in relation to participation in the ruling apparatus of this society. The accepted fields of sociology—organizational theory, political sociology, the sociology of work, the sociology of mental illness, deviance, and the like—have been defined from the perspective of the professional, managerial, and administrative structures and in terms of their concerns. The specialized functions and organizations of control over society have defined both the themes and relevances of sociology and to a considerable extent its subject matter. Indeed, the universe of sociological phenomenon, the world it knows, is to a large extent constructed in the working relations of this ruling apparatus with the people whose lives it organizes and controls.

The organization of our work as sociologists begins from and returns to the relevances and organization of the field as zones of interpretive and internal phenomenal coherence. We proceed from within the received conceptual apparatus serving to define the phenomenal prospect before us —mental illness, motivation, work satisfaction, instrumental versus expressive, roles, and so on. The world that appears before the sociologist in her sociological capacity is already structured conceptually in its phenomenal aspect. We do not perhaps recognize the degree to which our knowledge of the world is already located at a conceptual level prior to the development of a theoretical apparatus. In effect, it is the organization of the discourse that generates for sociology as a whole, as well as for its different subfields and schools, the organization of the phenomenal world that it claims to study. We make use of the world as it is as a resource from which we "return," bringing our "findings" back to the discourse as sociological findings, a contribution to the sociological work and process. The world *as we know it sociologically* is largely organized by the articulation of the discourse to the ruling apparatus of which it is part.

To a large extent and until recently the nature of this relation has remained invisible precisely because sociology has operated with a conceptual apparatus that has served to detach the phenomena from the working contexts of the social process constituting the phenomena thus named. Mental illness, for example, as a phenomenon arises in the relation between psychiatric agencies of various kinds and what becomes relevant to psychiatry. This is an organized social relation, which, like sociology, has two aspects. One is whatever it is that is happening to people which gets socially organized by the institutional processes of psychiatry. The other is exactly that set of institutional processes themselves as an organized practice. "Mental illness" as a phenomenon arises at the conjunction of the two. But sociology has taken the perspective of the institutional process which organizes the world as it appears for those whose professional business it is. In the context of their work the phenomena constituting its jurisdiction are seen as present in or as properties of the world *out there* to be acted on. Sociology shares this perspective and these presuppositions. It takes up mental illness, for example, as a problematic phenomenon for which causes have to be found. Earlier stages of breaking out of this way of thinking in sociology saw psychiatric agencies as causing mental illness by assigning people to this role.[32] It has taken much further work, including the important critique of ethnomethodology, for sociologists to begin to relocate the phenomenal universe in the actual working practices of the agencies and institutions that constitute it.[33]

Women are outside the frame. They are largely silent in the discourse that develops the conceptual apparatus, the relevances, and themes. They are not a speaking part of the workings of the professional, administrative, and managerial apparatus into which sociology is locked. Indeed the positions typically occupied by women in the society are positions of subordination to this apparatus. As we have seen, much of the critique made by women's movements locates women's oppression in the relation of women to its various parts—welfare, medical, and psychiatric agencies, as well as the ideological apparatus which is our chief focus here. In beginning, therefore, to speak from where we are as women, we can begin to make observable at least some of the assumptions built into the sociological discourse. Its own organized practices upon the world have treated these assumptions as features of the world itself. We have thus inserted into the world as *its* structure, organization, etc., the working relations and organization *of the discourse*.

The agentic approach in research described by Bernard, on the basis of work by Carlson,[34] as distinctively male would appear to have its base in this organization of the discourse. It is an approach that "operates by way of mastery and control."[35] Bernard has here isolated one of a family of "assumptions" which we find in various forms built into models of the social actor. Parsons, for example, represents the actor as a maker of choices among means in relation to ends; Harré and Secord's more recent model assumes that a "human being has the power to initiate change."[36] These assumptions are grounded in a mode of action in which the power to act and coordinate in a planned and rational manner and to exercise control over conditions and means are taken for granted.

Or take Schutz's description of the fear of death as a fundamental anxiety governing each individual's system of relevance in the working world. I have always stopped short at this assumption, since I do not personally experience this anxiety. Before I learned from the women's movement, I used to transform it into a metaphysical statement unsupported by experience, but Schutz does not mean it that way. He writes thus: "From the fundamental anxiety spring the many interrelated systems of hopes and fears, of wants and satisfactions, of chances and risks which incite man within the natural attitude to attempt the mastery of the world, to overcome obstacles, to draft projects, and to realize them."[37] This too, like the other assumptions mentioned above, is grounded in a mode of action in which the power to act and coordinate in a planned and rational manner and to exercise control as an individual over conditions and means are taken for granted.

Further, the lack of sociological interest in the social structuring of emotions to which Hochschild has drawn attention[38] also appears to be grounded in a sociological ontology that is isomorphic, with rational modes of action characteristic of this form of "ruling." The rational actor choosing and calculating is the abstracted model of organizational or bureaucratic man, whose motives, methods, and ego structure are organized by the formal rationality structuring his work role. At work his feelings have no place. Rationality is a normative practice organizing and prescribing determinate modes of action within the bureaucratic or professional form. Responses that do not conform to these modes of action, by virtue of how they are excluded from these domains, are constituted residually as a distinct mode of response and being. They are defined by

A Sociology for Women

contrast with what excludes them, the rational mode of action.[39] In the *Structure of Social Action,* Parsons specifically depends on the isomorphy of sociological practice and rationality. In arriving at a determination of its subject matter, sociology has simply conformed to the contours of the institutionalized boundaries it presupposes. It is no accident that women are identified with the world of feeling and emotion, not only as being more emotional than men, but also as creating and preserving for men who participate in this mode of action a place to feel.

These assumptions and the social organization in which they are grounded are drawn into question when we begin from the experience and actualities of women's situation. For then we locate our enterprises with knowers whose perspective is organized by exactly how it is they are outside these structures, how they are excluded from participation, what their concrete situation is and its relation to the ruling apparatus of which sociology is a part. If we began from women's experience of the world, we would not find these assumptions built into its sociology, since they do not conform to the organization of our experience. Characteristically for women (as also for others in the society similarly excluded), the organization of daily experience, the work routines and the structuring of our lives through time, has been and to a very large extent still is determined and ordered by processes external to, and beyond, our everyday world. I think I would be by no means alone in seeing in my past not so much a career as a series of contingencies, of accidents, so that I seem to have become who I am almost by chance.

The experience of marriage, of immigration closely following marriage, of the arrival of children, of the departure of a husband rather early one morning, of the jobs that became available—all these were moments in which I had in fact little choice and certainly little foreknowledge. I had little opportunity of calculating rationally what it means to have a child, what it means to leave your own country and live among strangers, what it means to be married, and how each of these experiences would be a major transformation. When I read in autobiographies or fiction of the lives of other women, I find these same qualities and the surprises in store for the subject about whom she may become. I do not find them in the same way in the autobiographies of men.

In general, women's work routines and the organization of their daily lives do not conform to the "voluntaristic" model or to the model upon which an agentic style of sociology might be based. Women have little opportunity for the exercise of mastery and control. Their working lives are not structured in terms of a project of their own. The housewife, for example, becomes rather highly skilled at holding together and coordinating the threads and shreds of several lines of action, the projects of more than one individual, while herself pursuing none. The conflicts academic and professional women experience when they are also housewives are partly conflicts between opposing modes of organizing consciousness. Typically, the lives and daily routines of women are structured by an organization of action and events originating externally to the domestic zone of action and externally to the positions which women usually occupy in hierarchical structures outside the home (indeed, it seems probable that one important aspect of organizational work roles for women is that they are designed specifically to constitute a class of persons who do not become "part of the action"). Women are generally means to the enterprises of others, or means to the enterprise built into an organizational process. They hold only a piece of the action, sometimes a piece essential to the action, but they are not at its center. The consciousness required in this type of relation is organized quite differently from the agentic model. What is required is a subordination of attentiveness to self and a focus on others, the lack of development of an independent project organizing relevances and, in contrast, an openness and attentiveness to cues and indications of others' needs. A housewife, holding in place the simultaneous and divergent schedules and activities of a family, depends upon a diffuse and open organization of consciousness available to the various strands, which are coordinated only in her head and by her work and do not coordinate otherwise in the world. And again, we who have done or do both types of work can report on how the individually undertaken project of our work can seriously impair and disorganize our ability to sustain the modes of consciousness required for a peak performance in the role of housewife.

Over a lifetime and in the daily routines, women's lives tend to show a loose, episodic structure that reflects the ways in which their lives are organized and determined externally to them and the situations they order and control. This lack of control over their lives and what happens to them can be found represented in a number of important contemporary novels about women. In *Them*, for example, Oates has made a dramatic and intense amalgam of the disorder and disintegration of the lives of women and the working class.[40] When recently in Vancouver a series of plays were performed, written, and directed by women, they shared distinctively episodic structures—though otherwise their themes were quite different. The exclusively male reviewers of these plays consistently failed to make sense of how they were put together and complained of their lack of "plot." They could not find, as the women in the audience had no difficulty in finding, the expression of the structure of their own experience in the structure of the plays. Joan Didion in her extraordinary novel *Play It As It Lays* made use of the episodic structure of a film script as a stylistic device realizing exactly the episodic discontinuities of the life of her protagonist.[41]

An important further difference between the frameworks relevant to the lives and experiences of men and those of women (as they are typically located in this society) emerged for me as a result of reading Huw Beynon's *Working for Ford*.[42] This book comes about as close as I can imagine to doing a sociology from the perspective of working-class men. True it does not become clear in that book what is implied by beginning from such a position, where a sociology which began there might go, or just what kinds of further consequences would follow (questions are and must be raised about the fundamentally academic enterprise of doing merely a sociology). But this book does describe and analyze not just workingmen's work experience but their work experience in the context of the organization, managerial practices, and economic relations of Ford. From my reading of it, I came to the conclusion that there would be quite important differences between a sociological perspective based on the position of working-class men and one based on the position of women (in general). Working-class men are provided or may be provided with an adequate accounting of their lives from within the organizational framework of company and union. The types of oppression experienced by working-class men and the actual determinations of their work experience are a function of a directly present managerial structure set up in line with company policies, responsive to changes in the economic situation. The sociological researcher may not always be able to identify what the policies are; but that there are policies, management, managerial authority and power and its uses in relation to policy and planning, is fundamental to the interpretive framework used in describing and analyzing what happens. The work lives and experience of those who work at Ford is determined by direct subordination to a managerial hierarchy, which shapes, among other matters, the union agenda. The standard sociological conceptual framework will work because essentially the same processes are the focus. But women's existence cannot be comprehended within such frames (nor perhaps, with this example to follow, should we take it for granted that men's can). Society has organized for women a different relation to the world. Attempts to apply a conceptual apparatus drawn uncritically from the standard sociological frames in these areas rest uneasily on the actual experience and situation of women as a means of analysis. Oakley, in her use of the conceptual apparatus from the sociology of work to focus on work satisfaction in the study of housework, adopts a framework which presupposes the wage relation—that is, a relation in which a worker sells his labor to an enterprise and in which his labor must therefore be managed for the benefit of the enterprise. This underlying structure—which is presupposed in the endless work that has been done on motivation in industrial settings—is simply not present in the relation of the housewife either to her husband or to her work.[43] Similarly, applications of time-budget methods to comparisons between the amount of work women do in the home and the amount of work men do outside and inside the home have simply adapted the distinction between work and leisure in such a way that the kinds of responsibilities women take in relation to the home and to the children simply do not appear.[44] The work-leisure organization applies to employment. The sociological concepts are borrowed directly from it. If we started with housework as a basis, the categories of "work" and "leisure" would never emerge. And indeed, it is hard to imagine how, using housework as our basic framework, it would be possible to make "work" and "leisure" observable. The social organization of the role of housewife, mother, and wife does not conform to the divisions between being at work and not being at work. Even the concept of housework as work leaves what we do as mothers without a conceptual home.

Traditionally in sociology, the problem of subordinating extramanagerial forms to the conceptual hegemony of rational administrative forms of organization has been worked out by applying functionalist theory. Functionalism makes possible the application of a model of rational action to social phenomena that could not be assimilated to that model empirically. Unfortunately, much contemporary Marxist thinking on women and the household follows an essentially functionalist procedure by "reducing" women's characteristic work and social relations in the household and family to concepts that analyze them in terms of their relation to capitalist *economic* processes.[45] But the work life of women escapes the scope of the bureaucratic, professional, and administrative princedoms of "the active society."[46] The phenomena of women's situation and experience fall between or outside the institutional spheres.[47] It is thus not adequate to do as Oakley suggests and divide women up as topics among the various existing subject-areas in sociology, defined—as Oakley herself recognizes—by the various managerial and professional jurisdictions of the ruling apparatus. Beginning from women's experience calls into question more than the distribution of topics as between women and men. Further, the ways in which women's experience has been introduced has been largely as a resource in entering new topics or eking out old ones. But the sociological agenda and the forms of thought organized by the location of the discourse within the ruling apparatus remain unmoved. Though Bernard and others have proposed a radical critique of methods,[48] we have not known—as poets, painters, and sculptors have known—how to begin from our own center, how to begin from our own experience, how to make ourselves as women the subjects of the sociological act of knowing.

A Sociology for Women

The Sociological Relation and the Abstracted Conceptual Mode

To help us analyze further the problem of women's relation as subjects or knowers to the sociological discourse, I want to draw on Alfred Schutz's description of the finite provinces of meaning and of the changes in the organization of consciousness associated with shifts from one province to another. The fundamental province of meaning is the paramount reality, the original and ultimate locus of consciousness, in which the subject's consciousness is organized by her own actual position in the world. In the paramount reality, the subject is located in that stratum of reality corresponding to the everyday world of working. Schutz describes this organization of consciousness thus:

> The wide-awake man within the natural attitude is primarily interested in that sector of the world of his everyday life which is within his scope and which is centered in space and time around himself. The place which my body occupies within the world, my actual Here is the starting point from which I take my bearings in space. It is, so to speak, the center 0 of my system of coordinates. Relative to my body I group the elements of my surroundings under the categories of right and left, before and behind, above and below, near and far, and so on. And in a similar way my actual Now is the origin of all the time perspectives under which I organize the events within the world, such as the categories of fore and after, past and future, simultaneity and succession, etc.[49]

This organization of the world in consciousness locates the null point, the center 0, in an actual and particular locality. The subject is located by her bodily situation in the world, and her coordinates shift in relation to her as center, changing as her position changes, changing as her "position" in time changes. It is consciousness located materially and in activities which enter the world of working.

Schutz analyzes other finite provinces of meaning. Among them (and of special relevance here) is the finite province of scientific attitude. In entering the "world" of science, consciousness is reorganized to drop away the particular and local organization from subject as center, as well as relevances arising out of work or activity in relation to the subject's own interests or projects in the everyday world. Consciousness organized in the finite province of meaning of science sets aside the anxieties and hopes and fears arising in the paramount reality. The *epoché* peculiar to the scientific attitude has these characteristics:

> In this *epoché* there is "bracketed" (suspended): 1) the subjectivity of the thinker as a man among fellow-men, including his bodily existence as a psychophysical human being within the world; 2) the system of orientation by which the world of everyday life is grouped in zones within actual, re-

storable, attainable reach, etc.; 3) the fundamental anxiety and the system of pragmatic relevances originating therein.[50]

Entry into the world of scientific theory organizes consciousness into a mode detached from the everyday world of working. In it "we" takes on a universal character, and the categories of before and after, etc., are organized by the temporal and "spatial" organization of the discourse rather than by the subject's bodily location in the world.

What Schutz is describing, in part, is the organization of consciousness in the work of "doing" science, which necessarily involves attention to a domain constituted separately from the particular and immediate interests and concerns of the individual located in her body. It is that zone which she enters in doing the kind of work we are doing now. But more than that, Schutz ascribes to this a definite cognitive domain organizing the subjectivity of its participant into a mode in which her particular position —the view from the center—is discarded and replaced by an impartial, detached mode. The grammatical subject identifies no particular person. Temporal and spatial coordinates which structure the referencing work of indexicals (before, after, etc.) do not intersect in a particular center.[51]

In taking up the scientific attitude as that mode in which their work is done, sociologists have sought to practice an objectivity constituted in relation to an "Archimedian" point—that is, a point external to any particular position in society. Objectivity for the social scientist has involved continual attention to the methodological and epistemological problems arising from the fact that the cognitive domain of sociology has to be organized in, and—in a sense—out of, the lived reality of the world the sociologist participates in in her total being. The scientific attitude sometimes enforces an exclusion of concerns and interests—an exclusion that seems artificial, strange, and wrong. The contrast between the professional starting point and an interested position identified with women can be seen in the following account by Russell of her experience at a conference among psychologists, psychiatrists, social workers, and sociologists concerning battered wives. She describes the character of the scientific attitude in this context in such a way that we can see how it locates her as subject outside herself and constitutes a social relationship of a distinct kind, not only in organizing her relation to the subject matter, battered wives, but also in organizing her relations with others so that she takes up her position in the hierarchical structure of the professions and separates herself from those whose partial and "emotional" involvement prevents "detached" and "logical" discussion of the problem. The account from which these quotes are drawn appeared in a feminist newspaper. Catherine Russell writes:

My attitudes on arriving at the conference were fairly consistent with those of the majority. I was there to learn by absorbing theories and facts about the specific phenomenon of violence in the family, particularly as experienced by battered wives. My purpose was to collect information that would contribute to my being a more effective worker at Transition House [a refuge in Vancouver, B.C., for women who have been violently treated at home]. Not knowing much, I accepted a position of being low on the hierarchy of people at the symposium; power and worthiness derived from being able to clearly articulate an intellectual perception of a social phenomenon and a theoretical solution to the problem.

My first emotional response at the symposium was to Gene Errington's speech. She made a strong, angry statement of her reaction to the conference and to the orientation of professionals. I was very uncomfortable and felt antagonistic toward her for making a speech that stirred up the symposium and antagonized a large number of delegates. I didn't want to be identified with the feminists who were giving her a standing ovation—even though I was sitting with that group whose interests coincided with mine. I was accepting the norm that says: "Let's be calm and logical about this. There's no need to get angry." And, by so doing, I was denying the validity of Gene's anger.

The next day I started to realise how I had been affected by the norms of the majority. And in the process had been denying others the expression of their feelings and had been valuing people's contributions predominantly on the basis of intellectual consistency, articulation and coolness.

In the first workshop, one woman—in an emotional and somewhat rambling statement—expressed her feeling of being battered by the conference itself. The expression of her feelings was only briefly responded to by the workshop speaker. However, she had spoken for a lot of women at that workshop, in that there was a lot of frustration being experienced—and not spoken of—at the tone of the conference. Her speaking led other women to speak from their feelings.

And that's when I really started feeling angry. I recognized that my acceptance of the professionals' norms had been a critical factor in my discounting and criticizing Gene the previous day and others during the course of the symposium, and consequently in my feeling separated from people. Those norms value intellectual perception so highly and emotions so lowly; they are a basic cause of the violence in our culture. And that was not being dealt with.[52]

In this account distinctive properties of the scientific attitude in the social sciences come into view. By suspending the subjectivity of the thinker as a woman among sister-woman (*cf.* Schutz above) she is related in a particular mode, to women who have experienced violence from the men with whom they live. That relation is packaged in a social organization which aligns her with other professionals sharing the same orientation and alienates her from groups representing directly the concerns and interests of women in that situation.

The relation between the knower and the object of her knowledge (constituted as such in the relation) is a socially organized practice. The cognitive domain of science is itself a social relation. Knowledge itself is a social accomplishment.[53] The conceptual practices, methodologies, instrumentalities, and so on, which in the concrete instance organize the cognitive domain of the particular science in which the subject is practitioner, are not merely tools to be picked up and laid down at will. They are together those practices which organize and bring into being the phenomena *as such* in the knower's relation to the known as object. In the example above it becomes clear that knowledge in the social sciences has this further character, namely that both terms of the 'knowledge relation' are human. The methods of inquiry and of thinking are integral not only to the relation among knowers in a discourse but constitute also a determinate social relation among knowers and the human objects of their knowledge. Sociology is an organization of practices that structure our relation to others in the society of whom we speak and write, concerning whom we make assertions, into whose lives and experience we inquire, who are the objects of our study, and whose behavior we aim to explain.

That the parties to this relation are rendered specifically anonymous by procedures taken for granted in our methodologies must be viewed as a definite feature of this social relation rather than as suspending its social character. Anonymity, impersonality, detachment, impartiality, objectivity itself, are accomplished by socially organized practices that bring into being a relation of a definite form between knowers and known. Integral to the relation thus formed is its organization to suspend the particular subjectivities of knower and known in such a way that its character as a social relation disappears—very much in the way in which, according to Marx, the activities of people disappear in the social relation constituted in the commodity form, such that relations between actual people appear as relations of exchange between things, money, and commodities.

In working as sociologists within established methods of thinking and inquiry, we "enter" a social relation organizing our relations with others into determinate forms. We get into this mode very much as the driver of a car gets into the driving seat. It is true that we do the driving and can choose the direction and destination; but the way in which the car is put together, how it works, and how and where it will travel structure our relation to the world we travel in. In entering the discourse as practitioners we enter it as subjects of the kinds of sentences it can properly generate, the assertions it can make. We have learned in our training to proceed from within the conceptual frameworks, the epistemological presuppositions, as well as to find our way around in the organization of camps, schools, and factions, of the discourse. We have learned to discard our experienced worlds as a source of concerns, information, and understandings of the actualities of the social world and to confine and focus our "insights" within the conceptual frameworks and relevances given in the discipline. Should we think otherwise or experience the world in different ways, with edges or horizons passing beyond what could be conceptualized in the established forms, we have learned to practice a discipline which disattends them or to find some way of making them over so that they will fit. We have learned a way of thinking about the world, a way of knowing it, that is recognizable to its practitioners as a sociological way of thinking, and we have come to identify ourselves as professionals in these terms.

In this way the discourse organizes our social relations with those who become the objects of our study. Ordinarily, as sociologists we function in and operate this social relation in the absence of another whose looking back on us makes us aware of its character as a social relation. Its methods are as effective in eliminating our subject's presence as they are in suspending our recognition of our own. Occasionally, when we are doing field work or interviewing, we experience this strange relation as an actual social interaction. But the conceptual procedures developed in sociology serve to suspend the presence of an actor in her actions; what people are doing, what they experience, what is happening to them, become "roles," "norms," "systems," "behaviors." We have learned a method of thinking which does away with the presence of the subjects in the phenomena which only subjects can accomplish.

In attempting to develop a sociology from the standpoint of women, we find a persistent difficulty that does not yield to the critique of standard themes and topics. In any of the many ways we might do a sociology of women, women remain the objects of study. Sociologies of sex roles, of gender relations, of women, constitute women as the object of inquiry. It never quite makes sense to do a sociology of men, nor is it clear how that would differ from the sociology we do. By insisting that women be entered into sociology as its subjects, we find that we cannot escape how its practices transform us into objects. As women we become objects to ourselves as subjects. We ourselves therefore can "look back"[54] as subjects constituted as objects in that relation, and in doing so, we disclose its essential contradiction. So long as "men," "he," and "his" appeared as the general and impersonal terms locating the subject of sociological assertions, the problem remained invisible. We had learned to "enter" our subjectivities into sentences beginning "he" and to disattend our sex under the convention—applying only to women since it is irrelevant for men—that the pronoun was in this context neutral. Once we had understood, however, that the male pronoun did indeed locate a male subject for whom women were constituted in the sociological relation outside the frame which organized his position, the appearance of impersonality went. The knower turns out after all not be "abstract knower" perching on an Archimedian point but a member of a definite social category occupying definite positions in the society.

The problem of how women cannot escape the status of object in the sociological relation thus enlivens a general issue. The methods of thinking, empirical inquiry, and the practices accomplishing the objectivity and the recognizably sociological features of sociological work organize an object world from the perspective of a determinate position in the society. They organize a determinate relation between those who occupy the positions from which it is known and those who become the objects of its method of knowing. In questioning the sociological relation from the standpoint of women, we find we have called into question the organization of the discourse in general, its location in the world, and the social relations organizing the positions of its subjects which its objectifying practices conceal. The specific character of the sociological mode of reflecting upon society, upon social relations, upon people, in suspending the actual and particular position of the knower must be understood as itself located. Sociology provides a mode in which people can relate to themselves and to others in a mode which locates them as subjects outside themselves, in which the coordinates are shifted to a general abstracted frame and the relation of actions, events, etc., to the local and particular is suspended or discarded. Bierstedt has celebrated the educational value of sociology thus: "Sociology can liberate the mind from time and space themselves and remove it to a new and transcendental realm where it no longer depends upon these Aristotelian categories."[55] What sociology teaches is precisely this mode of relating to the society in which it is practiced, but this mode of relating to others is not for everyone. It does not represent an impartial and general knowledge whose knower is truly Archimedian, nor does it represent knowers who might be any member of the society. We have found already that women are outside the frame and do not enter as its subjects. It is a partial view, a view which originates in a special kind of position in the society.

The basis of this position develops with the emergence of forms of corporate capitalism. Increasingly in the twentieth century we find the emergence of an abstracted conceptual mode of organization in which organizing functions become (a) differentiated as a distinct system of functions—whether as administration, management, or aspects of professional organization; (b) primarily communicative and informational (the "chief" of a

A Sociology for Women

corporation or a government department does not gather together the armed men of his clan and ride across the hills to attack his neighbor); (c) dependent increasingly on a secondhand knowledge organized conceptually as "facts," "information," and so on; (d) dependent increasingly on generalized systems of planning in the same mode. These practices are known as rational administrative practices[56] and the like. They constitute a generalized and generalizing practice of organization occupying an increasingly abstracted conceptual space, detached from the local and particular as the locus and center of the organizational processes.

The form of capitalism and indeed the most general form of enterprise in nineteenth-century Canada and the United States was the small-scale enterprise, whose owner also managed and controlled the enterprise. Such was the characteristic social organization of farming, as farming became more fully articulated to the market process; such was the organization of crafts, of shopkeeping, and of the various now relatively invisible roles in the market process (merchant, trader, jobber, etc.) Though the market appeared as an external force organizing relations and functioning independently of the choices and wishes of individual capitalists or workers *and* as the cumulated product of those choices, the immediate governance of the enterprise managed in relation to market exigencies and opportunities was *local*. Enterprises organized on a local basis also organized the relations of that local sector of the economy among themselves, including their relation to those who owned no property and participated in the productive process as sellers of labor. Class relations were locally based, and class organization had to build from that basis.

Towards the end of the nineteenth century, as capital accumulated, the earlier forms of individually owned enterprises organized on a local basis began to be superseded by the corporate form. An integral aspect of this was a change in the forms of property relations. Berle and Means have described this as a separation of ownership and control,[57] but it is more accurately understood as the emergence of a corporate form of property relations whereby the direct ownership of capital was vested in a corporation and the managerial process was a process of the corporation as an organizational form. The corporation is a determinate type of organizational process in which managerial practices become not only highly technical but also take on what Albert Sloan (who was one of the inventors and promulgators of this organizational form) describes as "objective organization," as contrasted with "subjective organization."[58] "Subjective" forms of organization he identified as the practices which had earlier prevailed, whereby decisions on financial issues and on how the assets of an enterprise should be committed had been made on the basis of hunches by individuals or of negotiations among heads of different departments or sectors functioning somewhat like fiefdoms. The forms of organization which began to emerge depended in the first place on marked technical developments in accounting practices and on the ability to analyze the economic environment and situation, as well as processes of demand and supply, in ways that made possible decisionmaking from which individual hunches, intuitions, bargaining, and personal edges or power were removed. The performance of different sections or departments became measurable in relation to one another with respect to how each contributed to the overall enterprise. Management, moreover, became self-conscious of the organizational process. Social relations, organizations, and so on became conceptualized as discrete and self-conscious processes quite separable as such from the particular individuals who performed and brought them into being as concrete social activities.

During this period of development a locus of organization became predominant, requiring a viewpoint of society and social relations which was extralocal something like a bird's-eye view, a viewpoint not situated in the local and particular places and not located in actual, particularistic social relations. A perspective was required that organized a world at a conceptual level abstracted from the local and particular and capable of locating the subjectivity of the knower in a view of society, and view of social relations, which she could not get from within her own null point, her own bodily location, where near and far, before and after, had to be organized in relation to herself as center. An institutionalized form of knowledge and practice of social control developed (in law, in psychiatry, in education, in universities, in the social sciences, in sociology in particular) which was externalized, objectified, and not locatable in a particular place, physical or social.

The version of ideology which Mannheim in particular represents constitutes just such a level of perspective on society—one detached from the partial perspectives of particular local groups, the rural village, the country town, the city, the political party, the particular class. Mannheim saw the work of the sociologist of knowledge not merely as that of the impersonal, disinterested, and scientific study of the social basis of knowledge or perspectives of the world. His methods of analysis were developed as means to the synthesis which would provide a "third" version, capable of rising above the contending views, drawn up out of combinations of the partial views into a total perspective from its local and particular basis in a particular section of social structure, in a particular group, class, locality.[59] The concept of ideology provided for him and, to a large extent, for sociologists who have followed him a way to separate a sociological or social scientific perspective from the biases of a particular and subjective account, rising above the contentious views of different classes.

Work of this kind gathered sociology up into the world in which activity, practice, methods, and social relations are the practices of mind, of the "head," of speaking, of writing, rather than of the body, the hand, the material work, the working world. A sociology was created with the capacity to transform actualities into the forms in which they could be thought of in the abstracted conceptual mode of ruling. These methods of working enabled sociologists to transform phenomena from their original actualities in concrete material processes into observables at the conceptual level. Thus the actual practices of social relations are transformed into "social roles," individuals' activities into "norms," and what people actually say in religious or political settings into "beliefs" and "values."

These methods of conceptualizing social processes articulate the local and particular worlds in which people are concretely located into the forms of thought which organize them in relation to the abstracted conceptual mode of "ruling." Of special importance so far as sociology is concerned is the capacity of people playing their parts in the ruling apparatus to think about people, to think about social relations, to think about social action, in terms of systems and in terms of social processes external to individuals. Sociological practices of thinking do indeed locate the consciousness of the thinker in just those ways which Bierstedt describes—outside the Aristotelian categories, detached from particularities, detached from the knower's location in the world. This has been part of the distinctive historical work of sociology. It provides, specifically, a mode of "entering" subjectivities into the abstracted conceptual modes of organizing this form of society. As a finite subprovince of meaning it structures a discard of the localized organization of consciousness from the "null point."[60] The knower starts already located outside her self. When we work as sociologists in this mode, we "enter" a sociology constituting our relation to the world in this way. We "enter" this relation.

The Standpoint of Women

When we take up the standpoint of women, we take up a standpoint outside this frame (as an organization of social consciousness). To begin from such a standpoint does not imply a common viewpoint among women. What we have in common is that organization of social relations which has accomplished our exclusion. Taking this up as a position for the subjects of a sociology, what is the critique? A critique is more than a negative statement. It is an attempt to define an alternative.

We have asked here how it is that sociology as we practice it and recognize its practices does not allow us to begin our work from our experience as women. Women's experience has been a resource, but it has not become the basis for a position from which sociology, as the systematic study of society and social relations, proceeds.

In *The Phenomenology of Mind*, Hegel analyzes the relation of master and servant.[61] This analysis was a model for Marx's analysis of the relation between a ruling class and the working class, including the dynamic process built into the relation which transforms it. Here we have use for a limited aspect of Hegel's "parable," the relation between the master's consciousness and the labor of the servant. Hegel describes how for the master the object of his desire is available to him in a simple and obvious manner such that he can leap directly from the desire to its object, from appetite to consummation, without an intervening labor. The object appears there for him in a simple and direct way. This appearance is, however, the result or product of the servant's labor. The servant produces the object for the master. In so doing the servant conforms to the will of the master, and his work is in that sense the master's consciousness realized. The servant in relation to the master does not constitute a distinct subject, a consciousness distinctly and authentically present who looks back and reflects the master's consciousness of his self to him. His labor is not independent of his master's will and has no autonomous existence. The servant's labor is present in the relation of the master to the object of his desire, the object of consciousness. The invisibility of that relation from the master's standpoint is a product of the organization of the relation between master and servant. That organization itself is not visible from the standpoint of the master. Within the consciousness of the master there is himself and the object and a servant who is merely a means. For the servant there is the master, the servant's labor producing the object, and there is the simplicity of the relation between the master and the object. The totality of the set of relations is visible.

This, I suggest, is how we should understand the way in which Marx viewed the relation between the consciousness of a ruling class as an ideological consciousness and a science of political economy proceeding from and grounded in the standpoint of the working class. Certainly this interpretation is one that enables us to take forward the implications of taking the standpoint of women. Interpretations of the relation between ideas and their social base which identify an ideological consciousness as determined by its social basis in class in a simple and direct way lead us to the unfortunate difficulty (which has been used to criticize Marx's work) that a political economy beginning from the standpoint of labor is subject to the same criticism. Identifying it with its social base in the working class invalidates it as a science from the outset. The claim to the primacy of this base over the base in the ruling class can then be treated either as an essentially arbitrary choice governed by a prior value judgment, hence invalid, or as Lukács did, by identifying it with a historical process in which truth emerges in the praxis of a class.[62] Both of these positions result from viewing class as a phenomenon which constitutes groups or collectivities *of essentially the same kind or order*, rather than as organized social relations which are differentiated vis-à-vis one another in a grand social division of labor—which is clearly how Marx viewed them (see *The German Ideology*).

The basis for a political economy from the standpoint of labor, according to Marx, is precisely that it is grounded in the work and activity of actual individuals producing their existence under definite material conditions. The standpoint of labor provides, therefore, a basis for knowledge corresponding to the position of the servant in Hegel's exemplary tale. From the servant's position the working of the whole process is available in principle since his actual practice brings into being the relation between self and object appearing as it does from the perspective of the master. From the point of view of the ruling class, the actual practices and the material conditions which form, organize, and provide for the "appearance" of direct action are not visible. Their activities, their work, their consciousness, appear simple and complete, their relations undetermined, because how they are determined is a product of the labor of the working class. The social organization of the forms of consciousness characteristic of a ruling class cannot be examined from the standpoint of the ruling class because that organization is not visible from that perspective or in that mode of action. Thus, when Marx draws attention to how Feuerbach's idealist philosophy disattends its essential dependence on the production of the philosopher's subsistence and hence his consciousness, upon the material processes of labor which produce the world he inhabits and its features (including the peach tree before his window, whose presence is itself a historical product of trading relations), he is not engaging in cheap gibes. He is drawing attention, rather, to the simplifications of idealism which view the transformation of social forms as taking place in and through conceptual transformations (and therefore as simple) and to how these very "simplifications" are organized, provided for, and produced by the productive relations and the productive activities, the labor of a working class standing in determinate relation to a ruling class, producing not merely its subsistence, but the basic organization which the social forms of consciousness of the ruling class take for granted.

Returning now to the question of sociology beginning from the standpoint of women, we can see an analogous relation. In the social division of labor the labor of articulating the local and particular existence of actors to the abstracted conceptual mode of ruling is done typically by women. The abstracted conceptual mode of ruling exists in and depends upon a world known immediately and directly in the bodily mode. The suppression of that mode of being as a focus, as thematic, depends upon a social organization which produces the conditions of its suppression. To exist as subject and to act in this abstracted mode depends upon an actual work and organization of work by others, who make the concrete, the particular, the bodily, the thematic of their work and who also produce the invisibility of that work. It is a condition of anyone's being able to enter, become and remain absorbed, in the conceptual mode of action that she does not need to focus her attention on her labors or on her bodily existence. The organization of work and work expectations in managerial and professional circles both constitutes and depends upon the alienation of members of this class from their bodily and local existence. The structure of work in this mode and the structure of career assume that individuals can sustain a mode of consciousness in which interest in the routine aspects of bodily maintenance is never focal, and can in general be suppressed. It is taken for granted in the organization of this work that such matters are provided for in a way which will not interfere with action and participation in the conceptual mode.

The sociologist enters the conceptual mode of action when she goes to work. She enters it as a member, and she enters it also as the mode in which she investigates it. She observes, analyzes, explains, and examines as if there were no problem in how that world becomes observable to her. She moves among the doings of organizations, governmental processes, bureaucracies, and so on, as a person who is at home in that medium. The nature of that world itself, how it is known to her, and the conditions of its existence or her relation to it are not called into question. Her methods of observation and inquiry extend to it as procedures which are essentially of the same order as those which bring about phenomena with which she is concerned, or which she is concerned to bring under the jurisdiction of that order. Her perspectives and interests may differ, but the substance is the same. She works with facts and information which have been worked up from actualities and appear in the form of documents, which are themselves the product of organizational processes, whether her own or administered by her or of some other agency. She fits that information back into a framework of entities and organizational processes which she takes for granted as known, without asking how it is that she knows them or what are the social processes by which the phenomena corresponding to or providing the empirical events, acts, decisions, etc., of that world, may be recognized. She passes beyond the particular and immediate setting in which she is always located in the body (the office she writes in, the libraries she consults, the streets she travels, the home she returns to) without any sense of having made a transition. She works in the same medium as she studies.

A Sociology for Women

But like everyone else she also exists in the body, in the place in which it is. This, then, is also the place of her sensory organization of immediate experience; the place where her coordinates of here and now, before and after, are organized around herself as center; the place where she confronts people face to face in the physical mode in which she expresses herself to them and they to her as more and other than either can speak. It is in this place that things smell. The irrelevant birds fly away in front of the window. Here she has flu. Here she gives birth. It is a place she dies in. Into this space must come as actual material events, whether as the sounds of speech, the scratchings on the surface of paper which is constituted as document, or directly, anything she knows of the world. It has to happen here somehow if she is to experience it at all.

Entering the governing mode of our kind of society lifts the actor out of the immediate local and particular place in which she is in the body. She uses what becomes present to her in this place as a means to pass beyond it to the conceptual order. This mode of action creates a bifurcation of consciousness, a bifurcation, of course, which is present for all those participating in this mode of action. It establishes two modes of knowing, experiencing, and acting, one located in the body and in the space which it occupies and moves into; the other, passing beyond it. And although I have made use of the feminine pronoun in general, it is primarily men who are *active* in this mode.

It is a condition of a person's being able to enter and become absorbed in the conceptual mode that attention to the local and bodily remain, as Schutz says, "horizonal" rather than focal or thematic. Schutz himself, that great ethnographer of the "head" world, provides an account of just this suppression which locates at least one form of women's work in organizing its own suppression. He writes:

> The corollary to the fact that we live simultaneously in various provinces of reality or meaning is the fact that we put into play various levels of our personality.... Only very superficial levels of our personality are involved in such performances as our habitual and even quasi-automatic "household chores," or eating, dressing, and (for normal adults) also in reading and performing simple arithmetical operations. To be sure, when we turn to such routine work, the activities connected with it are constituted as thematic, requiring and receiving our full attention if only momentarily.[63]

Without challenging Schutz's general picture of these various levels of personality and their organization in relation to projects in the world of working, we can also recognize what is presupposed in just that organization—namely, that the routine matters, the household chores, are not problematic, do not become a central focus of man's work, or at least "only momentarily." Once we are alerted to how women's work provides for this organization of consciousness, we can see how this structure depends in actual situations on the working relations of those providing for the logistics of the philosopher's bodily existence—those for whom household chores are not horizontal, but are thematic, and whose work makes possible for another the supression of all but passing attention to the bodily location of consciousness.

If men are to participate fully in the abstract mode of action, they must be liberated from having to attend to their needs in the concrete and particular. Organizing the society in an abstracted conceptual order, mediated symbolically, must be articulated to the concrete and local actualities in which it is necessarily and ineluctably located. That must be a work, must be a product of labor. To a very large extent the direct work of liberating men from the Aristotelian categories of which Bierstedt speaks has been and is the work of women.

The place of women, then, in relation to this mode of action is where the work is done to facilitate man's occupation of the conceptual mode of action. Women keep house, bear, and care for children, look after him when he is sick, and in general provide for the logistics of his bodily existence. But this marriage aspect of women's work is only one side of a more general relation. Women work in and around the professional and managerial scene in analogous ways.[64] They do those things which give concrete form to the conceptual activities. They do the clerical work, giving material form to the words or thoughts of the boss. They do the routine computer work, the interviewing for the survey, the nursing, the secretarial work. At almost every point women mediate for men the relation between the conceptual mode of action and the actual concrete forms on which it depends. Women's work is interposed between the abstracted modes and the local and particular actualities in which they are necessarily anchored. Also, women's work conceals from men acting in the abstract mode just this anchorage.

In the health profession, for example, the routine practices which mediate the actualities of the immediate experienced world and work them up into forms corresponding to the abstracted conceptual forms under which they may be professionally (or "scientifically") known are done largely by women. The psychiatric patient is indeed present to the psychiatrist as a "whole person," but the routines which limit the psychiatrist's relation to the patient, and hence define those aspects which come strictly within his professional focus, are performed in large part by women—nurses, laboratory technicians, social workers, clerks, and so on. To a large extent women have at various points direct and immediate contact with the actual life situation of the patient, before it has been cleaned and tidied up, in all its complexity—just as anyone's life situation is always complex, rooted in others' lives, and multifaceted. Through the work of those who reconstruct the patient's life as a case history, it is obliterated as it was experienced and lived.

By the time the patient gets to the psychiatrist, she is already an abstraction. She has been separated from the contexts in which what she was saying and doing were connected. Hence, the psychiatrist encounters the patient as one whose abstraction has already been socially organized. For him there is no war or tension between the direct experience he has in the settings of his work and the ideologies he uses to name, interpret, and order what he observes. He is not exposed to disjunctions between the nature of his psychiatric procedures and the actualities of his patients' lives. He is not exposed in his professional practice to the world before the practices of receptionists, nurses, secretaries, nurses' aides, social workers. Their work brings into being the forms in which what he does, thinks, and says make ordinary sense. His accomplishment of his work in the abstracted conceptual modes depends upon their work in ways which their work itself makes invisible.

Beginning from the standpoint of women locates a subject who begins in a material and local world. It shows the provinces of meaning described by Schutz (see above, pp. 155–56) not as alternatives—a paramount reality on the one hand and the scientific domain on the other—but rather as a bifurcation of consciousness, with a world directly experienced from oneself as center (in the body) on the one hand and a world organized in the abstracted conceptual mode, external to the local and particular places of one's bodily existence. The abstracted mode of the scientific province is always located in the local and material actualities. Participation in the "head" world is accomplished in actual concrete settings making use of definite material means. Suppression of interest in that setting is organized in a division of labor which accords to others the production and maintenance of the material aspects of a total process. To those who do this work, the local and concrete conditions of the abstracted mode are thematic. But women's standpoint locates a subject in the fundamental "item" of the twofold basis of knowing the world. The organization which divides the two becomes visible from this base. It is not visible from within the other.

We can see then how the silencing of women of which we spoke earlier suppresses not only women but the work they represent and the dimension of existence which locates, among other things, that fear of death which Schutz holds as the fundamental anxiety. The fear of death is the final announcement to the thinker that his occupancy of the conceptual mode of the bifurcated consciousness is necessarily temporary. He is precipitated into time. Women's lack of authority to speak, their exclusion from the circle of those who make the tradition, who make the discourse, means that the work that suppresses the concrete and material and the local, particular, and material locus of consciousness is also silenced. The modes of action in the conceptual mode depend upon this silence.

The theories, concepts, and methods of our discipline claim to be capable of accounting for and analyzing the same world as that which we experience directly. But these theories, concepts, and methods have been built up out of a way of knowing the world which takes for granted the boundaries of an experience in the same medium in which it is constituted. It takes for granted and subsumes without examining the conditions of its existence. Its object appears to it, as to Hegel's master, in a direct and simple relation. It is not capable of analyzing its own relation to its conditions nor of locating itself where the social relations organizing and providing for its existence can be seen. The sociologist as actual person in an actual concrete setting, the sociological knower, has been "cancelled" from the act of knowing by a procedure which objectifies and separates him from his knowledge. The essential linkage which is the first clue pointing back to the conditions of his knowledge is lacking.

Locating women's experience as a place to work from in sociology does not, if we follow this line of analysis, land us in a determinate type of position or identify a category of persons from whose various and typical positions in the world we must take our starting point. Women are variously located in society. Their situations are much more various than the topics we recognize somewhat stereotypically as women's topics would suggest. Their position also differs very greatly by class. Even among housewives, who appear to share a universal fate, there are rather wider differences in the conditions, practices, and organization of housework and the social relations in which it is embedded than our studies and the ways in which they have been framed would allow.

The identification of the bifurcated consciousness is a potential experience for women members of an intelligentsia or of women otherwise associated with the ruling apparatus which organizes the society. It is clearly not every woman's experience of the world. That is not the issue. At this point the concern is to develop a method of working in sociology that will make it possible to begin from where women in general are, doing the type of work with which we as a sex are identified. To develop a sociology from the standpoint of subjects located materially and in particular places does not involve simply the transfer from one conceptual frame to another, from, say, a Parsonian to a Marxist framework. It does something rather different. A Marxist framework can and has been quite readily assimilated into the modes of the sociological discourse which accord primacy to the conceptual categories and the forms of thought and subordinate the actualities of the world to them. Nor does the answer lie, as has sometimes been suggested, in the renunciation of the rational, conceptual, scientifically rigorous method or procedure. This is to treat the two sides of the bifurcated consciousness as if they were equal and to locate what is distinctively "feminine" in the subjective, emotional side, so that the alienative intellectual practices of sociology are eliminated rather than transformed. It has been suggested to me that a phenomenological sociology is a feminist sociology merely because it begins within the consciousness of the knower and is hence "subjective," but the phenomenological perspective remains within the conceptual abstracted world and begins from there, taking for granted the material and social organization of the bifurcated consciousness, and does not render its organization and conditions examinable.

The two sides of the divided consciousness are not equal. As Schutz makes clear and as even minimal attention to the actualities of our own functioning in the world makes clear (you can stop this moment in your reading and attend to the material properties of your reading: chair, paper, ink marks, your own bodily presence, etc.), there is no entry to the abstracted conceptual mode of working without passing through and making use of the concretely and immediately experienced. The symbolic structures which constitute the modes in which we act are necessarily material in transcending that materiality—the sounds we hear which we take up as speech, the scratches on the paper, the material organization which provides for how our consciousness can be thematized in this mode, as well as the social division of labor which sustains us in it. These are not merely essential as prerequisites; they are integral to the organization and existence of the abstracted conceptual mode. It is indeed part of how they are integral that they do not become thematic, that they remain horizontal. The other term of the bifurcated consciousness, which is located not merely in a subjectivity but in a subjectivity located in its body and located therefore in a definite and particular spatiotemporal existence, is irremediably in what Schutz describes rather ambiguously as the world of working. Beginning, then, from there locates the knower where knowledge must begin.

If we address the problem of the conditions as well as the perceived forms and organization of immediate experience, we should include in it the events as they actually happen or the ordinary material world which we and others encounter as what is happening to us, to them. When we examine these events, when we examine the actual material organization of our everyday experience, we find that there are many aspects of how these things are and come about of which we have very little, as sociologists, to say. We do not even know quite how to begin. We have a sense that the events which enter our experience originate somewhere in a human intention, but we are unable to track back to find it and to find out how it became and how it got from there to here. Take this room in which I work or that room in which you are reading and treat that as a problem. If we think about the conditions of our activity here, we could track back to how it is that there are chairs, table, walls, our clothing, our presence; how these places (yours and mine) are cleaned and maintained; etc. There are human activities, intentions, and relations which are not apparent as such in the actual material conditions of our work. The social organization of the setting is not wholly available to us in its appearance. What is here for us is the product of a social division of labor. If we heard in the things that we make use of—typewriter, paper, chair, table, walls—the voices of those who made them, we would hear the multitudinous voices of a whole society and beyond. Were it not for the time lapse involved, our own voices would be part of them. Locating our work as knowers in the first and fundamental term of the bifurcated consciousness also locates us in the standpoint of the working class, in the location from which Marx's political economy begins. Beginning from the standpoint of women does not follow in any direct way from beginning from the standpoint of labor, but once we have taken this other and momentous step, we can begin to take up the relation established by Marx. It becomes available to us in the mode in which it was originally conceived, namely as having its premises not in the conceptual, abstracted mode but in actual individuals, their work, their actual productive activities, and the material conditions produced by those activities which become their conditions.[65]

The Everyday World as Problematic

The critique of established sociological frameworks from the perspective of women's location leaves us with the problem of the structure of the sociological relation as it was described above. It does not, as such, serve to design for us a method of proceeding which offers an alternative to the concepts, relevances, and methods of a discourse which in its very use, organizes and shapes our work into its own forms and intentions regardless of what we mean to do. We must see this problem, I believe, in how our work returns to, is aimed at and repossessed by, knowers who are participants in the discourse or in other domains of the ruling apparatus, rather than knowers who are members of the society anywhere in it. Suppose then we began to devise a sociological enterprise not directed primarily towards the discourse and its knower, but capable of providing a sociology *for* women. We might attempt to develop *for* women analyses, descriptions, and understandings of their situation, of their everyday world, and of its determinations in the larger socioeconomic organization to which it is articulated. Then indeed we would be thinking about how to do a sociology relocating the sociological subject. Such a sociological enterprise presents an alternative conception of a science to that which depends upon a knower theoretically located in an Archimedian, i.e., purely formal space. It is a sociology whose knowers are members of the society and have positions in it outside that abstracted ruling apparatus—as an understanding of the bifurcating consciousness shows us everyone does—and who know the society from within their experience of it as an everyday world. Their experience locates for us the beginning of an inquiry. This is to constitute the everyday world as problematic, where the everyday world is taken to be various and differentiated matrices of experience—the place from within which the consciousness of the knower begins, the location of her null point.

Such a sociology would aim to make available to anyone a knowledge of the social organization and a determination of his or her directly experienced, everyday world. Its analyses would become part of our ordinary interpretations of experience and hence part of experience, just as our experience of the sun's sinking below the horizon has been transformed by our knowledge that the world turns and that our location in the world turns away from the sun—even though from where we are it seems to sink. The sociological knower, then, is not the sociologist as such. The work of the sociologist is to develop a sociology capable of explicating for members of the society the social organization of their experienced world, including in that experience the ways in which it passes beyond what is immediately and directly known, including also, therefore, the structure of a bifurcated consciousness.

Rather than explaining behavior, we begin from where people are in the world, explaining the social relations of the society of which we are part, explaining an organization which is not fully present in any one individual's everyday experience. Since the procedures, methods, and aims of present sociology give primacy to the concepts, relevances, and topics of the discourse, we cannot begin from within that frame. This would be to sustain the hegemony of the discourse over the actualities of the everyday experience of the world. It is precisely that relation that constitutes the break or fault disclosed by the women's movement.

An alternative is to turn this method on its head and to make the everyday world the locus of a sociological problematic. The everyday world is that world we experience directly. It is the world in which we are located physically and socially. Our experience arises in it as conditions, occasions, objects, possibilities, relevances, presences, and so on, organized in and by the practices and methods through which we supply and discover organization. It is necessarily local—because that is how *we* must be—and necessarily historical. Locating the sociological problematic in the everyday world does not mean confining the inquiry to the everyday world. Indeed, as we shall see, it is essential to this that the everyday world be seen as organized by social relations not observable within it. Thus, an inquiry confining itself to the everyday world of direct experience is not adequate to explicate its social organization.

One way in which the sociological discourse has maintained its hegemony over experience has been by insisting that we must begin with a conceptual apparatus or a theory drawn from the discipline if only because to embark on inquiry without such a conceptual framework exposes us to the wild incoherence of "history" or of the actualities of people's words. I am not suggesting, of course, that sociology can be done without knowing how to do it and that we can approach our work with a naïve consciousness. Indeed, I believe sociology to be rather more difficult than it has been made to seem. But the implication that the actualities of the everyday world are unformed and unorganized and that the sociologist cannot enter them without a conceptual framework to select, assemble, and order them is one that we can now understand in this special relation of a sociology constituted as part of a ruling apparatus vis-à-vis which the local and particular, the actualities of the world which is lived, are necessarily untamed, disordered, and incoherent. But we can begin from a different assumption when as premises we begin with the activities of actual individuals whose activity produces the social relations which they live.[66] Social phenomena are products of action and interpretation by actual women and men. Rational order itself, order itself, as ethnomethodologists have pointed out, is an accomplishment of members of society. The order, coherence, rationality, and sense of social situations and relations is an active work done prior to the presence and observational work of the sociologist. Further, her work itself is inseparable from such a social relation and in its preliminary phases must be constrained by the enterprise of explicating an organization of relations which is there prior to her inquiry and is to be discovered in its course.

Defining the everyday world as the locus of a sociological problematic is not the same as making it an object of study. A distinction must be made between the everyday world as problematic and as phenomenon. To aim at the everyday world as an object of study is to constitute it as a self-contained universe of inquiry. The effect of locating the knower in this way is to divorce the everyday world of experience from the larger social and economic relations which organize its distinctive character.

A Sociology for Women

Both Lefebvre and Kosik make the mistake of beginning with the abstracted conceptual mode and seek to grasp the everyday world as an object.[67] From this perspective its essential organization escapes. History, for example, is viewed as erupting into the everyday world[68] as if the two somehow existed alongside one another, largely independent except for occasional collisions. In constituting the everyday world as an object of sociological examination, we cut it off methodologically from the ways in which it is actually embedded in a socially organized context larger than may be directly known in that mode. Strategies such as Goffman's or Zimmerman and Pollner's constitute the everyday world as a phenomenon for investigation.[69] In so doing they serve to seal it off as a discrete phenomenon within the sociological universe. Goffman's dramaturgical metaphor does two kinds of work in this respect: one in providing a way of making features and processes of the everyday world visible as appearances; and the second (closely connected) in creating a set of categories (front and back stage, regions, settings, etc.) which organize a domain of inquiry to be treated as internally coherent and descriptively comprehensive. Though very different in approach, Zimmerman and Pollner's definition of the "occasioned corpus" also constitutes the everyday world as phenomenon. It is, in their approach, bounded by the constraint of observation and of knowledge arising in and as part of an "occasioned corpus." Thus, properties of organization and so on, conceived to be "in back of" the occasioned corpus, are treated as warrantably present for the observer only as they are accomplished in the present of her observation and become thereby features of the occasioned corpus. These and other strategies, focusing on the everyday world as phenomenon constitute it as an object of sociological inquiry and isolate it.

The concept of problematic is used to bring the sociologist and the sociological inquiry into a different relation to the experience of members of a society as knowers located in actual lived situations. It is used here to constitute the everyday world as that in which questions originate. The term *problematic* is ordinarily used to talk about matters at the level of concept or theory rather than at the level of experience and action (it should not, incidentally be confused with the concept of problem). As it is used here, we follow a procedure of going from a social actuality to develop a conceptual apparatus disclosing and explicating its properties. The problematic is property of the social organization of the everyday world. The concept of problematic explicates a property of the everyday world as a focus for sociological work. Constituting the social organization and determinations of the everyday world as a problematic is a method of guiding and focusing inquiry. The purpose and direction of inquiry is in part (and particularly at the outset of this approach to sociology) an explication or codification (to use Freire's term)[70] of a problematic that is implicit *in* the everyday world.

The concept of problematic is used here to direct attention to a *possible* set of questions which may not have been posed or a set of puzzles which do not yet exist in the form of puzzles but are "latent" in the actualities of the experienced world. The questions themselves, the inquiry, the puzzles, and perhaps the issues are the means of developing the problematic as an inquiry. What I have done in using this term, therefore, is to shift it out of its ordinary place within a scientific or philosophical discourse and treat it as a property of an actuality lived and practiced. This problematic is, I suggest, present in the everyday world as it is given to any of us to live. For the everyday world is neither transparent nor obvious. Fundamental to its organization for us in this form of society is that its inner determinations are not discoverable within it.

The everyday world, the world where people are located as they live, located bodily and in that organization of their known world as one that begins from their own location in it, is generated in its varieties by an organization of social relations which originate "elsewhere." It is like a dance in which the subject participates or in which she is placed. The "shapes" taken by the dance and the part she plays in it bring into being the dance as an actual organization of social relations through time. Whether she chooses to play a part or not, or the particular movements she elects in relation to the dance, its emerging and developing forms, are those that give shape to what she does. The dance, however, extends beyond the boundaries of her sight. She cannot from where she is recover its form or assess its character or movement. She picks it up as it moves its patterns into her scope of action, and she must be moved by or move with them. The conditions of our action and experience are organized by relations and processes outside them and beyond our power of control.

The everyday world is not fully understandable within its own scope. It is organized by social relations not fully apparent in it nor contained in it. This is the social organization of the sociological problematic in the actual work and practices of real individuals. Earlier forms of society do not have this double character. In simpler social forms, the character of the everyday world and its organization are fully visible. The ethnographic techniques of the anthropologist have depended upon this visibility.

You may perhaps have seen an ethnographic movie called *The Hunters*, which tells the story of the stalking and killing of a giraffe by a small group of Kalahari Bushmen. Though the movie provides a strongly male-oriented picture of the people—women are represented as waiting in the werf (camp) for the men to come home with the meat, and no indication is given of the substantial contribution women make to the food of the group—it illustrates a distinctive aspect of the social relations of production in this group. When the hunters have killed, the group brings the meat back to the camp and distributes it. All members of the group are present and part of the distribution. An old man passes it to small family groupings. Each little group takes its share, divides it further, and passes on a portion to other waiting groups of kinsfolk. The meat fans out through the camp, presumably channelled by degrees of relationship and types of obligation among kinsfolk. The origin of the meat is fully known. The territory which the hunters travelled is known to other members of the group. The path of meat from animal to pot to belly is made up of known persons standing in definite and known relations to one another as persons and performing tasks familiar and observable to anyone there. The determinations of social existence are fully present to the experience of its members and are coterminous with it.

The structures and transformation of the everyday world in our own form of society are not observable in the same way. The difference is more than a difference in size. It is only vaguely indicated in the notion of "complexity." There are important differences in the fundamental form of social organization. The problematic character of the everyday world is an essential property of this social form.

To exhibit one aspect of what I mean by the everyday world as problematic, I shall use the movie adaptation of Kurt Vonnegut's *Slaughterhouse Five*.[71] Vonnegut uses this problematic to display the senselessness of modern war. In the movie there is a sequence which leads up to the firebombing of Dresden. It is a straightforward sequence in contrast to the temporal discontinuities characteristic of much of the rest of the movie. There is a shot of the spires of Dresden in the morning mist and of people moving across a high bridge. Later we see the streets full of people marketing. We see children playing, some of them wearing the grotesque masks which are used in the movie to presage death. If you have read the book or know the history, you grasp these scenes in the shadow of what is to come. By the next morning most of the people will be dead. The temporal progression toward their doomsday is marked by a countdown printed as subtitles across the bottom of each scene as the day moves towards closure.

What Vonnegut does is to allow that sequence to stand juxtaposed to the next day, doomsmorning. As a whole the sequence makes no sense in terms of the everyday world. We cannot find how it was put together in what is available to us in the ordinary business which those people carried on the day before. Nothing that they did then motivated, caused, or otherwise brought about the next morning's scene of blackened and smoking ruins. Confining the sequence to the everyday world constitutes its senselessness. If Vonnegut had wanted to recover its "rationality," he would have done what so many British war movies do (you can see them on the late or late-late shows on TV)—given us the scene of the bombers taking off at dusk from somewhere in England. He would have shown the underground strategic bomber command headquarters. We would have been shown the organizational process connecting the two moments, of life and of death, in the everyday world.

This way in which events occur, their odd property of senselessness if our knowledge of them is confined to the everyday world, is not so very extraordinary. It is not out of this world. On the contrary, such events are part of a continual process transforming the environment of our lives, transforming our lives; notice next time, in this context, that hole in the ground so soon to become a highrise apartment, a gymnasium. Events occurring in this way are happening around us all the time. If we care to, we take them for granted. They are normal features of our world. If we cease to take them for granted, if we strip away everything that we imagine we know of how they come about (and ordinarily that is very little), if we examine them as they happen within the everyday world, they become fundamentally mysterious. If you allow them to stand there as Vonnegut does, they do not make sense within the domain of the everyday world. This is what I mean by a problematic *implicit* in the social organization of the everyday world.

These are events creating changes in or intruding on people's lives. The changes do not arise out of a logic of organization which is part of the local setting in which they occur. People who have lived for years in communities in the interior of British Columbia, in telling their lives and experiences, show us a typical layering sequence of change—the opening of the mine, the coming of the railroad, the market gardening enterprises established by local Indians to feed the miners, the closing of the mine, the decline of market gardening, the decline of the railroad, the dependence of the native people on the Indian Affairs Department, the building of a hydro plant, a brief period of employment for native peoples while it is being built, the refurbishing of the railroad, the development of a small tourist trade, the transformation of the settlement into a retirement village for hydro engineers. These changes do not arise from a logic within the local setting. They are like the flows of lava from a volcano, each transforming the landscape in radical ways, each laying over its predecessors, but unconnected with them other than by succession. The logic of transformation is elsewhere.

The sample problem is implicit in the social organization of present relations in any such actual community, as well as in the events which become its history. The present structure of local social relations is orga-

A Sociology for Women

nized by social relations external to it. Noticeable in the community I am thinking of is a lack of internal coherence in relations, a lack of working relations among members of the community, within the community as such. It is stratified ethnically by the Indian reservation and the employment opportunities for native people on the one hand and by the retirement homes of professionals from the nearby hydro plant on the other. The stratification is of a special and contemporary kind, the disconnected relations of people who live alongside one another in the same locality, but whose social relations are organized by social relations external to the local area and not appearing directly in it. This is the problematic of the everyday world.

The problematic can be characterized in a preliminary way as an abstraction of organization from the everyday world and the location of organizing processes in externally structured and differentiated relations. We return, indeed, to the same processes we identified in the organizational processes differentiating the local from the abstracted conceptual modes of consciousness, though we are no longer focusing solely on the apparatus of ruling. We are addressing a more general property of the social relations of capitalism and, specifically, of corporate or monopoly capitalism, for it is in capitalism that the socially organized forms, in and through which individuals depend upon one another, become externalized as a differentiated system of relations. In drawing a contrast between feudal and capitalist forms of social relation, Marx analyzes the capitalist form as follows:

> So far from constituting the removal of a 'state of dependence,' these external relationships represent its disintegration into a general form, or better, they are the elaboration of the general *basis* of personal states of dependence. Here too individuals come into relation with one another only in a determined role. These material states of dependence, as opposed to the personal states, are also characterized by the fact that *individuals are now controlled only by abstractions,* whereas earlier they depended on one another. The material state of dependence is no more than autonomous social relationships opposed to apparently independent individuals.[72]

Marx locates the organization of individual relations in a system of "autonomous social relations." These are *material* states of dependence—those which Marx analyzes more fully in his development of the concept of commodity in *Capital*.[73] They are social relations which appear in relations of market exchange as relations between things—the products of labor socially organized as commodities. Marx's analysis, both in this passage from the *Grundrisse* and in *Capital*, locates the determination of people's lives beyond and outside the places where they confront one another directly in the same local settings. Their relations in the local setting are organized elsewhere. The conditions of their action and experience are organized by relations external to the everyday world and beyond the power of individuals to control.

In the discussion so far, I have talked as if what is being described is merely a leaching out, a "depletion" by an extractive process, which produces an essential disorganization of the relations of the everyday world. I would emphasize, however, that this must, rather, be understood as a particular form of social organization and that the local and directly known world is extensively and increasingly penetrated by these processes of material and social organization. That organization may be *experienced* as disorganization, incoherence, lack of sense, but it *is* organization in that the processes of social relations at the abstracted level can be viewed as generating the organization of the everyday world. The relations among men hanging around on Tally's corner[74] and the relations of women to those men can be seen as organized by the development of capitalism to the level at which work for laborers is strictly casual and at which a segregated labor force organizes an urban pool of undifferentiated workers who are on call, and by the way in which the state, through its welfare agencies, regulates the relations between women and men, and women, men, and children.

The episodic character of women's lives—the uprooting, for example, of upper- and middle-class women from localities in which their relations have been formed, to follow their husband's careers (of which Seidenburg has written)—corresponds to an organization of corporate systems of careers and advancement at the level of managerial personnel. The wives of construction workers or of mineworkers who confront the exigencies of the primary resource market must be prepared to pack up and move on, resettling the children and the household in the next place where there is employment.

The structures of daily life and activity organized by this form of society are peculiarly desultory and bounded temporally to the occasion. Sex is detached from conception and birth—as in Didion's novel of disintegration and socially organized incoherence, where the protagonist may not even come to rest in the continuity and purpose of her own body in pregnancy, but is forced to abort. In the same book we see how activity arises out of the instrument, the tool, the equipment, so that the thing ceases to be a means to get things done but becomes a motive for what it has the capacity to do. So the gun becomes a motive for shooting; the automobile and freeway a motive for driving; the camera a motive for the taking of a picture. Ideological forms and images derived from the media generate forms of action aimed at their realization and unarticulated to a

A Sociology for Women

practical organization of working relations among people. The life world disintegrates into a collection of episodes. An organizing "logic" is located elsewhere than in an individual's own activity and experience.

The organization of social life as occasions or episodes built into some styles of contemporary sociological theory (Harré and Second, for example) and even of the self as a discontinuous presentation of appearances is not universal nor to be taken for granted. What has been left unexamined (and is indeed unexaminable within the method which focuses upon the everyday world as phenomenon) is the social organization which generates these actual properties of experience observed and named (for example) by Goffman.[75] The intermittances of relations, the structuring of regions into front and back, the lack of biographical anchorage of the self in present witnesses to the individual past—these and other features so aptly analyzed by the dramaturgical metaphor are socially organized prior to and beyond the processes which it makes observable.

Locating the subject in one's everyday world means locating oneself in one's bodily and material existence. The everyday world is not an abstracted formal "setting" transposed by the sociologist's conceptual work to an abstracted formal existence. It is an actual material setting, an actual local and particular place in the world. Its formal and generalized properties are generated as such by the social organization and the material forms produced to accomplish its formal and generalizable properties. The equivalence of actual settings which provides for their being seen readily as conceptually substitutable (the public toilets, the restaurants, the motels, etc.) is itself a product of social and material organization accomplishing the substitutability of different actual local and particular places. The social organization of the abstracted conceptual practices of ruling is provided for by a determinate material organization, a standardization of environments both as a condition of the work and as the application of technologies of various kinds to the material and social world as a means to transform it towards forms corresponding to the categories and concepts of the organizing processes of the ruling apparatus.

Conclusion

In the course of this inquiry the social relation now explicated as the problematic of the everyday world has been considered under different aspects. At the outset, in posing the starting point of this inquiry, I identified a "line of fault" in the social consciousness separating women's experience from the social forms of thought available in which to express it and make it actionable. The disjuncture arises because women have been excluded from the making of ideological forms produced as part of the apparatus by which this form of society is ruled. Patriarchy is a metaphor of this characteristic relation of power among women and men, in which direct and personal relations are organized and determined by an impersonal apparatus. At this stage in examining these social relations, we can define the standpoint of women only in negation to the ideological forms from which their experience as subjects has been excluded.

In exploring the distinctive ways in which sociology excludes the concerns and perspectives of women, we can observe women's standpoint as a determinate position from which society may be known. The concepts and methods of sociology as a discourse constitute women as object rather than subject. Subject is then seen, not as situated on an Archimedian point outside the world, but as a position within the ruling apparatus. The social relations explicated as the problematic here came into view in a new form. Sociology was seen as part of a differentiated practice of organizing a society constituted in an abstracted conceptual mode detached from the actual local and particular places in which individuals necessarily exist (and in which social relations themselves are necessarily grounded). Sociology as an ideological mode provides means of thinking social relations and social action into this abstracted conceptual mode. Locating ourselves as subjects in this relation places our knowledge of society and social relations outside experience and cuts us off from the actual grounding of our world.

The ideological relation formed by sociology also locates ourselves as subjects outside our experience and outside the local and particular places in which our knowing necessarily originates. The practices mediating and accomplishing the differentiation of the abstracted conceptual mode as a mode of action from the local and particular places of our bodily existence are not visible from within it. But since women's work has been characteristically that which directly mediates at the personal and individual level, the relation between women's two standpoints brings this relation into view.

My final step, then, has been to propose a method of relocating the sociological subject as actual individuals located in an everyday world. The conception of an everyday world as a sociological problematic presents a basis for a sociology which, like Marx and Engels's conception of the materialist method, begins not within the discourse but in the actual daily social relations between individuals. The problematic explicates, as the basis of inquiry, an actual socially organized relation between the everyday world of experience and the social relations of capitalism. The conceptualization of the problematic is intended to "hold" a relation between the sociological subject and a (possible) sociology (a systematic knowledge of the social relations of her society) in which the latter may become a means

A Sociology for Women

to disclose to the former the social relations determining her everyday world. The standpoint of women becomes now defined fully in such a way that we see that it has been a "transformer" rather than a final position. It has served to direct the inquiry and at each point has made us restless with solutions which fail to meet the criteria it imposes. In arriving at the formulation of the everyday world as problematic, we find a sociological subject who may be anyone, but who is always located just as she or he *is* actually located in a particular material setting.

The constitution of the problematic of the everyday world establishes something like a Copernican shift in sociology. The significance of Copernican innovations was less that the sun rather than the earth was declared to be the center of the solar system than that the position of the observer was no longer fixed and could no longer be disattended in interpreting observations. She had no longer a fixed, central position but had to be seen as located in a position itself in motion in relation to what she observed. Hence, the observed movements of the planets could no longer be seen simply as their movements, but had to be understood as movements seen from a moving position. The effect of locating the knower in the everyday world of experience pulls what we know as the "microsociological" level of the everyday world and the "macrosociological" level, which we make observable as "power elites," "formal organization," "stratification," and the "state," into a determinate relation. From a standpoint within the ruling apparatus, the actual organization of these relations remains unexaminable and disorganized to thought by the conceptual apparatus which constitutes its observability. The pieces of a world—"power elites," "formal organization," "stratification," "social class," the "state"—are thus littered all over a sociological landscape. Locating the knower in the everyday world and constituting our inquiry in terms of the problematic arising from how it is actually organized in a social process enable us to see the "micro" and "macro" sociological levels in a determinate relation—though it is one which scarcely makes sense any more in these terms. The actual character of the relation and how our worlds are determined by processes which do not appear fully in them is a matter for investigation and inquiry, not for speculation. Making the everyday world our problematic instructs us to look for the "inner" organization generating its ordinary features, its orders and disorders, its contingencies and conditions, and to look for that inner organization in the externalized and abstracted relations of economic processes and of the ruling apparatus in general. Our inquiry then can begin from the position of women, of women in whatever relation determines their experience as it is. It can begin from the position of any member of the society, explicating the problematic of her/his experience as a sociological problematic. The implications of a sociology for women in contemporary corporate capitalist society poses again, though with a different grounding, the problematic originally formulated by Marx and Engels: "Individuals always started, and always start, from themselves. Their relations are the relations of real life. How does it happen that their relations assume an independent existence over against them? And that the forces of their own life overpower them?"[76]

NOTES

I am very much indebted to Lynda Yantz, who helped type and assemble the first draft, and to Donna McClement for her exceptional skill and her work in the preparation and typing of both the first and final drafts.

1 Simone de Beauvoir, *The Second Sex* (New York, 1961); Betty Friedan, *The Feminine Mystique* (New York, 1963); Kate Millett, *Sexual Politics* (New York, 1971).
2 Jessie Bernard, *Academic Women* (New York, 1964).
3 Pauline Bart, "Sexism in Social Science: From the Iron Cage to the Gilded Cage—The Perils of Pauline," *Journal of Marriage and the Family* 33 (November 1971): 742.
4 Doris Lessing, "The Old Chief Msh Langa," in *The Black Madonna*, (St. Albans, Herts, 1966), pp. 83–106.
5 Sheila Rowbotham, *Woman's Consciousness, Man's World* (London, 1973), p. 41.
6 De Beauvoir, *The Second Sex*, p. xv.
7 Media Women's Association, comp., and Ethel Strainchamps, ed., *Rooms with No View: A Woman's Guide to the Man's World of the Media* (New York, 1974).
8 Gerda Lerner, "New Approaches to the Study of Women in American History," and "Placing Women in History," in *Liberating Women's History*, ed. Bernice A. Carroll (Urbana, 1976); Dorothy E. Smith, "Some Implications for a Sociology for Women," in *Woman in a Man-Made World*, 2nd ed., ed. Nona Glazer and Helen Y. Waehrer (New York, 1976).
9 Mary Daly, *Beyond God the Father: Towards a Philosophy of Women's Liberation* (Boston, 1973); Rosemary R. Ruether, *Religion and Sexism: Images of Women in the Jewish and Christian Traditions* (New York, 1974).
10 See, among others, Jessie Bernard, "My Four Revolutions: An Autobiographical History of the ASA," in *Changing Women in a Changing Society*, ed. Joan Huber (Chicago, 1973); Naomi Weisstein, "Psychology Constructs the Female, or the Fantasy Life of the Male Psychologist," in *The Roles Women Play*, ed. Michele Hoffnug Garskof (Belmont, Calif., 1971); Sandra L. Bem and Daryl J. Bem, "Training the Woman to Know Her Place: The Power of Nonconscious Ideology," in Garskof, *The Roles Women Play*; Dorothy E.

Smith, "Women's Perspective as a Radical Critique of Sociology," *Sociological Inquiry* 4 (1974): 7–13; Meredith Kimball, "Women, Sex Role Stereotypes, and Mental Health: Catch 22," in *Women Look at Psychiatry*, ed. Dorothy E. Smith and Sara J. David (Vancouver, 1975); Ann Oakley, *The Sociology of Housework* (London, 1975).

11 Judy Chicago, *Through the Flower* (New York, 1975); Lucy R. Lippard, *From the Center: Feminist Essays on Women's Art* (New York, 1973).

12 Boston Women's Health Book Collective, *Our Bodies, Ourselves* (New York, 1973); and others.

13 Barbara Ehrenreich and Diedre English, "Complaints and Disorders: The Sexual Politics of Sickness," *Glass Mountain Pamphlet*, no. 2 (New York, 1973); idem, "Witches, Midwives, and Nurses," *Glass Mountain Pamphlet* no. 1 (New York, 1973); Ann Oakley, "Wise Woman and Medicine Man: Changes in the Management of Childbirth," in *The Rights and Wrongs of Women*, ed. Juliet Mitchell and Ann Oakley (Harmondsworth, Middlesex, 1976); Jean Donnison, *Midwives and Medical Men: A History of Interprofessional Rivalries and Women's Rights* (London, 1977).

14 Phyllis Chesler, *Women and Madness* (New York, 1972); Pauline Bart, "Sexism in Social Science," pp. 734–45; Dorothy E. Smith, "Women and Psychiatry," in Smith and David, *Women Look at Psychiatry*.

15 Sara J. David, "Becoming a Non-Sexist Therapist," in Smith and David, *Women Look at Psychiatry*.

16 Karl Marx and Frederick Engels, *The German Ideology* pt. 1 (New York, 1970).

17 Karl Mannheim, *Ideology and Utopia* (New York, 1965).

18 Marx and Engels, *The German Ideology*, pt. 1.

19 Rowbotham, *Woman's Consciousness, Man's World*, p. 33.

20 Mary Ellman, *Thinking about Women* (New York, 1968).

21 Chicago, *Through the Flower*.

22 Adrienne Rich, *Poems: Selected and New, 1950–1974* (New York, 1975); Suzanne Juhasz, *Naked and Fiery Forms: Modern American Poetry by Women, A New Tradition* (New York, 1976).

23 Dorothy Richardson, *Pilgrimage* (New York, 1976).

24 Chicago, *Through the Flower*, pp. 79–80.

25 Lippard, *From the Center*.

26 Juhasz, *Naked and Fiery Forms*, p. 205. Emphasis mine.

27 Lerner, "New Approaches to the Study of Women"; Smith, "Some Implications for a Sociology for Women."

28 Michel Foucault, *The Archaelogy of Knowledge* (London, 1974).

29 Bernard, "My Four Revolutions."

30 Oakley, *The Sociology of Housework*, p. 4.

31 Thelma McCormack, "Towards a Non-Sexist Perspective on Social and Political Change," in *Another Voice: Feminist Perspectives on Social Life and Social Sciences*, ed. Marcia Millman and Rosabeth Moss Kanter (Garden City, N.Y., 1975).

32 Thomas J. Scheff, *Being Mentally Ill: A Sociological Theory* (Chicago, 1962);

R. D. Laing, *The Divided Self: A Study of Sanity and Madness* (Chicago, 1960).

33 Aaron V. Cicourel, *The Social Organization of Juvenile Justice* (New York, 1968); Dorothy E. Smith, "The Statistics on Mental Illness: What They Will Not Tell Us and Why," in Smith and David, *Women Look at Psychiatry*.

34 Rae Carlson, "Understanding Women: Implications for Personality Theory and Research," *Journal of Social Issues* 28, no. 2 (1972): pp. 17–32.

35 Bernard, "My Four Revolutions," p. 23.

36 Talcott Parsons, *The Structure of Social Action*, vol. 1 (New York, 1968); Romano Harré and Paul F. Secord, *The Explanation of Social Behavior* (Oxford, 1972).

37 Alfred Schutz, *Collected Papers*, 1 (The Hague, 1962): 228.

38 Arlie Russell Hochschild, "The Sociology of Feeling and Emotion: Selected Possibilities," in Millman and Kanter, *Another Voice: Feminist Perspectives*.

39 Max Weber, *The Theory of Social and Economic Organization* (New York, 1964), p. 6.

40 Joyce Carol Oates, *Them* (New York, 1970).

41 Joan Didion, *Play It As It Lays* (New York, 1971).

42 Huw Beynon, *Working for Ford* (Harmondsworth, Middlesex, 1973).

43 Oakley, *Sociology of Housework*, p. 4.

44 Meissner et al., "No Exit for Wives: Sexual Division of Labor and the Cumulation of Household Demands," *Canadian Review of Sociology and Anthropology* 12 (1975); 424–39.

45 Wally Seccombe, "The Housewife and Her Labour under Capitalism" *New Left Review*, no. 83, January–February 1974, pp. 3–24, also published as a pamphlet with a postscript by the author (London: IMG Publications, n.d.); Jean Gardiner, "The Role of Domestic Labour," *New Left Review*, no. 89, February, 1975, pp. 47–58; Marlene Dixon, "Women's Liberation: Opening Chapter Two," *Canadian Dimension* 10 (June 1975): 56–68; Margaret Coulson, Branka Magas, and Hilary Wainwright, "The Housewife and Her Labour under Capitalism: A Critique," *New Left Review*, no. 89, January–February 1975, pp. 59–71.

46 Amitai Etzioni, *The Active Society: A Theory of Societal and Political Process* (New York, 1968).

47 McCormack, "Towards a Non-Sexist Perspective."

48 Bernard, "My Four Revolutions."

49 Schutz, *Collected Papers*, 1: 222–23.

50 Ibid., p. 249.

51 Dorothy E. Smith, "The Intersubjective Structuring of Time" forthcoming in *Analytic Sociology*, 1979.

52 Catherine Russell, article in *Kinesis* (Vancouver) 6 (February 1977): 5.

53 Roy Turner, "Introduction," in *Ethnomethodology*, ed. Roy Turner (Harmondsworth, Middlesex, 1974).

54 De Beauvoir, *The Second Sex*, p. xvii–xiv.

55 Robert Bierstedt, "Sociology and General Education," in *Sociology and Contemporary Education*, ed. Charles H. Page (New York, 1966), p.

56 Weber, *Theory of Social and Economic Organization.*
57 Adolphe A. Berle and Gardiner C. Means, *The Modern Corporation and Private Property* (New York, 1968).
58 Albert Sloan, *My Years with General Motors* (New York, 1964); Alfred D. Chandler, Jr., *Strategy and Structure: Chapters in the History of American Industrial Enterprise* (New York, 1966).
59 Mannheim, *Ideology and Utopia.*
60 Schutz, *Collected Papers.*
61 Georg Wilhelm Friedrich Hegel, *The Phenomenology of Mind,* trans. A. V. Miller (Oxford, 1977).
62 Ggyörgy Lukács, *History and Class Conciousness* (London, 1971).
63 Alfred Schutz, *Reflections on the Problem of Relevance,* ed. Richard Zaner (New Haven, 1970), p. 11.
64 Rosabeth Moss Kantor, *Men and Women in Corporations* (New York, 1977).
65 Marx and Engels, *The German Ideology.*
66 Ibid.
67 Henri Lefebvre, *Everyday Life in the Modern World* (London, 1971); Karel Kosik, *Dialectics of the Concrete: A Study on Problems of Man and World,* Boston Studies in the Philosophy of Science, vol. 52 (Dordrecht, Holland, 1976).
68 Kosik, *Dialectics of the Concrete,* pp. 42–56.
69 Erving Goffman, *The Presentation of Self in Everyday Life* (New York, 1959); Don H. Zimmerman and Melvin Pollner, "The Everyday World as a Phenomenon," in *Understanding Everyday Life: Towards the Reconstruction of Sociological Knowledge,* ed. Jack Douglas (London, 1971).
70 Paulo Freire, *Cultural Action for Freedom* (Harmondsworth, Middlesex, 1972).
71 Kurt Vonnegut, *Slaughterhouse Five, or The Children's Crusade: A Duty-Dance with Death* (New York, 1969).
72 Karl Marx, *Grundrisse: Foundations of the Critique of Political Economy,* trans. Martin Nicolaus (Harmondsworth, Middlesex, 1973), p. 73. Second emphasis mine.
73 Karl Marx, *Capital: A Critical Analysis of Capitalistic Production,* 1 (Moscow, 1954): 71–83.
74 Elliot Liebow, *Tally's Corner: A Study of Negro Streetcorner Men,* with a foreword by Hylan Lewis (Boston, 1976).
75 Goffman, *The Presentation of Self.*
76 Karl Marx and Frederick Engels, *Feuerbach: Opposition of the Materialist and Idealist Outlooks* (London, 1973), p. 90.

KATHRYN PYNE PARSONS

Moral Revolution

Part I: Introduction

■ Has a covert bias been introduced into our world view by the near exclusion of women from the domain of intellectual pursuits?
Philosophers and scientists both have argued long and hard that it is a virtue of science that the sex, race, ethnic background, or creed of the investigator is irrelevant to scientific results, provided only that scientific method is practiced correctly. They have taken that to be one consequence of the *objectivity* of science, and some have even felt that the remedy for bias is to become *more* scientific. Although philosophers and scientists generally conclude that there is no bias, the question somehow keeps arising. One reason it cannot be laid to rest is that detecting bias is itself a philosophic or scientific enterprise, and the methods used in the detection may themselves be questioned as to bias.
When I was a graduate student in the early 1960s at Stanford, those of us in the philosophy of science course had to write a paper on the question, Does the scientist *qua* scientist make value judgments? Our discussions turned on whether, in the normal course of talking or writing about scientific theories and lab results, the scientist made assertions which contained value terms, and if not, whether the assertions made logically *entailed* statements containing value terms. We concluded that the scientist did have to make value judgments about simplicity, conformity to scientific standards of good investigation, and so on; and that he or she did have to evaluate results. But *qua* scientist he or she did not make *moral* value judgements. We felt a scientist who did that, wasn't talking *qua* scientist, but as an ordinary human being.
We reached these comforting conclusions by noticing that it was part of the scientific method that the laws and assertions of science were fac-

Copyright © 1978 by Kathryn Pyne Parsons.

tual and that the terms described things in the world which could be factually determined. The presupposition was that factual statements and factually determinable terms are not evaluative. Another presupposition was that factual statements do not *entail* value statements. If we look for bias only among the assertions which the scientist makes *qua* scientist, and if we make these presuppositions, then there is precious little science or philosophy which does have bias.

The presuppositions have been challenged, or rather, the philosophy of language and logic on which they rest has been challenged. To name only one sort of challenge, some philosophers have insisted that criteria for judging whether something has a certain characteristic may be entirely factual, and yet the characteristic be evaluative. Phillipa Foot argued this for the evaluative term *rude*.[1] We might give a similar argument for the evaluative term *IQ*. This method claims that there are evaluative consequences of networks of factual concepts, and some of the evaluative consequences may be moral.

Even if we accept this view in language and logic, still there will be precious few sciences which show this sort of bias. In fact, I should say, we would be overlooking some of the most important sorts of bias, including sex bias, if we look through the lens of that method. So before talking about bias introduced via the "intellectual pursuits," let's talk a little about varieties of bias—via their remedies. Then we can turn to asking about what sorts of methods might work for revealing bias.

Remedies for Bias

Sometimes bias in intellectual work has taken the form of doing "bad science," or "bad philosophy." In principle, the work is biased because of the biases of the investigators using the theory. Let me give an example from Judith Jarvis Thomson's paper, "A Defense of Abortion,"[2] which I'll consider in some detail in Part II below. In this paper, she says that most philosophical discussions of abortion have taken the point of view of a third party (lawgiver, abortionist, interested onlooker) and not the point of view of the pregnant woman. She argues that the moral decision from the point of view of the pregnant woman is quite different and that we can't generalize from the third-party point of view to hers. This is because something like considerations of self-defense may enter for the pregnant woman when they don't enter for an outsider. This criticism Judith Thomson raises shows bias in the *application* of the philosophical theory she is working with. It doesn't correct the philosophical theory itself. Her criticism shows that other papers on abortion have been biased *in the use of the theory*. The bias would be corrected by reforming the way the theory is applied.

Some criticisms of bias in the use of a theory show that fairly basic assumptions of the theory may need to be corrected to do "good science" with it. Let's take an example from sociology. Arlene Daniels reports on a paper by Joan Acker:

> [Joan Acker] points out that stratification literature—whether written by functionalists, Marxists, or others—contains assumptions about the social position of women that are quite inadequate. The first assumption is that the family is the unit in the stratification system. From this view, a number of other assumptions are derived, such as that the social position of a family is determined by the male head of household or that the status of females living in families is determined by the males to whom they are attached. But these assumptions do not accurately reflect the actual state of relationships for large segments of the population. There are many females and female heads of households who are not attached to males. Why should such persons be ignored or placed in some residual category indicating their irrelevance to any major analysis of the stratification system? No male stratification theorists have previously questioned the usefulness of a world view that excludes the conditions of so much of the population from consideration. But it has been convenient to assume that females have no relevant role in stratification processes independent of their ties to men.[3]

In this passage, Arlene Daniels isn't suggesting that the functionalist or Marxist theories have to be thrown out because they are sexist. She is saying that they contain inadequate assumptions about the social position of women, and that those assumptions need to be corrected by reforming the theory.

There is a more radical kind of bias that may infect a theory, a kind which can't be corrected by reforming the application of the theory or a few of its assumptions. To reform this kind of bias, we need a scientific revolution in which the old theory is scrapped and a new theory introduced. Let me give another example from sociology. In *Another Voice*, Lyn Lofland reviewed urban sociology. She says:

> ... women in that portion of the literature of urban sociology here under review are mostly and simply, just there. They are part of the locale or neighborhood or area—described like other important aspects of the setting such as income, ecology, or demography—but largely irrelevant to the analytic *action*. ... To the degree that urban researchers have taken seriously (and of course many have not) the Blumerian injunction to "look upon human group life as chiefly a vast interpretive process in which people, singly and collectively, *guide themselves* by *defining* the objects, events and situations they encounter," they have done so primarily for the male participants in the human group life. The female participants are "just there."[4]

Lyn Lofland feels a radical change in urban sociology is necessary to correct this bias and that no mere reform will do. She says: . . . the problems which lead to the portrayal of women as 'only there' are among the central conceptual, focal, and methodological difficulties of urban sociology itself."[5] She suggests that to remedy this bias, completely new models, concepts, and variables would have to be developed out of studies which gave proper investigation to women; the resulting theory, she feels, would very likely differ in a radical way from the one currently used by many urban sociologists. Such a radical change in theory is a *scientific revolution*.

Since the publication of Thomas Kuhn's *Structure of Scientific Revolutions* in 1962, a good deal of research has been done on scientific revolutions.[6] Charles Darwin's evolutionary theory constituted a scientific revolution of very great magnitude, since it brought with it a revolution in patterns of thinking in philosophy of science and many other sciences in addition to biology. Lavoisier's revolution, which transformed alchemy to chemistry, was important but of smaller magnitude. The Copernican revolution in astronomy and the Newtonian in physics were also far-reaching.

The bias which Lyn Lofland found in urban sociology has ancient roots. In this paper, as a philosopher, I shall be investigating a bias of the third sort in contemporary American moral philosophy. A main bias in moral philosophy for two millenia has been the bias which Lyn Lofland points out in urban sociology: the moral-social world has been taken to be the world as men know it. A meaningful life (or a "good life") has been a life seen from the perspective of males and open only to males—and in fact, only to higher-class white adult males, so that the bias is classist and racist and agist as well as sexist. I believe a moral, social, and philosophical revolution is necessary to change it.

Revolutions of Various Sorts

The method my graduate school philosophy class used to find bias just won't do to reveal bias that requires a revolutionary change of theory. What method will do? Rather than name or describe a method, let me give a persuasive example, that of Darwinian evolutionary theory.

In 1859, Charles Darwin's *Origin of Species* was published. The model (or metaphor) which implicitly underlay this theory was that of nature as a self-regulating machine. This model embodies a pattern of thinking quite different from that which underlay scientific and social thinking in the earlier parts of the modern era: the model of the universe as a great clockwork designed by God. Howard Gruber remarks:

> . . . before the 18th century, European inventors interested in automatic machines designed devices that followed rigid clockwork patterns. In the

18th century, there was a marked increase in the development of self-regulating machines (float regulators, temperature regulators, centrifugal governors, etc.), designed to make corrections for external disturbances so that the machine can maintain some desired state. It was during the same period that the concept of society as a self-regulating system became prominent in the work of Adam Smith and others, as against the more static idea of rigid, centralized control which dominated earlier social theories. Both the technological innovations and the new kind of social theory were essential features of the industrial revolution. They cannot be said to have caused it or to have caused each other: together with a host of real social and economic changes, they *were* the revolution. But it took almost another century before the same conception of a self-regulating system was powerfully reflected in biological theory.[7]

The pattern of thinking was embodied in Darwin's concept of *natural selection*. In fact, Darwin came to the insight which underlay the concept through reading economist Malthus—as did the codiscoverer of the theory Alfred Russel Wallace. The concept of natural selection eliminates the explanation that God designed the great clockwork that is nature by using utterly different principles of explanation, although it of course leaves it open that God might have had the smaller job of designing the first organism, or perhaps only the chemical elements.

The pattern of thinking embodied in the Darwinian theory yields value consequences of that theory. It supports classical (capitalist) economics, and it supports the social, political, and moral theories associated with that economic theory. By this I don't mean that the Darwinian theory logically entails other theories. Not at all. But it isn't merely a psychological connection either—that we human beings tend to think along the same lines in all our theories, whenever possible. Rather, it is a value consequence arising from certain basic principles in science. Scientists are supposed to select theories according to the principle of simplicity of explanation, for example. One factor in simplicity is that the same model of thinking is embodied in a new theory as is used in a number of other established theories. This means that the model of thinking is *more widely confirmed*. Using the model in something as fundamentally important as Darwinian theory became thus lent confirmation to those other theories which use the model to describe the natural or the human world. The same is true of the view of living organism and nature which is made explicit in the Darwinian concept of natural selection. That coheres with the concept of the marketplace filled with economic agents in classical economics, and to a certain degree with our present view of the law and legal agents and the moral law and moral agents under the moral philosophy, I'll be examining in the body of this paper.[8]

Besides giving scientific support to these economic and social-political theories through confirming the model of thinking and the model of environment and agent, the Darwinian theory also gave scientific support to theories which presuppose *materialism*. Darwinian theory explains the evolution of man in the same way that it explains the evolution of any other living thing—in terms of biological, not spiritual, evolution. We need no soul or spirit to explain human beings, any more than we need a God whose eye is on the sparrow. This aspect of Darwinian theory historically had the effect of discrediting social and biological theories like William Whewell's, which relied on the spiritual or vital principles in their explanations. It thus removed support for Christian sorts of religions, and it led to the philosophic and scientific theories based on materialism. Again, this is not an entailment but a connection through scientific principles of confirmation and simplicity.

These are value consequences. To establish them as a bias would mean taking a standpoint in a competing tradition. For example, the empiricist philosophers whose tradition rode to triumph after the victory of Darwinian theory were able to argue that previous philosophers of science, and many scientists themselves, showed bias in supporting religious superstitions by using "metaphysical principles" like those of vital forces, or souls, or minds which were not scientifically observable (in accord, of course, with materialist principles of observation in their own science). Fundamentalist Christians today argue in the other direction, that Darwinian theory is biased and that the Supreme Court is acting out of biased tradition in forcing that theory to be taught in the public schools. This is a foundation of patterns of thought, of models of man, society, and nature, of basic principles like materialism. When this foundation is embedded in a social system, it constitutes a world view. The foundation associated with Darwinian theory has, in fact, constituted a part of our *official* world view. In what follows, I shall examine the moral philosophy that is associated with that world view. That tradition in moral philosophy also has value consequences—much the same, in fact, as the value consequences of Darwinian theory. To show that this constitutes a bias, I'll introduce a competing "tradition," one based on a women's liberation abortion service called Jane. I'll also use that competing tradition to show another sort of value consequence of the tradition in moral philosophy—that of concealing data. Let me illustrate what I mean through the example of Darwinian evolutionary theory.

Concealing Data

A characteristic of most pre-Darwinian biological theories was that species were construed as *ideal Types*.[9] The philosophical view underlying this was first expressed by Plato when he set out the principles of his science about twenty-five hundred years ago: what is real are the Forms, and they are perfect types, or patterns, which imperfect things here on earth participate in (or resemble). William Whewell was the most influential philosopher of science in England in the pre-Darwinian period, and his was a variety of Platonism, an intelligent variety ably worked into the basis of modern science. The "ideal Type" view is clearly supportive of a God-designed universe, with Types given reality as ideas God embodies in the world.

According to such a Type view, variations in individuals are mere imperfections. The scientist seeks the Type and ignores these irregular differences. In an evolutionary theory based on these Types, the problem of explaining development of new species is overwhelming, and there do not seem to be satisfactory solutions. Are we to say that individuals themselves change Type (as Lamarck did: the giraffe stretches its neck to reach high leaves and passes the longer neck to offspring)? Or are we to say that an individual of one Type gives birth to an offspring of another? Darwin succeeded in solving the evolutionary problem by cutting the Gordian knot—or rather, by cutting off from the tradition which made the problem a Gordian knot and which concealed data relevant to solving the problem:

> Darwin's revolution lay in turning his attention away from the type of the species and concentrating on the actual individuals that made it up. Rather than regarding the variation between individuals as obscuring the essential difference between species, he took the actual variation between individuals to be the proper object of study. Variation became the thing-in-itself. Instead of regarding individual variation and differences between species as ontogenetically distinct and opposed to each other, he took them to be directly related causally. *Darwin's revolutionary theory was that the differences between organisms within a species are converted to the differences between species in space and time.* Thus the differences between species are already latent within them, and all that is required is a motive force for the conversion of the variation. That force is *natural selection.*[10]

The concept of species-as-Types which was used by previous evolutionary (and even nonevolutionary) theories and the world view which underpinned it turned biologists' eyes away from the data to be gained from observing variations among individuals. The data were made invisible, irrelevant to the scientific problems being faced. Darwinian theory revealed them.

The revolution accompanying Darwinian theory overthrew a world view. With the new world view, a philosophical outlook triumphed: philosophical empiricism. The tradition I shall examine and criticize is a part of this philosophical empiricism which triumphed with Darwin.[11] Part of my criticism will be that the moral philosophy associated with this tradition conceals data. In concealing data, it makes impossible the solution to certain moral problems—particularly the problem of sexism.

Part II: A Defense of Abortion

In September 1971, the first issue of *Philosophy and Public Affairs* was published. It was a very different kind of journal from the philosophy journals existing then. Its purpose was to highlight the philosophical dimension in issues of public concern and to encourage "philosophically inclined writers from various disciplines . . . [to] bring their distinctive methods to bear on problems that concern everyone." The journal was founded in the spirit of the late 1960s and early 1970s. Philosophy journals existing at that time did not aim at dealing with problems which "concern everyone." That meant that there was an extremely limited outlet for papers applying philosophic methods to current social, political, and moral problems, a severe stricture given the "publish or perish" mystique in the universities. Limited outlet meant limited number of papers written, limited discussion, and limited development of new methods to deal with "problems that concern everyone." So, the establishment of the journal had an effect on the direction of work in philosophy.

In the first issue of *Philosophy and Public Affairs*, there was a paper by Judith Jarvis Thomson titled "A Defense of Abortion." In the paper, Judith Thomson considers whether or not abortion is ever morally justifiable, concluding that it sometimes is. In the years since this paper was published, it has become one of the classic works used when the abortion problem is considered in philosophy courses and in medicine and ethics courses. It is an example of excellent work in its tradition—which I'll call the "Judith Thomson tradition," even though its roots lie in the seventeenth century, and even though some philosophers in the tradition today disagree with some of Judith Thomson's analyses.

Analyzing Arguments

There is a particular pattern of analysis, a particular method, which philosophers in Judith Thomson's tradition use, and there is a particular pattern of thinking which they take to be *moral reasoning*. *Moral reasoning* constitutes a technical category within this philosophic tradition, but it is really supposed to capture the kind of thinking people would do in moral matters if they were thinking properly. Let me go over the Judith Thomson paper to show the method and to indicate what moral reasoning is supposed to be.

In the introduction to an anthology in which Judith Thomson's abortion paper is reprinted, editor Joel Feinberg says: "Abortion raises subtle problems for private conscience, public policy, and constitutional law. Most of these problems are essentially philosophical, requiring a degree of clarity about basic concepts that is seldom achieved in legislative debates and letters to the newspaper."[12] As the analytic philosopher sees it, matters of private conscience have to do with a *moral agent* doing whatever *moral reasoning* is necessary to decide whether a *moral act* (or kind of moral act) is *morally justifiable*. Moral reasoning may show that an act is morally unjustifiable as well, of course. One way of showing that an act is justifiable is by finding a *moral principle* which covers it. One moral principle that Judith Thomson considers is "Every person has a right to life." Often, though, the matter is much more complicated, and the moral reasoning requires a *moral argument*.

Philosophers in this tradition spend a great deal of time analyzing arguments. It is a main part of their method. In the process of examining arguments, the philosopher clarifies and develops concepts, and often establishes the basis for a new position. Superficially, the widely used tactic of examining arguments makes this philosophy seem destructive and merely critical. But this is misleading. Razing buildings in a city would look merely destructive unless you realized that the buildings were unsafe for people to live in and that, perhaps, the neighborhood people wanted to build a park on the site.

Here is the line of argument Judith Thomson criticizes:

   A. The fetus is a *person* from the moment of conception.
   B. Every person has a *right to life*.
∴ C. The fetus has a *right to life*.
   D. The mother has a *right* to decide what will happen in and to her body.
   E. A person's *right to life* is stronger and more stringent than the mother's *right* to decide what happens in and to her own body and so outweighs it.
∴ F. The fetus may not be killed.

Since aborting the birth amounts (in nearly all cases) to killing the fetus, the conclusion of interest is

∴ G. Abortion is impermissible.

Using the word *mother* here reflects a bias—not Judith Thomson's bias, since she is just citing an argument which some "right-to-lifers" give. A pregnant woman is not a mother, nor is a woman giving birth a mother, except in the barest of biological senses. In the context of this argument, using *mother* constitutes an emotional and moral bias, and it begs the question. So I'll use the term *pregnant woman*.

The method of examining arguments is an exact science in philosophy, and there are various questions to ask in doing the examination. For example, a foremost question to ask is whether the argument is *valid*. That amounts to asking whether the conclusion follows by the laws of logic from the premisses.[13] In the argument I set out above, which Judith Thomson will be examining, C is a conclusion from premisses A and B. Conclusions may also be premisses, and C is in fact a premiss in the argument which has F as a conclusion. So a question which Judith Thomson raises is whether the argument having A, B, C, D, and E as premisses, and F as conclusion is valid.

In fact, that argument is not valid. Like nearly all arguments given in real life, it is *enthymematic*—that is, it has many suppressed premisses not set out explicitly in the argument. If our arguments in real life weren't enthymematic, we would all die of boredom because the premisses which have to be made explicit include enormous numbers of trivial premisses that everyone would agree to and which everyone realized are presupposed. Sometimes, however, the suppressed premisses are not at all obvious, and they may include unacknowledged prejudices and presuppositions which would be rejected if they were brought to light. For example, Judith Thomson's criticism of many arguments about abortion which I mentioned in the introduction to this paper—that they assume that the pregnant woman's moral decision is on a par with the decision of any other moral agent—is a criticism which reveals an unacknowledged prejudice and presupposition. There are other suppressed premisses, or "gaps," in the argument from A to E to conclusion F which Judith Thomson reveals in the course of her paper.

Using Hypothetical Cases

One tactic which Judith Thomson used, and one which is a staple in her tradition, is that of introducing hypothetical cases. Philosophers in this tradition suppose moral agents understand the arguments they are using, although that understanding may need clarification; and they suppose moral agents grasp the concepts involved in the arguments. The philosopher (so they say) merely clarifies the thinking and the concepts which the moral agent already grasps. The philosopher adds nothing new. In fact, adding something new would not be doing philosophy, they claim. It would be doing substantive morality, or moral persuasion. Sometimes philosophers talk of this in terms of clarifying the *meaning of the moral terms*. In that phrasing, it may seem even more obvious that the philosopher is merely dealing with what the moral agents already understand, and clarifying it.

Let me give the main hypothetical case which Judith Thomson uses in her paper:

> . . . let me ask you to imagine this. You wake up in the morning and find yourself in bed with an unconscious violinist. A famous violinist. He has been found to have a fatal kidney ailment, and the Society of Music Lovers has canvassed all the available medical records and found that you alone have the right blood type to help. They have therefore kidnapped you, and last night the violinist's circulator system was plugged into yours, so that your kidneys can be used to extract poisons from his blood as well as your own. The director of the hospital now tells you, "Look, we're sorry the Society of Music Lovers did this to you—we would never have permitted it if we had known." But still, they did it, and the violinist now is plugged into you. To unplug you would be to kill him. But never mind, it's only for nine months. By then he will have recovered from his ailment, and can safely be unplugged from you. (Pp. 48-49)

Judith Thomson takes this hypothetical case to have obvious analogies to the abortion case, analogies she will use in examining the antiabortion argument. I'll trace the outline of her discussion.

The conclusion of the antiabortion argument is

F. Abortion is impermissible.

Does this mean that the abortion is impermissible absolutely, under any and all circumstances? Or does it mean that it is impermissible under normal circumstances, but that there are extraordinary circumstances in which it might be permissible? To work that out, Judith Thomson begins clarifying premiss E.

E. A person's right to life is stronger and more stringent than the mother's right to decide what happens in and to her own body and outweighs it.

But, she asks, what if the pregnant woman will die if the fetus is not aborted? In that case, we have the pregnant woman's right to life balanced against the fetal right to life. Judith Thomson insists that in order for the valid conclusion to be that abortion is absolutely impermissible, two important, suppressed premisses have to be made explicit. They are

E(1) Performing an abortion would be *directly killing* the fetus and doing nothing will merely be *letting* the mother *die*.

E(2) Directly killing an innocent person is always and absolutely impermissible.

Judith Thomson now tests premiss E(2) by bringing in the hypothetical violinist example. Suppose your kidneys will break down under the strain of purifying the violinist's blood and your own? If someone walks in and unplugs the violinist from you, he will be directly killing the violinist, which is impermissible, by E(2). But, she asks, what if you turn around and unplug *yourself* from the violinist. Is that impermissible? A low murmur rises from all the comfortable nooks in which people are reading Judith Thomson's paper. "Surely not," goes the murmur. "Surely unplugging *yourself* is not impermissible." The moral principle embodied in E(2), that directly killing an innocent person is absolutely impermissible, is overridden by a principle of self-defense (or perhaps qualified by a principle of self-defense). We can see this clearly in the violinist example. But the abortion case also falls under E(2). So if it is not impermissible for you to unplug yourself from the violinist in the hypothetical case, then it is not impermissible for the pregnant woman to abort the fetus.

In the course of her discussion of the pregnant woman's decision to abort, Judith Thomson criticized other writings on aborting for having what amounts to a sexist bias (though she doesn't use that term):

> The main focus of attention in writings on abortion has been on what a third party may or may not do in answer to a request from a woman for an abortion. . . . So, the question asked is what a third party may do, and what the mother may do is decided, almost as an afterthought, from what it is concluded that the third party may do. But it seems to me that to treat the matter in this way is to refuse to grant to the mother that very status of person which is so firmly insisted on for the fetus. (P. 52)

This is a prime example of a woman working within the methods of a particular tradition in philosophy and correcting a bias which has its roots in sexism.

Clarifying Concepts

So far, we see that abortion is not *absolutely* impermissible. The pregnant woman may abort herself—or at least her decision to do so is morally justifiable. Now Judith Thomson goes on to argue that the pregnant woman's right to life and the fetus's right to life aren't on a par. She does this by using an analogy. The pregnant woman and the child, she says, aren't simply like "two tenants in a small house which has, by unfortunate mistake, been rented to both. The mother *owns* the house" (p. 53). She goes on to clarify this with another hypothetical example: "If Jones has found and fastened on a certain coat which he needs to keep him from freezing, but which Smith also needs to keep him from freezing, then it is not impartiality that says, 'I cannot choose between you' when Smith owns the coat.

Women have said again and again, 'This body is *my* body!'" (p. 53). At this point, some readers may raise their eyebrows and ask what owning a house or coat has to do with the right to life. Many philosophers, including Judith Thomson, would say that property rights are the very model we work with in discussing rights, that our picture of what rights are, and our understanding of what they are, is gained by focusing on property rights.[14] The reader should pay heed also to the fact that Judith Thomson analyzes the pregnant woman's relation to her body by analogy with the legal relation of property ownership (as distinct from the legal relation of tenancy). She then uses this clarification in terms of property relations to help clarify the question of whether abortion is impermissible.

At this point, the murmur rising from the comfortable nooks may show ripples of shock. "Does this mean *I* have an obligation to seize the coat from Jones so that Smith won't freeze to death?" (Or, by analogy, to seize the woman's body back from the fetus by helping her with an abortion?) Judith Thomson saves us from such actions. We *decide* that it is right that Smith have the coat (or that the woman have her body), but we need not ourselves be the agent who does the confiscating. We must grant, she says, that a person has a right to refuse to confiscate that coat: "But then what should be said is . . . 'I will not *act*,' leaving it open that somebody else can or should and, in particular, that anyone in a position of authority with the job of securing people's rights, both can and should" (p. 54).

Judith Thomson's process of clarifying concepts here has been to show their links with other concepts in the broad conceptual scheme which we moral agents allegedly work within. This network includes the concept of *property* and also the concept of the *law*, which is presupposed in the concepts of property and tenancy (those being legalistic concepts). She also links the concept of rights to the concept of a *legitimate authority* who has the *responsibility* for seeing that rights are secured. We shall see later that these linkages are important. But at the moment, the concept of the right to life needs further clarification—a clarification which involves bringing in the additional moral concept of *justice*.

The Right to Life

Investigating the concept of a right to life is part of clarifying premisses B and E of the antiabortion argument:

B. Every person has a *right to life*.
E. A person's *right to life* is stronger and more stringent than the mother's *right to decide* what happens in and to her own body and so outweighs it.

Judith Thomson investigates the concept of the right to life in stages. First she asks, "Does having a right to life mean that you have the right to be given the bare minimum you need to continue life?" This is a specific application of the general question of whether having a right to something means that a person has the right to the means to that something, and is one of the very general clarifications of rights which she will make. Looking at the violinist example again, she concludes that although the violinist has a right to life, and he may need to use my kidneys as his means to keep on living, he has no right to their use. What is important here is that Judith Thomson has distinguished between having the right to something and having the right to the means to that something. She claims it is a feature of all rights and something any adequate account of rights must deal with (p. 56).

If the right to life doesn't necessarily involve the right to the means essential to life, what does it involve? Judith Thomson finally concludes that the right to life must simply be the right not to be killed *unjustly*. She then clarifies the concept of justice she is using by a hypothetical example, once again leaning on the concept of property rights (p. 60).

Suppose two brothers are given a single box of chocolates for Christmas, that is, it is their joint possession. Suppose further that the big brother grabs the box, won't let the little brother have any of the chocolates, and instead eats them all himself. We would all surely agree, she says, that the big brother is treating the little one unjustly, because the little brother has been given a right to half of them (p. 56). She goes on with the example. Suppose the older brother had been given the chocolates for his very own and he ate them all himself, refusing to give the little brother even a single one. He wouldn't be treating the little boy unjustly unless he had somehow given him a right to some of the chocolates. The big boy might be greedy, stingy, callous, and mean. But he would not be unjust.[15]

There are many different concepts of justice, and some of them certainly bear a resemblance to this one, which Judith Thomson claims is one we moral agents use. But according to her concept of justice, one may have a right to something by owning it, or by having been given a right to it (by its rightful owner or perhaps by God or by whatever gives natural rights). To act unjustly, then, seems to mean not letting someone have or use something that person has a right to. Having a right to life comes down to not being deprived of life unjustly.

The question of whether abortion is permissible in a given case, then, seems to turn on whether the woman has given the fetus a right to use her body. Once the area of explicit legal contract and long-standing custom is left behind, it becomes very difficult to decide under what conditions someone has given someone else a right to use something. In trying to clarify this in the abortion case, Judith Thomson brings in some of her most memorable hypothetical examples, about people seeds which float in through the living room windows and root themselves in the carpets. But the upshot is that there are cases of pregnancy in which the woman has not given the fetus a right to use her body and in which the fetus may be aborted without killing it unjustly. And so there are cases in which abortion is not impermissible.

Matters of Public Policy

I have discussed work in the Judith Thomson tradition so far as matters of private conscience go. But Joel Feinberg also said that the abortion issue raised questions for public policy and constitutional law, so it would seem that the tradition deals with moral aspects of those things too. I won't take up the question of constitutional law, but it is important to say some things about the way the tradition handles the moral aspects of matters of public policy.[16]

In Judith Thomson's discussion of rights, a person makes his or her decision of private conscience against a background environment that is fixed so far as the distinction of rights goes. Some rights everyone has, like the right to life. Other rights not everyone has, particularly rights to property or rights to some of the means which are necessary to exercise rights which everyone has. The result is that not everyone can exercise even the rights that everyone has. This background distribution may be changed by actions based on individual conscience; for example, the pregnant woman may decide that she ought to give the fetus a right to use her body. In the main, however, the distribution is changed by public policy; for example, the legislature or the courts may decide that public funds must be used to pay for the abortions of indigent women.

Interestingly enough, philosophers in this tradition clarify questions of public policy in the same way as they clarify questions of private conscience. The only difference they see is that in private conscience, individuals without special status are making decisions about their personal lives; and in public policy, individuals who are acting in certain offices (congressmen, circuit court justices, heads of public health divisions) are making policy decisions which will have effects on the public at large. These philosophers suppose that the process of moral reasoning is the same in both cases. In the public case, each individual supposedly clarifies his or her conscience and then votes. In cases of legislation or in board decisions this is exactly what happens. Executive decisions may be construed as decisions of one-member groups. In this view, public policy is made by aggregates of individuals each of whom reasons his or her way through the moral arguments and then votes.

This should serve as enough of a discussion of work in the Judith Thomson tradition to give the reader a feel for the style and to set out enough of the method, categories, and concepts so that I may later argue for bias in the tradition. I'll now turn to an altogether different sort of discussion of abortion.

Part III: Jane

In 1969, most state laws prohibited abortion unless the life of the pregnant woman was threatened.[17] A few states had reformed their abortion laws to allow abortion by doctors in hospitals in cases of threat to the health of the woman, threat of fetal deformity, or rape.[18] In the mid-1960s, the estimated death rate for abortions performed in hospitals was 3 deaths per 100,000 abortions; the rate for illegal abortions was guessed to be over eight times that—30 deaths per 100,000 abortions was a rough estimate and almost certainly conservative.[19] For minority and poorer women, it was certainly very much higher.

The women's liberation movement was in its infancy in 1969. In that year, a group of Chicago women who had been active in radical politics formed an organization called Jane. Over the next year and a half, Jane evolved from an abortion counseling and referral service to a service in which abortions were actually performed by the Jane members themselves. By 1973 when they closed the service, over 12,000 abortions had been performed under Jane's auspices. The medical record equaled that of abortions done under legal, licensed conditions by physicians in hospitals. The service charged on a sliding scale; eventually all abortions were cheaper than the going rate, and some women paid nothing. Jane served many poor women, black women, and very young women who could not have had an abortion otherwise.

My discussion of Jane is based on one newspaper article and an interview with one member. Perhaps not all Jane members will agree with this member's interpretation, but that isn't the point here because I'm not doing a sociological study. I am investigating patterns of moral thinking and acting which the Judith Thomson tradition makes invisible, and that one person's thinking and action is concealed is enough to show bias. Pauline B. Bart has done a broader based study.[20]

What Jane Did

This is the way Jane operated, as reported in the June 1973 Hyde Park-Kenwood *Voices* article on the organization: "Jane was the pseudonym we chose to represent the service. A phone was opened in her name and an answering service secured, later replaced by a tape recorder. Jane kept all records and served as control-central." "Jane" was not a particular woman but the code name for whichever counselor was taking calls and coordinating activities on a given day.

> For four years, Jane kept the same phone number. . . . At first she received only eight to ten calls a week. A year later she was receiving well more than 100 calls a week.
>
> All phoned in messages were returned the same day: "Hello, Marcia. This is Jane from women's liberation returning your call. We can't talk freely over the phone, but I want you to know that we can help you."
>
> Then Jane would refer the name to a counselor, who would meet personally with the woman and talk with her at length about available alternatives.
>
> The counselor would also help the woman arrange finances and, whenever possible, collect a $25 donation for the service loan fund. The counseling session was also a screening process for detecting conflicts and potential legal threats.[21]

Jane worked with several male abortionists. One of these was "Dr. C." Dr. C worked alone with his nurse in motel rooms until the day an abortion was interrupted by a pounding on the door and a man's voice shouting, "Come on out of there, baby killer!" After a wild chase between buildings and down alleys, Dr. C escaped the irate husband. When he caught his breath, he decided that it might be better to quit working in motels.

Jane members then began renting apartments for Dr. C and his nurse to work in. Jane describes the first day they used a rented apartment: "Seven women were done that day, in a setting where they could relax and talk with other women in a similar predicament. And when the first woman walked out of the bedroom, feeling fine and no longer pregnant, the other six were noticably relieved. They asked her questions and got firsthand answers."[22] Another advantage of the new arrangement was that Jane counselors were with a woman during the abortion, giving her psychological and moral support and explaining what was going on to her. Still another was that the counselors gradually began assisting Dr. C in the abortion itself, and he began training them in the abortion procedures.

After a few months of operation, members of Jane had begun inducing miscarriages for women more than twelve weeks pregnant.[23] Thursday mornings were set aside as "women's day," the day when Jane women induced miscarriages in other women. It is a simpler procedure for the abortionist to induce a miscarriage than to do a direct abortion, but it is more difficult for the woman:

> The woman had to deal with a process that would take days instead of minutes and involve more pain, more risk and often more money.
>
> . . . there was no way to keep the abortion a secret from intolerant par-

ents or boyfriends, husband or employer. Women on welfare stood to lose their payments if the caseworker found out they had an abortion. Women had to find baby sitters and arrange for time off work—often this meant loss of job or income.

The counselor would have to be on call around the clock till the woman safely miscarried. She would have to arrange a place for the woman to stay while she was in labor; or if the woman had no one else to turn to, the counselor would have to fill in as babysitter, housekeeper and midwife, till the ordeal was over.[24]

During this time, Dr. C was teaching the women of Jane more and more about the process of doing direct abortions. Finally, some counselors were doing the entire direct abortion themselves, under Dr. C's eye. In the midst of all this, they learned that Dr. C was no doctor at all, but just a man who had become an expert in the giving of abortions. Then something happened on one of the "women's days."

Four counselors were working at the apartment one Thursday breaking water bags [placentas] and inserting Leumbach paste for long-term miscarriages. The fourth and last patient for the day was a 19-year-old black woman, about 14 weeks pregnant, fully counseled and prepared for a labor and miscarriage.

We were all glad this was the last patient—four in one day was a lot of responsibility and severe emotional drain. We were not fully sure of ourselves yet, even for this simple procedure. We dilated the patient and reached in with a forceps to break the membrane. Two other counselors were talking to the patient and watching.

There was the usual gush of water—slightly pink with blood—and in the teeth of the forceps the arm of a 14-week fetus.

The counselor who was doing the abortion looked silently at the forceps and its contents for a full ten seconds. The other counselors were silent . . . watching.

Finally the woman asked, "Is anything wrong?"

"Not at all," the counselor replied. "In fact, I think we'll do you direct and get the whole thing over with today."[25]

This was the first direct abortion members of Jane performed without leaning on the authority of Dr. C. They shortly broke off the relationship with Dr. C and began doing all of their own abortions. For good or ill, this meant that they had a sudden abundance of funds, since the abortion fee went to Jane instead of to Dr. C. In the eyes of the law, they became fullfledged abortionists: "We could no longer hide behind the label of 'counselor' or expect 'Dr. C' to act as a buffer, with his know-how and ready cash for dealing with a bust."[26] Jane members were arrested only once, although they were harassed by the police.[27]

The change in the abortion service meant that Jane members had to accept the full consequences of what they were doing—even if it resulted in illness, personal tragedy, or death—and they had to bear this without the protection that the doctor's professionalism gives him.[28] They worked under these conditions until 1 April 1973. Then, two months after the United States Supreme Court passed its opinion on the constitutionality of restrictive abortion laws, Jane officially closed.

What Jane Meant

In describing what Jane did, I selected data to a certain purpose. It was a selection different in many respects from the selection someone in Judith Thomson's tradition would have made. I didn't, however, use any special technical concepts or categories from some philosophical theory. In this section, I shall use Jane as a basis for constructing a moral theory which competes with theories of the Judith Thomson tradition, in order to reveal value implications of bias in that tradition.

Jane was an abortion clinic, and the women of Jane were working out moral and political beliefs and activities, not constructing a theory. I want to try to give a fragment of a theory which is able to capture their thinking and their work. The theory should be taken as an *hypothesis* about what Jane meant, subject to correction through further investigation of Jane and groups like Jane, and through seeing what comes of acting on the theory. I believe the theory is based on anarchist, or anarchist-feminist principles, but I won't discuss that. Instead I'll call the tradition out of which the theory arises the Jane tradition, to contrast with the Judith Thomson tradition.

In March 1977, I interviewed one of the founders of Jane. She said that the women who founded the organization had been active in civil rights or anti-war work in the late 1960s. They wanted to begin work in the newly born women's liberation movement. But how should they begin? What should they do? Someone suggested abortion as an issue. It was a difficult decision, and they struggled over it for months. Deciding on an issue required an analysis of a network of larger issues, and of the place of the abortion issue in that network. According to the woman I interviewed, the question was one of a woman's opportunities for life choices: "It was a question of free choice about reproduction, free choice about life style, because the old roles for women weren't viable any more. In frontier times, childbearing was valuable and important. So was housework. But that role is gone. The old ways are gone. We felt nothing *could* come in to replace them unless women could make a choice about childbearing. That seemed necessary for any other choice." These alternatives had to be *created* within our social system. The members of Jane hoped that other groups within the women's movement would work on other alternatives —offering alternative living arrangements, working on ways that women could become economically independent, and so on—while Jane members tried to offer the alternative of choosing not to have the child by aborting. That is, they thought in terms of a division of labor among women working to change the society so that women would have real alternatives for meaningful lives.

As I mentioned in the introduction, the concept of a *meaningful life* (more often called "a good life") has traditionally been a central concept in moral philosophy. The pattern of thinking Jane members use requires a holistic analysis of the society in terms of the resources it actually offers for women to have meaningful lives, plus an analysis of how to change the society so that it can offer such resources. I'll take this up in more detail in Part IV.

In offering the alternative of abortion, Jane was offering a service that was badly needed. The alternative was open to all kinds of women—rich and poor, older and young, white and nonwhite, but it was a service most desperately needed by the poorer, younger, and minority women. One author says:

> In a comparison of blacks and whites, both for premarital and marital conceptions, we find that whites have higher percentages ending in induced abortions at the lower educational levels, while at the higher educational levels there is little or no difference between blacks and whites . . . the data point to the greater reliance upon abortion on the part of whites over blacks and on the part of the more affluent or more educated over the less affluent and less educated.[29]

When they did turn to illegal abortion methods, poorer and nonwhite women came out far worse. Nationally in 1968, the black death rate from abortion was six times that of the white death rate. In New York in the early 1960s, 42 percent of the pregnancy-related deaths resulted from illegal abortions; and of those women who died, half were black and 44 percent were Puerto Rican. Only 6 percent were white.[30]

More affluent women were also able to pay the high fees which all good, illegal abortionists charged.[31] Jane overcame this by calculating fees on a sliding scale according to income. Some women paid nothing.

Jane's purpose, however, was not simply to provide a service for women, however valuable that service might be. The Jane group could not provide abortions to all Chicago women who needed them. More than that, Jane members knew that when abortion was legalized, their service would have to disappear. Jane's purpose was to show women a much broader alternative than simply not having a baby, to show that by acting together, women can change society so that all women can have an opportunity to choose a meaningful life. They tried to show this in different ways. One way was through the sliding scale for fees. Counselors explained to a woman paying $300 that she was helping pay the cost for a woman who could pay only $5.00. She was, in a small way, helping to undercut the unfairness of a society which would allow her an abortion but not the poorer woman.

Jane itself was the most dramatic demonstration of an alternative for women acting together. Jane members were themselves future or past candidates for abortion, and in the present, they were doing something dangerous, exhausting, and illegal for the sake of changing society for all women. Jane showed that women could take change into their own hands. By coming to Jane for their abortions, other women were also acting for this change. They were trusting women to do things which traditionally were done by men in their society, and legally done only by doctors (overwhelmingly male) within the rigid, hierarchically ordered medical profession. This was a leap of trust.

In the structure of their service, Jane members were trying to build an alternative kind of medical structure as well.[32]

> We—the counselors—we learned the medical mystiques are just bullshit. That was a great up for us. Do you know, you're required to have a license as a nurse just to give a shot. Nurses can't even give an intravenous on their own. That takes a different kind of license. We would just explain to our workers how you had to fill the syringe, and how to be certain there was no air in it, and why that was important, and so on. We'd spend a lot of time explaining it. Then we would say to the patient, "Well this is the first time that Sue is giving anyone a shot. Maybe you can help her, and be patient with her." The patient was part of what was happening too. Part of the whole team.
>
> Sometimes in the middle of an abortion, we would switch positions to show that everyone in the service could do things, to show that the woman who was counseling could give a shot, and the one who was giving a shot could counsel too. We did it to make people see that they could do it too. They have the power to learn to counsel and give a shot. They have the power to change things and build alternatives.

We here come to the central analysis within the Jane tradition, as it is expressed in Jane's practice. The analysis operates in a very general way to criticize our society and to offer direction to move toward change. Let me state it first in terms of the social structure of the institution of medicine in the United States today.

In the United States, medical people operate within a hierarchical system of dominance and subordination. Those higher in the hierarchy have power which those lower do not have—and the power to order those lower ones around is the least of it. One key aspect of that power is what Howard Becker calls "the right to define the nature of reality." He uses the notion of a "hierarchy of credibility": "In any system of ranked groups, participants take it as given that members of the highest group have the right to define the way things really are."[33] I would argue that this "right of definition" means not only that the word of the higher has heavier weight than that of the lower (teacher over student, doctor over intern or aide) but that the very categories and concepts that are used, the "official" descriptions of reality, are descriptions from the point of view of the dominant persons in the hierarchy. What counts as knowledge itself is defined in terms of that viewpoint, and the definition further legitimates the power of the dominant person.

The power of those in dominant positions in the hierarchy is *legitimate authority*. This contrasts with the *natural authority* of a person who, regardless of position, happens to have a great deal of knowledge, experience, or wisdom about a subject. A doctor's authority is legitimated by the criteria, standards, and institutions which control access to his place in the hierarchy. These criteria and requirements for training on the one hand are aimed at insuring that those with legitimate authority in the hierarchy also have the natural authority required to do the jobs they are doing. Although we all know there are incompetent doctors, these criteria do operate to screen out incompetence *as defined from the top of the hierarchy*. Do they insure that those at the top have natural authority? I think not, and that is because *legitimate authority* carries with it a definition of what counts as knowledge: the definition from the top of the hierarchy, the "official" point of view.

In our medical system what constitutes health, illness, and cure are almost entirely defined in terms of the training and knowledge of physicians. And so, for example, a woman giving birth has been treated like an appendectomy patient—drugged unconscious, laid out on a table in a sterile operating room, flat on her back. Menopause is described as "the most extensive disease of the endocrine glands," and as "estrogen starvation," when in fact it is the normal functioning of a human body. Drug and surgical cures are used instead of dietary measures because those higher in the hierarchy are trained in drug cures and are ignorant about nutritional health and healing. And so on.[34]

This outlook on knowledge is sometimes called "objective" or "the scientific outlook" of experts. In fact, it is absolutist, and when the definition of reality is given in terms of the tradition of the dominant in a dominant-subordinate structure, the outlook is, in fact, biased.

In part, Jane members were operating from the viewpoint of a subordinate group in our society: women. They were using this viewpoint to try to create new social structures which were not based on dominance and subordination and in which authority was natural authority—knowledge which suits the situation to the best degree that we know at the moment. When the woman I interviewed said that the members of Jane tried to show other women that they "have the power to learn to counsel and give a shot" and that they have the power to change things and build alternatives," she is talking not only about the natural authority of knowledge but what we might call natural *moral* power, or *moral* authority.

In structuring the abortion service as they did, the members of Jane were developing an alternative to hierarchy, but they were also overcoming the vices of dependency and feelings of ignorance and impotence by showing women that they did have the power to learn and do things themselves.[35] The Jane organization itself was built on nonauthoritarian, nonhierarchical principles, and Jane members tried to run it as a collective.

> We tried to make it as nonauthoritarian as we could. We had rotating chairs. There wasn't a high value placed on one kind of work and a low value on another. Every position was so important to what we were doing, and it was treated as equally important, to the highest degree possible. This meant every one of us could do what she was best at. You didn't have people competing to do what was important, or feeling what they were doing wasn't valuable.

In April of 1973, the women of Jane asked themselves, "What next?" Whether abortion had been a good issue to move on or not, there was no place for an illegal abortion service now that abortions were legal. Some of the women went on to found a "well woman clinic," the Emma Goldman Clinic. They hoped to run the clinic on the nonauthoritarian, nonhierarchical model used by Jane.[36] The clinic was organized around the concept of self-help, in which the "patients" are trained too in the kind of medical knowledge they need to understand and care for their own bodies for a large range of normal functions and slight disorders.

Part IV: Bias in the World View

In the biological case I discussed in the introduction, there was a certain problem that needed to be solved which we might call the problem of evolutionary change. The problem can't be named much more specifically than that, because to do that would mean describing it either in terms of the pre-Darwinian tradition, under which it is not soluble, or in terms of the Darwinian tradition, which solved it. The solution to the Darwinian problem was natural selection. But that solution involved a change in basic models (or metaphors), a change in basic patterns of thought, and a change in key traditions of the world view. The problem of evolutionary change required a revolution to be answerable.

What is the problem which both the Judith Thomson tradition and the Jane tradition share? In my discussion here, both were dealing with the problem of abortion. Neither would take it to be *the* problem. Abortion is a subsidiary problem chosen because of its connection with more central concerns. For Judith Thomson, it is a question of rights—we might even say a question of equal rights.[37] But it cannot be described that way for the Jane tradition without begging questions.

Within the Jane tradition, the problem was taken to be one of meaningful lives for women, or of free choice among genuine alternatives for meaningful lives. Some phrasing of the general problem in these terms seems appropriate to both traditions. Let me quote Betty Friedan, an activist who stands within traditions associated with Judith Thomson's:

> It is my thesis that the core of the problem for women today is not sexual but a problem of identity—a stunting or evasion of growth that is perpetuated by the feminine mystique. It is my thesis that as the Victorian culture did not permit women to accept or gratify their basic sexual needs, our culture does not permit women to accept or gratify their basic need to grow and fulfill their potentialities as human beings, a need which is not solely defined by their sexual roles.[38]

The statement of purpose of the liberal feminist National Organization for Women (NOW) also concerns opportunities for a meaningful life and moral development as a human being: NOW pledges to "take action to bring women into full participation in the mainstream of American society now, exercising all the privileges and responsibilities thereof, in truly equal partnership with men."[39] This makes it appear that for both traditions, the problem may be stated as one of equality, particularly equality so far as it relates to the moral questions of being a full human being and of having a meaningful (or good) life. I believe that this is a central concern of those within the Judith Thomson tradition. But it may be that the problem cannot be resolved under that tradition or its associated world view.

Concealing Data

In Part III, I presented the moral activity of the organization Jane under one tradition. If we look at the Jane organization under the Judith Thomson tradition, we get a different selection of data. Here's a quotation from the newspaper article:

Moral Revolution

> From the beginning, we discussed the moral implications of abortion from all angles. We listened to right-to-lifers, Catholic clergy, population-control freaks and women's liberationists.
>
> We heard legislators and lobbyists and political commentators arguing fine points of "fetal viability." When does a fetus become a person? When it can survive outside the womb (after six months)? When it begins to move (after four months)? Or from the moment of conception?
>
> Many opponents of abortion called it "murder." We argued the logical counterarguments: If a fetus is a person, then why aren't abortionists and women who have abortions charged with murder?
>
> Or, if the fetus has the rights of a person, then does the woman who carries it become subject to its rights? What happens when the rights of the woman and those of the fetus come into conflict?
>
> All philosophical and legalistic positions lost relevance when we began doing and viewing abortions . . . we knew that we were grappling with matters of life and death and no philosophical arguments could alter that belief.[40]

Judith Thomson, or someone from her tradition, would have been a great help to the Jane women in these early discussions on abortion. On the other hand, these early discussions had no clear relevance to the central moral activity the women of Jane were engaging in—*by their own judgment.* The terms in which they saw the problem were different. Their perception and their moral activity constitute data which are important to solving the problem of equality, but the Judith Thomson tradition not only ignores that data: it makes them invisible. Let's look at some of the mechanisms by which the data are concealed.

One way the tradition conceals data is through the concepts and categories it uses. The Judith Thomson tradition would focus on the Jane discussions of rights. It would ignore the discussions of hierarchy, dominance, and subordination; and perhaps some within the tradition would not take these as morally relevant discussions at all. Any theory must use concepts. Through their very use, some data are selected and some ignored. Yet the question of whether the concepts properly capture the data, or of whether they are *appropriate,* is a central, critical question about the adequacy of any tradition. For example, the pre-Darwinian concept of species was not appropriate, and the tradition with which it was associated was not adequate to solve the problem of evolutionary change.

In a similar way, the categories a tradition uses to organize data reveal some and conceal others. For example, the Judith Thomson tradition uses the categories of moral agent and of groups of moral agents as aggregates. The tradition also uses a division of moral phenomena into questions of individual conscience and those of public policy, where the latter is a matter of *official* public policy, made by those with legitimate authority. I don't want to argue that the tradition *rules out* other sorts of moral phenomena. But using those categories, it cannot capture the sort of moral phenomena Jane members took as central: those in a subordinate position acting to create a set of social relations which are not structured by dominance and subordination, through the subordinates' coming to know their own power (as opposed to legitimate authority) through acting in collectives (not aggregates).

But am I being fair to the Judith Thomson tradition? After all, they don't claim to cover *all* moral phenomena. Few theories claim to cover everything within their purview, and even within chemistry there are divisions into organic and inorganic. Mightn't there be divisions within the field of moral phenomena so that another part of the tradition might deal with Jane's moral activity and thus reveal it?

Perhaps any new moral tradition we develop will have to have something to do with the concept of rights (and associated concepts), and deal in some way with groups as aggregates and with public policy as officially handed down. But that new tradition could not be the Judith Thomson tradition, for a revolutionary change in the methodology of her tradition is necessary to uncover data like Jane.

The Judith Thomson tradition supposes that there exists a set of moral concepts embedded in moral principles which "we" all know and understand. In her paper, Judith Thomson herself is clarifying concepts "we" grasp by the standard method of the tradition: the use of hypothetical cases. This method presupposes a very mentalistic view of concepts and word meanings—mentalistic in the way philosophical empiricists are mentalistic in their views on meanings as "ideas."[41] The concepts exist in the speaker's understanding. If someone understands the concept, he or she knows whether it applies in any given case.[42] Considering hypothetical cases (in this view) points out cases the speaker might have overlooked; but once they are brought to his or her attention, the speaker allegedly knows whether the concepts apply or not, and so his or her explicit understanding of the concept is clarified. Similarly, one's explicit understanding of "our" moral principles is supposed to be clarified by considering hypothetical cases.

The most obvious thing to say about this method is that although bringing up hypothetical cases may clarify our understanding of concepts and principles, everyone knows that the selection of hypothetical cases also biases understanding. This bias may be (unintentionally) systematic. For example, Judith Thomson gives a case where Jones faces a frosty death because Smith owns the coat. Why not, instead, use a case where men, women, and children face poor diets, poor housing, and loss of dignity because the owner of a mill decides to move it out of one region into another having cheaper labor and lower tax rates? Philosophers may say the second example is too complicated, but the selection is not a trivial matter of simplicity. The coat example ignores an essential distinction in kinds of property ownership which the mill example reveals.

The method rules out empirical investigation to see what sorts of hypothetical cases might capture what is morally important to persons in a variety of circumstances in the United States. There seems to be no way whatsoever to insure that a fair consideration of hypothetical cases is made to reduce the bias. One can't develop a sampling procedure for hypothetical cases.

Worst of all, the method rules out empirical investigation to discover whether the moral concepts and principles the philosophers are dealing with are really the moral concepts which people use in the United States. It rules out empirical investigation to discover whether those concepts and those moral principles are relevant to the lives of people in different walks of life, investigation to discover whether they are relevant to solving those people's problems of human dignity and a meaningful life *as those people perceive* those problems.

The method itself has the mere appearance of being plausible only for ancient systems of concepts which are well worked out. It has not even the appearance of plausibility for a case like Jane's, in which people are in the process of creating new concepts through creating new social forms. The fundamental theory of meaning, of understanding, and of concept formation on which the method is based is not only inadequate: it is false.

All of this means that to encompass the Jane data, a revolutionary change is necessary in the methodology of the Judith Thomson tradition. Without it, the data remain concealed.

The data being concealed concern human moral activity and the possibilities of changing society. This constitutes a direct and very important value consequence. The Judith Thomson tradition dominates philosophy departments in the prestigious American universities, and even teachers in nonprestigious colleges are trained within it. This means that students are taught to see moral activity within that tradition. Activity requiring patterns of thinking and concepts and categories like Jane's is made invisible to them.

Official Points of View

From its beginnings, the tradition Judith Thomson works within has been centrally concerned with equality. People in this tradition have particularly been concerned that all human beings be equal under the moral law and under the positive law of the state. Equality before the moral or positive law means that the same laws and principles apply to all. Whether or not this is enlightened depends on which laws and principles one chooses and the society in which they apply.

The question of equality which those in the Jane tradition raise is one which takes dominant-subordinate structures in the society as *creators* of inequality. Their solution to the problem of equality is the use of the perception and power of the subordinate to eliminate dominant-subordinate structures through the creation of new social forms which do not have that structure. Those in the Judith Thomson tradition do not raise questions of dominance and subordination except in the moral, legal, and political spheres, where they are seen in terms of moral, legal, and political equality. Particularly, they do not raise the question of whether equality before the moral or positive law may not be rendered empty because of the dominant-subordinate structures in the economic or social (e.g., family) spheres.

Let me raise the issue from the point of view of the Jane tradition, leaving the positive law aside and concentrating on the moral law. The Judith Thomson tradition takes there to be one set of moral concepts and one set of moral principles which hold for all human beings. Does that set of concepts and principles represent an "official point of view" from the top of some dominant-subordinate structure? In what remains of this paper, I shall argue that it does, and that this constitutes a bias in the Judith Thomson tradition that makes the problem of equality insoluble.

In the United States today, there are four central and interconnected structures of dominance and subordination: those of class, sex, race, and age. I believe the Judith Thomson tradition represents an "official point of view" for the dominant in all four structures, but I'll discuss the question only for the class and sex structures.

Class Dominance

From Judith Thomson's abortion paper, we see that the concepts of rights is understood on the model of property rights. Given her distinction that having the right to something doesn't involve having the right to the means to that something, we see that in her analysis, the system of concepts involving rights represents the point of view of the property owner. In fact, that point of view is much more explicit in earlier parts of the tradition. John Locke, in his *Second Treatise on Government*, takes the main function of the state to be that of protecting property. It is still the main function of our state.

There is a distinction in kinds of property which is essential to our economic system. It is used to distinguish those in the dominant position in the capitalist class structure. Capitalists are those who own the kind of property that constitutes an investment and turns a profit. Members of the subordinate class are those who must sell their labor power to live, but who own property which they use (like coats and, if they are lucky, cars and homes). The class system in the United States is not the simple capitalist-worker system of street-corner Marxism. But despite the confusion introduced by hierarchies in the managerial and professional structures, and by stock-owning grandmothers, there is still a pretty clear distinction between those who must live by their labor and those who need not, even though they may choose, like Nelson or David Rockefeller, to labor in powerful positions in government or finance.

In representing the point of view of the property owner in a capitalist society, Judith Thomson's tradition *as a matter of fact* also represents the point of view of the dominant in the class structure, the owners of the kind of property called capital. But the connections between the Judith Thomson tradition and the class dominant-subordinate order are more intrinsic than that because the connection with capitalist economics is more intrinsic than that.

The Judith Thomson tradition uses the model of a human being as a separate atom, and the model of groups as aggregates which are central models in capitalist economic theory. In doing so, this tradition receives confirmation from the economic theory and, in its turn, confirms the model of a human being and of human groups which the economic theory uses. Some people may consider me foolish to say that a moral theory receives confirmation. But a moral theory must use a concept of a human being and a concept of human society. These concepts are (and must be) confirmed by a variety of scientific theories. That the concepts work in other traditions in the world view, like the moral tradition, confirms their validity within the scientific traditions.

Male Dominance

The Judith Thomson tradition is also associated with a male-dominant point of view and with the structure of sexism. There are a number of ways this comes about, but here let me mention only the connection with capitalism in the United States.

When principles of John Locke's political theory were embodied in our society after the American Revolution, political society was seen as a patriarchy consisting of male-headed households, with male political participation (for property-owning males only) counting as household participation. Since that time, our political theory and our society have been transformed, and politically, households are no longer taken as the unit: individuals are. Yet the capitalistic economic tradition, as embedded in our society, still does use households as units.

Under our complex economic system, workers are paid for the labor they sell in the marketplace (including the factory, the government, the academy, and so on). Other work that is essential to the economic system is not sold on the marketplace and is not paid for. This includes the work of creating a home for workers, taking care of their nutritional, health, sexual, and emotional needs. It includes reproducing the work force, through bearing and taking care of children. It includes managing the consumption of the household unit—and in our economy, which relies on expanding consumption, that is a very important economic function.[43]

The household requires a steady income from some source or other, and the large majority of households get this income by one or more household members' selling their labor power, that is, becoming paid workers. One of the requirements of capital is a steady, disciplined work force. In our version of capitalism, control of the production process itself has been taken out of the hands of workers (better to serve the interests of capital) and put into the hands of a hierarchy of managers who do the "mental labor" and the planning of the work process.[44] These factors have the effect on a household of making one member's paid work primary and the other member's paid work secondary. In many households, they have the effect that one senior member does all the paid work while the other senior member does nearly all the unpaid work.

Putting the problem in such language makes it sound abstract, theoretical, and of doubtful validity. But we all know the process firsthand. We all know that if you want to be hired as anything but a laborer paid by the day, your work record can't show that you work awhile, quit awhile, and work awhile again (unless you are a woman). You have to be a reliable, steady worker. Increase in your pay depends on your being reliable and steady. Being kept on in layoffs depends upon your seniority. This means the household does better if one member is regularly the paid worker, and if the household stays put in the geographic location of that worker's job, even if in some cases the other household workers can't find employment. On the other hand, capitalist economics in theory as well as practice requires a labor force which will pull up roots and change geographic location according to the needs of capitalist investment. This almost always requires the secondary worker to follow the primary worker in geographic work changes, even when there is little likelihood that the secondary worker will find a job in the new area.

All of this is intensified when the household is upwardly mobile. The paid worker climbing the success ladder has to stick with his company until the key moment comes for a switch that will better him in his job. Promotions often involve changing geographic location. In managerial and professional work, hiring practices make it explicit that there be one primary worker (the paid worker) and one secondary:

> Large, complex institutions employing highly educated men . . . develop their own version of the two-person career pattern among their employees [communicating] certain expectations to the wives. These expectations serve the dual function of reinforcing the husband's commitment to the institution and of demanding certain types of role performance from the wife which will benefit the institution in a number of ways. A pattern of pressures is generated for both members of the couple which is closely related to social mobility, mobility within the employing institution, loyalty, and interpersonal rivalry.[45]

I spoke of primary and secondary workers in a sex-neutral way, and this quotation speaks of husbands as primary workers and wives as secondary. This is no case of simple sex discrimination on the part of corporations, to be solved by changing the attitudes of the hiring personnel. To fill its needs for a disciplined labor force, our capitalist economic system requires a primary, paid worker in the household, with other workers being secondary. Historically, women have been subordinate to men. Socially and psychologically they are raised to take a second place. Biologically they bear children and nurse them. That biological fact alone means that women must take *some* time off from work, giving men the edge as primary workers. The upshot of all these factors is male dominance.

Many feminists have explained what the official point of view is in such a male-dominant society. Simone de Beauvoir, in the book which ushered in the "second wave" of feminism, said that in the male-dominant world, woman was "the other," not the actor, not the definer of a world, but "the other" whom the actor faced.[46] One of the clearest, most heartbreaking expressions of what this means was made by the wife of a business executive: "I bask in my husband's reflected glory. I don't have to be anything myself. His status is my status. Sometimes I feel he's living his life to the fullest, and I'm living his life to the fullest."[47]

The male-dominant definition of reality shows in the stereotype of women as dependent, emotional, subjective, submissive, illogical, unambitious, not businesslike, unworldly, etc.[48] It would be possible (though hardly worthwhile) to gather literal bushels full of quotations from learned, famous men, saints, philosophers, and men in the street which attribute those subordinate traits to women.[49] The fact that they are *stereotypic* of women means that women themselves are defined from the official male-dominant viewpoint.

Now those philosophers in the Judith Thomson tradition are genuinely interested in equality, and it is very unlikely that we would find one of them attributing these stereotyped characteristics to women. Still, the tradition represents an official viewpoint in the male-dominant order.

As I argued above, the tradition represents the dominant viewpoint in the class order. Capitalist economics as embodied in our society needs the subordination of women in the household, and so is a direct support of the male-dominant order. The Judith Thomson tradition is intrinsically associated with capitalist economics, in ways enumerated above. So the tradition represents the official point of view of the male-dominant order, even though its philosophers would not stereotype women as subordinates. This isn't mere guilt by association.

Judith Thomson's tradition deals with questions of political equality, or of moral equality narrowly conceived. The tradition in its very conceptual foundations ignores equality in the economic and social spheres, except insofar as these involve questions of political or moral equality. By its very methods and concepts, the tradition makes invisible the roots of the male-dominant and class-dominant orders. This makes a solution to the moral question of equality impossible.

The Question of Equality

The link between the moral question of equality and the male-dominant order has been made by feminists of many persuasions. One way the link has been made is in pointing out that the *portion* of the resources of our society for a good life that has gone to women has been very small. The lion's share has gone to middle- and upper-class men, to the point of depriving women of opportunities to be fully human. Another way the link has been made is to consider resources available in the society as a whole. Our society, for example, does not offer the resources to anyone which Renaissance Florence was able to offer to its aristocrats. This is not primarily a matter of scarcity of resources—except in cases of severe scarcity of material resources like food, shelter, or clothing. For us in the United States, it is a question of the social relationships which are available in the society as a whole: *not the limited number of positions open in the various relationships, but the nature of the relationships themselves.*

Our economic system requires a dominant-subordinate order in which most people must live by selling their labor power. Our work structure requires that many people must labor in jobs that allow them no chance to develop their abilities or to become what Betty Friedan called "fully human." It is not only that the work is repetitive and uninteresting, it also requires people to develop the characteristics of *subordinates*.

With very few exceptions, in our society women are only offered positions of subordination, either in the workplace or out of it. Those few exceptions have to struggle to avoid deforming themselves as they try to fit into a work structure designed for men. In fact, in such a society the resources available even to those who come out as dominant in all the interconnected structures (adult, white, higher-class males) allow only a truncated human being, as men's liberationists have argued. The dominant suffer from moral poverty at least as much as the subordinate.

These dominant-subordinate structures affect most of the sciences, and they are responsible for biases I mentioned in the introduction. For example, Arlene Daniels criticized stratification theorists for taking the status of women to be determined by the men to whom they are attached. A root cause for that bias is that our economic system rests on the male-dominant system and upon households, not individuals, as units. This, of course, is part of the social structure.

Lynn Lofland criticized urban sociology for dealing tenderly with male social activities and treating women as part of the environment. This is part of the total world view in science and philosophy which takes there to be one "objective" perspective on things, or one "correct and true" set of concepts and categories, one perspective which is *the* scientific or moral one, but which takes it *uncritically*. In a world structured by dominance and subordination, the one perspective will often be the official perspective of the dominant. In the social life of cities, it is the male-dominant viewpoint which prevails; thus the bias in urban sociology.

The dominance of the "official viewpoint" is, in the end, the most immoral part of the inequality in a society formed by dominant-subordinate structures. Judith Thomson's tradition has been much concerned with paternalism—conceived as state or social interference with a person's actions "for the person's own good." That paternalism is nothing compared to the imperialist paternalism which officially defines the reality of the world of the subordinate, for the subordinate, from the point of view of the dominant. It violates the central moral injunction for respecting other human beings:

> . . . look upon human group life as chiefly a vast interpretive process in which people, singly and collectively, *guide themselves* by *defining* the objects, events and situations they encounter.[50]

NOTES

I must thank many people for their help with this paper. For help with the paper as a whole, I am grateful to my research assistants Amy Hines and Shawn Pyne. Howard Becker was a wonderful help and also my main source for references in sociology. I must also thank John Connolly, Sandra Harding, Murray Kiteley, David Lyons, M. B. E. Smith, and Judith Jarvis Thomson (in alphabetical order) for their kind and very helpful criticisms of various drafts.

Thanks for more specific help are expressed in notes to subsections of the paper, but I want here to thank Vicky Spelman and the students in our Fall 1977 Women and Philosophy class for many wonderful discussions that were a help in putting Part IV together.

1. Phillipa Foot, "Moral Arguments," *Mind* 67 (1958): 502–13.
2. Judith Jarvis Thomson, "A Defense of Abortion," *Philosophy and Public Affairs* 1 (September 1971): 47–66.
3. Arlene Kaplan Daniels, "Feminist Perspectives in Sociological Research," in *Another Voice*, ed. Marcia Millman and Rosabeth Moss Kanter (Garden City, New York, 1975), p. 345. Daniels cites Joan Acker, "Women and Social Stratification: A Base of Intellectual Sexism," *American Journal of Sociology* 78 (1973): 936–45. *Another Voice* is a collection of essays revealing sex bias in sociological theories and in sociology. I believe the connection of stratification theory may not be as simple as Daniels indicates, and that the case may be nearer to the urban sociology case Lyn Lofland discusses (see below, n. 4).
4. Lyn Lofland, "The 'Thereness' of Women: A Selective Review of Urban Sociology," in Millman and Kanter, *Another Voice*, pp. 145–46, citing Herbert Blumer, *Symbolic Interactionism* (Englewood Cliffs, N.J., 1969), p. 132.
5. Lofland, "The 'Thereness' of Women," p. 162.
6. Thomas Kuhn, *The Structure of Scientific Revolutions*, 2nd ed. (Chicago, 1970).
7. Howard E. Gruber, *Darwin on Man* (New York, 1974), p. 13. Gruber continues: "Darwin's thinking, both in biology and in geology, was permeated with the idea of such self-regulating systems. But as far as I can tell, he never did use the analogy of natural selection and man-made feedback devices. Alfred Russel Wallace, however, co-discoverer of the theory of evolution through natural selection, wrote, 'The action of this principle is exactly like that of the centrifugal governor of the steam engine, which checks and corrects any irregularities almost before they become evident.'"
8. In Darwinian theory, organisms are described as surviving and reproducing, even though the organism's desires and wants, and its understanding of what it is doing may have nothing to do with survival or reproduction. This undercuts the vitalist explanations of competing biological theories of Darwin's time. Darwin's organisms are biological agents performing acts of surviving and performing acts of reproducing. In classical economics, human beings are economic agents buying and selling in the market. Some economists talk of the "profit motive," but this is not a human motive, and economics does not deal with the world perception of human beings. People may be doing things out of love of humanity or out of greed, out of free-spirited adventure or out of religious fanaticism. It makes no difference. Their behavior must be describable as buying or selling in the market or they are not acting as economic agents. Other motives are irrelevant to the theory, and people don't actually have to have the motive of buying or selling for a profit. In the tradition of moral philosophy I'll be discussing, moral agents are taken as performing acts which are subsumed under principles concerning rights and obligations, and these acts

are considered wrong or right, just or unjust, etc. This subsumption takes place whether or not the person would use that description, and ignoring things the person might think were morally more important. In this way it is like our legal system. I discuss this in detail in the first section of Part IV. What's important here is that persons are reduced to agents doing kinds of acts which are defined in terms of the moral theory in an environment defined in terms of the moral theory.

9 Alvar Ellegard offers a lively discussion of these matters in *Darwin and the General Reader*, Goteborgs Universitets Arsskrift, vol. 64 (Goteborg, 1958). He also discusses the impact of the Darwinian ideas on the world view.

10 R. C. Lewontin, "Darwin and Mendel. The Materialist Revolution," in *The Heritage of Copernicus*, ed. J. Neyman (Cambridge, Mass., 1974), p. 170. This article is short and couched in language understandable to the layperson, and I recommend it. The discussion of Mendel is even better than that of Darwin for understanding how traditions conceal data.

11 Jean Bethke Elshtain also criticizes this tradition in her essay in this volume.

12 Joel Feinberg, ed., *The Problem of Abortion* (Belmont, Calif., 1973), p. 1. All subsequent quotations from Judith Thomson's essay are from this edition.

13 It amounts to asking that only because we are talking about this informal argument in English on analogy with an argument in some formal, artificial language for which explicit rules of logic have been set out (reflecting the "laws of logic"), which rules have been shown to be complete and consistent. That the rules are shown to be complete means that all valid formulas which can be expressed in the language are also provable under its rules. That they are shown consistent means that only valid formulas are provable. Another way of saying this is to say that all and only valid formulas are theorems. Expressing it in terms of arguments instead of formulas we get "Every argument which is properly constructed according to the rules of the system is a valid argument"; i.e., if the premises of the argument are true, then the conclusion is true. This way of saying it is connected with the other way of saying it by the fact that every argument can be turned into a statement by taking the premises as antecedent (in an "if . . . then . . . " sentence) and the conclusion as consequence. I offer these comments to bring home to the reader that an enormously sophisticated tradition in language and logic is associated with the Judith Thomson tradition in ethics.

14 John Locke's work forms an important foundation to this tradition, and the centrality of the concept of property to the concept of rights is explicit in his *Second Treatise of Government*.

15 Both the Marxists and the Freudians among us will raise their eyebrows at the use of this hypothetical case to explain the concept of justice. Plato, of course, would turn over in his grave.

16 Some repercussions for constitutional law are discussed in Betty Sarvis and Hyman Rodman, *The Abortion Controversy* (New York, 1974).

17 For their help in this part of the paper, I thank Howard Becker for his assistance with references on abortion and Shawn Pyne for her zeal and imagina-

tion in searching the library. I am much indebted to Shawn Pyne for very helpful conversations and to her unpublished paper "Alternatives to the Health System" (May 1977).

18 For a discussion of abortion laws see Sarvis and Rodman, *The Abortion Controversy*. An excellent and more detailed discussion is given by Kristin Booth Glen in "Abortion in the Courts: A Laywoman's Historical Guide to the New Disaster Area," *Feminist Studies* (January 1978): 1–26. Glen traces the political implications of the fact that the decision turned on the right of physicians to make medical decisions, not on the rights of women.

The Supreme Court declared state laws restricting abortion unconstitutional on 22 January 1973.

19 See Willard Cates and R. W. Rochat, "Illegal Abortion in the United States: 1972–74," *Family Planning Perspectives* 8 (March-April 1976): 86–92.

20 Pauline B. Bart, Abraham Lincoln School of Medicine, University of Illinois, Chicago, "Seizing the Means of Reproduction," unpublished manuscript based on interviews with forty-two members of the Jane collective. I did not know of this study in time to incorporate it into my discussion in this section. I am grateful to Pauline Bart for reading this paper and suggesting two places where my informant's perception differed from the majority perception so that I might delete them.

21 Jane, "The Most Remarkable Abortion Story Ever Told," *Hyde Park–Kenwood Voices*, June 1973, p. 2.

22 Ibid.

23 At this time, most abortionists refused to handle women more than twelve weeks pregnant. Nancy Howell Lee, *Search for an Abortionist* (Chicago, 1969), p. 6.

24 Jane, "The Most Remarkable Abortion Story Ever Told," Part IV, *Voices*, September 1973, p. 2. Often women with induced miscarriages had to go to the hospital. Even for educated white women, this could turn into a very difficult ordeal. One married college student induced a miscarriage upon herself by using a catheter. "The bleeding was so profuse that her husband again called an ambulance to take her to the hospital. She remained in the hospital for five days, where she was questioned by police and hospital authorities on suspicion of deliberate abortion, but no charges were brought. She felt extremely badly treated, especially by the nurses at the hospital." Lee, *Search for an Abortionist*, p. 80. Minority women face the danger of being sterilized, with the hospital personnel getting their permission for hysterectomy in circumstances in which they are confused by pain or drugs as well as by the authoritarian atmosphere of the hospital, or in which they do not understand the middle-class-white dialect spoken by the person explaining things to them.

25 Jane, "The Most Remarkable Abortion Story," Part IV, p. 4.

26 Ibid., Part VI, November 1973, p. 3.

27 The arrest was in the third year of the service. It appears to have been a renegade action by a few policemen, not a planned political arrest.

28 Jane members had to take on other duties too. Each week during its peak, the service used fifty ampules of ergotrate, ten bottles of xylocaine, a hundred dis-

posable syringes, and six hundred tablets each of tetracycline and ergotrate. For a while, Dr. C's nurse had obtained the drugs. Eventually, Jane members had to devise ways of getting illegal supplies.

29 Lee, *Search for an Abortionist,* p. 161. In New York in the early 1960s, 93 percent of legal, therapeutic abortions were performed on white, private patients. During that period in the United States as a whole, the rate of legal abortions per 1,000 live births was 3.17 for private patients and 0.87 for clinic patients (those entering the hospital without a private physician). In Georgia in 1970, twenty-four times as many legal abortions were performed on unmarried white women as on unmarried black women. Sarvis and Rodman, *The Abortion Controversy,* p. 159.

30 Lee, *Search for an Abortionist,* pp. 169-70.

31 Information about illegal abortionists is spread through informal networks of acquaintances. More affluent women have more access to information about illegal abortionists of quality because they have acquaintances (some of them physicians) who have this information. Jane overcame this by publishing the telephone number of the service in underground newspapers and otherwise publicly spreading word about the service, through brochures, the Chicago Women's Liberation Union, and so on. See Lee, *Search for an Abortionist,* for extensive discussions on this.

32 I spoke with two women who worked with Jane, although only one interview is used in this paper. Both said that patients waited in the *living room.* They never called it the waiting room—although professionals using a house or apartment as an office, e.g., psychotherapists, call the living room the waiting room. Both said that abortions were done in the *bedroom.* They never used the term *operating room* or anything similar. This was part of the attempt to demystify medicine. Some other abortionists made great efforts to cloak themselves in medical mystique—Dr. C is an example, since he called himself "Doctor" when he was not. For a description of one service which smothered the patient in medical mystique (and for a glaring contrast with Jane), see Donald W. Ball, "An Abortion Clinic Ethnography," *Social Problems* 14 (Winter 1967): 293-301.

33 Howard Becker, "Whose Side Are We On?" *Sociological Work* (New Brunswick, N.J., 1977), p. 126.

34 See Barbara Ehrenreich and Barbara English, *Nurses, Witches, and Midwives* (Old Westbury, N.Y., 1972).

35 For an interesting look at subordinate "vices" and dominant "virtues" see Paul Rosenkrantz, Susan Vogel, Helen L. Bee, Inge Broverman, and David Broverman, "Sex-Role Stereotypes and Self-Concepts in College Students," *Journal of Consulting and Clinical Psychology,* 32 (1968): 287-95; and Inge Broverman, Donald Broverman, Frank Clarkson, Paul Rosenkrantz, and Susan Vogel, "Sex-Role Stereotypes and Clinical Judgments of Mental Health," *Journal of Consulting and Clinical Psychology* 34 (1970): 1-7. They find that certain traits are stereotypically assigned to women; those traits are also, for the most part, stereotypically assigned to children and minority group members (particularly Blacks) in the United States, that is, of members of age-

subordinate and race-subordinate groups, as well as members of the sex-subordinate group.

36 From what I had learned from other sources, it seemed to me that Emma Goldman had been less successful as a nonauthoritarian, nonhierarchical collective activity offering first-quality service. I asked Jane about this. She said that because the abortion service was illegal, it was free of many authoritarian and hierarchal pressures from the medical profession. Because Emma Goldman was a legal clinic, it had to accommodate itself to the medical profession—by maintaining relations with physicians, for example, who would let the clinic use their licenses. This introduced factors of authority because of the licensing procedure, and with it, hierarchy. For a discussion of self-help, see Boston Women's Health Book Collective, *Our Bodies, Ourselves*. 3rd ed. (New York, 1976), pp. 361–68.

37 For example, her interpreting women's remark, "This body is *my* body" by analogy with rights involved in property ownership parallels the great initial step toward equality made by John Locke when he interpreted a man's relation to his body and labor power by analogy with rights involved in property ownership.

38 Betty Friedan, *The Feminine Mystique* (New York, 1974), p. 69. The work, originally published in 1963, was a major force in initiating the "second wave" in feminism.

39 Ibid., p. 270. Betty Friedan was one of the founders of NOW. Liberal feminists share important parts of a world view with those in the Judith Thomson tradition. They are much more radical than the philosophers, however, in part because they are feminists, in part because they are activists.

40 Jane, "The Most Remarkable Abortion Story," Part VI, *Voices*, November 1973, p. 3.

41 This mentalism also exists in science, and it operates there too as a defense against accusations of bias. It is most evident in those sciences in which practitioners think they can "define" the key scientific terms of their theories, as though the meaning of a scientific term could be set out forever in an act of definition, as though we could then contain the meaning in our understanding. Mentalism underlies psychologists' defenses against claims that their concept of IQ is value-laden. They assert that the term *intelligence quotient* as used in their theories is defined in terms of tests and means nothing more than what their theory says it means in terms of test results. Most psychologists have become more sophisticated than that in recent years.

42 Unless the concept is vague, in which case no one knows whether it applies in certain cases until some sort of definitional decision is made on whether it applies.

43 Other functions are discussed by Mariarosa Dalla Costa in *Women and the Subversion of the Community* (1973), obtainable from The Falling Wall Press, Ltd., 79 Richmond Rd., Montpelier, Bristol BSG 5EP, England.

44 Kathryn Stone, "The Origin of Job Structures in the Steel Industry," *Review of Radical Political Economics* 6 (Summer 1974): 61–97. Harry Braverman, *Labor and Monopoly Capitalism* (New York, 1974).

45 Rosabeth Moss Kanter, *Men and Women of the Corporation* (New York, 1977), p. 111.
46 Simone de Beauvoir, *The Second Sex* (New York, 1952).
47 Kanter, *Men and Women of the Corporation*, p. 110.
48 Rosenkrantz et al., "Sex-Role Stereotypes and Self-Concepts;" and Broverman et al., "Sex-Role Stereotypes and Clinical Judgments."
49 Martha Lee Osborne, *Women in Western Thought* (New York, 1979).
50 Blumer, *Symbolic Interactionism*, p. 132.

JEAN BETHKE ELSHTAIN

Methodological Sophistication and Conceptual Confusion
A Critique of Mainstream Political Science

■ American political analysts work within a polity which has been denuded systematically of shared public moral values; a polity in which inequality of class, sex, and race are constituent features of the status quo; a polity in which the private sphere is seen as a haven from the competitive realities of the world of work and as the single arena within which the expression of sentiment and values as idiosyncratic private preferences is acceptable. I shall argue that this cluster of often unstated assumptions is imbedded within the framework of analysis adopted by political scientists who represent the mainstream of their discipline. The tacit categorizations of women as apolitical creatures and of politics as the pursuit and exercise of that public power whose chief purpose is to meet "legitimate" group interests and demands are imperatives which restrict the scope and subject matter of political discourse and thus have an effect upon the practice of politics itself.

Any final definition of or limitation on the scope of what constitutes politics may (and does) hide the fact that interests are served by these very limitations. The analyst who begins a discussion with the assumption that politics has to do with tough bargaining processes for which men, for a variety of reasons, are most suited, and that moral values are part of the "softer" virtues relegated to churches, women, and private lives, will be blinded to certain features of the social and political world which an observer who is critical of the status quo will see as problems to be explained rather than givens needing no explanation.

To examine the relationship of women to politics and of both to values one must, first, ascertain the ground upon which contemporary political inquiry and methodology rests. If one probes beneath the surface of facts labeled "objective" and hypotheses termed "scientific," one discovers interlocked images of human nature and politics which form the foundation for the "facts" and hypotheses on the surface. The responsible political analyst should open up to public scrutiny and review all the dimensions which cohere within his or her explanatory theory of politics, a perspective. A perspective, according to William E. Connolly, includes a set of fundamental (if tacit) assumptions about the "normal" operations of politics and an integrated set of concepts through which the analyst interprets the political and social world.[1] The analyst's initial expectations shape the conceptual system he or she adopts. These concepts, in turn, enable analysts to absorb or to ignore (if, indeed, they even see) "deviations" from their original presumptions.[2] "A perspective," Connolly writes,

> is a set of presumptions about social and political life derived from selective social experience; the conceptual system it sustains focuses on those aspects of the environment most congruent with those presumptions and tends to divert attention away from other possible dimensions. Since the investigator is seldom sharply aware of his own perspective and its role in inquiry, he is likely to ignore or underplay its tendency to push his interpretations in a particular direction.[3]

Practitioners of contemporary political science tend to presume and to celebrate their own commitment to neutral, scientific objectivity. To this end they have expunged values as a central feature of political study. Women, as the traditional bearers of morality and virtue within the Western culture, are identified with a private sphere which is seen as apolitical and infused with affect. The conceptual association of women with values understood as privatized, subjective preferences which are neither rationally defensible nor amenable to coherent adjudication is not a contingent but a necessary feature within mainstream political explanation. A framework of explanation which factors out women and values includes among its devotees behaviorists who assume political science is a value-free enterprise and those empirical political theorists who admit values, shrunken to "opinions, attitudes, and preferences," into their calculations. (These empirical theorists accept the designation "behavioralist" for their enterprise in order to distinguish themselves from the behaviorists, who do not concern themselves with values at all.)

I shall begin my examination of mainstream political inquiry with David Easton, a leading exponent of the behavioralist persuasion. Easton holds that most students of politics would probably agree about the general nature of the assumptions and objectives of behavioralism. These assumptions and objectives include the presumption that there are "discoverable uniformities in political behavior"; that these regularities are akin to the laws of physics; and that they provide the grounding for explanatory theories in political science which are verifiable (or falsifiable) empirically and have predictive value. The behavioralist effort, Easton declares, shares the scientific rigor of its counterparts in the physical and natural sciences; moreover, the facts of political life and the values one appends to those facts are "two different kinds of propositions that, for the sake of clarity, should be kept analytically distinct."[4] Easton's assertions are correct in this sense: students of politics, including many who claim they do not share behavioralist assumptions, can be seen, under scrutiny, to have adopted its key propositions. The separation between ethical evaluation and empirical explanation, between descriptive and evaluative statements, is widely, if implicitly, accepted and infuses political explanations with what Charles Taylor terms a particular "value slope."[5] Because the practitioners of an ostensibly value-free social science deny that their work is infused with values, they cannot recognize, and thus cannot articulate, the implications of their conclusions for human wants, needs, and purposes within political and social life. In this manner much contemporary political science is both a priori and presumptuous.

I shall expose several of the unexamined assumptions of mainstream political inquiry with specific attention to its implications for women and politics. First, what are the assumptions about human nature and human action which underlie contemporary political inquiry? No theory of human nature, as Ellen Wood points out, is empirically verifiable.[6] Yet theories of human nature, of what it *is* or means to be human, are central to social and political thought. Aristotle, Hobbes, Locke, and Rousseau, for example, formulated and defended theories of persons and related these persons to politics; indeed, without the articulation of what persons are, or can become, a theory of politics remains, at best, incomplete. The important question for our purposes is whether or not it is possible to discern a *particular* notion of human nature and mind within contemporary accounts of politics.

Perhaps the best way to begin is to ask, On *what* set of assumptions concerning human nature and action *must* contemporary inquiry be based if its conclusions are to be logical and internally consistent? For example: suppose I were to declare in an obdurate and uncompromising manner that people are by nature amicable, sociable creatures who cooperate voluntarily without any external coercion, who spontaneously engage in meaningful group action within social contexts (that is, the action has a common meaning for the purposive, intentional agents who undertake it); that these beings recognize that their way of life is constituted, in part, by their beliefs; and that these beings, finally, celebrate a life of thought and reason as an important activity. Suppose further, that at the request of a community of such beings I am commissioned to write up plans for a governing system for these peace-loving social beings. I devote myself to the task of determining how beings like themselves would order their life in common. The plan I come up with is called *The Leviathan* (my name, you see, is Thomas Hobbes). I begin my tract with the argument that, in the absence of authoritarian control by a single ruler, political life would dissolve into a war of all against all.

The response from the community of peace-loving beings who commissioned me to create a form of government in their behalf would no doubt be one of confusion and extreme consternation, as these cooperative beings had never engaged in a war of all against all. If I were to continue to insist that although I saw human beings as cooperative and peace-loving, as they did, I nevertheless found it necessary to create a polity ruled by a sovereign with absolute, unchecked power to make all judgements, determine all laws, and set forth the "truth" to his subjects, I would either be sent away for a prolonged visit to some tranquil spot in the country until such time as I regained the power of coherent thought, or I would be tolerated as someone engaged in a not-terribly-funny ruse. The more mistrustful members of the community might suspect that I was some sort of enemy agent hired by another society to undermine the morale of this community's naturally cooperative way of life.

The point of this tale is to indicate that there is a direct, if implicit, link between a theorist's views on what human beings are, how these beings come to learn and to reason and to act in common, and his or her logic of inquiry and political explanation. The conclusions about politics will flow in large measure from some prior commitment to a theory about the nature of persons. That political analysts refuse to lay all their prior commitments on the table does not mean they have none up their sleeves. At this point I can only suggest briefly certain connections between particular theories of human nature and the prevailing mode in political science. Modern political inquiry occurs within a particular context. That context includes a society characterized by sexual, as well as by class and racial, inequality. The view of human nature and the human mind which informs and helps to legitimate such inequities can be traced from certain dimensions within classical liberal political theory which emerged in conjunction with empiricist accounts of the operations of the human mind. Contemporary political scientists, for the most part, are unaware of the philosophical foundations of their enterprise and thus cannot even consider the contestable assumptions concerning human nature imbedded within their frameworks of analysis. Indeed, the problem "What kind of being does your analysis presuppose?" is neither a question to be asked nor an issue to be explored for modern political scientists, whose images of persons remain a series of unreflective prior commitments.

The human being who is the subject matter of political inquiry and the

Methodological Sophistication and Conceptual Confusion   233

object of mainstream pluralist political science is best characterized in paradigmatic form as an *abstract individual* who is said to be *sovereign*. For classical liberal thinkers a human being is real to the extent that she or he is posited as ontologically prior to society and alone.[7] He or she is a social atom whose relevant features "are assumed as given, independently of a social context. This givenness of fixed and invariant human psychological features leads to an abstract conception of the individual who is seen merely as the bearer of those features, which determine his [or her] behavior, and specify his interests, needs and rights."[8] The relationship between one abstract atom and the next, and between an aggregate (not a community!) of such atoms and their society, is external and instrumental. Society is an artificial aggregate which exists to serve specific instrumental purposes—called "group interests."

Abstract Man's* involvement with others in society is measured by a calculus James Glass has termed "the phenomenology of liberal externality," a mode of perception tied to what Hobbes called "reckoning consequences."[9] Abstract Man behaves or acts from a calculated, prudent self-interest which, in the liberal view, redounds ultimately to the good of all. Neither Hobbes nor Locke nor contemporary political scientists believe that persons are changed in any *fundamental* way by living among one another in a society rather than singly, say, on hundreds of desert islands, each populated by a single Abstract Man. The life of Abstract Man is characterized by a rigid split not only between the public and the private but between the economic and political spheres; indeed, the presumption of such splits is parasitical upon the atomistic self the theory presupposes. A theory of Abstract Man cannot take social contexts of meaning into account systematically. The social world is given and is featured variously as an entity which may threaten to destroy the sovereign individual's liberties and must be watched carefully, or as a powerful conglomerate of means which can be deployed on behalf of private interests. Classical liberal theory cannot provide the grounding for a shared political life in common. As Robert Paul Wolff points out, the liberal theory of the Abstract Man assumes that all values are simple private values or aggregates of private values.[10] In contemporary political science, Abstract Man is further reduced to a being with roles and functions as even more of his or her social attributes are stripped away.

The human mind featured in classical liberal and contemporary main-

---

*The term "Abstract Man" has been retained because of the historical context of the discussion; in contemporary writing a more inclusive term, such as Abstract Human, would be used.

stream accounts is also construed as asocial. According to defenders of "autonomous rationality," persons are free beings who constitute their own "universe of meaning."[11] There is an ineradicable solipsism—an ontology of atomistic individuals who alone are basic and real, who are the only true and "ultimate constituents of the social world."[12] The minds of such atomized beings, according to the empiricist epistemology which has predominated in Western discourse since Locke, Berkeley, and Hume, can apprehend self-evident facts (which, apparently, are sprinkled generously about in unadorned fashion) and reach conclusions on the basis of this evidence. The empiricist version holds that the mind works in much the way a Xerox machine replicates a sheet of printed matter: it makes copies or images of the impressions it receives, and these are "ideas." This particular theory of mind (part and parcel, remember, of the liberal theory of the individual) concludes that once the mind has an image or a copy of an impression given to the senses, it, too, can produce copies. New sets of ideas may be derived from solipsistic introspection, which involves a private definition of external reality.[13]

Abstract Man's mind, like his world, is bifurcated neatly: on the one hand, it contains an aspect associated with dispositions or desires; on the other hand, it is capable of cognition based on a passive capacity to "copy" the outside world. He reacts to forces and pressures from the outside. One aspect of reaction may be a piece of behavior which other passive humans who happen to be studying him observe and note down as data. But the behavior in which this subject engages also includes a subjective aspect, that is, the individual reacts to situations in one way or another depending upon biases, subjective preferences, attitudes, likes, dislikes, and so on. The combined behaviors of a number of passive, abstract human subjects will mean something different to each one, depending upon the idiosyncratic and private preferences of each. There is and can be no shared world of common meaning within this perspective.

Mainstream political inquiry cannot be understood apart from these links to the empiricist theory of mind and the classical liberal theory of Abstract Man. These views on human nature, thought, and action remain imbedded within contemporary accounts. The ideal subject of so-called scientific observation in political science is not (and cannot be) a self-reflexive, purposeful agent who engages the world actively and helps to shape it with thought and action, but is a narrowly calculating being who adapts, conforms, and engages in self-interested behavior, rather than in action with a social as well as a private meaning. The behavioralist enterprise rests on a set of tacit assumptions shared by those who labor within its framework of explanation. These include the conviction that human behavior is a relatively reliable variable within a scientific hypothesis. The idea, a simplistic one, is that an aggregate of human beings, exposed to a particular external force, will react and behave in ways that are predictable in advance; thus behavioralist "hypotheses" conform to the requirements of a method which assumes the possibility of prediction in the first place, given its narrow understanding of human reason and its mechanistic account of human emotion and action.[14]

The goal of behavioralist explanation is neither the *understanding* of human beings and their social and political world, nor the *interpretation* of that world of self and others, but the construction of verifiable hypotheses with the power to predict. In order to predict, one needs behavioral regularity which follows an inexorable logic; behavior, in other words, must be *caused*. The test of lawlike generalizations within political and social life is implicit within a logic of explanation which assumes the possibility of prediction and regularity. Behavioralism may be called the Calvinism of cognition: the aim is to strip away the apparent complexities of political life and human action, to get rid of anything untidy, so that one might engage in a search for lawlikeness in political life. The political and social context itself is accepted as a given rather than questioned or criticized. Issues of political justice; legitimacy; sexual, racial, and class inequality; and political reform or revolt cannot arise as problems, for these issues call the context into question and make the behavior of social participants less amenable to lawlike predictability. All resonant themes and issues must either be expunged from view before the analyst begins work (the context-as-a-given), or, for the more scrupulous who are somewhat aware of these matters, contested issues may be incorporated in a way which fits within the boundaries of their logic of explanation.[15] Within a pluralist society such as our own, for example, a mainstream analyst might accept the possibility that a few running repairs are needed here and there. This, in turn, will lead to demands and activities on the part of certain groups. But these groups and movements (dubbed "interest groups," thus narrowing all group efforts to the level of self-interestedness) are treated differently depending on whether they play by the "rules of the game"—that is, are rational and reasonable on the pluralist model—or whether they refuse to play by the rules and behave in ways which provide evidence of immaturity and rabid ideological commitments. (Once ideologues have matured and rid themselves of *parti pris*, they, too, may be admitted into the game on good behavior.) The analyst who grasps the particulars of the political system under the description proffered above excludes grasping them under a divergent description.

How do mainstream political scientists characterize their enterprise? What are the implications of this enterprise? What are the implications of this enterprise for women and politics? First, the analyst starts from what

Steven Lukes terms rock bottom and Charles Taylor calls brute-data identifiable behavior. For example, Heinz Eulau, a leading figure in the behavioralist revolution in political science, declares that any science of politics "which deserves its name" must be built "from the bottom up by asking simple questions that can, in principle, be answered; it cannot be built from the top down by asking questions that, one has reason to suspect, cannot be answered at all, at least not by the methods of science. An empirical discipline is built by the slow, modest, and piecemeal cumulation of relevant theories and data."[16]

Scientific inquiry in politics starts from the bottom with simple questions presumed to be objective and neutral. T. D. Weldon discusses what this demand for objectivity entails: "In fact the demand for 'objective' standards in politics and in morals is simply a demand for a criterion which enables us to grade people and institutions with the same sort of certainty and confidence as that with which, with very minor qualifications, we can grade physical bodies in terms of size and weight."[17]

Within the epistemological presumptions of behavioralist political thinking, to describe and to evaluate, to state what is and to state what ought to be, are *two entirely separable activities*. Those who mix the two are considered fuzzy-minded, impressionistic, and incapable of rigorous analysis—a description not unlike stereotypic characterizations of female thinking processes. A bifurcation between descriptive and evaluative statements is essential to behavioralist inquiry. The hypotheses formulated and the tests constructed to verify (or falsify) these same hypotheses are all contingent upon a prior separation of statements.[18] The goal of behavioralism, its *raison d'être*, lies in "coming as close as possible" to a description of the political world as it *really* is, stripped to the bare bones of objectivity. "Values, biases, attitudes, and emotional preferences"—subjective dimensions—may be appended later if the analyst chooses.

Laborers in the mainstream vineyard assume that in statements other than those which cannot be falsified (or analytic statements which entail a nonfalsifiable correspondence between subject and predicate by definition—for example, "All married women are wives"), the political analyst is presented with a problem of linking, or establishing a relationship between, subject and predicate which can be explored and adjudicated only through empirical investigation. This investigation will demonstrate (the assumption goes) a correlation between the subject of the statement and its predicate. Two statements requiring investigation might be "All married women purchase Crunchy Creatures for breakfast," or, more troubling but not so problematic as to give pause to the intrepid, "All married women are happy." The relationship between "married women" and the predicates in each sentence is called a "synthetic" one and is stated in quantitative terms. The nearer the investigator comes to a correlation of 1.0 the closer he or she is presumed to be to the truth and the greater the power of the statement, couched as a hypothesis, to predict. The researcher must strive to reduce or to bracket ambiguity, imprecision, complexity, and ambivalence in order to come as close as possible to symmetry between naming (the subject) and meaning (the predicate which expresses the truth of the statement). In the sample sentence "All married women are happy," for example, a researcher set on precision (and a high correlation) must first arrive at final cloture on a definition of *happy*, a notoriously rich, open-ended, and imprecise term of ordinary discourse. Despite the open-endedness of usage of a term within a way of life, the logic of this method forces the behavioralist to adopt a series of arbitrary and fixed definitions so as to construct the hypotheses. The result is a particularly crude verificationist theory of meaning.[19]

The theory of meaning imbedded in mainstream political inquiry claims as a central presumption that the *meaning* of synthetic statements ("All married women are happy") is *exhausted* once a relationship between the subject and predicate has been established *via* correlations. Yet even before such tests begin, the hypothesis has been impoverished by the arbitrary reduction of rich, reactive terms central to human social relationships (*happy*) to one among a number of possible definitions. Thus the definition of *happy* in my example constitutes an a priori. In Taylor's words, "The profound option of mainstream social scientists for the empiricist conception of knowledge and science makes it inevitable that they should accept the verification model of political science and the categorical principles that this entails. This means in turn that a study of our civilization in terms of its intersubjective and common meanings is ruled out. Rather this whole level of study is made invisible."[20] Should the critics of mainstream inquiry cavil at the "results" which emerge from such research, they are often confronted with the self-serving insistence that the tests are neutral and prove something whether others like it or not.

"Liking" or "not liking" the results of someone's research is not the point at all. What is the point is that test procedures, and what counts as evidence, are inseparable from a framework of analysis which provides for such tests in the first place. But this framework goes unexamined and thus unchallenged within mainstream literature.[21] Methodology can never be free-floating; it grows out of epistemological commitments. Those obvious facts which dot the pages of contemporary political science emerge within a perspective which holds that facts can stand naked and alone — that there is an unbridgeable gulf between descriptions and evaluation.

Yet, as Julius Kovesi argues in a compelling critique of the presumptions undergirding behavioralist political inquiry, these presumptions have normative implications for persons and politics, for there is no such thing as mere description.[22] Description is always from a point of view and hence is evaluative.[23] We describe situations on the basis of those aspects of that situation we deem relevant or important. In this way, we "always evaluate under a certain description."[24] Contrary to behavioralism, the most important contrast is not between description and evaluation but between "description from the moral point of view as opposed to other points of view."[25] Description is always to a purpose. This purpose may, and often does, remain hidden from view—imbedded in a series of tacit prior commitments the analyst or researcher does not acknowledge and therefore need not defend.

Three contrasting descriptions of the process of modern industrial wage labor will serve to demonstrate the evaluations for persons and social life which flow from the language of description itself (emphasis mine).

1. What dominates the labor process and all work processes which are performed in the mode of laboring is neither man's purposeful effort nor the product he may desire, but the motion of the process itself and the rhythm it imposes upon the laborers. Labor implements are drawn into this rhythm until body and tool swing in the same repetitive movement, that is, until the use of machines, which of all implements are best suited to the performance of the *animal laborans*, it is no longer the body's movement that determines the implement's movement but the machine's movement which enforces the movements of the body. *The point is that nothing can be mechanized more easily and less artificially than the rhythm of the labor process, which, in turn corresponds to the equally automatic repetitive rhythm of the life process and its metabolism with nature . . . . complaints about the "artificial" rhythm which the machines impose upon the laborer . . . characteristically, are relatively rare among the laborers themselves, who, on the contrary, seem to find the same amount of pleasure in repetitive machine work as in other repetitive labor . . . . They prefer [it] because it is mechanical and does not demand attention, so that while performing it they can think of something else.*[26]

2. When a workman is increasingly and exclusively engaged in the fabrication of one thing, he ultimately does his work with singular dexterity; but at the same time, he loses the general faculty of applying his mind to the direction of his work. He everyday becomes more adroit and less industrious. *In proportion as the principle of the division of labor is more extensively applied the workman becomes more weak, more narrow minded, and more dependent. The art advances, the artisan recedes.*[27]

3. The capitalist mode of production (essentially the production of surplus-value, the absorption of surplus-labour) produces thus, with the extention of the working day, not only the deterioration of human labour-power, by robbing it of its normal, moral and physical, conditions of development

and function, it produces also the premature exhaustion and death of this labour-power itself. *It extends the labourer's time of production during a given period by shortening his actual life-time.*[28]

The first description of the division of labor in assembly-line production conveys, through the language chosen for description, the assurance that such wage-labor is natural and pleasurable to those who engage in it. The analyst whose description provides this uncritical reassurance, Hannah Arendt in *The Human Condition*, does not preface her description of the work process with a caveat to the reader that she accepts and celebrates a stratified system of inequality which relegates a portion of its population, male and female, to daily repetitive labor and denies to that portion the social goods which routinely set the contours of life for the more privileged. Yet her description of the process as natural and pleasurable constitutes an evaluation of assembly-line work as good—as no imposition whatever on *animal laborans*. If one accepts Arendt's description of the work process and its benign and soothing correspondence with the body's rhythms, the effects of that process upon persons will not be called into question, and the social placement of such persons will remain hidden from critical scrutiny.

The second description, proffered by Alexis de Tocqueville, uses language which implicates him in an evaluation of the work process as one often harmful and ultimately demeaning to those who must engage in it. De Tocqueville's depiction has imbedded within it an evaluative dimension that allows the reader to question the beneficence of a highly specialized division of labor. With the third characterization of wage-labor production, drawn from Karl Marx's *Capital*, volume 1, the reader is confronted with a descriptive vocabulary consisting of a number of powerful critical terms. These terms allow the reader to probe beneath the appearance of things in order to explore, from a critical and skeptical stance, what may be deeper meanings and realities. Marx speaks of human deterioration under the circumstances of wage-labor, of robbing the worker of "normal, moral and physical" development and functions. Thus, de Tocqueville's and Marx's descriptions implicate them in criticism of, or dissent from, a process which is an integral feature of the capitalist socioeconomic and political status quo. Because the second and third descriptions make reference to human beings as purposive and intentional agents with wants, needs, and the capacity to feel pain, they can be said to be formed from a moral point of view. De Tocqueville and Marx are disturbed or outraged by a process which undermines human dignity and self-respect and vitiates the capacity for creative or independent work. Arendt's description, however, is formed without regard to a moral point of view. Those who remain within the language of Arendt's description cannot make reference to questions of respect for persons, or human beings as intentional and purposeful agents.

Despite the nexus between description and evaluation demonstrated by the examples above, the behavioralist imperative remains that of bifurcating statements of fact from statements of value, of exempting description from evaluation. The assumption is that the analyst describes objectively a problem or situation or issue in political life or thought, verifies the truth or meaning of hypotheses grounded in this objective characterization, and then, if he or she chooses, layers a patina of value judgments on top of neutral descriptions and the objective facts. Opinions, biases, and values (all are presumed to be rationally indefensible within the rigors of this logic) are related to facts and descriptions in much the way that clothing and accoutrements are related to a department store mannequin. A window decorator begins with an unadorned mannequin and dresses or undresses it as he or she (and the store manager) sees fit. In much the same way, the political analyst may add values to the objective facts which constitute his or her description of political life and social reality. These facts, like so many immobile, silent mannequins, remain unaltered through such external operations.

Ramifications of the behavioralist presumptions flow into moral theory as well. A link between political inquiry and moral imperatives was presumed explicitly by classical theorists in the history of political thought; however, contemporary political science tends to divide politics from moral considerations. This is yet another base from which a critique of the perspective can be mounted. Focusing on a moral dilemma should serve to illustrate further the inadequacy of the bifurcation between description and evaluation. Imagine that a group of persons are gathered around listening to a description of a brutal event in which young children were tortured systematically by sadistic adults. The account is replete with details of the desperate implorings of the children and the impervious cruelty of their torturers. One of those who hears this tale of terror and tragedy is a social scientist who accepts the dichotomy between description and evaluation. The social scientist insists, once the speaker has recounted the tale in all its graphic horror, that the group now be told whether the actions of the torturers are approved!

Would such a demand make sense? Remember, the situation is characterized by the speaker on the basis of those aspects considered relevant. These included the details of the suffering of the children at the hands of torturers depicted as brutal and sadistic. The *description* of events constituted an evaluation from a moral point of view. A person devoid of moral perspective would have described these events in different language

—in language not designed to arouse compassion, sorrow, moral indignation, and outrage from the listener.

If we place these considerations within the context of contemporary political inquiry, we find that those analysts who adopt a moral point of view from which to describe, and thereby evaluate, political reality—including inequality, the plight of the poor, indignities suffered by the elderly, and the indifference suffered by the mentally handicapped—characterize social reality in very different language from that deployed by those analysts who presume they have at their disposal a "neutral" language of description. Precisely the obverse pertains: we evaluate the world through our descriptive notions. In Kovesi's language, "Moral notions describe the world of evaluation."[29] Behavioralist "neutral" language is simply language not formed from a moral, or critical, point of view.

The response of mainstream scholars to the criticisms proffered above would be that researchers do have their own values, often termed biases. "We know," they would argue, "that biases and our own values are a problem. We have developed test procedures to cope with this problem, to correct for our values—to neutralize them for purposes of research." Values are left in a shadowy realm from which they may inform or push the analyst towards "constructive research." Easton goes so far as to admit values as a component, or variable, within his model. The "major kinds of propositions," for Easton, are factual, moral, applied, and theoretical. Although moral propositions help analysts to build "constructive theoretical research," ultimately the validity and utility of empirical political theory rests upon its correspondence with political reality.[30] Analysts, in this view, must isolate and bracket values as they go about their work. Values remain on a par with preferences, expressions of taste or distaste, or emotions and feelings presumed not to be rationally defensible. Moral notions are just one type of opinion among many.[31]

Those committed to the view that moral notions, opinions, biases, and beliefs can be stated apart from description and research methods and findings, that such notions are indefensible rationally, and that they can be bracketed after they have pushed the researcher towards certain questions have adopted tacitly a theory of morality known as *emotivism*. Emotivism is an account of moral notions compatible with and imbedded in behavioralist presumptions. Emotivist accounts hold that such terms of moral evaluation as *good* or *bad* are purely emotive. That is, these terms stand "for nothing whatever" and merely "serve as an emotive sign expressing our attitude . . . and perhaps evoking similar attitudes in other persons."[32]

According to the emotivist account, that which is called good depends upon one's values or biases. Should individuals commend a course of action to us as "good" they are merely recounting their biases or feelings or tastes—none of which comprises an evaluation for which reasons can be adduced and given. Should my own taste happen to concur, I will be likely to accept the commendation as "good." But suppose I am confronted with a moral dilemma. One day I find myself sequestered with a sadist who delights in lighting afire the tails of captured stray dogs. Wishing to draw me into the enterprise of maltreating and abusing animals, this person tells me, "It is *good* to torture helpless creatures and to make them feel pain." Why is it good? Because this individual feels it to be—and "feels good" when engaging in the torture of animals, and thus, commends these actions to others so that they, too, might "feel good." How am I to respond to these claims? I could try to get out of the problem by declaring the puppy-torturer a psychopath whose views must perforce be ignored. But perhaps the torturer's behavior betrays no signs of irrationality; indeed, the person is calm and cool throughout. All that is left me, if I am a consistent emotivist, is the reply: "Well, you have your opinion as to what is good and I have mine. Personally, I do not feel it is good to torture animals. My feelings are different from yours. So why don't we agree to disagree, and I'll leave now if it's all the same to you."

The emotivist account of moral notions, imbedded within the behavioralist perspective, requires that all arguments for or against social structures and arrangements formed from a moral point of view (through the language of injustice, oppression, exploitation, discrimination, etc.) be allowed to fall through the sieve of those who claim value-neutrality for their work, and those who insist that they do incorporate or defend values if by values one means rationally indefensible personal preferences.[33]

My central point is this: problems presented by questions of biases or values cannot be dealt with simply by admitting, as mainstream political scientists long ago began doing, to one's bias and claiming to set these biases to the side for purposes of research.[34] This response does not touch the heart of the matter, namely, an epistemology which requires the severance of fact from value.[35] The problem is more complex and fundamental than any charge of bias! *It is that every explanatory theory of politics supports a particular set of normative conclusions.* To have an explanatory theory, the analyst must adopt a framework linked, implicitly if not explicitly, to notions of human nature and human purposes. This framework sets the boundaries of the phenomena to be investigated. Some factors of social life will be incorporated, and others will be expunged from view before research begins. The framework gears choices, celebrates some interests, excludes others, and precludes seeing the political world under an alternative characterization.

What has all this to do with women, politics, and values? The relationships are on the level of depth connections within a tradition of moral and political discourse which has linked women traditionally to values trivialized as emotive and subjective preferences; which ties political behavior to a narrow view of rationality associated with a belief in predictable behavior (women, as irrational creatures, are shoved to the periphery of rational political behavior as thus understood); which sees the polity as an aggregate set-up to serve instrumental purposes or interests which is bifurcated conceptually and objectively from the private world of emotions, feelings, and noninstrumental relations. Women express values reduced to subjective, private, irrational, and emotional beliefs or affects and reign in some natural realm outside politics, power, and the world of rationalistic, calculated decisionmaking.

An alternative explanatory theory must deploy divergent criteria as to what counts as a political activity or issue and what does not. These criteria are imbedded within the concepts and the descriptive terms the analyst utilizes. Despite the smug self-assurance which emanates from the pages of so much contemporary political inquiry, no definition of *politics*, its range and purpose, is given either simply or a priori. Concepts and contests about what politics is slice up the world of thought and action in certain ways. Within mainstream political science, what has been described traditionally as politics tends to factor women out of the activity and has excluded for many years the questions raised by feminists. Such questions are relegated to a sphere outside organized political activity and are dismissed as private "troubles." Women have had to struggle not only against political policies, structures, and arrangements but against definitions of politics and modes of political explanation as well.

The view of politics proffered by several well-known practiners of contemporary political science will clarify my argument. Harold Lasswell, in his classic book on influence (*Politics: Who Gets What, When, How*) describes politics as the study of the influential. Who are the influential? They are those who get more of what there is to get: deference, income, safety. "The science of politics states conditions; the philosophy of politics justifies preferences. *This book, restricted to political analysis, declares no preferences. It states conditions.*"[36] Yet the title Lasswell chose for his book tells us in advance that politics is about who gets what, when, and how. By relegating politics to the study of the influential, Lasswell adopts complacency towards the reality that disproportionate numbers of women, minorities, and working-class persons fall into the category of the uninfluential and are thus defined out of politics (save as those over whom influence is exerted).

Bernard Crick, in his *In Defence of Politics*, published in 1964 when politics-as-usual was under challenge from civil rights activists and student rebels, calls for a reaffirmation of the traditional view that politics "can be simply defined as the activity by which differing interests within a given unit of rule are conciliated by giving them a share in power in proportion to their importance to the welfare and survival of the whole community."[37] Women do not represent a differing interest to be conciliated for Crick because their traditional activities fall outside Crick's political purview. Crick denies explicitly that personal relationships, marriage, and the family have anything to do with politics. Politics is the "master science among men. . . . a preoccupation of free men." But Crick's free men, as they go about their "preoccupation," are compelled to justify wide-ranging social inequality and injustice if they accept his definition of the activity and purpose of politics. If differing interests are conciliated by giving these interests a share in power "in proportion to their importance to the welfare and survival of the whole community," large segments within a given population are defined out of politics by fiat. Those who hold power are placed by Crick in a position to determine who shall or shall not be conciliated, depending upon their relative importance or unimportance to the welfare and survival of the unit of rule. Women, perhaps, might struggle to make their case within Crick's tidy universe, but the severely disadvantaged, the diseased, the infirm, the handicapped, could not. Perhaps Crick would allow them charity if not conciliation. In any case, the range over which he allows politics to operate restricts incorporating the concerns of the socially abused and disadvantaged into the heart of political debates.

Seymour Martin Lipset, a political sociologist whose most important book remains his 1963 volume, *Political Man: The Social Bases of Politics*, seems at first glance to meet criticism of the Lasswell-Crick approach to politics as too restrictive and narrow. He expands politics by defining it as a set of processes which are nothing more than "special cases of more general sociological and psychological relationships."[38] Unfortunately, Lipset's definition is so diffuse that the distinguishable activity one designates as "politics" gets lost in a blur of social undifferentiation. Lipset, too, manages to factor women out of political participation as measured by indices of voter participation. Lipset cites evidence for the relative nonparticipation of women in politics as a sign of female apathy and overweening concern with social values. Absorbed within these traditional family and community activities Lipset clearly accepts as their natural sphere, women are unconcerned with politics save when a "morality" issue like gambling or prohibition is at stake.[39] Lipset construes women's apathy as evidence of the *satisfaction* of women with their lot; thus, women's nonparticipation fails to become a problem to be explained.

For Lipset only issues that are organized around bargaining groups within a pluralist polity need to be explained and analyzed. He fails to recognize that a *nonissue* may be the outcome of a political process which skews the results of that process towards those who already have access to the system of rewards. He accepts as apolitical or nonpolitical all issues he locates at the level of personal troubles, problems, or values. Suppose, instead, an analyst viewed apathy or nonparticipation (utilizing the same data cited by Lipset) as a political issue or problem rather than a nonissue or an expression of personal values or problems. From some alternative perspective, apathy might indicate erosion of support for a political system rather than serving as proof that people are so (relatively) satisfied they can afford to be apathetic.[40]

Lipset's understanding of politics and of the apathetic underwrites his justification of the exclusion of the lower classes from political participation. He assigns to lower-class apathy and political silence an important function as a prop upon which systems stability rests. If too many participated too often about too much, it would result in political instability. As it is (one thinks of women, slaves, and under classes as Aristotle's "necessary conditions" for the existence of the *polis),* lower-class people are "much less committed to democracy," as evidenced by their "lower voter turnout."[41] Lipset does not recognize (or, if he does, he makes a secret of this realization) that his conclusions reflect his attachment to a particular political status quo and serve simultaneously to justify and to legitimate stratified and inegalitarian social structures and arrangements. He rests his case on the facts of apathy and nonparticipation by women and lower classes in politics. Then he utilizes these facts to make the case that the situation is all right because the lower class is less committed to democracy than the middle class, and women are immersed in their apolitical social values and their divergent social roles.

Two observations are necessary. First, politics and the power which flows from holding political responsibilities may be reflected in *limiting* the scope of the political process in the service of a given status quo. This limitation may be couched in the guise of preserving traditional values, or protecting politics from extremists who would pervert it should they gain power. There is often some truth to such charges. But the salient point for our consideration is that certain specific interests are served by these limitations and that this fact is hidden or remains opaque. Peter Bachrach and Morton S. Baratz, in their ground-breaking 1962 critique of pluralism, "Two Faces of Power," observed that although some issues are organized into politics and others are not, *power* is implicated in eliminating certain areas from explicit political consideration, just as it is involved in adjudicating between extant interest groups.[42] Power, they argued, is not limited to public debates and decisionmaking but is deployed in confining the scope of the political to consideration of issues not threatening to those interests who do not wish to see certain problems and issues opened up for political debate.

The women's movement has thrust issues previously declared private or nonpolitical into the midst of political debates. Together with the other liberation movements which emerged in the 1960s, the women's movement helped to forge a redefinition of political power to include both dimensions of unintentional power, and power as productive of unintended consequences.[43] Power as unintentional, or as productive of consequences which may be unintended, is that possessed by a particular class, group, or sex by virtue of its position within a set of social structures and arrangements—a position from which that group derives benefits and privileges but which it did not intentionally seek to create. For example, a white individual in a racist society may himself be nonracist, but in that society he possesses greater unintentional power than a black individual. Similarly, men *qua* men have greater unintentional power than women in a sexist society. An avid anti-Suffragist, writing in 1889, observed that husbands could not avoid possessing power over their wives: "He has not assumed it: it has existed as a consequence of the natures and constitutions of the two sexes. True, he need not exercise the power, but notwithstanding this, he cannot emancipate his wife therefrom.[44] This concept of unintentional power, in turn, may be tied up with notions of authority and legitimacy, concepts traditionally deployed as characterizations of the state or the highest level of political power. Yet familial relations involve (although they are not defined exclusively by) both power and authority. Men and women alike may exercise power as coercion, manipulation, or persuasion within the boundary of an intimate relationship, but the male is the sole possessor of unintentional power with a public meaning having political consequences. When he exerts power, it is considered legitimate—perhaps neither wise nor beneficent, but legitimate.[45] The women's movement, in this sense, is a legitimation crisis. Certainly not all instances of unintended consequences involve power. The important point is that by narrowing the scope of politics in the ways I have criticized, leading analysts representing mainstream social science have lent their support to forces who benefit from inegalitarian social arrangements and who seek to maintain and to defend the politics which helps them to get more of what there is to get.

A political scientist who denies to the majority of women, minorities, and poor a central role in politics because he or she has defined politics in a manner which eliminates those not already ensconced within the system of rewards and benefits is not engaged in some mere reflection or neutral description of political reality: he or she is providing a normative justification for an extant way of life. Women must fight both political reality and purportedly neutral statements about that reality, which, in fact, secrete normative dimensions supportive of the status quo. Mainstream political science, consciously or unconsciously, tacitly or openly, has adopted an interrelated set of presumptions; thus, it must be held responsible for the outcomes which flow from them.

An analyst who accepts the framework I have explicated and criticized in this essay is forced, through the logic of explanation, to accept all or some of the following presumptions: (a) a narrow definition of politics which excludes by fiat the cluster of issues, problems, and values focused on the family or private live; (b) a concept of political participation which involves a standard of an ideal, active political citizen and judges individuals against that norm without seriously considering factors which mitigate against participation or, having considered such factors, decides that participation is not necessarily desirable for everyone; (c) a focus on interest groups and pluralist bargaining, given the liberal dogma of politics as a sphere within which individual self-interest or aggregations of self-interest are articulated and adjudicated; (d) a privatization and trivialization of moral concerns or values as these relate to public, social issues; (e) a justification or rationalization of a system of stratification by sex, race, class, age, and so on, so long as system stability is maintained.

It would be difficult to find a political scientist who would own up to supporting all of these presumptions; nevertheless, if a perspective leads the analyst to accept any *one* of these dimensions, he or she is committed, in complex, tacit ways, to aspects of all the others. Despite the flurries, debates, and surface changes of the recent past, contemporary political inquiry continues to rest upon a philosophical foundation inhospitable at its core to rigorous, critical exploration of the deeper relations between women, politics, and values. Its practitioners continue, as they must, to toot the horns of scientific rigor and predictability, despite the remarkable fact that their colleagues in the natural sciences long ago junked such unacceptable constraints to creative scientific research. The physicist, for example, faces the astonishing truth that it is impossible to predict the behavior of subatomic particles. Behavioralist inquiry eviscerates our understanding of the complexity of human beings and the astonishing multilayered textures of their social world, for it cannot accommodate a logic of political explanation which incorporates a critical theory of both persons and politics formed from the moral point of view.

That the majority of women in contemporary political science have been trained within and have thus adopted the very presumptions which served and still serve to legitimate sexual inequality so long as it, in turn, serves the status quo indicates the strength and power of the dominant paradigm and the distance we have to go to achieve an equitable pursuit of knowledge. So long as feminist criticism of bias in scholarship takes place within the presumptions of the dominant mode of political inquiry, feminist scholars will fail to create a powerful alternative framework of explanation. Mainstream political science claims it has already dealt with the matter of bias by adopting an impoverished set of values even as it retained the conceptually fatal bifurcation between description and evaluation. Within the mainstream perspective, a feminist scholar can lodge charges of bias, or set forth her own biases, to her heart's content, but she cannot articulate serious moral claims which would serve to describe and to evaluate her society and her discipline.

Feminist scholars must not be fooled by the few victories women have achieved in those minor skirmishes over whether Professor So-and-So's data on female nonparticipation really correlates at the level claimed, or whether some other Professor So-and-So's research model or design fails to control for variables x, y, or z. Such victories are in the nature of family feuds: they occur within what Wittgenstein would call a single language game, an arena, in this instance characterized by refined and sophisticated techniques coupled with conceptual confusion. Perhaps this combination of sophistication and confusion helps to explain why so much contemporary political science is so trivial and leaves us so cold.

To move towards a critical perspective of politics we must begin as I have done in this essay: we must, first, bring the predominant presumptions of the discipline to the surface and, second, subject them to rigorous and unflinching scrutiny. As our tacit commitments are brought out into the open where they can be debated, we uncover internal inconsistencies, incoherence, and confusion in our own position as well as in the positions of others. A critical science of politics, in contradistinction to that which now wraps itself in the cocoon of neutral objectivity, incorporates interpretive self-criticism as a central feature of its logic. It is only through self-aware reinterpretations of thought and action that human beings can replace confused, tedious, and conformist accounts of the political and social world with more coherent, rational, lively, and critical accounts. Until we move to adopt a rich descriptive vocabulary with which to characterize and evaluate critically political life and thought, we must remain, whatever our stated and heartfelt intents and our radical noises, stuck within a framework of inquiry which neither transcends nor understands but simply reflects (and thus justifies) what is.

The equitable pursuit of knowledge will always involve a political struggle. The relationship between persons of critical mind and society and discipline will always be marked by tension. As traditional, unreflective positions are opened to scrutiny and debate, as critical awareness is attained painfully and arduously, the scholar finds it to be neither a passive nor an altogether pleasant experience. But this dynamic process of breaking through and breaking down the encrusted blur of "political science as usual" is a necessary step on the road towards critical interpretation. In our perplexing era, any method of political inquiry which thinks to find peace within itself, or between itself and society, has nothing to do with a restless, searching inquiry which intensifies political struggles and methodological debates as part and parcel of the pursuit of equity in knowledge and in social life.

To adopt the dictum that political science has to do with closed definitions, impoverished meanings, passive human actors, functions and interests, who gets what, when, and how, interest group articulation, inputs, outputs, managerial techniques and game theory scenarios, is to forsake the authentic heart and soul of politics and political contexts as couched in our resonant conceptual language—the language of justice, freedom, liberty, peace, exploitation, equality, liberation, community, the polity. Our long and turbulent history of politics and political discourse is punctuated, as is all history, with ennobling visions of great minds and ignoble machinations of tyrants and petty sycophants, with heroism and cowardice, the grandeur of the high and mighty and the stoic, mute suffering of the oppressed. The vision of politics I here recall predates its taming under the banner of value-free social science: sometimes bogus, always boring. Feminist political scholars can perform no greater service than to move beyond mainstream constrictions by tapping some of the verve, audacity, and pathos of our shared political tradition. One place to begin is with Jean-Jacques Rousseau's resounding declaration: "Those who wish to separate politics from morals will never understand either."

NOTES

1 William E. Connolly, "Theoretical Self-Consciousness," *Polity* 6 (Fall, 1973): 5–25, passim. A perspective in politics is analogous to a paradigm in scientific inquiry—an "ideal of the natural order."
2 Ibid., p. 13.
3 Ibid., p. 25.
4 Behavioralists, oversimply but not inaccurately, hold that the only valid data of political analysis is observable behavior. Behavioralism is a variation on the theme of epistemological positivism. For positivists all true knowledge is based on positive, observable facts or data given to the senses. See David Easton, "The Current Meaning of 'Behavioralism' in Political Science," in *The Limits*

of *Behavior,* ed. J. C. Charlesworth (Philadelphia, 1962), p. 5. After reading Easton's piece, turn to Alasdair MacIntyre's pithy critique of the fallacies involved in the quest for lawlike explanation as part of a general theory of politics, "Is a Science of Comparative Politics Possible?" in his collection *Against the Self-Images of the Age* (New York, 1967), pp. 222-79. See also Connolly, "Theoretical Self-Consciousness," and two seminal critical essays by Charles Taylor, "Interpretation and the Sciences of Man," *Review of Metaphysics* 26 (1971): 4-51, and "Neutrality in Political Science," in *Philosophy, Politics, and Society,* ed. Peter Laslett and W. G. Runciman (New York, 1967), pp. 25-57. For studies which exemplify the genre I am criticizing, turn to any current issue of the *American Political Science Review,* where examples abound.

5 Taylor, "Neutrality in Political Science," pp. 25-27.
6 Ellen Meiksins Wood, *Mind and Politics* (Berkeley, 1972), p. 4.
7 Ibid.
8 Steven Lukes, *Individualism* (New York, 1973), p. 73.
9 James Glass, "Schizophrenia and Perception: A Critique of the Liberal Theory of Externality," *Inquiry* 5 (1972): 116.
10 Robert Paul Wolff, *The Poverty of Liberalism* (Boston, 1969), p. 197.
11 David M. Rasmussen, "Between Autonomy and Sociality," *Cultural Hermeneutics* 1 (1973): 8-10.
12 Lukes, *Individualism,* p. 116. Lukes's exposition of methodological individualism serves as a critique of much contemporary behaviorist and behavioralist political science. Methodological individualists can incorporate only individual predicates, which by definition have "minimal social reference," into their logic of explanation.
13 Norman Malcolm, *Problems of Mind: Descartes to Wittgenstein* (London, 1972), pp. 2-16 passim. In the view of empiricist philosophers of mind we can never be certain that minds other than our own exist, although we can make arguments for their existence from analogy.
14 Cf. Wood, *Mind and Politics,* pp. 182-85. For an articulation and defense of lawlike generalizations in political and social life see Carl G. Hempel, "The Function of General Laws in History," *The Journal of Philosophy* 39 (1942): 37-48. See also the critiques by MacIntyre, Connolly, and Taylor already cited.
15 The reaction of mainstream political scientists to the student activism of the 1960s ran from rather condescending chiding to hysterical condemnation—with such notable exceptions as Sheldon Wolin at Berkeley. The volume by Bernard Crick cited later in this essay contains a reprimand and a warning in the matter of student politics.
16 Quoted in Sheldon Wolin, *Politics and Experience* (Boston, 1970), p. 127.
17 T. D. Weldon, *The Vocabulary of Politics* (Baltimore, 1953), p. 148. Physicists in our post-Heisenberg age would be bemused at Weldon's outmoded misconceptions concerning the nature of "hard" science.
18 See Connolly, "Theoretical Self-Consciousness," as well as his *The Terms of Political Discourse* (Lexington, Mass., 1974), for a full and rigorous articulation of the depth connections between explanatory theories, test procedures, and normative implications.

19 Lukes, *Individualism*, pp. 166ff.
20 Taylor, "Interpretation and Sciences of Man," p. 33.
21 Connolly, "Theoretical Self-Consciousness," p. 11.
22 But see, for example, David Easton's insistence, in *The Political System* (New York, 1965), p. 221, that facts and values "are logically heterogeneous. . . . The moral aspect of a proposition, however, expresses only the emotional responses of an individual to a state of real or presumed facts."
23 Julius Kovesi, *Moral Notions* (London, 1967), pp. 151-52, 156.
24 Ibid., p. 151.
25 Ibid., p. 63.
26 Hannah Arendt, *The Human Condition* (Chicago, 1972), note 8, pp. 145-46.
27 Alexis de Tocqueville, *Democracy in America*, ed. Richard D. Heffner (New York, 1956), pp. 217-18.
28 Karl Marx, *Capital*, vol. 1, ed. by Frederick Engels (New York, 1975), p. 265.
29 Kovesi, *Moral Notions*, p. 161.
30 Easton, *The Political System*, p. 226.
31 See W. H. Hudson, *Modern Moral Philosophy* (Garden City, N.Y., 1970); especially helpful is sect. 3 of this book, containing "Stevenson's Account of Emotivism," pp. 121-25. Kovesi's *Moral Notions* is a powerful work, which articulates a nonemotivist account of moral notions. Kurt Baier, "The Moral Point of View," in *The Definition of Morality*, ed. G. Wallace and A. D. M. Walker (London, 1970), pp. 188-210, is worth reading, as is Bernard Williams, *Utilitarianism: For and Against* (Cambridge, 1973), esp. pp. 77-150.
32 Quoted in Hudson, *Modern Moral Philosophy*, p. 125. Wolff, in *The Poverty of Liberalism*, p. 90, argues that the identification of goals with feelings and means with reason leads to that "much-celebrated value neutrality with which modern liberal social scientists emasculate their research. They are unable, for example, to see that a society which fails even to set itself certain social goals . . . is to that extent an *irrational* society. Naturally, since they cannot see this fact, they cannot undertake as social scientists to explain it. Hence, they remain at the level of predicting variations in public preferences among toothpastes of presidential candidates."
33 See Malcolm's *Problems of Mind*, especially his section on logical behavioralism, pp. 80-103.
34 Read Stuart Hampshire, *Thought and Action* (New York, 1959), particularly chap. 4, "Criticism and Regret."
35 Taylor, "Interpretation and Sciences of Man," p. 21.
36 Harold Lasswell, *Politics: Who Gets What, When, How* (Cleveland, 1958), p. 13 Emphasis mine.
37 Bernard Crick, *In Defence of Politics* (Baltimore, 1964), p. 21. As Christian Bay observes, the view that politics is a system of rules for facilitating peaceful battles between competing private interests is "professedly conservative." Bay, "Politics and Pseudopolitics: A Critical Evaluation of Some Behavioral Literature," *American Political Science Review* 59 (May 1965): 40.
38 Seymour Martin Lipset, *Political Man: The Social Bases of Politics* (Garden City, N.Y., 1963), p. 339.

39 Ibid., pp. 216–17.
40 Ibid., p. 14. Lipset's countermodel to our "healthy" apathy is the highly politicized, dangerously unstable Weinmar Germany prior to the Nazi take-over. The Germans had very high levels of political participation, he appears to argue, and what happened? They got Hitler. Lipset provides no consideration of the vagaries of German history, including the fact that the Germans had no tradition of democratic self-rule; nor does he discuss the disastrous nature of the post–World War I period, in which Germany faced disastrous inflation coupled with depression, enormous war debts, and the official burden of guilt for the war itself. Yet Lipset's abstract and ahistorical reference to Germany of the 1930s is supposed to convince mid-twentieth-century Americans that the price of high political participation is volatility at best, a Hitler at worst.
41 Ibid., p. 27.
42 Peter Bachrach and Morton S. Baratz, "Two Faces of Power," *American Political Science Review* 56 (December 1962): 948–49.
43 See William E. Connolly, ed., *The Bias of Pluralism* (Chicago, 1972), for a series of critiques on pluralistic theory.
44 Quoted from Hervert Leonidas Hart, *Women's Suffrage and National Danger: A Plea for the Ascendancy of Man* (London, 1889), p. 118.
45 Alexander Passerin d'Entrèves, *The Notion of the State* (Oxford, 1967), p. 141. D'Entrèves points out that the word *authority* derives from the Latin word meaning "to augment" and posits the notion of possession of a special qualification which authorizes whoever is invested with it to exercise a particular power or right.

VIRGINIA SAPIRO

Women's Studies and Political Conflict

■ Imagine a language lacking in political concepts. Forget such words as *power, equality, rights, ideology, law, public policy,* and *authority.* Erase the concepts of public goods and public welfare, democracy and patriarchy, conflict and cooperation. Using this new language, explain the problems of women and offer solutions. Use of synonyms is not allowed.

Politics and political analysis are central to any conception of women's studies and feminism. But until recently, political scientists have done little to focus their tools and skills on the "woman problem." Further, although one would not wish to argue that any given set of concepts is the exclusive domain of a particular discipline, the intensely political character of women's studies and its subject matter leads many scholars in the field to use political concepts in a rather promiscuous manner. As a result, both political science and women's studies suffer. This essay outlines some of the reasons for the lack of political research on women and offers a political analysis of the growth of women's studies.

Beyond Simple Accusations of Sexism: The Traditional Treatment of Women

Most academic disciplines which focus on human characteristics, activities, or thought have witnessed a substantial increase in the number of gender-relevant studies in the past few years. An inevitable by-product of the growth of a new focus, approach, or subfield within a discipline is the production of articles like those in this volume, devoted to criticism of past scholarship. Feminist political scientists have not been laggards in this respect; a number of published articles focus exclusively on criticism of sexism in past political scholarship.[1] Similar critical works are found in almost every academic discipline. These essays are more than the venting of personal frustration; they constitute an important phase in the process of political change.

Politics as used by political scientists takes on a variety of meanings—the presentation of handfuls of alternatives in most introductory courses in the field drives students to doodling—but there are core concepts central to most. Politics assumes a community of people linked in varying degrees of interdependence by geography, goals, tasks, kinship, or historical quirk. Politics also includes the assumption that decisions are or must be made regarding the distribution of goods or values (the latter including such things as status) within the community. Politics also focuses on conflict and conflict resolution. Concepts crucial to any understanding of distribution or conflict are power and authority.

Alteration of an academic field of inquiry is an essentially political process, regardless of the substantive content involved. First, academia as a whole as well as each specific discipline are communities in the sense suggested above. Second, one of the functions internal to the community is the distribution of goods and values, including status (credentials and promotions) and jobs. All academic disciplines have formal authority structures and informal power patterns. One of the values distributed within the academic political community, through power and authority structures, is designation of truth. This is done in part through the establishment of what may be seen as a judicial system: the procedures by which members of the community are supposed to judge the validity of a piece of research (methodology and epistemology).

My comments thus far are not intended to point out anything new; they are translations of parts of the arguments of many observers of science and academics, including, among others, Mannheim, Kuhn, and Merton.[2] My intention is to provide, not an analogy with, but a translation into the terms of political analysis in order to discuss the changes wrought by the development of women's studies.

The growth of women's studies has created conflict over the validity of established goals and procedures within every discipline it has touched. Women's studies exists in at least partial opposition to those working within the ideology (Mannheim) or normal science (Kuhn) or ethos (Merton) of the home discipline.[3] Women's studies scholars in every field are demanding a greater share of status and recognition in their fields. Although the specifics of the conflict vary from one field to another, the form of each of them contains many of the characteristics generally recognizable as political conflict. We may compare the dissension over the study of women with Coleman's landmark observations of community conflict and conflict resolution, for example.[4] He discerned general patterns of change in issues and social organization that accompany community conflict regardless of the specific focus or origin of the battle. In terms of issue change, he notes a shift from specific issues ("Why did you laugh when I said you should read Mill's *Subjection of Women* as well as *On Liberty*?") to more general issues ("You don't grant respect to anything having to do with women, do you?"). Along with the expansion to more general issues he saw the inclusion of new specific issues ("For example, I notice you never pay attention when I try to say something at faculty meetings"). Finally, with the increase in both generality and the number of specific issues, what began as a disagreement turns into personal antagonism ("Goddamn sexist"). Thus, as Coleman points out, a regular part of community conflict is alteration of personal relations and social organization. New social bonds are created and old bonds are broken as sides are taken. The new bonds are likely to result not simply in new friendships, but in partisan organization. Witness the number of academic women's caucuses established in the last five years. Finally, where once there were only the leaders or power holders in the mainstream, there is a recognizable development of leadership in the opposition. Despite the best efforts of the anti-star-system feminists, women's studies leaders in each discipline are recognized not only for their scholarship but for their partisan leadership—their power.

To return to the original point, then, the development of written criticisms devoted not to the generation of new knowledge but to criticism of the old is not a product of "idle" frustration. It is part of the process of the development of partisan consciousness essential to change. It helps a group with a grievance locate and develop a shared sense of specific and general grievances and goals. But because this is an activity of the relatively powerless, of the minority, immense frustration with the lack of fruits of this labor is a danger. Energy spent on criticism cannot be spent on creation; frustration and anger inhibit the ability to reason. Reason is one of the few resources of the relatively powerless in academics. The more powerful do not need the force of reason as much as do the less powerful. The former have the force of their power and authority. Ironically, those whose situation most debilitates reason have the most desperate need for it.[5]

How do we use this information to confront a discipline and attempt to resolve conflict in our favor? For one thing, we must pay careful attention to the way in which we formulate our charges of sexism. As we well know, the most insidious form of sexism is nonconscious. Thus, if we point the finger and say, "You are sexist; you discriminate," the accused may, in all "honesty," deny the charges. Psychologists have pointed out the variety of tricks our minds play in an attempt to order the world in congruence with our preconceptions of it. By nonconsciously applying stricter standards to studies of women than to other types of studies, the sexist may declare women's studies below par. By processes of categorization and self-definition a field may easily facilitate the exclusion of women. These processes must be understood. Further, by locating points of stress and conflict within a field, we may create a strategy for change.

The Study of Women in Political Science

The narrowest and least useful interpretation of the domain of political science is that what we study is government. This approach conjures up images of civics textbooks with archetypal diagrams of little men with briefcases busily turning bills into laws. Particularly popular in the 1940s, this definition led political scientists to concentrate on theories of who should govern and how, on structures of states and constitutions, and on public administration in a fairly narrow sense. The reason for the exclusion of women was obvious: women do not appear in large numbers among those who govern. Constitutions that might include declarations of the rights of man rarely have references to the rights of woman. Whether political scientists chose to study government directly or chose to study the thought of past philosophers, women were not considered relevant. Of course, even this narrow definition does not justify excluding women. There were not many women in elected public offices, but they performed important and often specialized functions within political parties. Only myopic sexism kept students of political philosophy from studying women; even if they limited themselves to the traditionally considered philosophers, most of the "great men" of political philosophy devoted some of their time to discussions of women. The development and expansion of governmental action in social welfare provided ample opportunities for analysis of women and "women's issues." The opportunities were rarely taken.

Political scientists grew tired of structures and constitutions. They found that the most extensive study of structures and legalisms could not tell us much about politics or even government. Thus, they turned to the study of human beliefs, motivations, attitudes, perceptions, and behavior in an attempt to understand the political world. Rather than concentrating solely on the beliefs, perceptions, and understanding of the intellectual elite, like Plato, Hobbes, Rousseau, Mill, Marx, and Weber, they began to attempt a more direct focus on the beliefs, perceptions, and understanding of "everyday people." There are some severe problems with the "behavioral" approach to political analysis, as Elshtain points out in this volume, but it was this style of political analysis that altered the definition of politics enough to let women in.

Political science began declaring that "politics is concerned with the conditions and consequences of human action."[6]

> Certainly . . . verbs do not define politics. But they do refer to those of man's acts that are at the core of what we study when we talk about politics. . . . If human behavior is the root of politics, they are more useful in studying political things than nouns like authority, power, conflict, allocation, or government. It seems to me that behavior comes first: ruling before government, obeying before authority, voting before decision, demanding before value, fearing before sanction, coercing before power, persuading before influence, fighting before conflict, believing before ideology.[7]

The shift in substantive focus demanded a change in methodology. Many political scientists were no longer content with observing human behavior from within the walls of the university library. The behavioralists searched for a way to let citizens speak for themselves, for "the physical scientist seems to have one great advantage over the political scientist: whatever meanings he may give his objects of study, they do not talk back to him. Atoms, neutrons, or electrons do not care how they are defined; political actors do mind."[8] Thus, the dominant analytic strategy of the behavioralist is the survey technique. The intent, though expressed in other words, was the reestablishment of a humanistic social science.

The plan, such as it was, went awry, but in a manner that gives feminist scholars ammunition they need to enter the field. First, the dream of a humanistic social science was not fulfilled. In their search for a way to let "political actors speak for themselves," political scientists found the logic of positivism. Political scientists attempted to restrict their analysis to the clearly observable, thus, they assumed, avoiding the imposition of their own beliefs on the people they studied. The problem generated by this strategy is threefold. Many of the phenomena—especially the psychological—they wished to study are not directly observable. As a result, the field of vision was narrowed to behavior itself and usually to very specific political attitudes. Political scientists also tended to lose sight of the fact that in creating a study, determining the question to be asked, selecting the phenomena to be observed, and choosing a particular analytical strategy, the researcher necessarily imposes personal values on the subject of study. In addition a whole generation of political scientists became unduly impressed with the brand new toys—computers and esoteric statistical models—at their disposal. The object for many appeared to be playing with the toys, not understanding politics. Scores of articles in the field appear to be techniques in search of substance.

A second major problem that developed in political science as a result of the growth of behavioralism was a renewed debate over the role of the "scientist" in politics; specifically, should political scientists use their knowledge and analytical abilities to criticize or advocate personal political preferences on issues or policies? The debate is nothing short of ironic. The discipline was born at the beginning of this century in part as a response to a political reform movement. The progressive impulse led to a desire for reform based on knowledge gained from an enlightened science of politics. From the days of the civic reformers to the Kissingers and Brzezinskis, political scientists have always been involved in political advocacy. And this advocacy has not been restricted to extracurricular political activity. Advocacy—or at least expression of values—remains an intrinsic part of almost any political research.

A last major effect of the "behavioral revolution" in political science was the need for a new definition of the domain of the political. Politics was no longer simply a narrow circle around government, but could it include *every* "condition and consequence of human behavior"? Could every situation that contains elements of power, competition, decisionmaking, or conflict be defined as political? Most political scientists were not imperialistic enough about their field of inquiry to assent to such a definition. Most of us suspect that a definition of a concept that includes everything means nothing. The new domain, therefore, was defined not as "governmental" but as "public."

What does "public" mean? It includes more than government, but where is the distinction between the public and private? Political scientists include within the appropriate domain of their study such nongovernmental topics as the internal politics of labor unions, the family as an agent of political socialization, and the behavior of college students while playing n-person games. By looking at some of the phenomena not included within the domain of political science, we can see the public-private distinction and the way it has affected the (lack of) study of women. Political science has ignored power, authority, conflict, and decisionmaking as such within the family. Little energy has been spent exploring these issues with regard to social relationships and groups. Sexuality and sexual preference have been omitted almost entirely from the purview of the political scientist. Children are considered only as objects of political teaching or as objects of public policy. Political scientists focus on the relationship between power and achievement motives and political involvement, but have not thought of a possible nurturance motive and its relation to social welfare attitudes. (A few years ago there was a debate about public and private regardingness which seemed to assume that wealthy proponents of social welfare spending were "irrational.") It is very difficult to define exactly where public matters end and private matters begin, but one thing is sure: the family and traditionally "feminine" domains of life are private and, therefore, nonpolitical in the eyes of many political scientists. Even where women are observed involving themselves in politics, their motives, styles, and activities are construed as somehow less political (more personal) than have been those of men.[9]

Although the behavioral trend has served to exclude consideration of gender-relevant issues in political science, it has also helped open the way for the study of gender and politics. As the practice of political science moved further away from the ideal, as political scientists within and without the framework of behavioralism become increasingly bored and frustrated with its pretensions, and as the crises of the sixties broke the self-contentment of a discipline that had grown too proud of itself, women began to be heard. Women who are trained in the techniques of empirical political science have little trouble pointing out the flaws of traditional behavioral work on women on its own terms. We are now turning our attention to putting traditional assumptions made about women to the test as well as testing the theories and hypotheses of feminist scholars. In doing so we reveal traditional political scientists as people who have not transcended the values, norms, and prejudices of their political cultures as well as they had thought. Finally, along with numerous other political scientists who have grown discontented with the public-private distinction, feminist political scientists turn their attention to people and things previously considered private and therefore nonpolitical. Increasing numbers of political scientists include women within the political world.

One need not be a Marxist to see that the increasing awareness of severe contradictions within the field provided an opportunity for change. Awareness of flaws in a field of inquiry is not enough to engender widespread dissent, conflict, and ultimately, radical change. As Kuhn points out, progress within "normal science" is built on corrections of and tinkering with small flaws and gaps.[10] As long as political scientists restricted their conception of politics to a narrow understanding of government, it was not entirely unreasonable to ignore women. As long as political science did not state clearly its intention to be value-free and politically disinterested, there was little to force the status quo orientation of political science to the attention of its practitioners. Only when the humanistically oriented Young Turks who declared that the "root" of politics is "man" appeared to turn into an Old Guard with hardening of the intellectual arteries did it become clear that "man" was narrowly conceived and certainly did not include a political conception of woman.

They Can't Govern If You Can't See Them: A Portrait

Few studies provide such a clear example of the treatment of women in political science as does Robert Dahl's *Who Governs?*, one of the best-known books in contemporary political science.[11] Analysis of the treatment of women in this volume offers important insights into the nature of the contradictions within political science for a number of reasons. First, Dahl is one of the major theoreticians of the behavioral movement in political science. Indeed, he was the first to declare this trend a "successful protest."[12] Further, Dahl may be taken as representative of the discipline insofar as he was granted its stamp of approval and certification of leadership when it elected him president of the American Political Science Association in 1967. Third, *Who Governs?* was taken for a long time as providing the definitive evidence that the United States is a pluralistic, relatively egalitarian political system. Finally, his data do include important information about women; only "sexist blinders" keep him from drawing the obvious conclusions.

Dahl sought to determine the degree to which local governors are drawn from relatively small, homogeneous, high-status groups or, conversely, are representative of the citizenry at large. He assessed the influence of a wide range of social groups on decisionmaking in New Haven by identifying the social background and socioeconomic status of locally influential people. He focused on a fairly wide range of indicators of social position, including ethnicity, religion, race, and occupation. Sex was not included. The core of the book is an analysis of three issue areas important in New Haven at the time of the study. Dahl's rather curious treatment of women enters into his analysis of one of those areas: education. Here, women are actually the subjects of his analysis, but he does not seem to recognize this fact. Where he makes assertions about the role of women in local politics he provides little or no evidence. Where he provides evidence of the role of women he does so unwittingly, missing important points that contradict his final conclusions and main thesis.

Women enter the picture in a discussion of the PTA as an educational interest group in a section entitled "Democratic Ritual: The Followings." Ironically, Dahl avoids an issue he actually recognizes at some lower level: women elites are found disproportionately in ritual or ceremonial positions. He discusses the PTA which has a very large female membership, as an organization which often serves as a loyal following for a school official who needs support. After discussing some of the reasons for this function of the PTA, without mentioning the sexual composition of the organization and its activists, Dahl's final—and presumably most convincing—argument is that for

> many women, in fact, the PTA is obviously an outlet for social needs; PTA meetings furnish opportunities to escape from the home for a few hours, meet neighbors, make new friends, gossip, talk about children, partake of coffee and pastry, and achieve a fugitive sense of social purpose. Some

female Machiavellians even look upon PTA activity as a way of assuring favorable treatment for their own children. (*Who Governs?*, p. 156)

This passage is particularly revealing. First, it is a demonstration of sloppy empirical work. Nothing—especially motives for and functions of social activity—is "obvious" to a careful social scientist in the absence of empirical evidence, which Dahl does not provide. Interestingly, he draws no conclusions about the reasons for male involvement. Second, his only direct reference to women in the PTA is to explain their behavior in terms of private, social concerns. Indeed, he uses his observation of women's behavior to explain why a "shrewd principal" can manipulate the PTA according to "his" will. Moreover, Dahl appears convinced that the organization has no real social purpose. Finally, we learn that some women ("Machiavellians") use their membership in a social organization to protect their interests, or at least those of their children. Whether this is notable because men do not do this, or because we should assume that women cannot engage in self-interested instrumental activities, or because a member of a PTA should not be expected to use the organization for the benefit of a child who is a student in the school, we do not know.

The effect of Dahl's sexist blinders becomes even more apparent when he discusses the PTA as a recruitment pool for political office. In the paragraph following his analysis of women in the PTA, Dahl writes:

> The PTA is also a legitimate channel through which potential leaders may enter into the school system, test themselves, gain experience, and pass into the ranks of the leaders. It is a remarkable fact that three recent appointees to the New Haven Board of Education all became involved in the politics of the public schools via the PTA. To be sure, each of these men had already possessed a strong prior interest in education. But it was when the education of their own children was at stake that they became active in their PTA. (P. 157)

The PTA, like other civic organizations, is indeed an important political recruitment channel, often—and unremarkably, we might add—leading to involvement in school board politics. Further, we would expect this organization to provide a logical channel through which women in particular might pass into political office. But Dahl does not notice his transition from discussion of social butterflies and female Machiavellians to his discussion of "these men" who were chosen for public office. He does not even notice the parallel motivations he ascribes to the men and women: women who become activists in the PTA may do so because they are concerned about their children and are thus "female Machiavellians"; men who become active for the same reason are not described in those terms.

Dahl's observations further highlight the discriminatory, antipluralistic nature of the recruitment process. One member of the school board recruited from the PTA stated:

> I became President of the PTA out there. They make it a habit to have men, most schools have women, and the supply of men is short and so they ask around. That's how they got on to me. So I started my stint. . . . Well, I noticed right away, when I started going into the school in any kind of detail, it was in a really dreadful condition. . . . And so . . . we got together a committee of parents consisting of a doctor and an engineer and so on. (P. 157)

Here we have an unnoted case of outright discrimination. Further, although we can only speculate about the sex of the "doctor, engineer, and so on," it is likely that this public official used as the indication of the status of his committee not female activists, but men. Another one of Dahl's respondents indicated that during the first PTA meeting he ever attended

> one thing led to another and . . . the first thing that happened . . . I was asked to be president of the PTA. The principal called me one night and they were having a meeting and I was quite taken by surprise, I have never had anything to do with PTA before. . . . My wife usually went to the meetings. But prior to that, you see, our children had been small, and we didn't have any particular interest in PTA before they enrolled in school. So the first thing I knew, I was appointed—or elected—president of the PTA, and as president of the PTA, I had a good deal more to say than I ever had to say about educational affairs [before]. (Pp. 157–58)

The words of Dahl's respondents reveal one of the prototypic processes of local recruitment of political elites. Contrary to the public image of political leaders as uniformly scheming "politicos," a large proportion of our leaders enter politics in a way that may be more accurately described as drifting than as climbing. But another characteristic of recruitment and decisionmaking processes that Dahl ignored is the preferential treatment accorded to men, even in a traditionally female route to political influence.

Dahl does not make his case stronger when he points out that the recruitments of these PTA presidents "are the exceptional cases. Ordinarily a PTA president is a housewife who lacks the time, experience, interest and drive to move into the real centers of educational influence" (p. 158). If the typical PTA president lacks the time to get into politics, how does she have the time to be president of the PTA? If involvement in a PTA gives one experience and skills, as Dahl argued earlier, why is this not the case for women? If, as the words of his respondents as well as the findings of other studies indicate, involvement can increase one's drive, interest, and ultimately, ambition, why do more women not take this route to politics? In sum, focusing exclusively on self-selection reasons for women's lack of political influence ignores the evidence Dahl himself provides that those who were recruited from PTAs were recruited by others at least partly because they were male. Indeed, later in the book Dahl notes that "in a society where public life is still widely thought to be a man's world and where men rather than women are generally expected to occupy the positions of responsibility, it is not surprising that two-thirds of the subleaders are men" (p. 169). He notes further that subleaders are distinguished from the population from which they are drawn by "more than merely the conventional privileges of American manhood" (p. 169). Thus one form of political oppression of women is dismissed as a mere cultural convention.

Dahl's work leads him to a number of important conclusions. I shall focus on two that have special bearing on women. First, while clearly denying that the practice of American politics is as democratic or egalitarian as the ideal, Dahl sees in our complex system of leaders and subleaders, interest groups and competition, no systematic exclusion of any sector of the population. Yet the little evidence on women he provides is congruent with other evidence that women are systematically discriminated against and passed over in the political recruitment and promotion process. Second, Dahl places great faith in Americans' rather tenuous belief in basic democratic norms. Even if we accept the list of caveats Dahl enumerates, one major problem remains. Americans do not share basic democratic beliefs about questions of female power and influence. As late as the fall of 1976 (and Dahl's study was fielded in 1959) 56 percent of American men and 50 percent of American women agreed that "it's more natural for men to have the top responsible jobs in the country."[13] About women's potential there is no democratic consensus upon which to place faith.

The point of this portrait is a simple one. It often takes no radical feminist analysis, no elaborate new techniques, no resorting to a language mainstream scholars cannot understand, in order to point out the error of sexism and myopia in past research relevant to an understanding of the role of gender in political society. If women's studies research is valid, traditional research on women is wrong or incomplete. If women's studies research is valid, traditional research on women is, in many cases, simply bad scholarship, a charge we may feel free to level at any research that guides us away from truth.

Conclusion

Accusations of sexism—whether leveled at a field as a whole or at an individual's work—are accusations of poor scholarship. Scholars cannot make assumptions about women or ignore gender where it is relevant without violating their own canons of research. Women's studies, when done well, is simply good research. At the same time, however, it is a powerful source of conflict and thus a means to real political change.

Engaging in women's studies research at this time is a radical political enterprise for most of us. Outside small pockets of tolerance or enlightenment, work on women is a confrontation to dominant values. Women (especially) who do research on women place themselves at great risk, and must do so consciously and with intent. Even among women most dedicated to the meaning and role of gender in politics a very common piece of advice is "Don't stake your career on women's studies. Prove that you can do 'normal' research." In return for the conflict women's studies research stirs up, women are screened out by recruitment committees, review committees, journals, convention panel chairs, and publishers. Many of the people in these positions of authority do not even recognize what they are doing. When women complain, they are seen as annoying, unreasonable, amusing, trivial, and an affront to the "standards" of the field.

Understanding the political process of the development of women's studies leaves us with a note of caution. It may help delay—but probably not avoid—the development of a field of women's studies that acts too much like a traditional discipline. The growth in the number of women's studies journals, programs, departments, degrees, conventions, and the establishment of the National Women's Studies Association along with its regional branches testify to the degree to which the process of establishing women's studies as a field of inquiry is largely similar to the establishment of any new field. Too much self-congratulation about our new-found strength and analytical and critical abilities is unwarranted and dangerous. It would be no difficult task for women's studies to lose the vitality and openness with which it began. Revolutions that end are lost.

NOTES

1 See Susan Bourke and Jean Gorssholtz, "Politics as an Unnatural Practice: Political Science Looks at Female Participation," *Politics and Society* 4 (1974): 255–66; Bonnie Freeman, "Power, Patriarchy, and 'Political Primitives,'" in *Beyond Intellectual Sexism*, ed. Joan Roberts (New York, 1976), pp. 241–64; Murray Goot and Elizabeth Reid, *Women and Voting Studies: Mindless Matrons or Sexist Scientism?*" Sage Professional Papers in Political Sociology (Beverly Hills, 1975); Thelma McCormack, "Toward a Nonsexist Perspective on Social and Political Change," in *Another Voice,* ed. Marcia Millman and

Rosabeth Moss Kanter (Garden City, N.Y., 1975), pp. 1-34; and Mary Shanley and Victoria Schuck, "In Search of Political Woman," *Social Science Quarterly* 55 (1975): 632-44.

2 Karl Mannheim, *Ideology and Utopia* (New York, 1936); Thomas S. Kuhn, *The Structure of Scientific Revolutions* (Chicago, 1970); and Robert K. Merton, *The Sociology of Science* (Chicago, 1973).

3 I say "partial" because not all studies of women—not even all feminist studies of women—are all that confrontational to the mainstream in any given discipline. Women's studies scholars sometimes exaggerate the degree to which we are "radical," as I argue later in the essay.

4 James S. Coleman, *Community Conflict* (New York, 1957).

5 For a discussion of the effects of oppression on reason, see Virginia Sapiro, "Sex and Games: On Rationality and Oppression," *British Journal of Political Science* 9 (1979), forthcoming.

6 Eulau Heinz, *The Behavioral Persuasion in Politics* (New York, 1963), p. 5.

7 Ibid.

8 Ibid.

9 For a discussion of the public-private split and women, see Jean Bethke Elshtain, "Moral Woman and Immoral Man: A Consideration of the Public-Private Split and Its Political Ramifications," *Politics and Society* 4, (1975): 453-74.

10 Kuhn, *The Structure of Scientific Revolutions*.

11 Robert Dahl, *Who Governs?* (New Haven, 1961), cited hereafter by page number in the text.

12 Robert Dahl, "The Behavioral Approach in Political Science: Epitaph for a Monument to a Successful Protest," *American Political Science Review* 55 (1961): 763-72.

13 Unpublished analysis by author, Center for Political Studies 1976 American Election Study.

JESSIE BERNARD

Afterword

■ In a book published fifteen years ago I raised questions about female contributions to knowledge. "What, if any," I asked, "is the effect on learning of the sex of the transmitter of human knowledge? What is the effect, if any, of the sex of the innovator on the acceptance of ideas?[1] I did not claim to answer those questions. But they stimulated David Reisman to comment:

> . . . competitiveness is so very American—or, more broadly, Western—in its style that I am led to wonder whether it bears some relation to our progress in scientific work, or rather whether, if women had a larger influence on that work, other sorts of discoveries might not be made, other "laws" emphasized, and altered patterns of scientific and academic organization preferred or discovered. . . . It could be argued that it took a particular set of sex-role attitudes as well as specific religious and cultural values for Western science and technology to develop initially, although to *continue* the work, one might speculate as to whether a different pattern of attitudes might not be productive.[2]

The papers in the present volume, though they deal with the humanistic disciplines rather than solely with science, speak precisely to Reisman's point. They do attempt to answer the questions Reisman and I raised. They document rather than "speculate as to whether a different pattern of attitudes" from those of the past "might not be productive." Their answer proves to be a resounding yes, it would.

The title of the present book—*The Prism of Sex*—is an imaginative gem. It suggests that knowledge about a world seen through the eyes of one sex may not be the same as knowledge about a world seen through the eyes of the other. And the book itself suggests a way to overcome the distortions of the prism: encourage women to make their own contribution to the greatest of all human enterprises, the pursuit of knowledge.

The authors of the papers in this book point up the costs we have incurred by restricting the potential contribution of women scholars. We need not continue to incur such costs.

Wide as is the gamut of subject matter dealt with in this book, all the contributors have written the same paper in the sense that all document omissions and/or distortions in human knowledge as it has been developed up to now. All offer evidence of the inequity in the pursuit of knowledge which has resulted in these lacunae or biases. All, in different ways and with different data, have made the same point: the male prism through which the world has been viewed has resulted in severe inadequacies in the humanistic disciplines. They note the methodological styles which have had the effect of reducing women to the status of the "other," and thus of validating the sexual status quo in the academy. They note the bifurcation between the private and public worlds and the all-but-total disregard of the private, a defect which becomes increasingly serious as the boundaries between public and private suffer attrition. In brief, though the authors have addressed different specific questions and offered different specific answers, they have all arrived at the same overall conclusion: the male prism has not served their several disciplines well. Knowledgeable specialists in the disciplines dealt with here will no doubt produce thoughtful critiques of each of these papers. But it seems to me— a nonspecialist in all but one of the disciplines—that the authors have demonstrated that knowledge has been overwhelmingly male in subject matter, in assumptions, in methods, in interpretations; that a disproportionate share of human knowledge in all the disciplines has dealt with a world viewed through a male prism;[3] that not only equity but also the human legacy calls for a correction of this situation in order that lacunae be filled and distortions corrected.

Where, then, do we go from here? Several questions have to be dealt with before we can answer this question: (1) *Can* the pursuit of knowledge transcend sex? (2) Does the contribution of women merely substitute one bias for another? (3) Assuming a positive reply to the first of these questions and a negative one to the second, how can the results of female scholarship be placed in the mainstream of academic inquiry?

I once wrote a paper called "Can Science Transcend Culture?" My thesis was that although the questions scientists asked were culturally determined, the methods used to answer them contained their own protection against cultural and other—including class—biases. The main points made seem to me still valid. And if we substitute "sex" for, let us say, "class," the new statement makes as much sense as the original statement. I quote myself here, for example, substituting "male" for the Marxist term "bourgeois": "Male ideology was an elaborate rationale of the male posi-

Afterword

tion in society. It could be no other. It was impossible for male social thinkers to perceive or to think in other than male terms. The value premises of their research must inevitably reflect their male point of view." I noted that the terms of the ideological framework within which sciences develop had changed from class to cultural matrices. And I documented the ways in which culture determined not only the perception of data but also the perception of problems. I noted also that "the questions men do *not* ask are also determined by their culture" (read "sex"). I quote myself again, this time substituting "sex" for "culture": "There are certain problems which people immersed in their own sex never conceive. . . . It never occurs to them that such problems exist or are amenable to scientific treatment. It takes a sexual outsider to call such problems to their attention."[4] To overcome, in brief, their "benign" blindness, not, in the present context, due to class or culture but to sex.

I am not so sure today that my second conclusion—that scientific method contains its own protection against class and cultural bias—is necessarily also valid in the case of bias due to sex. It rested on the fact that

> human beings everywhere have pretty much the same kind of physical mechanisms for vision, audition, olfaction, gustation, and kinesthesia. Those who are below normal or below a certain standard in acuity can often be brought up to standard by means of lenses or other aids. . . . The normal human retina, regardless of class or culture or individual bias, responds to certain physical stimuli in a more or less stereotyped way. . . . Whether or not you want to admit that heat has been generated, your reflexes show that it has. . . . You can deny gravity, but you fall down nevertheless. Such phenomena as light and heat and gravity can be "proved" in spite of one's class, cultural, or personal biases.[5]

I granted that the problems were harder in the social and behavioral sciences but concluded that the same bases for objectivity were becoming available.[6]

It may be inevitable if not intrinsic that men and women will be disposed to see the world through different prisms.[7] They are biologically and socially programmed to be sensitive to different cues. I once used a package metaphor to make this point. The sensory and intellectual equipment of the sexes are "packaged" in different kinds of bodies.[8] I once also contrasted the kinesthetic differences experienced by a body carrying a heavy cape from the shoulders and a body carrying a heavy skirt from the hips.[9] Or contrast a body with earlier and greater awareness of sexual arousal (characteristic of a male body) with one with later and less specific awareness (characteristic of a female body).[10] The question is sometimes raised whether an author of one sex can create authentic characters of the other sex. A similar question may be raised in the present context.

Does the male body itself preclude the perception and understanding of problems related to women and the development of adequate methods for studying them?[11] Is there something in male skeletal musculature and sexual hormones that produces the "benign" blindness referred to by Stimpson in her paper? I am willing, on the basis of the comments made above, to grant that it might be difficult for men to overcome an initial handicap in perceiving the female world but not that it is impossible. Women have been able to do the reverse.

For whatever the case may be with respect to men, we know it is feasible for women to learn to see through the male prism—perhaps too feasible. The history of female scholarship and research is, in fact, one in which women have been taught to see the world—even their own experience—through male eyes. Many of them have been so well taught that they have been alienated from other women, "de-feminized," to apply a term used by Arlie Hochschild in a subtle analysis of the processes which have deflected women scholars from accepting their authenticity as women. She notes in the brief autobiographical accounts of the careers of twelve successful women in science—the comments would be equally valid for humanists—that although they gave examples of discrimination in their vignettes, they also denied any such discrimination. They did not see their own lives in autonomous terms. Such "de-feminization," Hochschild tells us, "can take the form of a compliment: 'She's a fine analyst. She doesn't think like a woman. . . .' To the extent that this seems like a compliment, [the recipient] experiences distance from other women. . . . In order to maintain a professional identity she must sometimes prove herself different. . . . She does her own subtle 'de-feminization.'"[12]

Smith's paper in this volume refers to Hegel's discussion of the master and the servant; it is also relevant here. The servant, Hegel noted, had a better view of the master's world than the master had of the servant's. Analogously it might be argued that women know more about the male world than men do about the female world. In any event, many women have been co-opted; that is, they have been trained to pursue knowledge in the male style, to study subjects approved of by men, to view the world through the male prism. True, the work done by women is rarely accorded the same recognition as work of the same quality done by men;[13] still, that work demonstrates that it is not impossible for women to see through the male prism.

There has, however, been a price paid for this accomplishment in addition to alienation: women have been deprived of the conviction of authenticity in pursuing knowledge in any but the male way. I refer to a statement made by Dorothy Smith:

Afterword 271

> ... the deprivation of authority and the ways in which women have been trained to practice the complement of male control of "topic development" have the effect of making it difficult for women to treat one another as relevant figures. We have difficulty in asserting authority for ourselves. We have difficulty in grasping authority for women's voices and for what women have to say. We are thus deprived of the essential basis for developing among ourselves the discourse out of which symbolic structures, concepts, images and knowledges might develop which would be adequate to our experience and to deviating forms of organization and action relevant to our situation and interests. In participating in the world of ideas as object rather than as subject we have come to take for granted that our thinking is to be authorized by an external (male) source of authority. . . . It has not been easy for women (any more than for men) to take what women have to say as authoritative nor is it easy to find our own voice convincing. It is hard for us to listen to ourselves. The voice of our own experience is equally defective. . . . We need . . . to learn how to treat what other women say as a source and basis for our own work and thinking.[14]

The answer to our first question, then, is that the pursuit of knowledge can in fact transcend sex, that it may be difficult for men to learn to see through the female prism but not impossible. In the case of women such transcendence may help to explain why so relatively little of human knowledge has come to us by way of the female prism.

My second question was, Are the authors in this volume merely arguing for the substitution of one bias for another? a feminist for a male bias? Not at all. Equity in the pursuit of knowledge does not at all call for the substitution of one bias for another. It can hardly be labeled a bias to have as goals the filling in of lacunae, the pointing out of distortions resulting from an almost exclusive concentration on the public or political or economic world, the noting of the pervasive neglect of women's contributions, the bringing in of new subjects. The idea is merely to render the pursuit of knowledge equitable, fair.

Still, as both Jean Bethke Elshtain and Kathryn Pyne Parsons remind us, in somewhat different contexts, fairness is not at all self-evident. Elshtain, for example, tackles the issue of bias. Does bias mean bias "against the best interests of women?" she asks, or "for the interests of male-dominated professions and knowledge?" That is, does research on women's concerns constitute a "good" bias? Isn't *any* perspective promoted by *any* identifiable group a biased one? Is bias the same as false-consciousness or ideology the same as a systematically distorted way of constructing social and individual reality? Is it possible to adjudicate between biased perspectives? Will women become more biased as they gain more power? How do we distinguish our biases from our values?

The specter of bias is one of the oldest bugbears in the history of the social and behavioral sciences. Male scholars and researchers have wrestled with it for decades, but, so far as I know, almost never with biases based on sex. One of the most valuable potential contributions of the papers in this book is the raising of this question among them. Perhaps I merely demonstrate my own biases when I answer the second question with a convinced no.

The problem is not so much that women scholars will merely introduce a different bias into the pursuit of knowledge as that their contribution to the supplying of missing data and the correction of distortions will be ignored, not integrated into the body of human and humane knowledge. The "benign blindness" referred to by Stimpson is no longer "benign," since it is dysfunctional. And it may as effectively destroy the insights and research of the female scholars as actual banning might. The problem is how to overcome the sometimes purposive "blindness" that relegates the new knowledge to a female ghetto or isolates it from the intellectual mainstream.[15]

Is the male "blindness" curable? Or is it part of the "biogrammar"?[16] My reply to the first of these rhetorical questions would be affirmative, to the second, negative. It may be harder for men to see the female world without help, but it should not be hard for them to see it after it has been described or analyzed by female scholars. Here, actually, we are not dealing with blindness so much as with neglect. We cannot explain it in terms of inability to perceive. More relevant perhaps is the male homosociality which Lipman-Blumen has analyzed so persuasively, or even the misogyny which Lionel Tiger tells us characterizes the male world.[17] Men find female scholarship dealing with women boring, dull, unimportant. It is not about them and hence not interesting. If it is critical of them, they find it painful. In any event, they look to one another for professional recognition, and mastery of the products of female scholarship will not win that recognition for them.

Several strategies suggest themselves for overcoming the barriers to placing female scholarship in the mainstream. Most activist would be a strategy of asserting the right to set standards. In a paper presented at the conference from which this book is drawn, Mary Daly raised the question in regard to theology, "evil by whose standards?" Women might well raise the same question with regard to the validity or importance of all the humanistic disciplines—namely, "valid or important by whose standards?" This question is related to Stimpson's "right to name." Why should the standards used in judging scholarship or in judging academic departments be those of the male world? Women might judge departments in the great universities on criteria they themselves establish, including per-

Afterword

haps how *au courant* the departments are in terms of courses dealing with female scholarship, how much of the female research in the disciplines is being disseminated in reading lists and textbooks, and how many male students are exposed to the results of female scholarship.

Also activist would be a strategy of intellectual "confrontation." Space might well be requested in professional journals to point out omissions and distortions and evidences of sexism which have appeared in books reviewed over a given year if the reviewers themselves have not noted them. Such critiques, it need hardly be noted, should be soberly documented and not polemical. If they are primarily polemical, they can, as Elshtain reminds us, easily be demolished.

Somewhat less activist would be a request that questions based on female-oriented research be incorporated in the Graduate Record Examination. It could be cogently argued that neglect of this corpus of knowledge is as serious as neglect of any branch of traditional knowledge. Qualifying examinations for graduate degrees might also include questions dealing with the feminist scholarship in the disciplines involved.

Another strategy might be called competitive, not in a male but in a female way. It would involve the power of sheer volume of research, analyses, interpretations, explanations. When the amount of female scholarship became large enough, it would become harder and harder to avoid recognizing it.[18]

Finally, there is a collaborative strategy. The general thrust here would be emphasis on improvement of the discipline rather than on the status of women in the academic world. Women would make their pitch not as activists, protagonists, antagonists, or agonists at all, but as disciplinarians, as theologians, as historians, as psychologists. The assumption would be that men share with women a genuine concern for the quality of their several disciplines, that men too, presumably, want their disciplines to be as good as they can be. The argument would be that women were seeking, not to supersede men in the pursuit of knowledge (as indeed, they are not), but rather to improve its product. Both male and female scholars share a common desideratum, that of correcting the omissions and distortions in their disciplines introduced by the male prism. No professor of any of the humanistic disciplines can afford to reject these corrections.

All of these suggestions presuppose that the knowledge resulting thereby is of a high quality, asks the most relevant questions, and supplies the least biased answers. Whether or not any of these strategies is followed, the effort to fill in the omissions and correct the distortions of human knowledge will, we hope, continue. Barriers to the equitable pursuit of knowledge will fall before the cogent critiques of scholars such as those represented in this book. More power to their pens.

Back, then, to the question raised earlier: where do we go from here? I would like to see a great deal of research devoted to a description, analysis, explanation, and interpretation of the female world, which all the papers in this book, implicitly or explicitly, recognize as important, although there is no consensus with respect to its nature. Some see it as a support system which makes the work possible; some, as a goal to strive for. Stimpson sees it as a necessary withdrawal for facilitating a female culture. Dye and Schulenburg see it as a private world vis-à-vis a public world. Parsons sees it as a world based on individual rights that can be exercised only when one has the means to exact them. In another paper I gave a brief overview of some relevant aspects of the concept in functional terms.[19] However conceptualized, we can learn about it by making full use of the female prism to create a body of knowledge complementary to as well as corrective of our present store. As Reisman has suggested, "Other sorts of discoveries might . . . be made, other 'laws' emphasized, and altered patterns of scientific and academic organization . . . discovered." This goal is well worth a try.

NOTES

1 Jessie Bernard, *Academic Women* (University Park, Pa., 1964), p. vii.
2 David Reisman, Introduction, ibid., pp. xix–xx.
3 Even when men have studied women, their focus has tended to be the status of women in the male world or the relations of women to men.
4 Jessie Bernard, "Can Science Transcend Culture?" *The Scientific Monthly* 61 (October 1950): 270, 271.
5 Ibid., p. 273.
6 "In the social sciences it is somewhat more difficult to secure such results because we are dealing with phases of the reacting organism that are not so standardized. It is not nearly so easy . . . to be sure that we all see or hear or perceive the same things in common stimuli. Here cultural biases and past experiences come sharply into play. Nevertheless, the creation of instruments, tests, sampling procedures, interviewing techniques, systems of recording, all the precautions for assuring accuracy, precision, for minimizing bias, for testing, for validating, for checking—the whole armory of scientific method—are now becoming available for social science data and standardizing our observations anywhere that agreed-upon questions are being asked." Ibid.
7 "It is . . . impossible for either sex to have the same experiences as those the other has. No matter what a culture may prescribe, the sexes are not reacted to the same way. The effect a woman has on a man is different from the effect she has on a woman, and the effect a man has on a woman is different from the effect he has on a man. They are rejected differently. They are deprived differ-

Afterword

ently, they are ignored differently; they are indulged differently. These are social phenomena and independent of culture. No culture can provide identical experiences to both sexes." Jessie Bernard, *The Sex Game* (Atheneum, 1972), p. 47.
8 Bernard, *Academic Women*, pp. 168–69.
9 Bernard, *The Sex Game*, p. 51.
10 More boys than girls are able to find the hidden pornography in cartoons.
11 See, for example, Rae Carlson, "Understanding Women: Implications for Personality Theory and Research," *Journal of Social Issues* 28 (1972): 17–32. Carlson makes the point that "agentic" research techniques, favored by males, are not the most suitable for studying women.
12 Arlie Hochschild, "Making It: Marginality and Obstacles to Minority Consciousness," in *Women & Success*, ed. Ruth Knudsin (New York, 1973), p. 196.
13 A scientist, asked to name the ten top people in his field, listed the names of ten men. When the names of several outstanding women were mentioned, he replied that yes, they were among the top ten; he had just never thought of them.
14 Dorothy Smith, "An Analysis of Ideological Structures and How Women Are Excluded: Considerations for Academic Women" (Paper presented at Conference on Women's Studies in Higher Education, University of Alberta, 1975).
15 Eleanor Sheldon, when asked to assess the influence of the feminist movement on social scientists' thinking, replied that there had been little, if any. The questioner, Cynthia Nelson of the American University in Cairo, did not agree; she believed that "in spite of Sheldon's assessment . . . our analysis of feminism and social science suggested that indeed this was not the case and that, to the contrary, feminists had generated some rather influential and significant ideas." Introduction to *Feminist Thought*, a special issue of *Catalyst* (1977), pp. 1–2.
16 The term *biogrammar* refers to a behavioral baseline from which cultural variation develops. It was conceptualized by Tiger and Fox on the basis of Earl W. Count's concept of the "biogram," the basic form of an animal's social life. See Lionel Tiger and Robin Fox, *The Imperial Animal* (New York, 1971); Earl W. Count, *Being and Becoming Human: Essays on the Biogram* (New York, 1973).
17 Jean Lipman-Blumen, "Toward a Homosocial Theory of Sex Roles: An Explanation of the Sex Segregation of Social Institutions," *Signs* 1 (Spring 1976): 15–32; Lionel Tiger, *Men in Groups* (New York, 1970), pp. 112, 150, 263.
18 One researcher, after ignoring the work of women in his area for some time, finally sent out an urgent request to a female colleague for a bibliography of feminist work in his area. He had thought that it would pass, *spurlos versunken*. When it grew and grew, he realized that he could no longer ignore it.
19 Jessie Bernard, "Models for the Relationship between the World of Women and the World of Men," in *Research on Social Movements, Conflicts, and Change*, ed. Louis Kriesberg (Greenwich, Conn., 1978).

Contributors

EVELYN TORTON BECK is Associate Professor of Comparative Literature, German, and Women's Studies at the University of Wisconsin-Madison. She is author of *Kafka and the Yiddish Theater*, co-author of *Interpretive Synthesis*, and co-editor of *Women in German*. In her teaching and research she focuses on literature and art by women whose work has been excluded from the traditional curriculum. She is especially concerned with the way art is used to perpetuate dominant cultural norms.

JESSIE BERNARD, Research Scholar Honoris Causa, Pennsylvania State University, is a sociologist who has written extensively in the area of women, marriage, and family and has also been interested in the sociology of knowledge. Her works include *Academic Women* (1964), *Women and the Public Interest: An Essay on Policy and Protest* (1971), *The Future of Marriage* (1973), *The Future of Motherhood* (1974), and *Women, Wives, Mothers: Values and Options* (1975).

NANCY SCHROM DYE is an Assistant Professor of History at the University of Kentucky. Her research interests include working women's history, Southern and Appalachian women's history, and the history of childbirth. She has published articles in *Feminist Studies* and *Radical America* and is completing a book on the New York Woman's Trade Union League.

JEAN BETHKE ELSHTAIN is an Associate Professor of Political Science at the University of Massachusetts, Amherst. Her articles have appeared in *Polity, Politics and Society, Telos, Politics, Political Theory, Quest, Commonweal*, and *The Nation*. She is the author of a forthcoming book, *The Public and the Private: Towards a Critical Theory of Women and Politics*.

SUSAN SNIADER LANSER teaches in the Women's Studies Program at the University of Wisconsin-Madison, where she holds a Ph.D. in Comparative Literature (1979). She is also a staff specialist with the

University of Wisconsin System's Undergraduate Teaching Improvement Project. Her most recent interests include women and language, feminist and lesbian fiction, and the relationship between gender and literary response.

KATHRYN PYNE PARSONS did her graduate work in philosophy at Stanford, and now teaches at Smith College and is an editor of *Feminist Studies*. She grew up in a family of Irish-Catholic workers and had her daughters Kay and Shawn before she started college.

VIRGINIA SAPIRO (Ph.D. University of Michigan, 1976) is an Assistant Professor of Political Science and Women's Studies at the University of Wisconsin-Madison. Her primary interest is political psychology, and she has written on gender role socialization, women as political elites, oppression, public opinion regarding women's status, and Mary Wollstonecraft.

JANE TIBBETTS SCHULENBURG received her Ph.D. in history from the University of Wisconsin and is presently Assistant Professor of History at the University of Wisconsin-Extension. She has published and lectured on women in the Middle Ages. She is currently working on a book about women saints in early medieval society.

CAROLYN WOOD SHERIF, Professor of Psychology, Pennsylvania State University, holds a Ph.D. from the University of Texas (Austin). Her publications include *Orientation in Social Psychology* (1976) and (with Muzafer Sherif) *Social Psychology* (1956, 1969), *Interdisciplinary Relations in the Social Sciences* (1969), *Attitude and Attitude Change* (1965), *Reference Groups* (1964), *Intergroup Conflict and Cooperation* (1961), and *Groups in Harmony and Tension* (1953).

JULIA A. SHERMAN, a director and founder of the Women's Research Institute of Wisconsin, Inc., now WRI, has been actively engaged in research, writing, and psychotherapy for and about women since 1965. She is author of *On the Psychology of Women* (1971), *Sex-Related Cognitive Differences* (1978), and numerous research articles, and is the editor of a forthcoming book, *Psychology of Women: Future Directions in Research*.

DOROTHY E. SMITH (B. Sc [Soc], University of London, 1955; Ph.D., University of California, Berkeley, 1964) is divorced and the parent of two sons. She emigrated to Canada in 1968 and has been at the Ontario Institute for Studies in Education since 1977. She is active in the women's movement politically and intellectually; her special sociological fields are Marxism and the social organization of knowledge.

CATHARINE R. STIMPSON is a member of the English Department of Barnard College; the editor of *Signs: Journal of Women in Culture and Society*; and the author of fiction and non-fiction.

Index

Abolitionism: role of American women in, 25
Abortion: moral justifications, 190; and public policy, 203, 214; statistics on, 204, 208. *See also* "Jane"; Philosophy; Thomson, Judith Jarvis
"Abstract Man," 233–35
Abstract thought. *See* Cognitive domain
Academia: tenure and women, 3; recency of discipline as a factor in nondiscrimination in, 18–19; feminist critique of, 254. *See also* Achievement; Bias; Scholarship; Sexism; and under names of individual fields of inquiry
Academic Women (Jessie Bernard), 136
Achievement: women's intellectual, 3, 36; invisibility of women's, 5, 35, 168–70. *See also* under names of individual fields of inquiry
Achievement motivation. *See* Psychology
Acker, Joan, 191
Adams, Henry, 11–17 *passim*
Adams, Herbert Baxter, 16
Affirmative action, 3
Agentic approach. *See* Sociology
American Historical Association, 13, 16, 18
American Men of Science (ed. J. McKeen Cattell), 94
American Political Science Association, 260
American Psychological Association, 97
Anastasi, Anne, 97
Androcentrism: in historiography, 37; and literary tradition, 79, 86; in psychology, 94–96, 121. *See also* Bias
Androgyny, 117

Annales school, 44–47
Another Voice (Lyn Lofland), 191
Anthropology, cultural: and sex differences, 116
Antinomian controversy, 24–25
Aptitude tests: and the military, 109–10
Archetype: Woman as, 17. *See also* Stereotypes
Arendt, Hannah, 70, 239
Aristotle, 231, 245
Authority. *See* Power
Avant-garde, the: and radicalism, 56; history of, 56–59; and change, 57; and art, 57–58; Bohemianism, 58–59; as producing feeling of rejection in reader, 58; and sexism, 58, 63, 72; and politics, 62; institutionalization of, 63. *See also* Feminism; Joyce, James; Stein, Gertrude; *Partisan Review*; *PMLA*
Avigdor, Rozet, 124–25

Bachrach, Peter, 245
Bancroft, George, 11, 15
Baratz, Morton S., 245
Bart, Pauline B., 136, 204
Beach, Sylvia, 58–59
Beard, Charles, 20
Beard, Mary, 20
Beauvoir, Simone de, 136, 138–39, 219
Becker, Howard, 210
Bede, the Venerable, 40–42
Beginning with O (Olga Broumas), 88
Behavioralism. *See* Political Science
Behaviorism. *See* Political Science; Psychology
Benedict, Ruth, 18, 116
Berkeley, George, 234

279

Berle, Adolphe, 161
Bernard, Jessie, 111, 114, 136, 150
Beynon, Huw, 153
Bias: in pursuit of knowledge, 15–18, 189, 190–92; unconscious distortion as revealing, 38; and aptitude tests, 110–11. *See also* Academia; Androcentrism; Heterocentrism; Sexism; and under names of individual fields of inquiry
Bierstadt, Robert, 160, 163
Bildungsroman, 87
Binet, Alfred B., 97
"Biographical Element in the Novels of Mary Wollstonecraft Shelley, The" (Walter Edwin Peck), 70
Biology: and hierarchical structure, 116
Bishop, Elizabeth, 70
Blake, Robert R., 124
Bloch, Marc, 38, 44–47
Boccaccio, Giovanni, 36
Bodkin, Maud, 80
Boring, E. G., 95
Bray, Helen, 126
Breton, André, 61
Brodsky, Annette, 126
Broumas, Olga, 88
Brown, Rita Mae, 88
Bryher, 57–58
Budgen, Frank, 67

Calkins, Mary, 94, 95
Capital (Karl Marx), 179, 239
Capitalism: organizing functions of, 140–41, 160–63; development of, in North America, 161; corporate property relations and objectivity, 161–62; social relations determined by, 179; and Darwinian theory, 193; ownership, 216–17; economics of, 217–20; and sexism, in United States, 217–20. *See also* Marx, Karl; Philosophy; Sociology
Carlson, Rae, 150
Cattell, J. McKeen, 94
Century of Struggle (Eleanor Flexner), 20
Chaucer, Geoffrey, 33
Chicago, Judy, 145
Childbirth: history of, 27
Chivalry: and women's loss of power in Middle Ages, 43–44
Christianity: influence on European history, 37; role of women in England's conversion to, 41; and evolutionary theory, 194. *See also* Church
Christine de Pisan, 34–35; use of "Women Worthies" by, 35–36; and male bias, 36; and hypocrisy of chivalry, 43–44, 49

Church: women in early medieval, 39–40. *See also* Christianity
City of Ladies (Christine de Pisan), 34–36, 44
Civic identity. *See* History, American
Clark, Kenneth B., 97
Class: and social mobility, 21; ideology, 142–43; and gender, 143; study of men in working, 153; relations, 164; *See also* Dominance-subordination
Classicism: and European history, 37
Cocteau, Jean, 58
Cognitive domain, 156, 158. *See also* Epistemology
Colby, Vineta, 83
Coleman, James S., 254–55
Colet, Louise, 80
Concerning Famous Women. See De claris mulieribus
Connolly, William E., 230
Consciousness: and literature, 56; organization of, 155; bifurcation of, 167–72
Conspiracy of Pontiac (Francis Parkman), 12
Contraception. *See* History, American
Creativity: intellectual, female exclusion from, 3, 4; and gender, 267
Crick, Bernard, 243–44
Criticism: and change, 255; in psychology, 120–23. *See also* Literary criticism
Critics: female, 79, 91; feminist, 84–85; Transcendentalist, 85
Culture: female, 11, 14, 26–27
—Western: and sexism, 55; and women, 230

Dacier, Anne Lefevre, 81–82
Dahl, Robert, 259–63
Dame Alice. *See* Wife of Bath
Daniels, Arlene, 191, 221
Darwin, Charles, 113; as scientific revolutionary, 192–95; natural selection theory, 193–95, 211; and materialism, 194; and concept of "ideal Types," 194–95
Darwinism, social: critics of, 18
Davis, Natalie Zemon, 49
De Beauvoir, Simone. *See* Beauvoir, Simone de
De claris mulieribus (Giovanni Boccaccio), 36
De-feminization: of women scholars, 270
"Defense of Abortion, A" (Judith Jarvis Thomson), 190, 196–204
Democracy: and American history, 16
De Pisan, Christine. *See* Christine de Pisan
De Staël, Madame. *See* Staël, Madame de

Index

De Tocqueville, Alexis. *See* Tocqueville, Alexis de
Dickinson, Emily, 145
Didion, Joan, 152, 180
Discrimination. *See* Bias
Doctrine of Spheres. *See* Sex roles
Dominance-subordination, structures of, 216-21. *See also* Bias; Capitalism; Patriarchy; Power; Sexism

Eagley, Alice, 107
Easton, David, 230-31
Economics. *See* Capitalism; Housework; Labor; Marx, Karl
Education, women's, 4, 17-19. *See also* Academia
Education of Henry Adams, The (Henry Adams), 17
Eliot, George, 81
Eliot, T. S., 84
Ellis, Havelock, 99, 120
Ellman, Mary, 85
Emma Goldman Clinic, 211
Emotions: social structuring of, 150
Emotivism. *See* Political Science
Empiricism. *See* Political Science
Engels, Frederick, 140-41, 182, 184
Environmental determinism. *See* Psychology
Epistemology: for women, 88; empiricist, 234; and political methodology, 237
L'Ere de soupçon (Nathalie Saurraute), 84
Erikson, Eric, 119-20
Ethnocentrism: in psychology, 94
Eulau, Heinz, 236
Evolutionary theory. *See* Darwin, Charles
"Exemplar history." *See* Gregory of Tours

Family, The (Elsie Clews Parsons), 19
Fear: of death as fundamental anxiety, 150, 169-70
Febvre, Lucien, 44
Feinberg, Joel, 197, 203
Feminine mystique: as repressive of women, 136
Feminine Mystique, The (Betty Friedan), 93, 136
Femininity: and nature, 12, 17; as symbol, 17, 69. *See also* Archetype; Stereotypes
Feminism: and the avant-garde, 57, 68-69; and *Partisan Review*, 57, 68. *See also* Literary criticism; Women's movement
Feudal Society (Marc Bloch), 46
Finnegan's Wake (James Joyce), 66-67
Flanner, Janet, 59

Flexner, Eleanor, 20
Foot, Phillipa, 190
French Historical Method: The Annales Paradigm (Traian Stoianovich), 45
Fresno Women's Program, 145
Freud, Anna, 119
Freud, Sigmund, 62, 96, 99, 119-20, 136, 144
Friedan, Betty, 136, 212, 220
Fuller, Margaret, 81, 85
Functionalism: in Marxist thought on women, 154

Galton, Sir Francis, 95, 115
Genius: and gender, 69
Genre: conceptions of, 87, 88
German Ideology, The (Karl Marx and Frederick Engels), 140
Germanic society: women in, 39
Gilman, Charlotte Perkins, 86
Glass, James, 233
Goffman, Erving, 175, 181
Graham, Kenneth, 83
Gregory of Tours, 39-40
Gruber, Howard, 192
Grundrisse (Karl Marx), 179
Guttentag, Marcia, 126
Gynocentricism: and feminism, 86

Hardwick, Elizabeth, 70
Harré, Romano, 150, 181
Häutungen (Verena Stefan), 88
Hefner, Robert, 127
Hegel, Georg Wilhelm Friedrich, 164-65, 170, 270
Hemingway, Ernest, 69
Heterocentrism: and literature, 88
Hierarchy. *See* Dominance-subordination; Psychology
Historians: American, characteristics of, 14-18; Progressive, 19-20; feminist, 25-28, 146. *See also* Historiography; History
Historian's Craft, The, 44
Historiography: American, 13; European, and androcentrism, 37, 49. *See also* Historians; History
History: as interpretation of public events, 9; values reflected by notions of significance in, 9; development of, as academic discipline, 11; writing of, as a male pursuit, 15, 18, 33-34; social, 21, 45; rewriting of, from female point of view, 26, 35; patriarchal values in, 33; written by clerics, 33, 38; medieval, 33-37; of women, 35, 38-48; compart-

Continued:
  mentalization of, 37; bias in, 38; French, 39–40; English, 40–41; written by aristocrats, 42–46; 18th-century, 44; 19th Century Romanticism, 44; 20th-century, 44–46; modern, 46–48; periodization of, and women's history, 47. *See also* Historians; Historiography; Literary history
—American: and politics, 9, 10, 16; absence of women from, 9–11, 13–15, 19, 21–22; and civic identity, 10; development of, as academic field, 11, 13–19; experience of triumph over wilderness in, 12; industrialization, 13; and social evolution, 13; the progressives and feminism, 19–20; 20th century, 19–28; social, 21; periodization of, as form of order, 21, 22–24; bias in, 21–25; and contraception, 23; and patriarchy, 25; modernization of, and effect on women, 23–24
History of the English Church and People (the Venerable Bede), 40, 41
History of Experimental Psychology (E. G. Boring), 95
History of the Franks (Gregory of Tours): as a universal chronicle, 40
History of Modern Criticism: 1750–1900 (René Wellek), 80–81
History of the Pacific States (George Bancroft), 15
History of the Rise, Progress, and Termination of the American Revolution (Mercy Warren), 15
Hobbes, Thomas, 231–33, 256
Hochschild, Arlie, 150, 270
Hofstadter, Richard, 9
Hollingsworth, Leta, 18, 95, 108
Homosexuality: and feminism, 69. *See also* Lesbianism
Housework: historical role of, 27; and women, 27; structure of, 153–54; Marxist view of, 154. *See also* Capitalism; Labor; Sociology
Human Condition, The (Hannah Arendt), 239
Hume, David, 234
Humphrey, Robert, 84
Hunters, The (film), 176–77
Hutchinson, Ann, 24–25

Ideology: feminist critique of, 136–40; Marxist analysis of, 140–46
In Defence of Politics (Bernard Crick), 243
Industrialization. *See* History, American

Institutions: feminist critique of, 139–40; and society, 142
Intelligentsia: role of, in Marxist analysis of ideology, 140–46

Jacklin, Carol, 114, 119, 123
Jacobi, Mary Putnam. *See* Putnam-Jacobi, Mary
James, Henry, 62, 83
James, William, 94, 117
Jameson, Anna Brownwell, 81
"Jane" (pseudonym of an abortion service): operation of, 204–7; tradition and moral theory, 207–11; tradition *vs*. Judith Thomson tradition, 212–20; and equality, 216. *See also* Thomson, Judith Jarvis; Abortion
Johnson, Samuel, 81, 82–83
Journal of Personality and Social Psychology, 102
Joyce, James: and the avant-garde, 58–69 *passim*; and the Partisan Review, 63, 65–67; on language, 64; on women, 64, 67; and *PMLA*, 64–65
Judith Thomson tradition, the: of moral reasoning, 196–204, 207; critique of, as incomplete, 212, 213–15; and equality, 215–16, 220–21; and capitalism, 216, 217–22. *See also* "Jane"; Thomson, Judith Jarvis
Juhasz, Suzanne, 145–46

Kellogg, Robert, 84
Kelly-Gadol, Joan, 47
Knowledge: and academia, 3; equitable pursuit of historical, 25–28; inequality in pursuit of, 36, 247–49; as political struggle, 248–49; female contributions to, 267; and gender, 267–68. *See also* Academia; Achievement; Creativity
Kosik, Karel, 175
Kovesi, Julius, 237, 241
Kuhn, Thomas, 192, 254, 259

Labor: and political economy, 164–66; descriptions of, 238–39
Ladd-Franklin, C., 94
Language: Gertrude Stein's rearrangement of, 68; bias in, 69, 190; and women, 143; as reflection of experience, 143–46. *See also* Judith Thomson tradition, the; Philosophy; Thomson, Judith Jarvis
Lasswell, Harold, 243
Law: and legitimate authority, 201; constitutional, and abortion, 203
Lawrence, D. H., 67, 136

Index

Leavis, Q. D., 81
Lee, Vernon (pseudonym of Violet Paget), 83
Lefebvre, Henri, 175
Lennox, Charlotte, 82, 83
Lerner, Gerda, 3, 24
Lerner, Tillie. *See* Olson, Tillie
Lesbianism: and literature, 88
Lessing, Doris, 70, 138
Levertov, Denise, 70
Leviathan, The (Thomas Hobbes), 232
Lewes, George Henry, 81
Lewin, Kurt, 97, 100, 123
Lipman-Blumen, Jean, 272
Lippard, Lucy, 57, 145
Lipset, Seymour Martin, 244-45
Literary criticism: traditions of, 79; absence of women in, 80; "practical criticism," 80; and bias, 81; 20th-century, 83
Literary history: and women's scholarship, 85-86
Literature: bias in, 55, 79; stream-of-consciousness, 84; comic mode, 87; lesbian, 88. *See also* Avant-garde; Feminism; *Nouveau roman*; Sexism
Locke, John, 216, 217, 231, 233, 234
Lofland, Lyn, 191-92, 221
Lukács, Ggyörgy, 165
Lukes, Steven, 236

McCarthy, Mary, 70, 84
Maccoby, Eleanor, 114, 119, 123
McCormack, Thelma, 148
Mack, Maynard, 56
"Manhood and Statehood" (Theodore Roosevelt), 16
Mannheim, Karl, 162, 254
Marriage, 26, 151
Marx, Karl, 62, 140, 141, 158, 164-65, 170, 172, 179, 182, 184, 239, 256, 268
Marxism: and sexism, 191
Masculinity: as symbol, 69. *See also* Stereotypes
Materialism: and Darwin, 194-95
Mead, Margaret, 116
Means, Gardiner C., 161
Mednick, Martha, 126
Menopause: as cause of deviant behavior, 210
Menstruation: study of, 95, 101, 108, 109
Mental illness: and psychiatry, 149
Merton, Robert, 254
Middle Ages, 37-38; Early, 39, 48; Central and Late, 42-44
Milgram, Stanley, 105-6

Military. *See* Psychology
Millett, Kate, 70, 136-37
Minnesota Multiphasic Personality Inventory, 110
Misogynism: in history, 34, 35, 37
Mitchell, Juliet, 70
Modern Language Association, 56, 59, 63, 71; and *PMLA*, 59-60, 70; and the avant-garde, 59-60, 68-70
Montagu, Elizabeth, 80
Moral reasoning. *See* Judith Thomson tradition, the
Moral theory. *See* Political Science
Morelock, Judy, 107
Mouton, Jane, 124
Murdoch, Iris, 70

National Organization of Women (NOW), 212
National Women's Studies Association, 264
Natural selection. *See* Darwin, Charles
Neilson, Nellie, 18
New Radicalism, the: and sexism, 69
Nouveau-roman, 84

Oakley, Ann, 147-48, 153-54
Oates, Joyce Carroll, 70, 152
Objectivity: as male attribute, 5; and history, 13; in psychology, 101, 104; in scientific inquiry, 156-58, 189, 230, 236
Oleshansky, Barbara, 127
Olson, Tillie, 70, 71
Origin of species by Means of Natural Selection, On the (Charles Darwin), 192
Orthodoxy: in psychology, 104
"Other," 136, 138, 219

Paget, Violet. *See* Lee, Vernon
Parent-Teacher Association (PTA): and women, 260; as political recruitment channel, 261-63; bias in, 262
Parkman, Francis, 11, 12
Parsons, Elsie Clews, 18, 19
Parsons, Talcott, 150-51
Partisan Review: history of, 60; goals of, 61; and the avant-garde, 62-64; and language bias, 69; and socialism, 69; and women, 70. *See also* Avant-garde, the; Joyce, James; Stein, Gertrude
Paternalism: and Judith Thomson tradition, 221. *See also* Dominance-subordination
Patriarchy: and literary history, 13-14, 85; as base of American culture, 17; and the Church, 33; as a relation of

Continued:
dominance, 136; and social organization, 140; and political theory, 217–20. *See also* Bias; Capitalism; Dominance-subordination; History; Sexism
Peck, Walter Edwin, 70
Phenomenology of the Mind, The (Georg Hegel), 164
Phillips, William: and the *Partisan Review*, 63
Philosophes, the: and the Enlightment, 44
Philosophy: of language, presuppositions challenged, 190; of abortion and ethics, 190, 196; bias in, 190–94; contemporary American moral, 192, 194; empiricist, 194–95, 214–15. *See also* Capitalism; "Jane"; Judith Thompson tradition, the; Political Science
Philosophy and Public Affairs, 196
Piaget, Jean, 122
Piercy, Marge, 70
Pilgrimage (Dorothy Richardson), 85
Plath, Sylvia, 70
Plato, 256; and ideal types, 194–95
Play It As It Lays (Joan Didion): use of episodic structure in, 152–53
Pluralism. *See* Politics
Plutarch: anthology of famous women by, 36
PMLA: history, 59–60; and the avant-garde, 62; and feminism, 68, 69. *See also* Avant-garde, the; Joyce, James; Stein, Gertrude
Podhoretz, Norman, 62
Political analysis: American, 229; and Women's Studies, 254; behavioral approach to, 256
Political inquiry: and implications for women, 231; assumptions of, 231–35; and behavioralism, 235–41; theory of meaning in mainstream, 237; description and evaluation of, 237–41; and moral theory, 240–42. *See also* "Jane"; Judith Thomson tradition, the; Marx, Karl
Political Man: The Social Bases of Politics (Seymour Martin Lipset), 244
Political methodology: grounds of, 229–33
Political Science: philosophical consideration of biases in, 190, 241–49; and philosophy, 232, 256; classical liberal theory of, 233–34; empirical, 234
—behavioralist, 230–35, 247, 256–59, 260; and behaviorism, 230–31; goals of, 235–36, 240; and moral theory, 240–41; moral theory and emotivism, 241–42; methodology, 257; and women, 257, 259; and the family, 258; and sexuality, 258; and public/private conflict, 258–59
Politics: and women, 229, 243; and power, 243, 245–46; women's exclusion from, 243–56; and pluralism, 245; and unintentional power, 246; and Women's Studies, 253; and feminism, 253, 259; and academia, 254; assumptions of, 254. *See also* Feminism; History; Parent-Teacher Association; Power; Sociology
Politics: Who Gets What, When, How (Harold Lasswell), 243
Pollner, Melvin, 175
Pour un nouveau roman (Alain Robbe-Grillet), 84
Poverty and Progress (Stephan Thernstrom), 21
Power: and legitimacy, 210, 214; unintentional, 246. *See also* Dominance-subordination; Feminism; "Jane"; Politics; Women's Studies
Power, Eileen, 43
Pregnancy, 26; as property ownership, 201; abortion as alternative to, 207–9. *See also* "Jane"; Judith Thomson tradition, the
Prescott, William, 11
Progress of Romance (Clara Reeve), 83
Psychiatry: feminist critique of, 139–40; as a rationalization of ideology, 144
Psychology: study of sex differences in, 93, 114–17; bias in, 93–94, 99, 107–9; social, 96; testing and statistical, 96; developmental, 97; applied, 98; ahistoricalism in, 98, 100; and academia, 99; history of, 99; scientific/humanistic conflict in, 100, 103–4; methodology, 100, 112–14; causation, 101, 116; and language, 101, 120; researcher bias, 104; achievement motivation, 106; suggestibility, 107; perpetuation of social myth, 107–9; and the military, 109; clinical, 111–12; animal behavior, 113; trait theory, 114–17; environmental determinism, 117–18; behaviorism, 117–19; and Freud, 119; psychodynamics, 119; cognitive revolution in, 122; and the women's movement, 126
Psychology of Women Quarterly, 120
Psychotherapy, 99
Public/private conflict, 13–14, 71; affects of, on women, 258–59
Putnam-Jacobi, Mary, 95, 101, 108

Index

Racism: and values, 192
Radicalism: the avant-garde as, 56
Rahv, Philip, 62, 67
Rebecca, Meda, 127
Reeve, Clara, 83–84
Reisman, David, 267, 274
Rhodes, James Ford, 13, 16
Rich, Adrienne, 70, 145
Richardson, Dorothy, 84–85, 145
Right to life: and the abortion argument, 197, 201–2
Rights: equal, 212; and property ownership, 216–17
Rise of American Civilization, The (Charles and Mary Beard), 20
Rise of the City, The (Arthur Schlesinger), 20
Rivera, Diego: and surrealism, 61
Robbe-Grillet, Alain, 84
"Role of Women in American History, The" (Arthur Schlesinger), 19
Roles. *See* Sex roles
Romanticism, 19th Century, 44
Room of One's Own, A (Virginia Woolf), 22, 34, 85
Roosevelt, Theodore, 15, 16
Rosenberg, Rosalind, 18
Rosenthal, Robert, 104
Rousseau, Jean-Jacques, 231, 256
Rowbotham, Sheila, 5, 137–38, 143, 144
Rubyfruit Jungle (Rita Mae Brown), 88
Russell, Catherine, 156–57

Saint-Simon, Duc de, 81–82
Salmon, Lucy Maynard, 18
Sanger, Margaret, 120
Sarraute, Nathalie, 84
Schlesinger, Arthur, 19, 20
Scholarship: as dominated by males, 3; within androcentric framework, 6, 17–18; feminist, and literary history, 79–80; strategies for success in, 272–73. *See also* Academia; Achievement; Bias; Creativity; Sexism
Scholes, Robert, 84
Schutz, Alfred, 150, 155–57, 167, 169, 171
Scientific revolution. *See* Darwin, Charles
Second Sex, The (Simone de Beauvoir), 136
Second Treatise on Government (John Locke), 216
Secord, Paul, 150, 181
Seward, Georgene, 93
Sex and the Social Order (Georgene Seward), 93

Sex differences. *See* Psychology
Sexism: in academia, 55; critique of, in sociology, 139; non-conscious, 255; as poor scholarship, 263–64. *See also* Avant-garde, the; Bias; Dominance-subordination; Misogyny; and under the names of individual fields of inquiry
Sex roles: female, 3, 12; and the doctrine of spheres, 14; early research on differences in, 19. *See also* Psychology
Sex Roles (journal), 120
Sexton, Anne, 70
Sexual Politics (Kate Millett), 136
Sherif, Muzafer, 124
Sherman, Julia A., 4, 114, 119, 125–26
Shields, Stephanie, 96
Simon, Theodore, 97
Sinha, Durganand, 112
Skinner, B. F., 99, 118
"Slaughterhouse Five" (Kurt Vonnegut), 177
Sloan, Albert, 161
Smedley, Agnes, 70
Smith-Rosenberg, Carroll, 14
"Social Devices for Impelling Women to Bear and Rear Children" (Leta S. Hollingsworth), 95
Sociobiology, 113
Sociology: and female experience, 135, 143–46, 163–72; for women, 135, 159, 163–72, 180–84; and ideology, 142, 162–63; and the "superstructure," 142; discourse of, 146–50, 157–59; absence of women in, 146–54; bias in, 147; fields of, 148; ethnomethodology in, 149; agentic approach in, 150, 151, 152; and rationality, 150–51; and housework, 151–54; and functionalism, 154; and capitalism, 161–63; and Marx, 164–65; and modes of action, 165–70; phenomenological, 171; everyday world as phenomenon for investigation by, 175; everyday world as problematic for, 175–85. *See also* Capitalism; Class; Housework; Ideology; Political Science
Sontag, Susan, 70
Staël, Madame de, 79, 81
Stein, Gertrude: and the avant-garde, 58, 63–64; and *PMLA*, 65, 68; and the *Partisan Review,* 66, 68; and language, 68; and feminism, 68, 69. *See also* Avant-garde, the; Joyce, James

Stereotypes: female, 12, 17, 20, 33, 219, 243; social, 123–25; in the media, 139
Stoianovich, Traian, 45–47
Stratification theory: and sexism, 221
Structure of Scientific Revolution (Thomas Kuhn), 192
Structure of Social Action, The (Talcott Parsons), 151
Subordination: of women, in society, 149, 210–11; of female self, in D. H. Lawrence's work, 136–37. *See also* Dominance-subordination
Success: and guilt, 4; fear of, 106
Suffrage, 14
Sukenich, Ronald, 68
Surrealism. *See* Avant-garde, the; Rivera, Diego; Cocteau, Jean

Taft, Jessie, 18
Task Force on Sex Bias and Sex-Role Stereotyping in Psychotherapeutic Practice, 121
Taylor, Charles, 231, 236
Tenure. *See* Academia
Them (Joyce C. Oates), 152
Thernstrom, Stephan, 21
Thomson, Judith Jarvis: defense of abortion by, 190, 196–204. *See also* "Jane"; Judith Thomson tradition, the
Thorndike, E. L., 95
Tiger, Lionel, 272
Tittler, Ben, 107
Tocqueville, Alexis de, 239
Transcendentalism: in literary criticism, 85
Trilling, Diana, 69
Trilling, Lionel, 69
"Two Faces of Power" (Peter Bachrach and Morton S. Baratz), 245
Tyler, Leona, 97

University of Iowa, 96, 97
Urban sociology: bias in, 191–92

Value judgments: in science, 189–90, 231, 240
Van Ghent, Dorothy, 70
Victor, Frances, 15
"Virgin, The." *See* Stereotypes; Femininity
Von Arnim, Bettina, 81

Vonnegut, Kurt, 177–78
Von Tieck, Ludwig, 87

Wallace, Alfred Russel, 193
Warren, Mercy Otis, 15
Washburn, Margaret, 94, 95
Watson, John, 117
Weaver, Harriet, 58
Weisstein, Naomi, 93
Weldon, T. D., 236
Welleck, René, 80, 81, 85
Whewell, William, 194
Who Governs? (Robert Dahl), 259–60
Wife of Bath, Dame Alice: on history's lack of famous women, 33–37 *passim*
Wilson, Edmund, 84
Wittgenstein, Ludwig, 248
Wolff, Robert Paul, 233
Woman as Force in History (Mary Beard), 20
Woman's Consciousness, Man's World (Sheila Rowbotham), 5
Women: as receivers of knowledge, 3; female Indians in American history, 12; in public life, 14; as institution-builders, 24; as Muse, 56; as "other," 136, 138; and men, 137–39, 146, 182; compared to working class, 143–44; as housewives, 151–54, 170; as objects in sociological relations, 159–60; as outside sphere of influence, 243–45, 263; *See also* Culture; Housework; Sexism; Stereotypes; and under names of individual fields of inquiry
Women's Christian Temperance Movement, 14
Women's movement, 126, 136; and changing ideology, 140. *See* Feminism.
Women's Studies, 6; and power, 255; and politics, 259–64; and research, 263–64. *See also* Academia; Bias; Politics; Sociology
Wood, Ellen, 231
Woolf, Virginia, 5, 22, 34, 44, 80, 81, 84, 85
Woolley, Helen Thompson, 18, 95
Working For Ford (Huy Beynon), 153
Wundt, Wilhelm, 94

Young, Karl, 82–83

Zimmerman, Don H., 175

DESIGNED BY GARY G. GORE
COMPOSED BY METRICOMP, GRUNDY CENTER, IOWA
MANUFACTURED BY THOMSON-SHORE, INC., DEXTER, MICHIGAN
TEXT IS SET IN PALATINO, DISPLAY LINES IN PALATINO AND OPTIMA

Library of Congress Cataloging in Publication Data
Main entry under title:
The Prism of sex.
Includes bibliographical references and index.
1. Sex discrimination against women—Congresses.
2. Women—Intellectual life—Congresses. 3. Women—
Social conditions—Congresses. I. Sherman, Julia Ann,
1934–   II. Beck, Evelyn Torton. III. WRI of Wisconsin, inc.
HQ1154.P74   301.41′2   79-3969
ISBN 0-299-08010-2

HQ1154 .P74

WITHDRAWN
From Bertrand Library

DATE DUE			
APR 29 80			
APR 14 80			
AUG 13 1981			
SEP 9 1981			
FEB 13 1985			
JUN 28 1985			
OCT 29 1991			
NOV 19 1991			
MAY 25 1993			
GAYLORD			PRINTED IN U.S.A